UNDERSTANDING PUBLIC POLICY

Ninth Edition

Thomas R. Dye

McKenzie Professor of Government and Public Policy
Florida State University

 Prentice Hall, Upper Saddle River, New Jersey 07458

Library of Congress Cataloging-in-Publication Data

Dye, Thomas R.
    Understanding public policy / Thomas R. Dye.—9th ed.
        p.   cm.
    Includes bibliographical references and index.
    ISBN 0–13–639105–2
        1. United States—Social policy.   2. United States—Social
    conditions—1980–   3. United States—Politics and government—20th
    century.   I. Title.
    HN65.D9   1998   97–25918
    361.6'1'0973—dc21   CIP

Editor-in-chief: Nancy Roberts
Senior acquisitions editor: Michael Bickerstaff
Production liaison: Fran Russello
Editorial production supervision and interior design: Joan Saidel/P.M. Gordon Associates, Inc.
Prepress and manufacturing buyer: Bob Anderson
Cover design: Pat Wosczyk
Electronic art creation: Asterisk Group Inc.
Director, Image Resource Center: Lori Morris-Nantz
Photo research supervisor: Melinda Lee Reo
Image permission supervisor: Kay Dellosa
Photo researcher: Beth Boyd
Marketing manager: Christopher DeJohn

This book was set in 10/12 Garamond by Stratford Publishing Services
and was printed and bound by Courier Companies, Inc.
The cover was printed by Phoenix Color Corp.

Printed in the United States of America

10   9   8   7   6   5   4   3   2   1

ISBN 0-13-639105-2

Prentice-Hall International (UK) Limited, *London*
Prentice-Hall of Australia Pty. Limited, *Sydney*
Prentice-Hall Canada Inc., *Toronto*
Prentice-Hall Hispanoamericana, S.A., *Mexico*
Prentice-Hall of India Private Limited, *New Delhi*
Prentice-Hall of Japan, Inc., *Tokyo*
Simon & Schuster Asia Pte. Ltd., *Singapore*
Editora Prentice-Hall do Brasil, Ltda., *Rio de Janiero*

CONTENTS

iii

Contents   v

vi   Contents

PREFACE

Policy analysis is concerned with "who gets what" in politics and, more importantly, "why" and "what difference it makes." We are concerned not only with what policies governments pursue but why governments pursue the policies they do and what the consequences of these policies are.

Political science, like other scientific disciplines, has developed a number of concepts and models to help describe and explain political life. These models are not really competitive in the sense that any one could be judged as the "best." Each focuses on separate elements of politics and each helps us to understand different things about political life.

We begin with a brief description of nine analytic models in political science and the potential contribution of each to the study of public policy:

Institutional model	Incremental model
Process model	Game theory model
Group model	Public choice model
Elite model	Systems model
Rational model	

We then attempt to describe and explain public policy by the use of these various analytic models. Readers are not only informed about public policy in a variety of key domestic policy areas; they are also encouraged to utilize these conceptual models in political science to explain the causes and consequences of public policies in these areas. The policy areas studied are

Civil rights	Economic policy
Criminal justice	Taxation
Health and welfare	National defense
Education	State and local spending and services
Environmental protection	International trade and immigration

Most public policies are a combination of rational planning, incrementalism, competition among groups, elite preferences, systemic forces, public choice, political processes, and institutional influences. Throughout this volume we employ these models, both singly and in combination, to describe and explain public policy. However, certain chapters rely more on one model than another.

Any of these policy areas might be studied by using more than one model. Frequently our selection of a particular analytic model to study a specific policy area was based as much on pedagogical considerations as on anything else. We simply wanted to demonstrate how political scientists employ analytic models. Once readers are familiar with the nature and uses of analytic models in political science, they may find it interesting to explore the utility of models other than the ones selected by the author in the explanation of particular policy outcomes. For example, we use an elitist model to discuss civil rights policy, but the reader may wish to view civil rights policy from the perspective of group theory. We employ public choice theory to discuss environmental policy, but the reader might prefer studying environmental problems from the perspective of the process model.

Each chapter concludes with a series of propositions, which are derived from one or more analytic models and which attempt to summarize the policies discussed. The purpose of these summaries is to suggest the kinds of policy explanations that can be derived from analytic models and to tie the policy material back to one or another of the models.

In short, this volume is not only an introduction to the study of public policy but also an introduction to the models political scientists use to describe and explain political life.

Thomas R. Dye
Florida State University

1

POLICY ANALYSIS
What Governments Do,
Why They Do It,
and What Difference It Makes

U.S. President Bill Clinton is sworn in for his second term by Supreme Court Justice William Rehnquist as Hillary and Chelsea look on. (Tim Clary/Agence France Presse/Corbis-Bettmann)

WHAT IS PUBLIC POLICY?

This book is about public policy. It is concerned with what governments do, why they do it, and what difference it makes. It is also about political science and the ability of this academic discipline to describe, analyze, and explain public policy.

Definition of Policy. Public policy is whatever governments choose to do or not to do. (See box, Defining Public Policy: Playing Word Games.) Governments do many things. They regulate conflict within society; they organize society to carry on conflict with other societies; they distribute a great variety of symbolic rewards and material services to members of the society; and they extract money from society, most often in the form of taxes. Thus public policies may regulate behavior, organize bureaucracies, distribute benefits, or extract taxes—or all these things at once.

Policy Expansion and Government Growth. Today people expect government to do a great many things for them. Indeed there is hardly any personal or societal problem for which some group will not demand a government solution, that is, a public policy designed to alleviate personal discomfort or societal unease. Over the years, as more and more Americans turned to government to resolve society's problems, government grew in size and public policy expanded in scope to encompass just about every sector of American life.

Throughout the twentieth century, government grew in both absolute size and in relation to the size of the national economy. The size of the economy is usually measured by the gross domestic product (GDP), the sum of all the goods and services produced in the United States in a year (see Figure 1–1). Governments accounted for only about 8 percent of the GDP at the beginning of the century, and most governmental activities were carried out by state and local governments. Two world wars, the New Deal programs devised during the Great Depression of the 1930s, and the growth of the Great Society programs of the 1960s and 1970s all greatly expanded the size of government, particularly the federal government. The rise in government growth relative to the economy leveled off during the Reagan presidency (1981–1989), and it has remained at about 35 percent of GDP in recent years. More than two-thirds of this government spending—about 24 percent of GDP—is accounted for by the *federal government* alone. The nation's fifty *state* governments and 86,000 *local* governments (cities, counties, towns and townships, school districts, and special districts) combined account for less than one-third of total government spending—about 11 percent of GDP.

Scope of Public Policy. Not everything that government does is reflected in governmental expenditures. *Regulatory activity*, for example, especially environmental regulations, imposes significant costs on individuals and businesses; these costs are *not* shown in government budgets. Nevertheless, government spending is a common indicator of governmental functions and priorities. For example, Figure 1–2 indicates that the *federal government* spends more on senior citizens—in Social Security and Medicare outlays—than on any other function, including national

DEFINING PUBLIC POLICY: PLAYING WORD GAMES

This book discourages academic discussions of the definition of public policy—we say simply that public policy is whatever governments choose to do or not to do. Books, essays, and discussions of a "proper" definition of public policy have proven futile, even exasperating, and they often divert attention from the study of public policy itself. Moreover, even the most elaborate definitions of public policy, on close examination, seem to boil down to the same thing. For example, political scientist David Easton defines public policy as "the authoritative allocation of values for the whole society"—but it turns out that only the government can "authoritatively" act on the "whole" society, and everything the government chooses to do or not to do results in the "allocation of values."

Political scientist Harold Lasswell and philosopher Abraham Kaplan define policy as "a projected program of goals, values, and practices," and political scientist Carl Friedrick says, "It is essential for the policy concept that there be a goal, objective, or purpose." These definitions imply a difference between specific government actions and an overall program of action toward a given goal. But the problem raised in insisting that government actions must have goals in order to be labeled "policy" is that we can never be sure whether or not a particular action has a goal, or if it does, what that goal is. Some people may assume that if a government chooses to do something there must be a goal, objective, or purpose, but all we can really observe is what governments choose to do or not to do. We may wish that governments act in a "purposeful, goal-oriented" fashion, but we know that all too frequently they do not.

Political scientists Heinz Eulau and Kenneth Prewitt supply still another definition of public policy: "Policy is defined as a 'standing decision' characterized by behavioral consistency and repetitiveness on the part of both those who make it and those who abide by it." Now certainly it would be a wonderful thing if government activities were characterized by "consistency and repetitiveness"; but it is doubtful that we would ever find "public policy" in government if we insist on these criteria. Much of what government does is inconsistent and nonrepetitive.

So we shall stick with our simple definition: *public policy is whatever governments choose to do or not to do*. Note that we are focusing not only on government action but also on government inaction, that is, what government chooses *not* to do. We contend that government *in*action can have just as great an impact on society as government action.

See David Easton, *The Political System* (New York: Knopf, 1953), p. 129; Harold D. Lasswell and Abraham Kaplan, *Power and Society* (New Haven, CT: Yale University Press, 1970), p. 71; Carl J. Friedrich, *Man and His Government* (New York: McGraw-Hill, 1963), p. 70; Heinz Eulau and Kenneth Prewitt, *Labyrinths of Democracy* (Indianapolis: Bobbs-Merrill, 1973), p. 465.

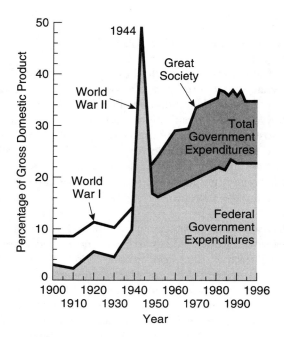

FIGURE 1–1   The Growth of Government

defense. The national debt is now so large that interest payments on it consume more than 15 percent of all federal spending. Federal welfare and health programs account for substantial budget outlays, but federal financial support of education is very modest. *State and local governments* in the United States bear the major burden of public education. Welfare and health functions consume larger shares of their budgets than highways and law enforcement do.

WHY STUDY PUBLIC POLICY?

Political science is the study of politics—the study of "who gets what when and how." It is more than the study of governmental institutions, that is, federalism, separation of powers, checks and balances, judicial review, the powers and duties of Congress, the president, and the courts. "Traditional" political science focuses primarily on these institutional arrangements as well as the philosophical justification of government. And political science is more than the study of political processes, that is, campaigns and elections, voting, lobbying, legislating, and adjudicating. Modern "behavioral" political science focuses primarily on these processes.

Political science is also the study of public policy—*the description and explanation of the causes and consequences of government activity*. This focus involves a

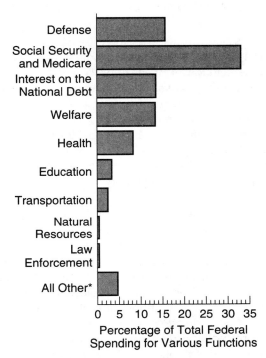

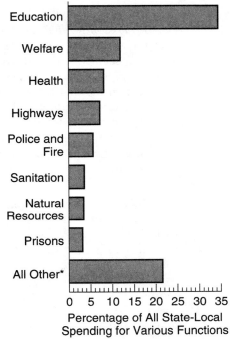

Source: Budget of the United States Government, 1997.

Source: Statistical Abstract of the United States, 1995.

FIGURE 1–2   Public Policy: What Governments Do

description of the content of public policy; an analysis of the impact of social, economic, and political forces on the content of public policy; an inquiry into the effect of various institutional arrangements and political processes on public policy; and an evaluation of the consequences of public policies on society, both expected and unexpected.

Public policy can be studied for a variety of reasons:

Scientific Understanding.   Understanding the causes and consequences of policy decisions improves our knowledge of society. Policy study helps us learn about the linkages between social and economic conditions in society, the responses of the political system to these conditions, and the effects, if any, of government activities on these conditions (see Figure 1–2). Policy studies incorporate the ideas and methods of economics, sociology, anthropology, psychology, history, law, and public administration, as well as political science. It adds to the breadth, significance, reliability, and theoretical development of the social sciences generally.

Professional Advice.   Public policy can also be studied for *professional reasons:* understanding the causes and consequences of public policy permits us to apply social science knowledge to the solution of practical problems. Factual knowledge is a prerequisite to prescribing for the ills of society. If certain ends are desired, the question of what policies would best implement them is a factual question requiring scientific study. In other words, policy studies can produce professional advice, in terms of "if . . . then . . . " statements, about how to achieve desired goals. Government agencies, as well as private policy research organizations ("think tanks"), are usually more concerned with the practical application of knowledge about policy than with the development of scientific theory.

Policy Recommendations.   Finally, public policy can be studied for *political purposes:* to ensure that the nation adopts the "right" policies to achieve the "right" goals. It is frequently argued that political science should not be silent or impotent in the face of great social and political crises and that political scientists have a moral obligation to advance specific public policies. An exclusive focus on institutions, processes, or behaviors is frequently looked on as "dry," "irrelevant," and "amoral" because it does not direct attention to the really important policy questions facing American society. Policy studies can be undertaken not only for scientific and professional purposes but also to inform political discussion, advance the level of political awareness, and improve the quality of public policy. Of course, these are very subjective purposes—Americans do not always agree on what constitutes the "right" policies or the "right" goals—but we will assume that knowledge is preferable to ignorance, even in politics.

WHAT CAN BE LEARNED FROM POLICY ANALYSIS?

Policy analysis is finding out what governments do, why they do it, and what difference, if any, it makes. What can be learned from policy analysis?

Description.   First, we can describe public policy—we can learn what government is doing (and not doing) in welfare, defense, education, civil rights, health, the environment, taxation, and so on. A factual basis of information about national policy is really an indispensable part of everyone's education. What does the Civil Rights Act of 1964 actually say about discrimination in employment? What did the Supreme Court rule in the *Bakke* case about affirmative action programs? What is the condition of the nation's Social Security program? What do the Medicaid and Medicare programs promise for the poor and the aged? What agreements have been reached between the United States and Russia regarding nuclear weapons? How much money are we paying in taxes? How much money does the federal government spend each year and what does it spend it on? How large is the national debt and how much does it grow each year? These are examples of descriptive questions.

Causes.   Second, we can inquire about the causes, or determinants, of public policy. Why is public policy what it is? Why do governments do what they do? We might inquire about the effects of political institutions, processes, and behaviors on public policies (Linkage B in Figure 1–3). For example, does it make any difference in tax and spending levels whether Democrats or Republicans control the presidency and Congress? What is the impact of lobbying by the special interests on efforts to reform the federal tax system? We can also inquire about the effects of social, economic, and cultural forces in shaping public policy (Linkage C in Figure 1–3). For example: What are the effects of changing public attitudes about race on civil rights

FIGURE 1–3   Studying Public Policy, Its Causes and Consequences

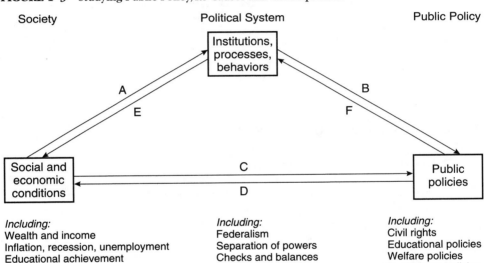

Linkage A: What are the effects of social economic conditions on political and governmental institutions, processes, and behaviors?
Linkage B: What are the effects of political and governmental institutions, processes, and behaviors on public policies?
Linkage C: What are the effects of social and economic conditions on public policies?
Linkage D: What are the effects (feedback) of public policies on social and economic conditions?
Linkage E: What are the effects (feedback) of political and governmental institutions, processes, and behaviors on social and economic conditions?
Linkage F: What are the effects (feedback) of public policies on political and governmental institutions, processes, and behaviors?

policy? What are the effects of recessions on government spending? What is the effect of an increasingly older population on the Social Security and Medicare programs? In scientific terms, when we study the causes of public policy, policies become the dependent variables, and their various political, social, economic, and cultural determinants become the independent variables.

Consequences.   Third, we can inquire about the consequences, or impacts, of public policy. Learning about the consequences of public policy is often referred to as *policy evaluation*. What difference, if any, does public policy make in people's lives? We might inquire about the effects of public policy on political institutions and processes (Linkage F in Figure 1–3). For example, what is the effect of welfare reform on Republican party fortunes in Congress? What is the impact of deficit reduction efforts on the president's popularity? We also want to examine the impact of public policies on conditions in society (Linkage D in Figure 1–3). For example, does capital punishment help to deter crime? Are welfare programs a disincentive to work? Do liberal welfare benefits result in larger numbers of poor people? Does increased educational spending produce higher student achievement scores? In scientific terms, when we study the consequences of public policy, policies become the independent variables, and their political, social, economic, and cultural impacts on society become the dependent variables.

POLICY ANALYSIS AND POLICY ADVOCACY

It is important to distinguish policy analysis from policy advocacy. *Explaining* the causes and consequences of various policies is not equivalent to *prescribing* what policies governments ought to pursue. Learning *why* governments do what they do and what the consequences of their actions are is not the same as saying *what* governments ought to do or bringing about changes in what they do. Policy advocacy requires the skills of rhetoric, persuasion, organization, and activism. Policy analysis encourages scholars and students to attack critical policy issues with the tools of systematic inquiry. There is an implied assumption in policy analysis that developing scientific knowledge about the forces shaping public policy and the consequences of public policy is itself a socially relevant activity and that such analysis is a prerequisite to prescription, advocacy, and activism.

Specifically, policy analysis involves

1. A *primary concern with explanation rather than prescription*. Policy recommendations—if they are made at all—are subordinate to description and explanation. There is an implicit judgment that understanding is a prerequisite to prescription and that understanding is best achieved through careful analysis rather than rhetoric or polemics.
2. A *rigorous search for the causes and consequences of public policies*. This search involves the use of scientific standards of inference. Sophisticated quan-

titative techniques may be helpful in establishing valid inferences about causes and consequences, but they are not essential.

3. *An effort to develop and test general propositions about the causes and consequences of public policy and to accumulate reliable research findings of general relevance.* The object is to develop general theories about public policy that are reliable and that apply to different government agencies and different policy areas. Policy analysts clearly prefer to develop explanations that fit more than one policy decision or case study—explanations that stand up over time in a variety of settings.

Policy issues are decided not by analysts but by political actors—elected and appointed government officials, interest groups, and occasionally even voters. Social science research often does not fare well in the political arena; it may be interpreted, misinterpreted, ignored, or even used as a weapon by political combatants. Policy analysis sometimes produces unexpected and even politically embarrassing findings. Public policies do not always work as intended. And political interests will accept, reject, or use findings to fit their own purposes.

POLICY ANALYSIS AND THE QUEST FOR SOLUTIONS TO AMERICA'S PROBLEMS

It is questionable that policy analysis can ever "solve" America's problems. Ignorance, crime, poverty, racial conflict, inequality, poor housing, ill health, pollution, congestion, and unhappy lives have afflicted people and societies for a long time. Of course, this is no excuse for failing to work toward a society free of these maladies. But our striving for a better society should be tempered with the realization that solutions to these problems may be very difficult to find. There are many reasons for tempering our enthusiasm for policy analysis, some of which are illustrated in the battle over educational policy.

Limits on Government Power.   First, it is easy to exaggerate the importance, both for good and for ill, of the policies of governments. It is not clear that government policies, however ingenious, could cure all or even most of society's ills. Governments are constrained by many powerful social forces—patterns of family life, class structure, child-rearing practices, religious beliefs, and so on. These forces are not easily managed by governments, nor could they be controlled even if it seemed desirable to do so. In the final chapter of this volume we will examine policy impacts, but it is safe to say here that some of society's problems are very intractable.

Disagreement over the Problem   Second, policy analysis cannot offer solutions to problems when there is no general agreement on what the problems are. For example, in educational policy some researchers assume that raising achievement levels (measures of verbal and quantitative abilities) is the problem to which our efforts should be directed. But educators often argue that the acquisition of verbal and quantitative skills is not the only, or even the most important, goal of the public schools. They contend that schools must also develop positive self-images among pupils of all races and backgrounds, encourage social awareness and the appreciation of multiple cultures, teach children to respect one another and to resolve their differences peacefully, raise children's awareness of the dangers of drugs and educate them about sex and sexually transmitted diseases, and so on. In other words, many educators define the problems confronting schools more broadly than raising achievement levels.

Policy analysis is not capable of resolving value conflicts. If there is little agreement on what values should be emphasized in educational policy, there is not much that policy research can contribute to policymaking. At best it can advise on how to achieve certain results, but it cannot determine what is truly valuable for society.

Subjectivity in Interpretation.   Third, policy analysis deals with very subjective topics and must rely on interpretation of results. Professional researchers frequently interpret the results of their analyses differently. Social science research cannot be value-free. Even the selection of the topic for research is affected by one's values about what is important in society and worthy of attention.

Limitations on Design of Human Research.   Another set of problems in systematic policy analysis centers around inherent limitations in the design of social science research. It is not really possible to conduct some forms of controlled experiments on human beings. For example, researchers cannot order children to go to poor schools for several years just to see if it adversely impacts their achievement levels. Instead, social researchers must find situations in which educational deprivation has been produced "naturally" in order to make the necessary observations about the causes of such deprivation. Because we cannot control all the factors in a real-world situation, it is difficult to pinpoint precisely what causes educational achievement or nonachievement. Moreover, even where some experimentation is permitted, human beings frequently modify their behavior simply because they know that they are being observed in an experimental situation. For example, in educational research it frequently turns out that children perform well under *any* new teaching method or curricular innovation. It is difficult to know whether the improvements observed are a product of the new teaching method or curricular improvement or merely a product of the experimental situation.

Complexity of Human Behavior.   Perhaps the most serious reservation about policy analysis is the fact that social problems are so complex that social scientists are unable to make accurate predictions about the impact of proposed policies. *Social scientists simply do not know enough about individual and group behavior to be able to give reliable advice to policymakers.* Occasionally policymakers turn to social scientists for "solutions," but social scientists do not have any. Most of society's problems are shaped by so many variables that a simple explanation of them, or remedy for them, is rarely possible. The fact that social scientists give so many contradictory recommendations is an indication of the absence of reliable scientific knowledge about social problems. Although some scholars argue that no advice is better than contradictory or inaccurate advice, policymakers still must make decisions, and it is probably better that they act in the light of whatever little knowledge social science can provide than that they act in the absence of any knowledge at all. Even if social scientists cannot predict the impact of future policies, they can at least attempt to measure the impact of current and past public policies and make this knowledge available to decision makers.

POLICY ANALYSIS AS ART AND CRAFT

Understanding public policy is both an art and a craft. It is an art because it requires insight, creativity, and imagination in identifying societal problems and describing them, in devising public policies that might alleviate them, and then in finding out whether these policies end up making things better or worse. It is a craft because these tasks usually require some knowledge of economics, political science, public administration, sociology, law, and statistics. Policy analysis is really an applied sub-field of all of these traditional academic disciplines.

We doubt that there is any "model of choice" in policy analysis—that is, a single model or method that is preferable to all others and that consistently renders the best solutions to public problems. Instead we agree with political scientist Aaron Wildavsky, who wrote:

> Policy analysis is one activity for which there can be no fixed program, for policy analysis is synonymous with creativity, which may be stimulated by theory and sharpened by practice, which can be learned but not taught.[1]

Wildavsky goes on to warn students that solutions to great public questions are not to be expected:

> In large part, it must be admitted, knowledge is negative. It tells us what we cannot do, where we cannot go, wherein we have been wrong, but not necessarily how to correct these errors. After all, if current efforts were judged wholly satisfactory, there would be little need for analysis and less for analysts.

There is no one model of choice to be found in this book, but if anyone wants to begin a debate about different ways of understanding public policy, this book is a good place to begin.

NOTE

1. Aaron Wildavsky, *Speaking Truth to Power* (New York: John Wiley, 1979), p. 3.

BIBLIOGRAPHY

ANDERSON, JAMES E. *Public Policymaking*. Boston: Houghton Mifflin, 1994.
COCHRAN, CLARKE E., LAWRENCE C. MAYER, T. R. CARR, and N. JOSEPH CAYER. *American Public Policy: An Introduction*. 5th ed. New York: St. Martin's Press, 1996.

DUNN, WILLIAM N. *Public Policy Analysis.* 2nd ed. Englewood Cliffs: 1994.

HEIDENHEIMER, ARNOLD T., ET AL. *Comparative Public Policy.* 3rd ed. New York: St. Martin's Press, 1990.

PALUMBO, DENNIS J. *Public Policy in America.* 2nd ed. New York: Harcourt Brace, 1994.

PETERS, B. GUY. *American Public Policy: Promise and Performance.* Chatham, N.J.: Chatham House, 1993.

STOKEY, EDITH, and RICHARD ZECKHAUSER. *A Primer for Policy Analysis.* New York: Norton, 1978.

WILDAVSKY, AARON. *Speaking Truth to Power.* New York: John Wiley, 1979.

2

MODELS OF POLITICS
Some Help in Thinking
about Public Policy

President Clinton, fourth from right, listens during a meeting with his Cabinet members at Blair House in Washington. (AP/Wide World Photos)

MODELS FOR POLICY ANALYSIS

A model is a simplified representation of some aspect of the real world. It may be an actual physical representation—a model airplane, for example, or the tabletop buildings that planners and architects use to show how things will look when proposed projects are completed. Or a model may be a diagram—a road map, for example, or a flow chart that political scientists use to show how a bill becomes law.

Uses of Models.   The models we shall use in studying policy are *conceptual models*. These are word models that try to

- Simplify and clarify our thinking about politics and public policy
- Identify important aspects of policy problems
- Help us to communicate with each other by focusing on essential features of political life
- Direct our efforts to understand public policy better by suggesting what is important and what is unimportant
- Suggest explanations for public policy and predict its consequences

Selected Policy Models.   Over the years, political science, like other scientific disciplines, has developed a number of models to help us understand political life. Throughout this volume we will try to see whether these models have any utility in the study of public policy. Specifically, we want to examine public policy from the perspective of the following models:

- Institutional model
- Process model
- Group model
- Elite model
- Rational model
- Incremental model
- Game theory model
- Public choice model
- Systems model

Each of these terms identifies a major conceptual model that can be found in the literature of political science. None of these models was derived especially to study public policy, yet each offers a separate way of thinking about policy and even suggests some of the general causes and consequences of public policy.

These models are not competitive in the sense that any one of them could be judged "best." Each one provides a separate focus on political life, and each can help us to understand different things about public policy. Although some policies appear at first glance to lend themselves to explanation by one particular model, most policies are a combination of rational planning, incrementalism, interest group activity, elite preferences, systemic forces, game playing, public choice, political processes, and institutional influences. In later chapters these models will be employed, singularly and in combination, to describe and explain specific policies. Following is a brief description of each model, with particular attention to the separate ways in which public policy can be viewed.

INSTITUTIONALISM: POLICY AS INSTITUTIONAL OUTPUT

Government institutions have long been a central focus of political science. Traditionally, political science has been defined as the study of government institutions. Political activities generally center around particular government institutions—Congress, the presidency, courts, bureaucracies, states, municipalities, and so on. Public policy is authoritatively determined, implemented, and enforced by these institutions.

The relationship between public policy and government institutions is very close. Strictly speaking, a policy does not become a public policy until it is adopted, implemented, and enforced by some government institution. Government institutions give public policy three distinctive characteristics. First, government lends *legitimacy* to policies. Government policies are generally regarded as legal obligations that command the loyalty of citizens. People may regard the policies of other groups and associations in society—corporations, churches, professional organizations, civic associations, and so forth—as important and even binding. But only government policies involve legal obligations. Second, government policies involve *universality*. Only government policies extend to all people in a society; the policies of other groups or organizations reach only a part of the society. Finally, government monopolizes *coercion* in society—only government can legitimately imprison violators of its policies. The sanctions that can be imposed by other groups or organizations in society are more limited. It is precisely this ability of government to command the loyalty of all its citizens, to enact policies governing the whole society, and to monopolize the legitimate use of force that encourages individuals and groups to work for enactment of their preferences into policy.

Traditionally, the institutional approach in political science did not devote much attention to the linkages between the structure of government institutions and the content of public policy. Instead, institutional studies usually described specific government institutions—their structures, organization, duties, and functions—without systematically inquiring about the impact of institutional characteristics on policy outputs. Constitutional and legal arrangements were described in detail, as were the myriad government offices and agencies at the federal, state, and local level. (See Figure 2–1 for a description of federal constitutional arrangements.) However, the linkage between institutional arrangements and policy remained largely unexamined.

Despite the narrow focus of early institutional studies in political science, the institutional approach is not necessarily unproductive. Government institutions are really structured patterns of behavior of individuals and groups. By "structured" we mean that these patterns of behavior tend to persist over time. These stable patterns

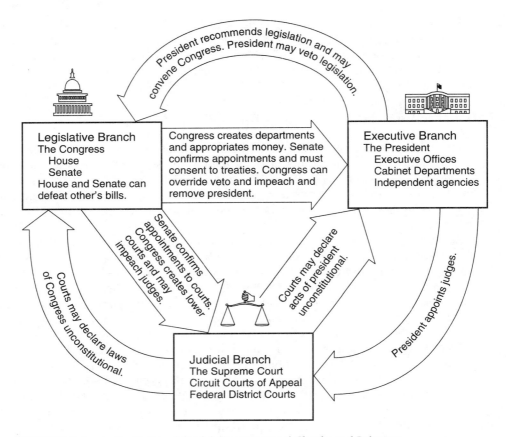

FIGURE 2–1   An Institutional Model: Constitutional Checks and Balances

of individual and group behavior may affect the content of public policy. Institutions may be so structured to facilitate certain policy outcomes and to obstruct other policy outcomes. They may give advantage to certain interests in society and withhold advantage from other interests. Certain individuals and groups may enjoy greater access to government power under one set of structural characteristics than under another set. In short, the structure of government institutions may have important policy consequences.

The institutional approach need not be narrow or descriptive. We can ask what relationships exist between institutional arrangements and the content of public policy, and we can investigate these relationships in a comparative, systematic fashion. For example, in the area of urban affairs we can ask: Are the policies of the federal government more responsive to popular preferences than the policies of state or local governments? How does the division of responsibility among federal, state, and local governments affect the content of public policy? These questions, which can be dealt with systematically, involve institutional arrangements.

INSTITUTIONALISM: APPLYING THE MODEL

Government institutions and organizations are mentioned throughout this book. But in Chapter 12, "American Federalism: Institutional Arrangements and Public Policy," we shall examine some of the problems of American federalism—the distribution of money and power among federal, state, and local governments.

It is important to remember that the impact of institutional arrangements on public policy is an empirical question that deserves investigation. Too frequently, enthusiastic reformers have asserted that a particular change in institutional structure would bring about changes in public policy without investigating the true relationship between structure and policy. They have fallen into the trap of assuming that institutional changes will bring about policy changes. We must be cautious in our assessment of the impact of structure on policy. We may discover that *both* structure and policy are largely determined by social or economic forces and that tinkering with institutional arrangements will have little independent impact on public policy if underlying forces remain constant.

PROCESS: POLICY AS POLITICAL ACTIVITY

Political processes and behaviors have been a central focus of political science for several decades. Modern "behavioral" political science since World War II has studied the activities of voters, interest groups, legislators, presidents, bureaucrats, judges, and other political actors. One of the main purposes has been to discover patterns of activities—or "processes." Recently some political scientists have tried to group various activities according to their relationship with public policy. The result is a set of *policy processes,* which usually follow this general outline:

Identifying problems	Expressing demands for government action
Setting the agenda for decision making	Deciding what issues will be decided and what problems to address
Formulating policy proposals	Developing policy proposals to resolve issues and problems
Legitimating policies	Selecting a proposal Building political support for it Enacting it as a law
Implementing policies	Organizing bureaucracies Providing payments or services Levying taxes

Evaluating policies   Studying programs
                                 Reporting outputs of
                                    government programs
                                 Evaluating impacts of programs
                                    on target and nontarget
                                    groups in society
                                 Suggesting changes and adjust-
                                    ments

In short, one can view the policy process as a series of political activities—problem identification, agenda setting, formulation, legitimation, implementation, and evaluation. A popular example of the process approach is shown in Table 2–1.

It has been argued that political scientists must limit their studies of public policy to these *processes* and avoid analyses of the *substance* of policies. According to political scientist Charles O. Jones,

> I maintain that the special purview of the political scientist is the political process and how it works. His or her interest in the substance of problems and policies, therefore, is in how it interacts with process, not necessarily in the substance itself . . . this also suggests that my remedies for the social system tend to be of the process variety—more access for more interest, providing for criticism and opposition, publicizing decisions, and how they are made.[1]

TABLE 2-1   The Policy Process—A Framework for Analysis

Functional Activities	Categorized in Government	And as Systems	With Output
Perception Definition Aggregation Organization Representation	Problems to Government	Problem Identification	Problem to Demand
Formulation Legitimation Appropriation	Action in Government	Program Development	Proposal to Budgeted Program
Organization Interpretation Application	Government to Problem	Program Implementation	Varies (service, payments, facilities, controls, etc.)
Specification Measurement Analysis	Program to Government	Program Evaluation	Varies (justification, recommendation, etc.)
Resolution/ Termination	Problem Resolution or Change	Program Termination	Solution or Change

Source: Charles O. Jones, *An Introduction to the Study of Public Policy,* 2nd ed. (Boston: Duxbury, 1978) p. 12. Copyright © 1977 by Wadsworth Publishing Co., Inc. Reprinted by permission of the publisher, Brooks/Cole Publishing Co., Monterey, CA.

This argument allows students of political science to study *how* decisions are made, and perhaps even how they *should* be made. But it does not permit them to comment on the substance of public policy—who gets what and why. Books organized around the process theme have sections on identifying problems, setting the agenda for decision making, formulating proposals, legitimating policies, and so on. It is not the *content* of public policy that is to be studied but rather the *processes* by which public policy is developed, implemented, and changed.

Despite the narrow focus of the process model, it is still useful in helping us to understand the various activities involved in policymaking. We want to keep in mind that *policymaking* involves agenda setting (capturing the attention of policymakers), formulating proposals (devising and selecting policy options), legitimating policy (developing political support; winning congressional, presidential, or court approval), implementing policy (creating bureaucracies, spending money, enforcing laws), and evaluating policy (finding out whether policies work, whether they are popular).

Indeed, it may even be the case that the way policies are made affects the content of public policy and vice versa. At least this is a question that deserves attention. But again, just as we warned readers in the discussion of the institutional model, we do not want to fall into the trap of assuming that a change in the process of policymaking will always bring about changes in the content of policy. It may turn out that social, economic, or technological constraints on policymakers are so great that it makes little or no difference in the content of policy whether the process of policymaking is open or closed, competitive or noncompetitive, pluralist or elitist, or whatever. Political scientists are fond of discussing how a bill becomes a law, and even how various interests succeed in winning battles over policy questions. But changing either the formal or informal processes of decision making may or may not change the content of public policy.

We all may prefer to live in a political system where everyone has an equal voice in policymaking; where many separate interests put forward solutions to public problems; where discussion, debate, and decision are open and accessible to all; where policy choices are made democratically; where implementation is reasonable, fair, and compassionate. But merely because we prefer such a political system does not necessarily mean that it would produce significantly different policies in national defense, education, welfare, health, or criminal justice. The linkages between *process* and *content* must still be investigated.

GROUP THEORY: POLICY AS GROUP EQUILIBRIUM

Group theory begins with the proposition that interaction among groups is the central fact of politics.[2] Individuals with common interests band together formally or informally to press their demands on government. According to political scientist David Truman, an interest group is "a shared-attitude group that makes certain claims upon other groups in the society"; such a group becomes political "if and when it makes a claim through or upon any of the institutions of government."[3] Individuals are important in politics only when they act as part of, or on behalf of,

---

PROCESSES: APPLYING THE MODEL

Political processes and behaviors are considered in each of the policy areas studied in this book. Additional commentary on the impact of political activity on public policy is found in Chapter 14, "The Policymaking Process: Getting inside the System."

---

group interests. The group becomes the essential bridge between the individual and the government. Politics is really the struggle among groups to influence public policy. The task of the political system is to *manage group conflict* by (1) establishing rules of the game in the group struggle, (2) arranging compromises and balancing interests, (3) enacting compromises in the form of public policy, and (4) enforcing these compromises.

According to group theorists, public policy at any given time is the equilibrium reached in the group struggle (see Figure 2–2). This equilibrium is determined by the relative influence of any interest groups. Changes in the relative influence of any interest groups can be expected to result in changes in public policy; policy will move in the direction desired by the groups gaining influence and away from the desires of groups losing influence. Political scientist Earl Latham described public policy from the group theory viewpoint as follows:

> What may be called public policy is actually the equilibrium reached in the group struggle at any given moment, and it represents a balance which the contending factions or groups constantly strive to tip in their favor. . . . The legislature referees the group struggle, ratifies the victories of the successful coalition, and records the terms of the surrenders, compromises, and conquests in the form of statutes.[4]

FIGURE 2–2   The Group Model

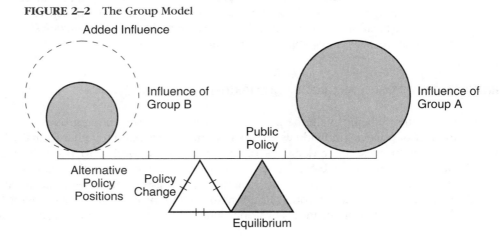

The influence of groups is determined by their numbers, wealth, organizational strength, leadership, access to decision makers, and internal cohesion.

Group theory purports to describe all meaningful, political activity in terms of the group struggle. Policymakers are viewed as constantly responding to group pressures—bargaining, negotiating, and compromising among competing demands of influential groups. Politicians attempt to form a majority coalition of groups. In so doing, they have some latitude in determining what groups are to be included in the majority coalition. The larger the constituency of the politician, the greater the number of diverse interests and the greater his or her latitude in selecting the groups to form a majority coalition. Thus, members of the House have less flexibility than senators, who have larger and generally more diverse constituencies; and the president has more flexibility than members of Congress and senators. Executive agencies are also understood in terms of their group constituencies.

Parties are viewed as coalitions of groups. The Democratic party coalition from the Roosevelt era until recently was made up of labor, central-city dwellers, ethnic groups, Catholics, the poor, liberal intellectuals, blacks, and Southerners. The difficulties of the Democratic party today can be traced largely to the weakening of this group coalition—the disaffection of the South and the group conflict between white labor and ethnic groups and blacks. The Republican coalition has consisted of rural and small-town residents, the middle class, whites, Protestants, white-collar workers, and suburbanites.

The whole interest group system—the political system itself—is held together in equilibrium by several forces. First, there is a large, nearly universal, *latent group* in American society that supports the constitutional system and prevailing rules of the game. This group is not always visible but can be activated to administer overwhelming rebuke to any group that attacks the system and threatens to destroy the equilibrium.

Second, *overlapping group membership* helps to maintain the equilibrium by preventing any one group from moving too far from prevailing values. Individuals who belong to any one group also belong to other groups, and this fact moderates the demands of groups who must avoid offending their members who have other group affiliations.

Finally, the *checking and balancing resulting from group competition* also helps to maintain equilibrium in the system. No single group constitutes a majority in American society. The power of each group is checked by the power of competing groups. "Countervailing" centers of power function to check the influence of any single group and protect the individual from exploitation.

ELITE THEORY: POLICY AS ELITE PREFERENCE

Public policy may also be viewed as the preferences and values of a governing elite.[5] Although it is often asserted that public policy reflects the demands of "the people," this may express the myth rather than the reality of American democracy. Elite theory suggests that the people are apathetic and ill informed about public policy, that elites actually shape mass opinion on policy questions more than masses

---

GROUP THEORY: APPLYING THE MODEL

Throughout this volume we will describe struggles over public policy. In Chapter 6, "Education: The Group Struggle," we will examine group conflict over public policy in the discussions of education and school issues. In Chapter 10, "Tax Policy: Battling the Special Interests," we will observe the power of interest groups in obtaining special treatments in the tax code and obstructing efforts to reform the nation's tax laws.

---

shape elite opinion. Thus, public policy really turns out to be the preferences of elites. Public officials and administrators merely carry out the policies decided on by the elite. Policies flow downward from elites to masses; they do not arise from mass demands (see Figure 2–3).

Elite theory can be summarized briefly as follows:

- Society is divided into the few who have power and the many who do not. Only a small number of persons allocate values for society; the masses do not decide public policy.

FIGURE 2–3 The Elite Model

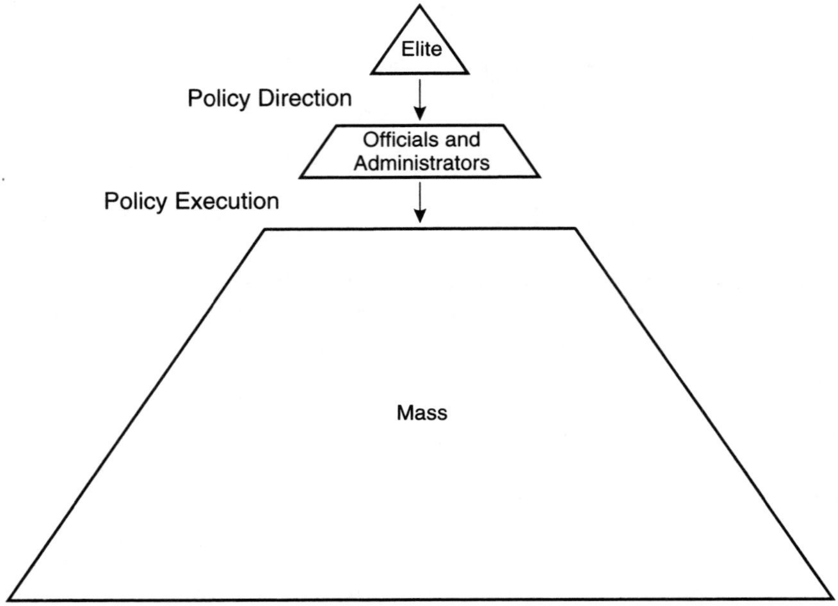

- The few who govern are not typical of the masses who are governed. Elites are drawn disproportionately from the upper socioeconomic strata of society.
- The movement of nonelites to elite positions must be slow and continuous to maintain stability and avoid revolution. Only nonelites who have accepted the basic elite consensus can be admitted to governing circles.
- Elites share consensus in behalf of the basic values of the social system and the preservation of the system. In America, the bases of elite consensus are the sanctity of private property, limited government, and individual liberty.
- Public policy does not reflect the demands of masses but rather the prevailing values of the elite. Changes in public policy will be incremental rather than revolutionary.
- Active elites are subject to relatively little direct influence from apathetic masses. Elites influence masses more than masses influence elites.

What are the implications of elite theory for policy analysis? First, elitism implies that public policy does not reflect the demands of the people so much as it does the interests and values of elites. Therefore, change and innovations in public policy come about as a result of redefinitions by elites of their own values. Because of the general conservatism of elites—that is, their interest in preserving the system—change in public policy will be incremental rather than revolutionary. Public policies are frequently modified but seldom replaced. Changes in the nature of the political system occur when events threaten the system, and elites, acting on the basis of enlightened self-interest, institute reforms to preserve the system and their place in it. The values of elites may be very "public regarding." A sense of noblesse oblige may permeate elite values, and the welfare of the masses may be an important element in elite decision making. Elitism does not mean that public policy will be against mass welfare but only that the responsibility for mass welfare rests on the shoulders of elites, not masses.

Second, elitism views the masses as largely passive, apathetic, and ill informed; mass sentiments are more often manipulated by elites, rather than elite values being influenced by the sentiments of masses; and for the most part, communication between elites and masses flows downward. Therefore, popular elections and party

---

ELITE THEORY: APPLYING THE MODEL

Chapter 3, "Civil Rights: Elite and Mass Interaction," portrays the civil rights movement as an effort by established national elites to extend equality of opportunity to blacks. Opposition to civil rights policies is found among white masses in the states. Chapter 11, "International Trade and Immigration: Elite-Mass Conflict" expands on the elite model by arguing that when elite preferences differ from those of the masses, the preferences of elites prevail.

RATIONALISM: APPLYING THE MODEL

Chapter 4, "Criminal Justice: Rationality and Irrationality in Public Policy," shows that rational policies to deter crime—policies ensuring certainty, swiftness, and severity of punishment—have seldom been implemented and that the nation's high crime rate is partly a product of this irrationality. The problems of achieving rationality in public policy are also discussed in Chapter 5, "Health and Welfare: The Search for Rational Strategies." We will consider the general design of alternative strategies in dealing with poverty, health, and welfare. We will observe how these strategies are implemented in public policy, and we will analyze some of the obstacles to the achievement of rationality in public policy.

---

competition do not enable the masses to govern. Policy questions are seldom decided by the people through elections or through the presentation of policy alternatives by political parties. For the most part these "democratic" institutions—elections and parties—are important only for their symbolic value. They help tie the masses to the political system by giving them a role to play on election day and a political party with which they can identify. Elitism contends that the masses have at best only an indirect influence over the decision-making behavior of elites.

Elitism also asserts that elites share in a consensus about fundamental norms underlying the social system, that elites agree on the basic rules of the game, as well as the continuation of the social system itself. The stability of the system, and even its survival, depends on elite consensus in behalf of the fundamental values of the system, and only policy alternatives that fall within the shared consensus will be given serious consideration. Of course, elitism does not mean that elite members never disagree or never compete with one another for preeminence. It is unlikely that there ever was a society in which there was no competition among elites. But elitism implies that competition centers on a very narrow range of issues and that elites agree more often than they disagree.

RATIONALISM: POLICY AS MAXIMUM SOCIAL GAIN

A rational policy is one that achieves "maximum social gain"; that is, governments should choose policies resulting in gains to society that exceed costs by the greatest amount, and governments should refrain from policies if costs are not exceeded by gains.

Note that there are really two important guidelines in this definition of maximum social gain. First, no policy should be adopted if its costs exceed its benefits. Second, among policy alternatives, decision makers should choose the policy that produces the greatest benefit over cost. In other words, a policy is rational when the difference between the values it achieves and the values it sacrifices is positive and greater than any other policy alternative. One should *not* view rationalism in a narrow dollars-and-cents framework, in which basic social values are sacrificed for dollar savings. Rationalism involves the calculation of *all* social, political, and economic values sacrificed or achieved by a public policy, not just those that can be measured in dollars.

To select a rational policy, policymakers must (1) know all the society's value preferences and their relative weights, (2) know all the policy alternatives available, (3) know all the consequences of each policy alternative, (4) calculate the ratio of benefits to costs for each policy alternative, and (5) select the most efficient policy alternative.[6] This rationality assumes that the value preferences of *society as a whole* can be known and weighted. It is not enough to know and weight the values of some groups and not others. There must be a complete understanding of societal values. Rational policymaking also requires *information* about alternative policies, the *predictive capacity* to foresee accurately the consequences of alternate policies, and the *intelligence* to calculate correctly the ratio of costs to benefits. Finally, rational policymaking requires a *decision-making system* that facilitates rationality in policy formation. A diagram of such a system is shown in Figure 2–4.

This model of maximum social gain is often used to think about the optimal size of government programs. Government budgets should increase until maximum net gain is achieved, and then no more should be spent. The model of maximum social gain is applied to public policymaking in benefit-cost analysis. The first applications were developed in the 1930s by the U.S. Corps of Engineers in programs for dams and river basin development. Today it is applied to virtually all government policies and programs. It is the principal analytic framework used to evaluate public spending decisions.

However, there are many barriers to rational decision making.[7] In fact, there are so many barriers to rational decision making that it rarely takes place at all in government. Yet the model remains important for analytic purposes because it helps to identify barriers to rationality. It assists in posing the question, Why is policymaking not a more rational process? At the outset we can hypothesize several important obstacles to rational policymaking:

- No societal benefits are usually agreed on but only benefits to specific groups and individuals, many of which are conflicting.
- The many conflicting benefits and costs cannot be compared or weighted; for example, it is impossible to compare or weigh the value of individual dignity against a tax increase.
- Policymakers are not motivated to make decisions on the basis of societal goals but instead try to maximize their own rewards—power, status, reelection, money, and so forth.
- Policymakers are not motivated to maximize net social gain but merely to satisfy demands for progress; they do not search until they find "the one best way"; instead they halt their search when they find an alternative that will work.
- Large investments in existing programs and policies (sunk costs) prevent policymakers from reconsidering alternatives foreclosed by previous decisions.

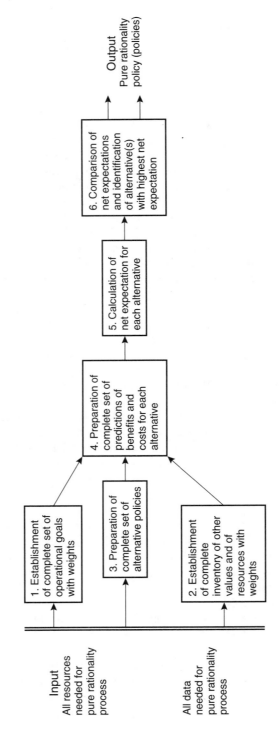

FIGURE 2–4   A Rational Model of a Decision System

- There are innumerable barriers to collecting all the information required to know all possible policy alternatives and the consequences of each, including the cost of information gathering, the availability of the information, and the time involved in its collection.
- Neither the predictive capacities of the social and behavioral sciences nor those of the physical and biological sciences are sufficiently advanced to enable policymakers to understand the full benefits or costs of each policy alternative.
- Policymakers, even with the most advanced computerized analytical techniques, do not have sufficient intelligence to calculate accurately costs and benefits when a large number of diverse political, social, economic, and cultural values are at stake.
- Uncertainty about the consequences of various policy alternatives compels policymakers to stick as closely as possible to previous policies to reduce the likelihood of disturbing, unanticipated consequences.
- The segmentalized nature of policymaking in large bureaucracies makes it difficult to coordinate decision making so that the input of all the various specialists is brought to bear at the point of decision.

INCREMENTALISM: POLICY AS VARIATIONS ON THE PAST

Incrementalism views public policy as a continuation of past government activities with only incremental modifications. Political scientist Charles E. Lindblom first presented the incremental model in the course of a critique of the traditional rational model of decision making.[8] According to Lindblom, decision makers do *not* annually review the whole range of existing and proposed policies, identify societal goals, research the benefits and costs of alternative policies in achieving these goals, rank order of preferences for each policy alternative in terms of the maximum net benefits, and then make a selection on the basis of all relevant information. On the contrary, constraints of time, information, and cost prevent policymakers from identifying the full range of policy alternatives and their consequences. Constraints of politics prevent the establishment of clear-cut societal goals and the accurate calculation of costs and benefits. The incremental model recognizes the impractical nature of "rational-comprehensive" policymaking, and describes a more conservative process of decision making.

Incrementalism is conservative in that existing programs, policies, and expenditures are considered as a base, and attention is concentrated on new programs and

---

INCREMENTALISM: APPLYING THE MODEL

Special attention to incrementalism is given in the discussion of government budgeting in Chapter 9, "Economic Policy: Incrementalism at Work."

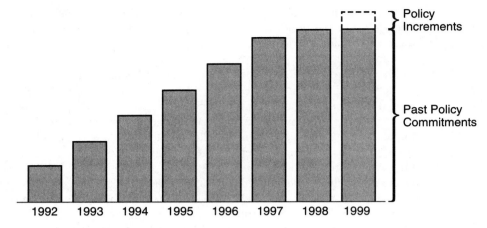

FIGURE 2-5 The Incremental Model

policies and on increases, decreases, or modifications of current programs. (For example, budgetary policy for any government activity or program for 1996 might be viewed incrementally, as shown in Figure 2–5.) Policymakers generally accept the legitimacy of established programs and tacitly agree to continue previous policies.

They do this, first, because they do not have the time, information, or money to investigate all the alternatives to existing policy. The cost of collecting all this information is too great. Policymakers do not have sufficient predictive capacities, even in the age of computers, to know what all the consequences of each alternative will be. Nor are they able to calculate cost-benefit ratios for alternative policies when many diverse political, social, economic, and cultural values are at stake. Thus completely "rational" policy may turn out to be "inefficient" (despite the contradiction in terms) if the time and cost of developing a rational policy are excessive.

Second, policymakers accept the legitimacy of previous policies because of the uncertainty about the consequences of completely new or different policies. It is safer to stick with known programs when the consequences of new programs cannot be predicted. Under conditions of uncertainty, policymakers continue past policies or programs whether or not they have proven effective.

Third, there may be heavy investments in existing programs (sunk costs), which preclude any really radical change. These investments may be in money, buildings, or other hard items, or they may be in psychological dispositions, administrative practices, or organizational structure. It is accepted wisdom, for example, that organizations tend to persist over time regardless of their utility, that they develop routines that are difficult to alter, and that individuals develop a personal stake in the continuation of organizations and practices, all of which makes radical change very difficult. Hence, not all policy alternatives can be seriously considered, but only those that cause little physical, economic, organizational, and administrative dislocation.

Fourth, incrementalism is politically expedient. Agreement comes easier in

GAME THEORY: APPLYING THE MODEL

Game theory is frequently applied in international conflicts. We will explore the utility of game theory in our own efforts to describe and explain in Chapter 8, "Defense
Policy: Strategies for Serious Games."

policymaking when the items in dispute are only increases or decreases in budgets
or modifications to existing programs. Conflict is heightened when decision making
focuses on major policy shifts involving great gains or losses, or "all-or-nothing,"
"yes-or-no" policy decisions. Because the political tension involved in getting new
programs or policies passed every year would be very great, past policy victories are
continued into future years unless there is a substantial political realignment. Thus,
incrementalism is important in reducing conflict, maintaining stability, and preserving the political system itself.

The characteristics of policymakers themselves also recommend the incremental model. Rarely do human beings act to maximize all their values; more often they
act to satisfy particular demands. People are pragmatic; they seldom search for the
"one best way" but instead end their search when they find "a way that will work."
This search usually begins with the familiar—that is, with policy alternatives close to
current policies. Only if these alternatives appear to be unsatisfactory will the policy-
maker venture out toward more radical policy innovation. In most cases modifica-
tion of existing programs will satisfy particular demands, and the major policy shifts
required to maximize values will be overlooked.

Finally, in the absence of any agreed-on societal goals or values, it is easier for
the government of a pluralist society to continue existing programs rather than to
engage in overall policy planning toward specific societal goals.

GAME THEORY: POLICY AS RATIONAL CHOICE
IN COMPETITIVE SITUATIONS

Game theory is the study of rational decisions in situations in which two or more
participants have choices to make and the outcome depends on the choices made
by each. It is applied to areas in policymaking in which there is no independently
"best" choice that one can make—in which the "best" outcomes depend upon what
others do.

The idea of "game" is that decision makers are involved in choices that are interdependent. "Players" must adjust their conduct to reflect not only their own desires and abilities but also their expectations about what others will do. Perhaps the
connotation of a "game" is unfortunate, suggesting that game theory is not really appropriate for serious conflict situations. But just the opposite is true: game theory

can be applied to decisions about war and peace, the use of nuclear weapons, international diplomacy, bargaining and coalition building in Congress or the United Nations, and to a variety of other important political situations. A "player" may be an individual, a group, or a national government—indeed, anybody with well-defined goals who is capable of rational action.

Game theory is an abstract and deductive model of policymaking. It does not describe how people actually make decisions but rather how they would go about making decisions in competitive situations if they were completely rational. Thus, game theory is a form of rationalism, but it is applied in competitive situations in which the outcome depends on what two or more participants do.

The rules of the game describe the choices that are available to all the players. The choices are frequently portrayed in a "matrix"—a diagram that presents the alternative choices of each player and all possible outcomes of the game. A two-by-two matrix is the simplest; there are only two players, and each player has only two alternatives to choose from:

		PLAYER A	
		Alternative A₁	*Alternative A₂*
PLAYER B	Alternative B₁	Outcome 1	Outcome 3
	Alternative B₂	Outcome 2	Outcome 4

There are four possible outcomes to this simple game, each represented by a cell in a matrix. The actual outcome depends on the choices of both Player A and Player B.

In game theory, *payoff* refers to the values that each player receives as a result of his or her choices and those of the opponent. Payoffs are frequently represented by numerical values; these numerical values are placed inside each cell of the matrix and presumably correspond to the values each player places on each outcome. Because players value different outcomes differently, there are two numerical values inside each cell—one for each player.

Consider the game of "chicken." Two adolescents drive their cars toward each other at a high speed, each with one set of wheels on the center line of the highway. If neither veers off course they will crash. Whoever veers is "chicken." Both drivers prefer to avoid death, but they also want to avoid the "dishonor" of being "chicken." The outcome depends on what both drivers do, and each driver must try to predict how the other will behave. This form of "brinkmanship" is common in international relations (see Figure 2–6).

Inspection of the payoff matrix suggests that it would be better for both drivers to veer in order to minimize the possibility of a great loss (-10). But the matrix is too simple. One or both players may place a different value on the outcomes than is suggested by the numbers. For example, one player may prefer death to dishonor in the game. Each player must try to calculate the values of the other, and neither has complete information about the values of the opponent. Moreover, bluffing or the deliberate misrepresentation of one's values or resources to an opponent is always a possibility. For example, a possible strategy in the game of chicken is to al-

| | | DRIVER A | |
		Stay on Course	Veer
DRIVER B	Stay on course	A: −10 B: −10	A: −5 B: +5
	Veer	A: +5 B: −5	A: −1 B: −1

FIGURE 2–6   A Game-Theoretic Matrix for the Game of Chicken. The game theorist himself or herself supplies the numerical values to the payoffs. If Driver A chooses to stay on course and Driver B chooses to stay on course also, the result might be scored as −10 for both players who wreck their cars. But if Driver A chooses to stay on course and Driver B veers, then Driver A might get +5 ("courage") and Driver B −5 ("dishonor"). If Driver A veers but Driver B stays on course, the results would be reversed. If both veer, each is dishonored slightly (−1), but not as much as when one or the other stayed on course.

low your opponent to see you drink heavily before the game, stumble drunkenly toward your car, and mumble something about having lived long enough in this rotten world. The effect of this communication on your opponent may increase his or her estimate of your likelihood of staying on course, and hence provide incentive for your opponent to veer and allow you to win.

A key concept in game theory is *strategy*. Strategy refers to rational decision making in which a set of moves is designed to achieve optimum payoff even after consideration of all of the opponent's possible moves. Game theorists employ the term *minimax* to refer to the rational strategy that either *minimizes the maximum loss or maximizes the minimum gain* for a player, regardless of what the opponent does. The minimax strategy is designed to protect a player against the opponent's best play. It might be viewed as a conservative strategy in that it is designed to reduce losses and ensure minimum gains rather than to seek maximum gains at the risk of great losses. But most game theorists view minimax as the best rational strategy. (The rational player in the game of chicken will veer because this choice minimizes the player's maximum loss.)

It should be clear from this discussion that game theory embraces both very complex and very simple ideas. The crucial question is whether any of them is really useful in studying public policy.

Game theory is more frequently proposed as an analytic tool by social scientists than as a practical guide to policymaking by government officials. The conditions of game theory are seldom approximated in real life. Seldom do policy alternatives present themselves neatly in a matrix. More important, seldom can policymakers know the real payoff values for themselves or their opponents of various policy alternatives. Finally, as we have already indicated, there are many obstacles to rational policymaking by governments.

Yet game theory provides an interesting way of thinking clearly about policy choices in conflict situations. Perhaps the real utility of game theory in policy analysis at the present time is in suggesting interesting questions and providing a vocabulary to deal with policymaking in conflict situations.

PUBLIC CHOICE THEORY: POLICY AS COLLECTIVE DECISION MAKING BY SELF-INTERESTED INDIVIDUALS

Public choice is the economic study of nonmarket decision making, especially the application of economic analyses to public policymaking. Traditionally, economics studied behavior in the marketplace and assumed that individuals pursued their private interests; political science studied behavior in the public arena and assumed that individuals pursued their own notion of the public interest. Thus, separate versions of human motivation developed in economics and political science: the idea of *homo economicus* assumed a self-interested actor seeking to maximize personal benefits; that of *homo politicus* assumed a public-spirited actor seeking to maximize societal welfare. But public choice theory challenges the notion that individuals act differently in politics than they do in the marketplace. This theory assumes that all political actors—voters, taxpayers, candidates, legislators, bureaucrats, interest groups, parties, bureaucracies, and governments—seek to maximize their personal benefits in politics as well as in the marketplace. James Buchanan, the Nobel-Prize-winning economist and leading scholar in modern public choice theory, argues that individuals come together in politics for their own mutual benefit, just as they come together in the marketplace; and by agreement (contract) among themselves they can enhance their own well-being, in the same way as by trading in the marketplace.[9] In short, people pursue their self-interest in both politics and the marketplace, but even with selfish motives they can mutually benefit through collective decision making.

Government itself arises from a social contract among individuals who agree for their mutual benefit to obey laws and support the government in exchange for protection of their own lives, liberties, and property. Thus, public choice theorists claim to be intellectual heirs to the English political philosopher John Locke, as well as to Thomas Jefferson, who incorporated this social contract notion into the American Declaration of Independence. Enlightened self-interest leads individuals to a constitutional contract establishing a government to protect life, liberty, and property.

Public choice theory recognizes that government must perform certain functions that the marketplace is unable to handle; that is, it must remedy certain "market failures." First, government must provide *public goods*—goods and services that must be supplied to everyone if they are supplied to anyone. The market cannot provide public goods because their costs exceed their value to any single buyer, and a single buyer would not be in a position to keep nonbuyers from using it. National defense is the most common example: protection from foreign invasion is too expensive for a single person to buy, and once it is provided no one can be excluded from its benefits. So people must act collectively through government to provide for the common defense. Second, *externalities* are another recognized market failure and justification for government intervention. An externality occurs when an activity of one individual, firm, or local government imposes uncompensated costs on others. The most common examples are air and water pollution: the discharge of air and water pollutants imposes costs on others. Governments respond by either regulating the activities that produce externalities or imposing penalties (fines) on these activities to compensate for their costs to society.

Public choice theory helps to explain why political parties and candidates generally fail to offer clear policy alternatives in election campaigns. Parties and candidates are not interested in advancing principles but rather in winning elections. They formulate their policy positions to win elections; they do not win elections to formulate policy. Thus each party and candidate seeks policy positions that will attract the greatest number of voters.[10] Given a unimodal distribution of opinion on any policy question (see Figure 2–7), parties and candidates will move toward the center to maximize votes. Only "ideologues" (irrational, ideologically motivated people) ignore the vote-maximizing centrist strategy.

But public choice theory has developed its own critique of the simple median-voter model by recognizing the separate interests of politicians and bureaucrats in contrast to the interest of voters. The interests of politicians and bureaucrats are to win reelection, garner generous campaign contributions, expand agency budgets, gain greater authority and prestige, and expand the power of government. The constitutional rules for government decision making do not always ensure that the interests of politicians and bureaucrats coincide with those of the median voter. Even a totally selfless, altruistic public official who tries diligently to implement the preferences of his or her constituents—the median voters—may find many obstacles. Government officials do not have continuous information to assess changing preferences of consumers-taxpayers. Unlike marketplace consumers, voter consumers do not engage in continuous voting. When politicians find out what the voters really

FIGURE 2–7 Public Choice: A Vote-maximizing Model of Party Competition

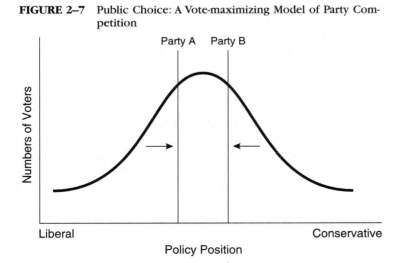

want, it may be too late, for the election will be won or lost. Even after the contest, elected officials can only guess at what they did right or wrong. Voting outcomes are not always policy informative.

In the absence of good information about citizen preferences, the "natural tendencies" of politicians and bureaucrats to expand their power in society are unchecked. They exaggerate the benefits of government spending programs and understate their costs. Various "fiscal illusions"—hidden taxes, payroll deductions, and deficit financing—contribute further to the citizens' underestimation of the costs of government. These "political failures" all contribute to the government's oversupply of public goods and services and to its overtaxing of the citizens.

Public choice theory also contributes to our understanding of interest groups and their effects on public policy. Most government programs provide "quasi-public goods"—services that benefit some groups in society more than others. It is rational for individuals seeking specific benefits, subsidies, privileges, or protections to organize themselves to pressure for government action. The costs of these specific benefits can be dispersed to all taxpayers, none of whom individually bears enough of the cost to merit spending time, energy, or money to organize in opposition to the expenditure. This concentration of benefits to the few and dispersal of costs to the many results in an interest group system that favors small, well-organized, homogenous interests seeking expansion of government activity at the expense of larger but less organized groups of citizens-taxpayers. Over long periods of time, the activities of many special interest groups, each seeking concentrated benefits to themselves and dispersed costs to others, results in an overproduction of government regulations, programs, and services. Indeed, the cumulative effect of interest group activity on society is "organizational sclerosis"—a political economy so encrusted with subsidies, benefits, regulations, protections, and special treatments for organized interest groups that work, productivity, and investment are discouraged.

To attract members and contributions, interest groups must dramatize and publicize their cause. Interest group leaders must compete for members and money by exaggerating the dangers to society of ignoring their demands. Even when governments meet their original demands, interest groups must generate new demands with new warnings of danger if they are to remain in business. In short, interest groups, like other political actors, pursue their self-interest in the political marketplace.

PUBLIC CHOICE: APPLYING THE MODEL

The public choice theory is employed in Chapter 7, "Environmental Policy: Externalities and Interests," to aid in recognizing environmental pollution as a problem in the control of externalities in human activity. Public choice theory also helps us to understand the behavior of environmental interest groups in dramatizing and publicizing their cause.

SYSTEMS THEORY: POLICY AS SYSTEM OUTPUT

Another way to conceive of public policy is to think of it as a response of a political system to forces brought to bear on it from the environment.[11] Forces generated in the environment that affect the political system are viewed as *inputs*. The *environment* is any condition or circumstance defined as external to the boundaries of the political system. The *political system* is that group of interrelated structures and processes that functions authoritatively to allocate values for a society. *Outputs* of the political system are authoritative value allocations of the system, and these allocations constitute *public policy*.

This conceptualization of political activity and public policy can be diagrammed as in Figure 2–8. This diagram is a simplified version of the idea of the political system described at great length by political scientist David Easton. The notion of a political system has been employed, either implicitly or explicitly, by many scholars who have analyzed the causes and consequences of public policy.

Systems theory portrays public policy as an output of the political system. The concept of *system* implies an identifiable set of institutions and activities in society that functions to transform demands into authoritative decisions requiring the support of the whole society. The concept of system also implies that elements of the system are interrelated, that the system can respond to forces in its environment, and that it will do so to preserve itself. Inputs are received into the political system in the form of both demands and support. Demands occur when individuals or groups, in response to real or perceived environmental conditions, act to affect public policy.

FIGURE 2–8   The Systems Model

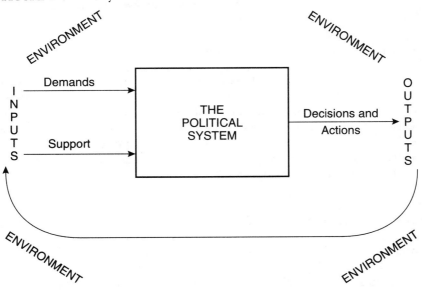

SYSTEMS THEORY: APPLYING THE MODEL

The systems model is particularly helpful in Chapter 13, "Inputs and Outputs: A Systems Analysis of State Policies," in examining public policies in the American states. By comparing states, we will assess the impact of various environmental conditions—particularly income—on levels of spending, benefits, and services in education, welfare, highways, police, corrections, and finance. We will see how federal policy sometimes tries to offset the impact of environmental variables on domestic policy in the states. We will examine the impact of political system characteristics—particularly party competition and voter participation—on levels of taxing, spending, benefits, and service, and we will compare the impact of these system characteristics on public policy with the impact of environmental conditions.

Support is rendered when individuals or groups accept the outcome of elections, obey the laws, pay their taxes, and generally conform to policy decisions. Any system absorbs a variety of demands, some of which conflict with another. To transform these demands into output (public policies), it must arrange settlements and enforce these settlements on the parties concerned. It is recognized that outputs (public policies) may have a modifying effect on the environment and the demands arising from it, and they may also have an effect on the character of the political system. The system preserves itself by (1) producing reasonably satisfying outputs; (2) relying on deeply rooted attachments to the system itself; and (3) using, or threatening to use, force.

The value of the systems model to policy analysis lies in the questions that it poses:

- What are the significant dimensions of the environment that generate demands on the political system?
- What are the significant characteristics of the political system that enable it to transform demands into public policy and to preserve itself over time?
- How do environmental inputs affect the character of the political system?
- How do characteristics of the political system affect the content of public policy?
- How do environmental inputs affect the content of public policy?
- How does public policy affect, through feedback, the environment and the character of the political system?

MODELS: HOW TO TELL IF THEY ARE HELPING OR NOT

A model is merely an abstraction or representation of political life. When we think of political systems or elites or groups or rational decision making or incrementalism or games, we are abstracting from the real world in an attempt to simplify, clarify, and understand what is really important about politics. Before we begin our study of public policy, let us set forth some general criteria for evaluating the usefulness of concepts and models.

Order and Simplify Reality.   Certainly the utility of a model lies in its ability to order and simplify political life so that we can think about it more clearly and understand the relationships we find in the real world. Yet too much simplification can led to inaccuracies in our thinking about reality. On the one hand, if a concept is too narrow or identifies only superficial phenomena, we may not be able to use it to explain public policy. On the other hand, if a concept is too broad and suggests overly complex relationships, it may become so complicated and unmanageable that it is not really an aid to understanding. In other words, some theories of politics may be too complex to be helpful, while others may be too simplistic.

Identify What Is Significant.   A model should also identify the really significant aspects of public policy. It should direct attention away from irrelevant variables or circumstances and focus on the real causes and significant consequences of public policy. Of course, what is "real," "relevant," or "significant" is to some extent a function of an individual's personal values. But we can all agree that the utility of a concept is related to its ability to identify what it is that is really important about politics.

Be Congruent with Reality.   Generally, a model should be congruent with reality—that is, it ought to have real empirical referents. We would expect to have difficulty with a concept that identifies a process that does not really occur or symbolizes phenomena that do not exist in the real world. However, we must not be too quick to dismiss unrealistic concepts *if* they succeed in directing our attention to why they are unrealistic. For example, no one contends that government decision making is completely rational—public officials do not always act to maximize societal values and minimize societal costs. Yet the concept of rational decision making may still be useful, albeit unrealistic, if it makes us realize how irrational government decision making really is and prompts us to inquire why.

Provide Meaningful Communication.   A concept or model should also communicate something meaningful. If too many people disagree over the meaning of a concept, its utility in communication is diminished. For example, if no one really agrees on what constitutes an elite, the concept of an elite does not mean the same thing to everyone. If one defines an elite as a group of democratically elected public officials who are representative of the general public, one is communicating a different idea in using the term than one who defines an elite as an unrepresentative minority that makes decisions for society based on its own interests.

Direct Inquiry and Research.   A model should help to direct inquiry and research into public policy. A concept should be operational—that is, it should refer directly to real-world phenomena that can be observed, measured, and verified. A concept, or a series of interrelated concepts (which we refer to as a model), should suggest relationships in the real world that can be tested and verified. If there is no way to prove or disprove the ideas suggested by a concept, the concept is not really useful in developing a science of politics.

Suggest Explanations. Finally, a model approach should suggest an explanation of public policy. It should suggest hypotheses about the causes and consequences of public policy—hypotheses that can be tested against real-world data. A concept that merely describes public policy is not as useful as a concept that explains public policy, or at least suggests some possible explanations.

NOTES

1. Charles O. Jones, *An Introduction to the Study of Public Policy,* 2nd ed. (Boston: Duxbury, 1978), p.6.
2. The classic statement on group theory is David B. Truman, *The Governmental Process* (New York: Knopf, 1951).
3. Ibid., p. 37.
4. Earl Latham, "The Group Basis of Politics," in *Political Behavior,* ed. Heinz Eulau, Samuel J. Eldersveld, and Morris Janowitz (New York: Free Press, 1956), p. 239.
5. Elite theory is explained at length in Thomas R. Dye and Harmon Zeigler, *The Irony of Democracy,* 10th ed. (Belmont, CA: Wadsworth, 1996).
6. See Yehezdel Dror, *Public Policy-Making Re-examined,* Part IV, An Optional Model of Public Policy-Making (San Francisco: Chandler, 1968).
7. See Charles E. Lindblom, "The Science of Muddling Through," *Public Administration Review,* 19 (Spring 1959), 79–88; Aaron Wildavsky, *The Politics of the Budgetary Process* (Boston: Little, Brown, 1964).
8. Lindblom, "The Science of Muddling Through."
9. James M. Buchanan and Gordon Tullock, *The Calculus of Consent* (Ann Arbor: University of Michigan Press, 1962).
10. Anthony Downs, *An Economic Theory of Democracy* (New York: Harper & Row, 1957).
11. This conceptualization was first put forth by David Easton, *A Framework for Political Analysis* (Englewood Cliffs, NJ: Prentice Hall, 1965).

BIBLIOGRAPHY

BUCHANAN, JAMES M., and GORDON TULLOCK. *The Calculus of Consent.* Ann Arbor: University of Michigan Press, 1962.

DOWNS, ANTHONY. *An Economic Theory of Democracy.* New York: Harper & Row, 1957.

DYE, THOMAS R., and HARMON ZEIGLER. *The Irony of Democracy.* 10th ed. Belmont, CA: Wadsworth, 1996.

EASTON, DAVID. *A Framework for Political Analysis.* Englewood Cliffs, NJ: Prentice Hall, 1965.

LINDBLOM, CHARLES E., and EDWARD J. WOODHOUSE. *The Policy-Making Process.* 3rd ed. Englewood Cliffs, NJ: Prentice Hall, 1993.

TRUMAN, DAVID B. *The Government Process.* New York: Knopf, 1954.

WILDAVSKY, AARON. *The New Politics of the Budgetary Process.* 2nd ed. New York: HarperCollins, 1992.

3

CIVIL RIGHTS
Elite and Mass Interaction

Reverend Martin Luther King, Jr., delivers his "I Have a Dream" speech at the Lincoln Memorial in Washington, D.C., in 1963, in support of the bill that became the Civil Rights Act of 1964. (UPI/Corbis–Bettmann)

ELITE AND MASS ATTITUDES AND RACE

Race has been the central domestic issue of American politics over the long history of the nation. In describing this issue we have relied heavily on the elite model—because elite and mass attitudes toward civil rights differ a great deal, and public policy appears to reflect the attitudes of elites rather than masses. Civil rights policy is a response of a national elite to conditions affecting a minority of Americans rather than a response of national leaders to majority sentiments. Policies of the national elite in civil rights have met with varying degrees of mass resistance at the state and local levels. We will contend that national policy has shaped mass opinion more than mass opinion has shaped national policy.

Black-White Opinion Differences. The attitudes of white masses toward blacks in America are ambivalent. Today most whites believe that there is little discrimination toward blacks in jobs, housing, or education and that any differences between whites and blacks in society is a result of lack of motivation among blacks (see Table 3–1). Blacks disagree. Most blacks believe that they are not treated equally in employment, housing, or education and that differences between blacks and whites in standards of living are "mainly due to discrimination." Whites constitute a large majority of the nation's population—about 87 percent. If public policy reflected the views of this majority, there would be very little civil rights legislation.

TABLE 3–1   White and Black Attitudes toward Discrimination

	Whites	Blacks
In your view, are racial minorities in the United States today routinely discriminated against, or not?"		
Yes	40%	74%
No	55%	22%
Do you feel that, compared to whites, blacks		
Get equal pay for equal work?	72%	31%
Are treated equally by the justice system?	51%	17%
On the average blacks have worse jobs, income, and housing than white people. Do you think these differences are		
Because most blacks do not have the motivation or willpower to pull themselves out of poverty?	62%	36%
Because most blacks don't have the education that it takes to rise out of poverty?	52%	68%
Most people agree that on the average, blacks have worse jobs, income, and housing than whites. Do you think the differences are mainly due to discrimination?	7%	70%

Source: Derived from data reported in *The American Enterprise,* January/February 1990, pp. 96–103, and *The Polling Report,* July 31, 1995.

This strongly suggests that civil rights policy is not a response of government to the demands of the white majority.

Mass Opinion Lags behind Policy.   White majority opinion has *followed* civil rights policy rather than inspired it. That is, public policy has shaped white opinion rather than white opinion shaping public policy. Consider the changes in opinion among whites toward school integration over the years. Between 1942 and 1985 samples of white Americans were asked this question: "Do you think white and black students should go to the same schools or separate schools?" (See Table 3–2.) In 1942, not one white American in three approved of integrated schools. In 1956, two years *after* the historic *Brown* v. *Topeka* court decision, white attitudes began to shift, although about half of all whites still favored segregation. By 1964, two out of every three whites supported integrated schools. Additional survey information suggests that whites are becoming increasingly accommodating toward equal rights for blacks over time in other areas as well. But, again, white opinion generally follows public policy rather than leads it.

Elite-Mass Differences.   There is a wide gap between the attitudes of masses and elites on the subject of black rights. The least favorable attitudes toward blacks are found among the less privileged, less educated whites. Whites of lower socioeconomic status are much less willing to have contact with blacks than those with higher socioeconomic status, whether it is a matter of using the same public restrooms, going to a movie or restaurant, or living next door. It is the affluent, well-educated white who is most concerned with discrimination and who is most willing to have contact with blacks. The political implication of this finding is obvious: opposition to civil rights legislation and to black advancement in education, jobs, income, housing, and so on is likely to be strongest among less educated and less affluent whites. Within the white community support for civil rights will continue to come from the educated and affluent.

There is very little support among white masses for preferential treatment for racial minorities. Moreover, a majority of whites today believes that we have enough federal laws and regulations aimed at reducing discrimination.

But civil rights policy does not reflect the views of the nation's white majority. Rather it reflects the views of governing elites—Congress, the president, the bureaucracy, and especially the U.S. Supreme Court.

TABLE 3–2   Changing White Attitudes toward School Integration

Question: "Do you think white students and black students should go to the same school or to separate schools?"

Same Schools						
	1942	1956	1964	1970	1972	1980	1985
Percent	30	48	65	74	80	86	92

Source: General Social Survey and Gallup Polls reported in Harold W. Stanley and Richard G. Niemi, *Vital Statistics on American Politics,* 5th ed. (Washington, DC: CQ Press, 1995), p. 367.

THE DEVELOPMENT OF CIVIL RIGHTS POLICY

The initial goal in the struggle for equality in America was the elimination of discrimination and segregation practiced by governments, particularly in voting and public education. Later, discrimination in both public and private life—in transportation, theaters, parks, stores, restaurants, businesses, employment, and housing—came under legal attack.

The Fourteenth Amendment.   The Fourteenth Amendment, passed by Congress after the Civil War and ratified in 1868, declares,

> All persons born or naturalized in the United States, and subject to the Jurisdiction thereof, are citizens of the United States and of the State wherein they reside. No State shall make or enforce any law which shall abridge the privileges or immunities of citizens of the United States; nor shall any State deprive any person of life, liberty, or property, without due process of law; nor deny to any person within its jurisdiction the equal protection of the laws.

The language of the Fourteenth Amendment and its historical context leave little doubt that its original purpose was to achieve the full measure of citizenship and equality for black Americans. During Reconstruction and the military occupation of the Southern states, some radical Republicans were prepared to carry out in Southern society the revolution this amendment implied. The early success of Reconstruction was evident in widespread black voting throughout the South and the election of blacks to federal and state offices. Congress even tried to legislate equal treatment in theaters, restaurants, hotels, and public transportation in the Civil Rights Act of 1875, only to have the Supreme Court declare the effort unconstitutional in 1883.[1]

By 1877, Reconstruction had been abandoned; the national government was not prepared to carry out the long, difficult, and disagreeable task of really reconstructing society in the eleven states of the former Confederacy. In the Compromise of 1877, the national government agreed to end military occupation of the South, gave up its efforts to rearrange Southern society, and lent tacit approval to white supremacy in that region. In return, the Southern states pledged their support of the Union; accepted national supremacy; and agreed to permit the Republican candidate, Rutherford B. Hayes, to assume the presidency, even though his Democratic opponent, Samuel J. Tilden, had won more popular votes in the disputed election of 1876.

Segregation.   The Supreme Court agreed to the terms of the compromise. The result was a complete inversion of the meaning of the Fourteenth Amendment so that it became a bulwark of segregation. State laws segregating the races were upheld. The constitutional argument on behalf of segregation under the Fourteenth Amendment was that the phrase "equal protection of the laws" did not prevent state-enforced separation of the races. Schools and other public facilities that were "separate but equal" won constitutional approval. This separate-but-equal doctrine became the Supreme Court's interpretation of the Equal Protection Clause of the Fourteenth Amendment in *Plessy* v. *Ferguson:*

> The object of the [14th] Amendment was undoubtedly to enforce the absolute equality of the two races before the law, but in the nature of things it could not have been intended to abolish distinctions based upon color, or to enforce social, as distinguished from political, equality, or a commingling of the two races upon terms unsatisfactory to either. Laws permitting, and even requiring, their separation in places where they are liable to be brought into contact do not necessarily imply the inferiority of either race to the other, and have been generally, if not universally, recognized as within the competency of the state legislatures in the exercise of their police power. The most common instance of this is connected with the establishment of separate schools for white and colored children, which has been held to be a valid exercise of the legislative power. . . .[2]

However, segregated facilities, including public schools, were seldom if ever equal, even in physical conditions. In practice, the doctrine of segregation was separate and *un*equal. The Supreme Court began to take notice of this after World War II. Although it declined to overrule the segregationist interpretation of the Fourteenth Amendment, it began to order the admission of individual blacks to white public universities when evidence indicated that separate black institutions were inferior or nonexistent.[3]

NAACP.   Leaders of the newly emerging civil rights movement in the 1940s and 1950s were not satisfied with court decisions that examined the circumstances in each case to determine if separate school facilities were really equal. Led by Roy Wilkins, executive director of the National Association for the Advancement of Colored People, and Thurgood Marshall, chief counsel for the NAACP, the civil rights movement pressed for a court decision that segregation itself meant inequality within the meaning of the Fourteenth Amendment, whether or not facilities were equal in all tangible respects. In short, they wanted a complete reversal of the separate-but-equal interpretation of the Fourteenth Amendment and a ruling that laws separating the races were unconstitutional.

The civil rights groups chose to bring suit for desegregation to Topeka, Kansas, where segregated black and white schools were equal in buildings, curricula, qualifications and salaries of teachers, and other tangible factors. The object was to prevent the Court from ordering the admission of blacks because tangible facilities were not equal and to force the Court to review the doctrine of segregation itself.

Brown v. *Topeka.*   The Court rendered its historic decision in *Brown* v. *Board of Education of Topeka, Kansas,* on May 17, 1954:

> Segregation of white and colored children in public schools has a detrimental effect upon the colored children. The impact is greater when it has the sanction of law, for the policy of separating the races is usually interpreted as denoting the inferiority of the Negro group. A form of inferiority affects the motivation of a child to learn. Segregation

with the sanction of law, therefore, has a tendency to retard the educational and mental development of Negro children and to deprive them of some of the benefits they would receive in a racially integrated school system.[4]

The original *Brown* v. *Topeka* decision was symbolically very important. Although it would be many years before a significant number of black children would attend formerly segregated white schools, the decision by the nation's highest court undoubtedly stimulated black hopes and expectations. Black sociologist Kenneth Clark writes,

> This [civil rights] movement would probably not have existed at all were it not for the 1954 Supreme Court school desegregation decision which provided a tremendous boost to the morale of Negroes by its *clear* affirmation that color is irrelevant to the rights of American citizens. Until this time the Southern Negro generally had accommodated to the separation of the black from the white society.[5]

Note that this first great step toward racial justice in the twentieth century was taken by the *nonelective* branch of the federal government. Nine men, secure in their positions with lifetime appointments, responded to the legal arguments of highly educated black leaders, one of whom—Thurgood Marshall—would later become a Supreme Court justice himself. The decision was made by a judicial elite, not by the people or their elected representatives.

MASS RESISTANCE TO DESEGREGATION

Although the Supreme Court had spoken forcefully in the *Brown* case in declaring segregation unconstitutional, from a political viewpoint the battle over segregation was just beginning. Segregation would remain a part of American life, regardless of its constitutionality, until effective elite power was brought to bear to end it. The Supreme Court, by virtue of the American system of federalism and separation of powers, has little formal power at its disposal. Congress, the president, state governors and legislatures, and even mobs of people have more power at their disposal than the federal judiciary. The Supreme Court must rely largely on the other branches of the federal government and on the states to enforce the law of the land.

Segregationist States. In 1954 the practice of segregation was widespread and deeply ingrained in American life (see Figure 3–1). Seventeen states *required* the segregation of the races in public schools:

Alabama	Mississippi	Texas	Maryland
Arkansas	North Carolina	Virginia	Missouri
Florida	South Carolina	Delaware	Oklahoma
Georgia	Tennessee	Kentucky	West Virginia
Louisiana			

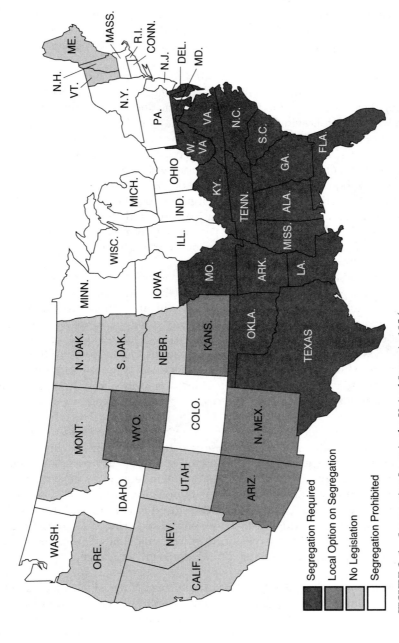

FIGURE 3–1 Segregation Laws in the United States in 1954

Segregation Required

Local Option on Segregation

No Legislation

Segregation Prohibited

The Congress of the United States required the segregation of the races in the public schools of the District of Columbia. Four additional states—Arizona, Kansas, New Mexico, and Wyoming—authorized segregation on the option of local school boards.

Thus, in deciding *Brown* v. *Topeka,* the Supreme Court struck down the laws of twenty-one states and the District of Columbia in a single opinion. Such a far-reaching decision was bound to meet with difficulties in implementation. In an opinion delivered the following year, the Supreme Court declined to order immediate nationwide desegregation but instead turned over the responsibility for desegregation to state and local authorities under the supervision of federal district courts. The way was open for extensive litigation, obstruction, and delay by states that chose to resist.

The six border states with segregated school systems—Delaware, Kentucky, Maryland, Missouri, Oklahoma, West Virginia—together with the school districts in Kansas, Arizona, and New Mexico that had operated segregated schools chose not to resist desegregation formally. The District of Columbia also desegregated its public schools the year following the Supreme Court's decision.

State Resistance.   However, resistance to school integration was the policy choice of the eleven states of the Old Confederacy. Refusal of a school district to desegregate until it was faced with a federal court injunction was the most common form of delay. State laws that were obviously designed to evade constitutional responsibilities to end segregation were struck down in federal courts; but court suits and delays slowed progress toward integration. On the whole, those states that chose to resist desegregation were quite successful in doing so from 1954 to 1964. In late 1964, ten years after the *Brown* decision, only about 2 percent of the black schoolchildren in the eleven southern states were attending integrated schools.

Congress and the Power of the Purse.   Congress entered the civil rights field in support of court efforts to achieve desegregation in the Civil Rights Act of 1964. Title VI provided that every federal department and agency must take action to end segregation in all programs or activities receiving federal financial assistance. It was specified that this action was to include termination of financial assistance if states and communities receiving federal funds refused to comply with federal desegregation orders. Thus, in addition to court orders requiring desegregation, states and communities faced administrative orders, or "guidelines," from federal executive agencies threatening loss of federal funds for noncompliance.

Presidential Use of Force.   The historic *Brown* decision might have been rendered meaningless had President Dwight Eisenhower not decided to use military force in 1957 to secure the enforcement of a federal court order to desegregate Little Rock's Central High School. Governor Orval Faubus had posted state units of the Arkansas National Guard at the high school to prevent federal marshals from carrying out federal court orders to admit black students. President Eisenhower officially called the Arkansas National Guard units into federal service, ordered them to leave the high school, and replaced them with units of the U.S. Eighty-second Airborne

Division under orders to enforce desegregation. Eisenhower had not publicly spoken on behalf of desegregation, but the direct threat to national power posed by a state governor caused the president to assert the power of the national elite. President John F. Kennedy also used federal troops to enforce desegregation at the University of Mississippi in 1962.

Unitary Schools.   The last legal excuse for delay in implementing school desegregation collapsed in 1969 when the Supreme Court rejected a request by Mississippi school officials for a delay in implementing school desegregation in that state. The Court declared that every school district was obligated to end dual school systems "at once" and "now and hereafter" to operate only unitary schools.[6] The effect of the decision, fifteen years after the original *Brown* case, was to eliminate any further legal justification for the continuation of segregation in public schools.

BUSING AND RACIAL BALANCING IN SCHOOLS

Although the nation's public schools have been desegregated by law for forty years, de facto segregation—black children attending public schools in which more than half the pupils are black—continues to characterize American education. Indeed, nationwide roughly two-thirds of all black public school pupils attend schools with a black majority. One-third of black pupils attend schools with 90 to 100 percent minority enrollment.[7] Years ago, the U.S. Civil Rights Commission reported that even when segregation was de facto—that is, a product of segregated housing patterns and neighborhood school attendance—the adverse effects on black students were still significant.[8]

Ending racial isolation in the public schools generally involves busing schoolchildren into and out of segregated neighborhoods. The objective is to achieve a racial balance in each public school, so that each has roughly the same percentage of blacks and whites as are found in the total population of the entire school district. Indeed, in some large cities where blacks make up the overwhelming majority of public school students, ending racial isolation may require city students to be bused to the suburbs and suburban students to be bused to the core city.

Federal Court Intervention.   Federal district judges enjoy wide freedom in fashioning remedies for past or present discriminatory practices by governments. If a federal district court anywhere in the United States finds that any actions by governments or school officials have contributed to racial imbalances (e.g., by drawing school district attendance lines), the judge may order the adoption of a desegregation plan to overcome racial imbalances produced by official action. A large number of cities have come under federal district court orders to improve racial balances in their schools through busing.

In the important case of *Swann* v. *Charlotte-Mecklenburg County Board of Education* (1971), the Supreme Court upheld (1) the use of racial balance requirements in schools and the assignment of pupils to schools based on race, (2) "close scrutiny" by judges of schools that are predominately of one race, (3) gerrymandering of school attendance zones as well as "clustering" or "grouping" of schools to achieve equal balance, and (4) court-ordered busing of pupils to achieve racial balance.[9] The Court was careful to note, however, that racial imbalance in schools is not itself grounds for ordering these remedies, unless it is also shown that some present or past government action contributed to the imbalance.

In the absence of any government actions contributing to racial imbalance, states and school districts are *not* required by the Fourteenth Amendment to integrate their schools. For example, where central-city schools are predominantly black and suburban schools are predominantly white because of residential patterns, cross-district busing is not required unless some official action brought about these racial imbalances. Thus, the Supreme Court threw out a lower federal court order for massive busing of students between Detroit and fifty-two suburban school districts. Although Detroit city schools were 70 percent black, none of the Detroit-area school districts segregated students within their own boundaries. Chief Justice Burger, writing for the majority, said, "Unless [Detroit officials] drew the district lines in a discriminatory fashion, or arranged for the white student residing in the Detroit district to attend schools in Oakland or Macomb counties, they were under no constitutional duty to make provision for Negro students to do so."[10] In a strong dissent, Justice Thurgood Marshall wrote, "In the short run it may seem to be the easiest course to allow our great metropolitan areas to be divided up each into cities—one white, the other black—but it is a course, I predict, our people will ultimately regret." This important decision means that the largely black central cities, surrounded by largely white suburbs, will remain segregated in practice because there are not enough white students living within the city to achieve integration.

Many school districts in the South and elsewhere have operated under federal court supervision for many years. How long should court supervision continue, and what standards are to be used in determining when desegregation has been achieved once and for all? The Rehnquist-led Supreme Court in recent years has undertaken to free some school districts from direct federal court supervision. When the last vestiges of state-sanctioned discrimination have been removed "as far as practicable," the Supreme Court has allowed lower federal courts to dissolve racial balancing plans even though imbalances due to residential patterns continue to exist.[11]

Mass Reaction to Busing.   Busing holds little appeal for white masses, especially when it involves sending their children to predominately black schools. Although white racial attitudes have moderated over the years, a majority of white parents continue to object to sending their children to black majority schools (see Table 3–3).

Mass opposition to busing has defeated the purpose of busing in many cities. In some cities where there was extensive busing, white flight from the public schools has been so widespread that the schools ended up more segregated than before busing was imposed.

The Boston experience indicates the extent of mass resistance to busing and how white flight defeated the original policy objective. In 1974 U.S. Federal District

TABLE 3-3   White Mass Attitudes toward School Integration by Racial Composition
of the School

Question: "Would you, yourself, have any objection to sending your children to a school
where more than half of the children are blacks?"

Percent Objecting

1958	1965	1970	1975	1980	1985	1990	1994
70	68	66	66	62	60	59	54

Source: General Social Survey and Gallup Polls reported in Harold W. Stanley and Richard G. Niemi,
Vital Statistics on American Politics, 5th ed. (Washington, DC: CQ Press, 1995), p. 368.

Court Judge W. Arthur Garrity found that Boston school authorities had knowingly
endeavored to keep their schools racially segregated. He ordered massive busing
throughout the city. When the Boston School Committee refused to cooperate, he
took over the governance of the school system himself. Serious racial conflict accompanied early attempts to bus students to and from high schools in working-class
white neighborhoods. But Judge Garrity stuck to his plans: "No amount of public or
parental opposition will excuse avoidance by school officials, of constitutionally imposed obligations."[12]

Prior to Judge Garrity's busing orders in 1973, Boston had 94,000 public school
students, 57 percent of whom were white. When Judge Garrity finally removed himself from the case in 1985 and returned control of the schools to elected city officials,
only 57,000 students remained in Boston's schools, and only 27 percent of them
were white.[13] There was no creditable evidence that black students had improved
their performance on standard test scores. Most white students in the Boston area attended either suburban schools or private schools.

THE CIVIL RIGHTS MOVEMENT

The early goal of the civil rights movement in America was to prevent discrimination and segregation by *governments,* particularly states, municipalities, and school
districts. But even while important victories for the civil rights movement were being recorded in the prevention of discrimination by governments, particularly in the
Brown case, the movement began to broaden its objectives to include the elimination of discrimination in *all* segments of American life, private as well as public.
Governments should not only cease discriminatory practices of their own, they
should also act to halt discrimination by private firms and individuals.

The goal of eliminating discrimination in private life creates a positive obligation of government to act forcefully in public accommodations, employment, housing, and many other sectors of society. When the civil rights movement turned to
combating private discrimination, it had to carry its fight into the legislative branch
of government. The federal courts could help restrict discrimination by state and local governments and school authorities, but only Congress, state legislatures, and
city councils could restrict discrimination practiced by private owners of restaurants,

hotels, and motels, private employers, landlords, real estate agents, and other individuals who were not government officials.

The Montgomery Bus Boycott.   The leadership in the struggle to eliminate discrimination and segregation from private life was provided by a young black minister, Martin Luther King, Jr. His father was the pastor of one of the South's largest and most influential congregations, the Ebenezer Baptist Church in Atlanta, Georgia. Martin Luther King, Jr., received his doctorate from Boston University and began his ministry in Montgomery, Alabama. In 1955 the black community of Montgomery began a year-long boycott, with frequent demonstrations against the Montgomery city buses over segregated seating. The dramatic appeal and the eventual success of the boycott in Montgomery brought nationwide attention to its leader and led to the creation in 1957 of the Southern Christian Leadership Conference.

Nonviolent Direct Action.   Under King's leadership the civil rights movement developed and refined political techniques for minorities in American politics, including nonviolent direct action, a form of protest that involves breaking "unjust" laws in an open, "loving," nonviolent fashion. The general notion of civil disobedience is not new; it has played an important role in American history, from the Boston Tea Party to the abolitionists who illegally hid runaway slaves, to the suffragettes who demonstrated for women's voting rights, to the labor organizers who formed the nation's major industrial unions, to the civil rights workers of the early 1960s who deliberately violated segregation laws. The purpose of the nonviolent direct action is to call attention, or to "bear witness," to the existence of injustice. In the words of King, civil disobedience "seeks to dramatize the issue so that it can no longer be ignored."[14]

There should be no violence in true civil disobedience, and only "unjust" laws are broken. Moreover, the law is broken "openly, lovingly" and with a willingness to accept the penalty. Punishment is actively sought rather than avoided since it will help to emphasize the injustice of the law. The object is to stir the conscience of an elite and win support for measures that will eliminate the injustices. By willingly accepting punishment for the violation of an unjust law, one demonstrates the strength of one's convictions. The dramatization of injustice makes news, the public's sympathy is won when injustices are spotlighted, and the willingness of demonstrators to accept punishment is visible evidence of their sincerity. Cruelty or violence directed against the demonstrators by police or others plays into the hands of the protesters by further emphasizing the injustices they are experiencing.

Martin Luther King, Jr.   In 1963 a group of Alabama clergymen petitioned Martin Luther King, Jr., to call off mass demonstrations in Birmingham. King, who had been arrested in the demonstrations, replied in his famous "Letter from Birmingham City Jail":

> In no sense do I advocate evading or defying the law as the rabid segregationist would do. This would lead to anarchy. One who breaks an unjust law must do it *openly, lov-*

ingly (not hatefully as the white mothers did in New Orleans when they were seen on television screaming "nigger, nigger, nigger") and with a willingness to accept the penalty. I submit that an individual who breaks a law that conscience tells him is unjust, and willingly accepts the penalty by staying in jail to arouse the conscience of the community over its injustice, is in reality expressing the very highest respect for law.

It is important to note that King's tactics relied primarily on an appeal to the conscience of white elites. The purpose of demonstrations was to call attention to injustice and stimulate established elites to remedy the injustice by lawful means. The purpose of civil disobedience was to dramatize injustice; only *unjust* laws were to be broken "openly and lovingly," and punishment was accepted to demonstrate sincerity. King did not urge black masses to remedy injustice themselves by any means necessary; and he did not urge the overthrow of established elites.

In 1964, Martin Luther King, Jr., received the Nobel Peace Price in recognition of his unique contributions to the development of nonviolent methods of social change.

Birmingham, 1963.   Perhaps the most dramatic confrontation between the civil rights movement and the southern segregationists occurred in Birmingham, Alabama, in the spring of 1963. In support of a request for desegregation of downtown eating places and the formation of a biracial committee to work out the integration of public schools, Martin Luther King, Jr., led several thousand Birmingham blacks in a series of orderly street marches. The demonstrators were met with strong police action, including fire hoses, police dogs, and electric cattle prods. Newspaper pictures of blacks being attacked by police and bitten by dogs were flashed all over the world. More than 25,000 demonstrators, including King, were jailed.

The year 1963 was probably the most important for nonviolent direct action. The Birmingham action set off demonstrations in many parts of the country; the theme remained one of nonviolence, and it was usually whites rather than blacks who resorted to violence in these demonstrations. Responsible black elites remained in control of the movement and won widespread support from the white liberal community.

"I Have a Dream."   The culmination of the nonviolent philosophy was a giant, yet orderly, march on Washington, held on August 28, 1963. More than 200,000 blacks and whites participated in the march, which was endorsed by many labor leaders, religious groups, and political figures. The march ended at the Lincoln Memorial where King delivered his most eloquent appeal, entitled "I Have a Dream": "I have a dream. It is a dream deeply rooted in the American dream. I have a dream that one day this nation will rise up and live out the true meaning of its creed: 'We hold these truths to be self-evident, that all men are created equal.' " In response President Kennedy sent a strong civil rights bill to Congress, which was passed after his death—the famous Civil Rights Act of 1964.

The Civil Rights Act of 1964.   The Civil Rights Act of 1964 passed both houses of Congress by better than a two-thirds favorable vote; it won the overwhelming support of both Republican and Democratic members of Congress. It was signed into law on July 4, 1964. It ranks with the Emancipation Proclamation, the Fourteenth Amendment, and *Brown* v. *Topeka* as one of the most important steps toward full equality for blacks in America. Among its most important provisions are the following:

Title II It is unlawful to discriminate or segregate persons on the grounds of race, color, religion, or national origin in any public accommodation, including hotels, motels, restaurants, movies, theaters, sports arenas, entertainment houses, and other places that offer to serve the public. This prohibition extends to all establishments whose operations affect interstate commerce or whose discriminatory practices are supported by state action.

Title VI Each federal department and agency shall take action to end discrimination in all programs or activities receiving federal financial assistance in any form. This action shall include termination of financial assistance.

Title VII It shall be unlawful for any employer or labor union to discriminate against any individual in any fashion in employment, because of his race, color, religion, sex, or national origin, and that an Equal Employment Opportunity Commission shall be established to enforce this provision by investigation, conference, conciliation, persuasion, and if need be, civil action in federal court.

The Civil Rights Act of 1968.   For many years fair housing had been considered the most sensitive area of civil rights legislation. Discrimination in the sale and rental of housing was the last major civil rights problem on which Congress took action. Discrimination in housing had not been mentioned in any previous legislation—not even in the comprehensive Civil Rights Act of 1964. Prohibiting discrimination in the sale or rental of housing affected the constituencies of northern members of Congress more than any of the earlier, southern-oriented legislation.

The prospects for a fair housing law were not very good at the beginning of 1968. However, when Martin Luther King, Jr., was assassinated on April 4, the mood of Congress and the nation changed dramatically. Congress passed a fair housing law as tribute to the slain civil rights leader.

The Civil Rights Act of 1968 prohibited the following forms of discrimination:

Refusal to sell or rent a dwelling to any person because of his race, color, religion, or national origin.

Discrimination against a person in the terms, conditions, or privileges of the sale or rental of a dwelling.

Advertising the sale or rental of a dwelling indicating a preference or discrimination based on race, color, religion, or national origin.

PUBLIC POLICY AND AFFIRMATIVE ACTION

Although the gains of the civil rights movement were immensely important, it must be recognized that they were primarily gains in *opportunity* rather than in *results*. Racial politics today center on the actual inequalities between blacks and whites in incomes, jobs, housing, health, education, and other conditions of life.

Continuing Inequalities.   The problem of inequality is often posed as differences in the "life chances" of blacks and whites. Figures can reveal only the bare outline of the black's life chances in American society (see Table 3–4). The average income of a black household is only 63 percent of the average white household income. More than 29 percent of all black families are below the recognized poverty line, while only 11 percent of white families live in poverty. The black unemployment rate is more than twice as high as the white unemployment rate. Blacks are less likely to hold prestigious white-collar jobs in professional, managerial, clerical,

TABLE 3-4   Minority Life Chances

Median Income of Households			
	1975	*1985*	*1995*
White	12,340	24,908	35,766
Black	7,408	14,819	22,393
Hispanic	8,865	17,465	22,860

Percent Persons below Poverty Level			
White	9.7	11.4	11.2
Black	31.3	31.3	29.3
Hispanic	26.9	29.0	30.3

Education: Percent Persons over 25 Completing (1990):		
	HIGH SCHOOL	*COLLEGE*
White	79	22
Black	65	11
Hispanic	51	9

Unemployment Rate			
	1980	*1985*	*1995*
White	6.3	6.2	5.2
Black	14.3	15.1	10.6
Hispanic	10.1	10.5	9.7

Source: *Statistical Abstract of the United States 1995;* updated U.S. Bureau of the Census, *1996 Current Population Survey.*

or sales work. They do not hold many skilled craft jobs in industry but are concentrated in operative, service, and laboring positions. The civil rights movement opened up new opportunities for black Americans. But equality of opportunity is not the same as equality of results.

Policy Changes.   What public policies should be pursued to achieve equality in America? Is it sufficient that government eliminate discrimination, guarantee equality of opportunity, and apply color-blind standards to both blacks and whites? Or should government take affirmative action to overcome the results of past unequal treatment of blacks—preferential or compensatory treatment that will favor black applications for university admissions and scholarships, job hiring and promotion, and other opportunities for advancement in life?

Opportunity versus Results.   Most Americans are concerned more with equality of opportunity than equality of results. Equality of opportunity refers to the ability to make of oneself what one can; to develop one's talents and abilities; and to be rewarded for work, initiative, and achievement. It means that everyone comes to the same starting line with the same chance of success, that whatever differences develop over time do so as a result of abilities, talents, initiative, hard work, and perhaps good luck. Equality of results refers to the equal sharing of income, jobs, contracts, and material rewards regardless of one's condition in life. It means that everyone starts and finishes the race together, regardless of ability, talent, initiative, or work.

Insofar as affirmative action programs seek to ensure equality of opportunity; to help everyone make the best of his or her life; to ensure that minorities are sought out and given a fair shot at jobs, educations, and promotions; to bring everyone up to the same starting line—then there is widespread support for these programs.[15] But when affirmative action programs seek to provide equality of results; to distribute jobs, education, or promotions according to racial quotas; to put race ahead of ability, talent, experience, or hard work—then affirmative action loses support among white masses.

Equal Opportunity versus Affirmative Action.   The earlier emphasis of government policy, of course, was nondiscrimination, or equal employment opportunity. "It was not a program to offer special privilege to any one group of persons because of their particular race, religion, sex, or national origin."[16] This appeared to conform to the original nondiscrimination approach, beginning with President Harry Truman's decision to desegregate the armed forces in 1946 and carrying through Title VI and Title VII of the Civil Rights Act of 1964 to eliminate discrimination in federally aided projects and private employment.

Gradually, however, the goal of the civil rights movement shifted from the traditional aim of equality of opportunity through nondiscrimination alone to affirmative action to establish "goals and timetables" to achieve absolute equality between blacks and whites. While avoiding the term *quota,* the notion of affirmative action tests the success of equal employment opportunity by observing whether blacks achieve admissions, jobs, and promotions in proportion to their numbers in the population.

Affirmative action programs were initially products of the federal bureaucracy. They were not begun by Congress. Instead, they were developed by the federal executive agencies that were authorized by the Civil Rights Act of 1964 to develop "rules and regulations" for desegregating activities receiving federal funds (Title VI) and private employment (Title VII). President Lyndon B. Johnson gave impetus to affirmative action with Executive Order No. 11246 in 1965, which covered employment and promotion in federal agencies and businesses contracting with the federal government. In 1972 the U.S. Office of Education issued guidelines that mandated "goals" for university admissions and faculty hiring of blacks and women. The Equal Employment Opportunity Commission, established by the Civil Rights Act of 1964 (Title VII) to eliminate discrimination in private employment, has carried the notion of affirmative action beyond federal contractors and recipients of federal aid into all sectors of private employment.

Federal officials generally measure "progress" in affirmative action in terms of the number of blacks admitted, employed, or promoted. The pressure to show progress and retain federal financial support can result in preferential treatment of blacks. It also puts pressure on traditional measures of qualifications—test scores and educational achievement.

THE SUPREME COURT AND AFFIRMATIVE ACTION

Affirmative action programs pose some important constitutional questions. Do these programs discriminate against whites in violation of the Equal Protection Clause of the Fourteenth Amendment? Do these programs discriminate against whites in violation of the Civil Rights Act of 1964, which prohibits discrimination "on account of race," not just discrimination against blacks? Clearly, these are questions for the Supreme Court to resolve, but unfortunately the Court has failed to develop clear-cut answers.

The Bakke Case.   In an early, controversial case, *Regents of the University of California* v. *Bakke* (1978), the Supreme Court struck down a special admissions program for minorities at a state medical school on the grounds that it excluded a white applicant because of his race and violated his rights under the equal protection clause.[17] Allan Bakke applied to the University of California Davis Medical School two consecutive years and was rejected; in both years black applicants with significantly lower grade point averages and medical aptitude test scores were accepted through a special admissions program that reserved sixteen minority places in a class of one hundred.* The University of California did not deny that its admissions decisions were based on race. Instead, it argued that its racial classification

---

* Bakke's grade point average was 3.51; his MCAT scores were verbal 96, quantitative 94, science 97, general information 72. The average for the special admissions students were grade point average 2.62, MCAT verbal 34, quantitative 30, science 37, general information 18.

was "benign," that is, designed to assist minorities, not to hinder them. The special admissions program was designed (1) to "reduce the historical deficit of traditionally disfavored minorities in medical schools and the medical profession," (2) to "counter the effects of societal discrimination," (3) to "increase the number of physicians who will practice in communities currently underserved," and (4) to "obtain the educational benefits that flow from an ethnically diverse student body."

The Court held that these objectives were legitimate and that race and ethnic origin may be considered in reviewing applications to a state school without violating the Equal Protection Clause. However, the Court also held that a separate admissions program for minorities with a specified quota of openings that were unavailable to white applicants did violate the Equal Protection Clause. The Court ordered Bakke admitted to medical school and the elimination of the special admissions program. It recommended that California consider developing an admissions program that considered disadvantaged racial or ethnic background as a "plus" in an overall evaluation of an application, but did not set numerical quotas or exclude any persons from competing for all positions.

The Bakke case failed to resolve the controversies over affirmative action. Supporters of affirmative action emphasized the Supreme Court's willingness to allow minority status to be considered a positive factor; opponents emphasized the Court's unwillingness to allow quotas that excluded whites from competing for a certain number of positions. Since Bakke had "won" the case, most observers felt that the Supreme Court was not going to permit racial quota systems.

Affirmative Action as a Remedy for Past Discrimination. However, the Supreme Court appears willing to approve affirmative action programs where there is evidence of past discriminatory actions. In *United Steelworkers of America* v. *Weber* (1979), the Court approved a plan developed by a private employer and a union to reserve 50 percent of higher-paying, skilled jobs for minorities. Kaiser Aluminum Corporation and the United Steelworkers Union, under federal government pressure, had established a program to get more blacks into skilled technical jobs; only 2 percent of the skilled jobs were held by blacks in the plant where Brian Weber worked, while 39 percent of the local work force was black. When Weber was excluded from the training program and blacks with less seniority and fewer qualifications were accepted, he filed suit in federal court claiming that he had been discriminated against because of his race in violation of Title VII of the Civil Rights Act of 1964.

But the Supreme Court held that Title VII of the Civil Rights Act of 1964 "left employers and unions in the private sector free to take such race-conscious steps to eliminate manifest racial imbalances in traditionally segregated job categories. We hold that Title VII does not prohibit such . . . affirmative action plans." Weber's reliance on the clear language of Title VII was "misplaced." According to the Court, it would be "ironic indeed" if the Civil Rights Act were used to prohibit voluntary, private race-conscious efforts to overcome the past effects of discrimination.[18]

Despite changing membership over time, the Supreme Court has not altered its policy regarding affirmative action as a remedy for past discrimination. In *United*

States v. *Paradise* (1987), the Court upheld a rigid 50 percent black quota system for promotions in the Alabama Department of Safety, which had excluded blacks from the ranks of state troopers before 1972 and had not promoted any blacks higher than corporal before 1984. In a 5-to-4 decision, the majority stressed the long history of discrimination in the agency as a reason for upholding the quota system. Whatever burdens were imposed on innocent parties were outweighed by the need to correct the effects of past discrimination.[19]

Cases Questioning Affirmative Action.   Yet in the absence of past discrimination, the Supreme Court has expressed concern about whites who are directly and adversely affected by government action solely because of their race. In *Firefighters Local Union* v. *Stotts* (1984), the Court ruled that a city could not lay off white firefighters in favor of black firefighters with less seniority.[20] In *Richmond* v. *Crosen* (1989), the Court held that a minority set-aside program in Richmond, Virginia, which mandates that 30 percent of all city construction contracts must go to "blacks, Spanish-speaking, Orientals, Indians, Eskimos, or Aleuts," violated the Equal Protection Clause of the Fourteenth Amendment.[21]

However, the Supreme Court has never adopted the *color-blind doctrine* first espoused by Justice John Harlan in his dissent from *Plessy* v. *Ferguson*—that "our constitution is color-blind and neither knows nor tolerates classes among cities."[22] If the Equal Protection Clause required that the laws of the United States and the states be truly color-blind, then *no* racial preferences, goals, or quotas would be tolerated. This view has occasionally been expressed in recent minority dissents, and concurring opinions.[23]

Proving Discrimination.   The Civil Rights Act of 1964, Title VII, bars racial or sexual discrimination in employment. But how can persons who feel that they have been passed over for jobs or promotions go about the task of proving that discrimination was involved? Evidence of direct discrimination is often difficult to obtain. Can underrepresentation of minorities or women in a workforce be used as evidence of discrimination, in the absence of any evidence of direct discriminatory practice? If an employer uses a requirement or test that has a disparate effect on minorities or women, who has the burden of proof that the requirement or test is relevant to effective job performance?

The Supreme Court responded to both of these questions in its interpretation of the Civil Rights Act in *Wards Cove Packing Co., Inc.* v. *Atonio* (1989).[24] In a controversial 5-to-4 decision, the Court held that statistical imbalances in race or gender in the workplace were not sufficient evidence by themselves to prove discrimination. The Court also ruled that it was up to the plaintiffs to prove that an employer had no business reason for requirements or tests that had an adverse impact on minorities or women. This decision clearly made it more difficult to prove job discrimination.

Congress Enters the Dispute.   Civil rights groups were highly critical of what they regarded as the Supreme Court's "narrowing" of the Civil Rights Act protections in employment. They turned to Congress to rewrite portions of the Civil Rights Act to restore these protections. Business lobbies, however, believed that accepting statistical imbalances as evidence of discrimination or shifting the burden of proof to employers would result in hiring by "quotas" simply to avoid lawsuits. After nearly two years of negotiations on Capital Hill and a reversal of President Bush's initial opposition, Congress crafted a policy in its Civil Rights and Women's Equity Act of 1991. Among the more important provisions of the act are the following:[25]

> **Statistical imbalances:** The mere existence of statistical imbalance in an employer's workforce is not, by itself, sufficient evidence to prove discrimination. However, statistical imbalances may be evidence of employment practices (rules, requirements, academic qualifications, tests) that have a "disparate impact" on minorities or women.
>
> **Disparate employment practices:** Employers bear the burden of proof that any practice that has a "disparate impact" is necessary and has "a significant and manifest relationship to the requirements for effective job performance."

"Strict Scrutiny."   In 1995, the Supreme Court held that racial classifications in law must be subject to "strict scrutiny." This means that race-based actions by government—any disparate treatment of the races by federal, state, or local public agencies—must be found necessary to remedy past proven discrimination, or to further clearly identified, compelling, and legitimate government objectives. Moreover, it must be "narrowly tailored" so as not to adversely affect the rights of individuals. In striking down a federal construction contract "set-aside" program for small businesses owned by racial minorities, the Court expressed skepticism about governmental racial classifications: "There is simply no way of determining what classifications are 'benign' and 'remedial' and what classifications are in fact motivated by illegitimate notions of racial inferiority or simple racial politics."[24]

Elites Divided.   The Supreme Court appears to be closely divided over the constitutional status of affirmative action. At least two justices (Scalia and Thomas) believe that the Constitution requires a color-blind standard: "Under our Constitution, the Government may not make distinctions based on race." Three justices (O'Connor, Rehnquist, and Kennedy) apparently require "strict scrutiny" of racial distinctions by governments. And four justices (Stevens, Ginsburg, Souter, and Breyer) appear willing to accept racial distinctions that are "benign" toward minorities even if these distinctions place an "incidental burden on some members of the majority."

Moreover, the Court's cumulative decisions about affirmative action have not provided the nation with a clear or coherent interpretation of the Constitution. All we can say is that affirmative action programs are *more likely to be found constitutional* when (a) they are adopted as a remedy to past proven discrimination, (b) they serve a clearly identified, compelling, and legitimate government objective, (c) they are "narrowly tailored" to achieve this objective, and (d) they do not absolutely bar majority members from participation.

MASS OPINION AND AFFIRMATIVE ACTION

Mass opinion generally supports "affirmative action" when it is defined as encouragement, training, and education for qualified minorities and women (see Table 3–5). However, black and white opinions differ sharply over preferences and "quotas" in hiring, promotions, and admissions. Whites oppose such measures by more than two to one, while blacks support them by comparable margins. But both blacks

TABLE 3-5   Mass Opinion on Affirmative Action

Do you favor or oppose the following?			
	ALL	*BLACKS*	*WHITES*
Companies making special efforts to find qualified minorities and women and then encouraging them to apply for jobs.			
Favor	73	87	71
Oppose	24	12	12
Providing job training programs for minorities and women to make them better qualified for jobs?			
Favor	82	94	80
Oppose	17	6	18
Providing special education classes for minorities and women to make them better qualified for college?			
Favor	75	90	73
Oppose	22	9	24
Establishing quotas that require businesses to hire a certain number of minorities and women?			
Favor	35	66	30
Oppose	63	31	68
Establishing quotas that require schools to admit a certain number of minorities and women as students?			
Favor	39	20	35
Oppose	52	27	61
Favoring a well-qualified minority applicant over an equally qualified white applicant when filling a job in a business that has few minority workers?			
Favor	48	51	47
Oppose	44	42	45
Favoring a minority who is less qualified than a white applicant when filling a job in a business that has few minority workers?			
Favor	13	22	11
Oppose	84	68	86

Source: As reported in *USA Today,* March 24, 1995.

and whites oppose preferences for "less qualified" minorities over "more qualified" whites.

Mass Opposition to Racial Preferences.   Opponents of affirmative action argue that government racial classifications violate the fundamental principle of equality under the law. It is argued that America cannot "make up" for past discrimination, by "discrimination in the opposite direction." Some early supporters of affirmative action have come to believe that race-conscious programs are no longer necessary, that disadvantages in society today are more class-based than race-based, and that if preferences are to be granted at all they should be based on economic disadvantage, not race. Moreover, misgivings have been expressed by some African Americans about unfair stigmatizing of the supposed beneficiaries of affirmative action—a resulting negative stereotyping that "stamps minorities with a badge of inferiority and may cause them to develop dependencies or to adopt an attitude that they are 'entitled' to preferences."[26] White resentment against the perceived unfairness of affirmative action aggravates racial conflict, creating an "angry white male" backlash that erodes support for civil rights generally.

Yet most Americans agree that discrimination still exists in American society. Many supporters of affirmative action would ideally prefer a society in which "our children will one day live in a nation where they will not be judged by the color of their skin but by the content of their character." Martin Luther King, Jr.'s dream remains the ultimate goal for the nation. Elites are more likely to see race-conscious policies as a continuing necessity to remedy current discrimination and the effects of past discrimination. America is not now nor has it ever been a "color-blind" society. "If we abandon affirmative action we return to the old white boy network."[27] They perceive affirmative action as a necessary tool in achieving equality of opportunity.

The California Civil Rights Initiative.   Opposition to racial and gender preferences inspired a citizens' initiative that was placed on the ballot in California in 1996. The California Civil Rights Initiative adds the following key phrase to that state's constitution:

> Neither the state of California nor any of its political subdivisions or agents shall use race, sex, color, ethnicity or national origin as a criterion for either discriminating against, or granting preferential treatment to, any individual or group in the operation of the State's system of public employment, public education or public contracting.

Supporters argue that this initiative leaves all existing federal and state civil rights protections intact. It simply extends the rights of specially protected groups to all of the state's citizens. Opponents argue that it sets back the civil rights movement, that it will end the progress of minorities in education and employment, and that it denies minorities the opportunity to seek assistance and protection from government. The initiative was approved by 54 percent of California's voters.

Following its adoption, opponents of the California Civil Rights Initiative filed suit in federal court arguing that it violated the Equal Protection Clause of the U.S. Constitution because it denied minorities and women an opportunity to seek preferential treatment by governments. But a federal Circuit Court of Appeals upheld the constitutionality of the initiative: "Impediments to preferential treatment do not deny equal protection."[25] The Court reasoned that the Constitution allows some race-based preferences to correct past discrimination, but it does not prevent states from banning racial preferences altogether.

The Effects of Eliminating Preferences.   The California citizens' initiative barring racial and gender preferences has inspired similar mass movements in other states. But college and university officials and most government office-holders continue to oppose measures they regard as anti-affirmative-action. At the University of California–Berkeley and University of Texas–Austin law schools, minority admissions dropped following the elimination of racial preferences. It is not clear whether minority students unable to gain admission to prestigious institutions will enroll at other schools or be lost altogether as educated professionals and role models. An alternative to racial preferences in undergraduate admissions may be the automatic admission of top academic students (perhaps the top 10 percent) at each high school in the state. Presumably this would allow students from schools with heavy minority enrollments to gain admission without reliance on standardized test scores. But opponents of this alternative argue that it "lets poor schools off the hook" and that the solution is to improve the performance of minority students in high schools everywhere.

GENDER EQUALITY AND THE CONSTITUTION

The historical context of the Fourteenth Amendment implies its intent to guarantee equality for newly freed slaves. But the wording of its equal protection clause applies to "any person." Thus the text of the Fourteenth Amendment *could* be interpreted to bar any gender differences in the law. However, the Supreme Court has never interpreted the Equal Protection Clause to give the same level of protection to gender equality as to racial equality. Indeed, the Supreme Court in the nineteenth century specifically rejected the argument that this clause applied to women; the Court once upheld a state law banning women from practicing law, arguing that "The natural and proper timidity and delicacy which belongs to the female sex evidently unfits it for many of the occupations of civil life."[28]

Early Feminist Politics.   The earliest active feminist organizations grew out of the pre–Civil War antislavery movement, in which the first generation of feminists learned to organize, hold public meetings, and conduct petition campaigns. After the Civil War, women were successful in changing many state laws that abridged the property rights of married women and otherwise treated them as chattel (property) of their husbands. Activists were also successful in winning some protections for women in the workplace, including state laws limiting hours of work, working conditions, and physical demands. At the time, these laws were regarded as progressive.

The most successful feminist efforts of the 1800s centered on the protection of women in families. The perceived threats to women's well-being were their husbands' drinking, gambling, and consorting with prostitutes. Women led the Anti-Saloon League and succeeded in outlawing gambling and prostitution in every state except Nevada and provided the major source of moral support for the Eighteenth Amendment (Prohibition).

In the early twentieth century, the feminist movement concentrated on women's suffrage—the drive to guarantee women the right to vote. The early suffragettes employed mass demonstrations, parades, picketing, and occasional disruption and civil disobedience—tactics similar to those of the civil rights movement of the 1960s. The culmination of their efforts was the 1920 passage of the Nineteenth Amendment to the Constitution: "The right of citizens of the United States to vote shall not be denied or abridged by the United States or by any state on account of sex."

Judicial Scrutiny of Gender Classifications.   In the 1970s, the Supreme Court became responsive to arguments that sex discrimination might violate the Equal Protection Clause of the Fourteenth Amendment. It ruled that sexual classifications in the law "must be reasonable and not arbitrary, and must rest on some ground of difference having fair and substantial relation to . . . important governmental objectives."[29] Thus, for example, the Court has ruled (1) that a state can no longer set different ages for men and women to become legal adults[30] or purchase alcoholic beverages,[31] (2) women cannot be barred from police or firefighting jobs by arbitrary height and weight requirements,[32] (3) insurance and retirement plans for women must pay the same monthly benefits (even though women on the average live longer),[33] and (4) schools must pay coaches in girls' sports the same as coaches in boys' sports.[34]

Equal Rights Amendment.   At the center of feminist activity in the 1970s was the Equal Rights Amendment (ERA) to the Constitution. The amendment stated simply, "Equality of rights under the law shall not be denied or abridged by the United States or by any state on account of sex." The ERA passed Congress easily in 1972 and was sent to the states for the necessary ratification by three-fourths (thirty-eight) of them. The amendment won quick ratification in half the states, but a developing "Stop ERA" movement slowed progress and eventually defeated the amendment itself. In 1979, the original seven-year time period for ratification—the period customarily set by Congress for ratification of constitutional amendments—expired. Proponents of the ERA persuaded Congress to extend the ratification period for three more years, to 1982. But despite heavy lobbying efforts in the states and public opinion polls showing national majorities favoring it, the amendment failed to win ratification by the necessary thirty-eight states.*

* By 1982, thirty-four states had ratified the ERA. Three of them—Idaho, Nebraska, and Tennessee—subsequently voted to "rescind" their ratification; but the U.S. Constitution does not mention rescinding votes. The states that had not ratified by 1982 were Nevada, Utah, Arizona, Oklahoma, Illinois, Indiana, Missouri, Arkansas, Louisiana, Mississippi, Alabama, Georgia, Florida, North Carolina, South Carolina, and Virginia.

Proponents of the ERA argued in the state legislatures that most of the progress women have made toward equality in marriage, property, employment, credit, education, and so on depends on state and federal *law*. The guarantee of equality of the sexes would be much more secure if this guarantee were made part of the U.S. Constitution. Moreover, the ERA would eliminate the need to pass separate laws in a wide variety of fields to ensure sexual equality. The ERA, as a permanent part of the U.S. Constitution, would provide a sweeping guarantee of equality, directly enforceable by court action. Finally, the ERA has taken on a great deal of symbolic meaning; even if federal and state laws prohibit sexual discrimination now, it is nonetheless important to many to see the ERA as part of the Constitution—"the supreme law of the land."

Opponents of the ERA charged that it would eliminate many legal protections for women, such as financial support by husbands, an interest in the husband's property, exemption from military service, and so forth. In addition to these specific objectives, opponents of "women's liberation" in general charged that the movement weakens the family institution and demoralizes women who wish to devote their lives to their families, husbands, and children.

GENDER EQUALITY AND THE ECONOMY

Today, women's participation in the labor force is not much lower than men's, and the gap is closing over time. More than 80 percent of women with college educations are working; more than 75 percent of married women with school age children are working; and more than 60 percent of married women with children under 6 years of age are working (see Table 3–6). The movement of women into the American workforce shifted feminist political activity toward economic concerns—gender equality in education, employment, pay, promotion, and credit.

Civil Rights Laws.   Title VII of the federal Civil Rights Act of 1964 prevents sexual (as well as racial) discrimination in hiring, pay, and promotions. The Equal Employment Opportunity Commission (EEOC), which is the federal agency charged with eliminating discrimination in employment, has established guidelines barring stereotyped classifications of "men's jobs" and "women's jobs." The courts have repeatedly struck down state laws and employer practices that differentiate between men and women in hours, pay, retirement age, and so forth.

The Federal Equal Credit Opportunity Act of 1974 prohibits sex discrimination in credit transactions. Federal law prevents banks, credit unions, savings and loan associations, retail stores, and credit card companies from denying credit because of sex or marital status. However, these businesses may still deny credit for a poor or nonexistent credit rating, and some women who have always maintained accounts in their husbands' name may still face credit problems if they apply in their own name.

Title IX of the federal Education Act Amendment of 1972 deals with sex discrimination in education. This federal law bars discrimination in admissions, housing, rules, financial aid, faculty and staff recruitment and pay, and—most troublesome of all—athletics. The last problem has proven very difficult because men's

TABLE 3-6   Women in the Workforce

Participation Rates: Percent in Labor Force		
	MALE	*FEMALE*
Total	75.5	61.0
Ages		
25–34	92.6	74.0
35–44	92.8	77.1
45–54	89.1	74.6
55–64	65.5	48.9
65 plus	16.8	9.2
Marital Status		
Single	73.7	66.7
Married	77.5	60.7
Education		
H.S. only	89.3	68.6
College	94.2	81.8
Women with Children	Single	Married
6–17	67.5	76.0
Under 6	52.2	61.7

Source: *Statistical Abstract of the United States 1996,* pp. 399–400.

football and basketball programs have traditionally brought in the money to finance all other sports, and men's football and basketball have received the largest share of school athletic budgets.

The Earnings Gap.   Overall, women's earnings remain substantially less than men's earnings. In 1994, for example, median annual earnings for men were $30,407 compared to $21,747 for women, indicating that women, on the average, earned only about 72 percent of men's earnings.[35] This earnings gap is not so much a product of direct discrimination, that is, women in the same job with the same skills, qualifications, experience, and work record being paid less than men. This form of direct discrimination has been illegal since the Civil Rights Act of 1964. Rather, the earnings gap is primarily a product of a division in the labor market between traditionally male and female jobs, with lower salaries paid in traditionally female occupations.

The initial efforts of the women's movement were directed toward ensuring that women enjoyed equal access to traditionally male "white-collar" occupations, for example, physician, lawyer, and engineer. Success in these efforts would automatically narrow the wage gap. And indeed, women have been very successful over the last several decades in increasing their representation in prestigious white collar occupations (see Table 3–7), although most of these occupational fields continue to be dominated by men.

TABLE 3-7   The Dual Labor Market

"White Collar"			
Women are increasingly entering white-collar occupation fields traditionally dominated by men.			
	1960	*1983*	*1995*
Architects	3	13	20
Computer analysts	11	28	32
College and university teachers	28	36	45
Engineers	1	6	8
Lawyers and judges	4	16	26
Physicians	10	16	24

"Pink Collar"			
Women continue to be concentrated in occupational fields traditionally dominated by women.			
	1970	*1980*	*1995*
Secretaries	98	99	98
Waitresses and waiters	91	88	79
Nurses	97	96	94
Office clerks	75	82	78

"Blue Collar"			
Women continue to be excluded from many blue-collar occupational fields traditionally dominated by men, although women bartenders now outnumber men.			
	1970	*1980*	*1995*
Truck drivers	1	2	5
Carpenters	1	1	2
Laborers	17	19	18
Auto mechanics	1	1	1
Bartenders	21	44	55

Sources: U.S. Department of Labor, *Employment in Perspective: Working Women* (Washington, DC: U.S. Government Printing Office, 1983); National Research Council, National Academy of Sciences, *Women's Work, Men's Work* (Washington, DC: National Academy Press, 1985); *Statistical Abstract of the United States 1996)*, pp. 405–407.

Dual Labor Market. Nonetheless, evidence of a "dual" labor market, with male dominated "blue-collar" jobs distinguishable from female-dominated "pink-collar" jobs, continues to be a major obstacle to economic equality between men and women. A study sponsored by the National Academy of Sciences concluded that most of the differences in men's and women's earnings could be attributed to sex segregation in occupations.[36] These occupational differences were attributed to cultural stereotyping, social conditioning, and premarket training and education, which narrow the choices available to women. Although significant progress has been made in recent years in reducing occupational sex segregation, nonetheless many observers doubt that sexually differentiated occupations will be eliminated in the foreseeable future.

Comparable Worth.   As a result of a growing recognition that the wage gap is more a result of occupational differentiation than direct discrimination, some feminist organizations have turned to a new approach—the demand that pay levels in various occupations be determined by "comparable worth" rather than by the labor market. Comparable worth means more than paying men and women equally for the same work; it means paying the same wages for jobs of comparable value to the employer. It means that traditionally male and female jobs would be evaluated by government agencies or courts to determine their "worth" to the employer, perhaps by considering responsibilities, effort, knowledge, and skill requirements. Jobs adjudged to be "comparable" would be paid equal wages. Government agencies or the courts would replace the free labor market in the determination of wage rates. But the EEOC has rejected the notion of comparable worth and declined to determine wages for traditionally male and female jobs. And so far the federal courts have *not* declared that differing wages in traditionally male and female occupations constitute evidence of sexual discrimination in violation of federal law. However, some government agencies and private employers have undertaken to review their own pay scales to determine if traditionally female occupations are underpaid.

The Glass Ceiling.   Few women have climbed the ladder to become president or chief executive officer or director of the nation's largest industrial corporations, banks, utilities, newspapers, or television networks.[37] Large numbers of women are entering the legal profession, but few have made it to senior partner in the nation's largest and most prestigious law firms. Women are more likely to be found in the president's cabinet than in the corporate boardroom.

The barriers to women's advancement to top positions are often very subtle, giving rise to the phrase *the glass ceiling.* In explaining "why women aren't getting to the top," one observer argues that "At senior management levels competence is assumed. What you're looking for is someone who fits, someone who gets along, someone you trust. Now that's subtle stuff. How does a group of men feel that a woman is going to fit? I think it's very hard."[38]

There are many other explanations and all of them are controversial: Women choose staff assignments rather than fast-track, operating-head assignments. Women are cautious and unaggressive in corporate politics. Women have lower expectations about peak earnings and positions, and these expectations become self-fulfilling. Women bear children, and even during relatively short maternity absences they fall behind their male counterparts. Women are less likely to want to change locations than men, and immobile executives are worth less to a corporation than mobile ones. Women executives in sensitive positions come under even more pressure than men in similar posts. Women executives believe that they get much more scrutiny than men and must work harder to succeed. Finally, it is important to note that affirmative action efforts by governments, notably the EEOC, are directed primarily at entry-level positions rather than senior management posts.

Sexual Harassment.   In recent years the women's movement has succeeded in placing the issue of sexual harassment on the national agenda. Title VII of the Civil Rights Act of 1964 protects employees from sexual discrimination "with respect to compensation, terms, conditions, or privileges of employment." The Supreme Court held in 1986 that "discriminatory intimidation" of employees could be "sufficiently severe" to alter the "conditions" of employment and therefore violate Title VII.[39]

Sexual harassment may take various forms. There seems to be little doubt that it includes (1) conditioning employment or promotion or privileges of employment on the granting of sexual favors by an employee and (2) "tangible" acts of touching, fondling, or forced sexual relations. But sexual harassment has also been defined to include (3) a "hostile working environment." This phrase may include offensive utterances, sexual innuendos, dirty jokes, the display of pornographic material, and unwanted proposals for dates. Several problems arise with this definition. First, it would appear to include speech and hence raise First Amendment questions regarding how far speech may be curtailed by law in the workplace. Second, the definition depends more on the subjective feelings of the individual employee about what is "offensive" and "unwanted" rather than on an objective standard of behavior that is easily understood by all. The Supreme Court wrestled with the definition of a "hostile work environment" in *Harris* v. *Forklift* in 1993. It held that a plaintiff need not show that the utterances caused psychological injury but only that a "reasonable person" would perceive the work environment as hostile or abusive. Presumably a single incident would not constitute harassment; rather courts should consider "the frequency of the discriminatory conduct," "its severity," and whether it "unreasonably interferes with an employee's work performance."

ABORTION AND THE RIGHT TO LIFE

Abortion is not an issue that can easily be compromised. The arguments touch on fundamental moral and religious principles. Proponents of abortion, who often refer to themselves as "pro choice," argue that a woman should be permitted to control her own body and should not be forced by law to have unwanted children. They cite the heavy toll in lives lost in criminal abortions and the psychological and emotional pain of an unwanted pregnancy. Opponents of abortion, who often refer to themselves as "pro life," generally base their belief on the sanctity of life, including the life of the unborn child, which they believe deserves the protection of law— "the right to life." Many believe that the killing of an unborn child for any reason other than the preservation of the life of the mother is murder.

Early State Laws.   Historically, abortions for any purpose other than saving the life of the mother were criminal offenses under state law. About a dozen states acted in the late 1960s to permit abortions in cases of rape or incest or to protect the physical health of the mother, and in some cases her mental health as well. Relatively few abortions were performed under these laws, however, because of the red tape involved—review of each case by several concurring physicians, approval of a hospital board, and so forth. Then in 1970, New York, Alaska, Hawaii, and Washington enacted laws that in effect permitted abortion at the request of the woman involved and the concurrence of her physician.

Roe v. Wade.   The U.S. Supreme Court's 1973 decision in *Roe* v. *Wade* was one of the most important and far-reaching in the Court's history.[40] The Court ruled that the constitutional guarantee of "liberty" in the Fifth and Fourteenth Amendments included a woman's decision to bear or not to bear a child. The Court also ruled that the word *person* in the Constitution did not include the unborn child. Therefore, the Fifth and Fourteenth Amendments to the Constitution, guaranteeing "life, liberty, and property," did not protect the "life" of the fetus. The Court also ruled that a state's power to protect the health and safety of the mother could not justify *any* restriction on abortion in the first three months of pregnancy. Between the third and sixth months of pregnancy, a state could set standards for abortion procedures to protect the health of women, but a state could not prohibit abortions. Only in the final three months could a state prohibit or regulate abortion to protect the unborn.

Government Funding of Abortions.   The Supreme Court's decision did not end the controversy over abortion. Congress defeated efforts to pass a constitutional amendment restricting abortion or declaring that the guarantee of life begins at conception. However, it banned the use of federal funds under Medicaid (medical care for the poor) for abortions except to protect the life of a woman. The Supreme Court upheld the constitutionality of federal and state laws denying tax funds for abortions. Although women retained the right to an abortion, the Court held that there was no constitutional obligation for governments to pay for abortions;[41] the decision about whether to pay for abortion from tax revenues was left to Congress and the states.

Early efforts by the states to restrict abortion ran into Supreme Court opposition. The Court held that states and cities may not interfere with, or try to influence, a woman's decision to terminate a pregnancy. Specifically, the Court held that states may not require all abortions to be performed in hospitals, require parental consent for all minors, require that physicians inform women of particular risks associated with abortion or provide information about fetal development, and require a 24-hour waiting period between authorizing and performing an abortion.[42]

Abortions in the United States.   About 1.6 million abortions are performed each year in the United States. This is about 44 percent of the number of live births. About 85 percent of all abortions are performed at abortion clinics; others are performed in physicians' offices or in hospitals, where the cost is significantly higher. Most of these abortions are performed in the first three months; about 10 percent are performed after the third month.

Abortion Battles.   Opponents of abortion won a victory in *Webster* v. *Reproductive Health Services* (1989), when the Supreme Court upheld a Missouri law restricting abortions.[43] The right to abortion under *Roe* v. *Wade* was not overturned, but the Court held that Missouri could deny public funds for abortions that were not necessary for the life of the women and could deny the use of public facilities or employees in performing or assisting in abortions. More important, the Court upheld the requirement for a test of "viability" after twenty weeks and a prohibition on abortions of a viable fetus except to save a woman's life. The Court recognized the state's "interest in the protection of human life when viability is possible." The effect of the *Webster* decision was to rekindle contentious debates over abortion in virtually all state capitols. Various legal restrictions on abortions have been passed in some states, including (1) prohibitions on public financing of abortions; (2) requirements for a test of viability and prohibitions on abortions of a viable fetus; (3) laws granting permission to doctors and hospitals to refuse to perform abortions; (4) laws requiring humane and sanitary disposal of fetal remains; (5) laws requiring physicians to inform patients about the development of the fetus and the availability of assistance in pregnancy; (6) laws requiring that parents of minors seeking abortion be informed; (7) laws requiring spouses to be informed; (8) laws requiring that late abortions be performed in hospitals; (9) laws setting standards of cleanliness and care in abortion clinics; (10) laws prohibiting abortion based on the gender of the fetus.

Reaffirming Roe v. *Wade.*   Abortion has become such a polarizing issue that pro-choice and pro-life groups are generally unwilling to search out a middle ground. Yet the Supreme Court appears to have chosen a policy of affirming a woman's right to abortion while upholding modest restrictions.

Pennsylvania is a state where pro-life forces won the support of the governor and legislature for a series of restrictions on abortion—physicians must inform women of risks and alternatives; a 24-hour waiting period is required; minors must have consent of parents or a judge; spouses must be notified. These restrictions reached the Supreme Court in the case of *Planned Parenthood of Pennsylvania* v. *Casey* in 1992.[44]

Justice Sandra Day O'Connor took the lead in forming a moderate, swing bloc on the Court; her majority opinion strongly reaffirmed the fundamental right of abortion:

> Our law affords constitutional protection to personal decisions relating to marriage, procreation, contraception, family relationships, child rearing and education. . . . These matters, involving the most intimate and personal choices a person may make in a lifetime, choices central to personal dignity and autonomy, are central to the liberty protected by the Fourteenth Amendment. . . . A woman's liberty is not so unlimited, however, that from the outset the State cannot show its concern for the life of the unborn, and at a later point in fetal development the State's interest in life has sufficient force so that the right of the woman to terminate the pregnancy can be restricted. We conclude the line should be drawn at viability, so that before that time the woman has a right to choose to terminate her pregnancy. . . .

Justice O'Connor went on to establish a new standard for constitutionally evaluating restrictions: They must not impose an "undue burden" on women seeking abortion or place "substantial obstacles" in her path. All of Pennsylvania's restrictions were upheld except spousal notification.

Congress and Abortion. "Pro-choice" and "pro-life" forces battle in Congress as well as the courts. "Pro-choice" forces regularly attempt to repeal the Hyde Amendment that prevents states from using federal Medicaid funds to pay for abortions. A Democratic-controlled Congress responded in a limited fashion in 1993 by making abortions in cases of rape and incest eligible for Medicaid payments. "Pro-life" forces fought a long battle in a Republican-controlled Congress in 1996 to outlaw late-term "partial birth" abortions—the killing of a living fetus during vaginal delivery before delivery is complete. This procedure is relatively rare, but "pro-choice" forces argued that the proposed law was the first step in a strategy to ban all abortions "procedure by procedure." Congress passed the bill, but President Clinton vetoed it.

SUMMARY

Let us try to set forth some propositions that are consistent with elite theory and help describe the development of civil rights policy.

1. Elites and masses in America differ in their attitudes toward blacks. Support for civil rights legislation has come from educated, affluent whites in leadership positions.
2. Mass opinion toward civil rights has generally *followed* public policy and not led it. Mass opinion did not oppose legally segregated schools until after elites had declared national policy in *Brown* v. *Topeka*.
3. The greatest impetus to the advancement of civil rights policy in this century was the U.S. Supreme Court's decision in *Brown* v. *Topeka*. Thus, it was the Supreme Court, nonelected and enjoying life terms in office, which assumed the initiative in civil rights policy. Congress did not take significant action until ten years later.
4. Resistance to the implementation of *Brown* v. *Topeka* was centered on states and communities. Resistance to national policy was remarkably effective for over a decade; blacks were not admitted to white schools in the South in large numbers until all segments of the national elite—Congress and the executive branch, as well as the judicial branch—acted in support of desegregation.
5. The elimination of legal discrimination and the guarantee of equality of opportunity in the Civil Rights Act of 1964 were achieved largely through the dramatic appeals of middle-class black leaders to the consciences of white elites. Black leaders did not attempt to overthrow the established order but rather to increase opportunities for blacks to achieve success within the American system.
6. Elite support for equality of opportunity does not satisfy the demands of black masses for equality of results. Inequalities between blacks and whites in life

chances—income, education, employment, health—persist, although the gap may be narrowing over the long run.

7. Affirmative action programs are pressed on governments, universities, and private employers by federal agencies seeking to reduce inequalities. But white masses generally reject preferences or quotas, which they believe to put working-class and middle-class white males at a disadvantage.

8. The Supreme Court has approved affirmative action programs with racial quotas when there is evidence of current or past discriminatory practices and when the program is narrowly defined to remedy the effects of previous discrimination. The Court has upheld some claims that racial preferences by governments violate the Fourteenth Amendment's guarantee of equal protection of laws when white males are excluded altogether solely on the basis of race.

9. Congress has been slower to address key issues raised by affirmative action programs than by the nonelected judicial and bureaucratic elites. Congress seeks to avoid publically endorsing "quotas" while at the same time allowing "statistical imbalances" to be used as evidence of discrimination and shifting the burden of proof to employers to show that employment practices with a "disparate impact" on women and minorities are required for effective job performance.

10. From its earliest beginnings, the feminist movement has frequently relied on the tactics of minorities—demonstrations, parades, and occasional civil disobedience—to convince governing elites to recognize women's rights. The Equal Rights Amendment won easy approval in Congress but failed to win ratification by three-quarters of the states.

11. Abortion was prohibited by most of the states until the Supreme Court decided in *Roe* v. *Wade* in 1973 that women have a constitutional right to terminate pregnancies. Thus, the Court established as a constitutional right what pro-choice forces had failed to gain through political processes.

12. Despite heated battles over abortion policy, the Supreme Court has steered a moderate policy, affirming a woman's right to abortion while upholding restrictions that do not impose an "undue burden" on women.

NOTES

1. *Civil Rights Cases,* 100 U.S. 3 (1883).
2. *Plessy* v. *Ferguson,* 163 U.S. 537 (1896).
3. *Sweatt* v. *Painter,* 339 U.S. 629 (1950).
4. *Brown* v. *Board of Education of Topeka, Kansas,* 347 U.S. 483 (1954).
5. Kenneth B. Clark, *Dark Ghetto* (New York: Harper & Row, 1965), pp. 77–78.
6. *Alexander* v. *Holmes County Board of Education,* 396 U.S. 19 (1969).
7. Gary Orfield and Franklin Monfort, *Status of School Desegregation* (Alexandria, VA: National School Board Association, 1993).
8. U.S. Commission on Civil Rights, *Racial Isolation in the Public Schools* (Washington, DC: U.S. Government Printing Office, 1966).
9. *Swann* v. *Charlotte-Mecklenburg County Board of Education,* 402 U.S. 1 (1971).
10. *Milliken* v. *Bradley,* 418 U.S. 717 (1974).
11. *Board of Education* v. *Dowell,* U.S. (1991), 111 S. Ct. 630.

12. George M. Metcalf, *From Little Rock to Boston: The History of School Desegregation* (Westport, CT: Greenwood Press, 1983), p. 202.
13. *New York Times,* September 15, 1985.
14. For an inspiring essay on nonviolent direct action and civil disobedience in a modern context, read Martin Luther King, Jr., "Letter from Birmingham City Jail," April 16, 1963.
15. Sidney Verba and Gary R. Owen, *Equality in America* (Cambridge, MA: Harvard University Press, 1985).
16. See David H. Rosenbloom, "The Civil Service Commission's Decision to Authorize the Use of Goals and Timetables in Federal Equal Employment Opportunity Programs," *Western Political Quarterly,* 26 (June 1973), 236–251.
17. *Regents of the University of California v. Bakke,* 438 U.S. 265 (1978).
18. *United Steelworkers v. Weber,* 443 U.S. 193 (1979).
19. *United States v. Paradise,* 480 U.S. 149 (1987).
20. *Firefighters Local Union v. Stotts,* 467 U.S. 561 (1984).
21. *Richmond v. Crosen,* 109 S. Ct. 706 (1989).
22. *Plessy v. Ferguson,* 163 U.S. 537 (1896), dissenting opinion.
23. See Justice Antonin Scalia's dissenting opinion in *Johnson v. Transportation Agency of Santa Clara County,* 480 U.S. 616 (1987).
24. *Wards Cove Packing Co., Inc. v. Atonio,* 490 U.S. 642 (1989).
25. *Coalition for Economic Equity, et al. v. Pete Wilson, et al.,* Ninth Circuit Court of Appeals (April 1997).
26. See concurring opinion of Justice Clarence Thomas *Adarand Construction v. Pena* (1995).
27. Quote from Connie Rice of the NAACP, reported in *U.S. News and World Report,* February 13, 1995, p. 35.
28. *Bradwell v. Illinois,* 16 Wall 130 (1873).
29. *Reed v. Reed.* 404 U.S. 71 (1971).
30. *Stanton v. Stanton,* 421 U.S. 7 (1975).
31. *Craig v. Borden,* 429 U.S. 190 (1976).
32. *Dothard v. Rawlinson,* 433 U.S. 321 (1977).
33. *Arizona v. Norris,* 103 S. Ct. 3492 (1983).
34. *EEOC v. Madison Community School District,* 55 U.S.L.W. 2644 (1987).
35. *Statistical Abstract of the United States 1995,* p. 435.
36. National Research Council, National Academy of Sciences, *Women's Work, Men's Work* (Washington, DC: National Academy Press, 1985).
37. See Thomas R. Dye, *Who's Running America,* 6th ed. (Englewood Cliffs, NJ: Prentice Hall, 1994).
38. Susan Fraker, "Why Women Aren't Getting to the Top," *Fortune,* April 16, 1984, pp. 40–45.
39. *Meritor Savings Bank v. Vinson* (1986).
40. *Roe v. Wade,* 410 U.S. 113 (1973).
41. *Harris v. McRae,* 448 U.S. 297 (1980).
42. *Planned Parenthood of Missouri v. Danforth,* 428 U.S. 52 (1976); *Bellotti v. Baird,* 443 U.S. 622 (1979); *Akron v. Akron Center for Reproductive Health,* 103 S. Ct. 2481 (1983).
43. *Webster v. Reproductive Health Services,* 492 U.S. 111 (1989).
44. *Planned Parenthood v. Casey,* 112 S. Ct. 2791 (1992).

BIBLIOGRAPHY

BARKER, LUCIUS J., and MACK H. JONES. *African Americans and the American Political System.* 3rd ed. Upper Saddle River NJ: Prentice Hall, 1994.
CONWAY, M. MARGARET. *Women and Public Policy.* Washington DC: C.Q. Press, 1994.
GLAZER, NATHAN. *Affirmative Discrimination.* New York: Basic Books, 1987.
HACKER, ANDREW. *Two Nations.* New York: Scribner, 1992.

MEZEY, SUSAN GLUCK. *In Pursuit of Equality: Women, Public Policy, and the Federal Courts.* New York: St. Martins Press, 1991.

SIGELMAN, LEE, and SUSAN WELCH. *Black Americans' Views of Racial Inequality.* Cambridge, MA: Cambridge University Press, 1991.

SOWELL, THOMAS. *Civil Rights: Rhetoric or Reality.* New York: William Morrow, 1984.

SOWELL, THOMAS. *Preferential Policies: An International Perspective.* New York: William Morrow, 1990.

4

CRIMINAL JUSTICE
Rationality and Irrationality in Public Policy

A member of the Metro Dade Police Department's "Street Narcotics Unit" searches a suspected crack dealer. (Chris Brown/SABA Press Photos, Inc.)

CRIME IN AMERICA

Crime is a central problem confronting any society. The rational strategy of crime fighting is known as *deterrence*. The goal is to make the costs of committing crimes far greater than any benefits potential criminals might derive from their acts. With advanced knowledge of these costs, rational individuals should be deterred from committing crimes. But before we describe the deterrence model and assess its effectiveness, let us examine the nature and extent of crime in America.

Measuring Crime. It is not easy to learn exactly how much crime occurs in society. The official crime rates are based on the Federal Bureau of Investigation's *Uniform Crime Reports,* but the FBI reports are based on figures supplied by state and local police agencies (see Table 4–1). The FBI has established a uniform classification of the number of serious crimes per 100,000 people that are reported to the police: *violent crimes* (crimes against persons)—murder and nonnegligent manslaughter, forcible rape, robbery, aggravated assault; and *property crimes* (crimes committed against property only)—burglary, larceny, arson, and theft, including auto theft. But one should be cautious in interpreting official crime rates. They are really a function of several factors: (1) the willingness of people to report crimes to the police, (2) the adequacy of the reporting system that tabulates crime, and (3) the amount of crime itself.

Trends in Crime Rates. The national crime rate rose dramatically between 1960 and 1980. Indeed, it more than doubled, and "law and order" became an important political issue. But in the early 1980s crime rates leveled off and even declined slightly from their record years. It was widely believed that the earlier rapid increase and later moderation was a product of age group changes in the population: the baby boom had expanded the size of the crime-prone age group in the population, people fifteen to twenty-four; later, crime rates leveled off when this age group was no longer increasing as a percentage of the population. Many analysts

TABLE 4-1   Crime Rates in the United States

	Offenses Reported to Police per 100,000 Population					
	1960	*1970*	*1980*	*1985*	*1990*	*1995*
Violent Crimes	160	360	581	557	732	689
Murder	5	8	10	8	9	8
Forcible Rape	9	18	36	37	41	37
Robbery	60	172	244	209	257	221
Assault	85	162	291	303	424	423
Property Crimes	1,716	3,599	5,319	4,651	4,903	4,611

Source: Federal Bureau of Investigation, *Uniform Crime Reports* (annual).

were looking forward to gradual decreases in crime rates based on smaller crime-prone age groups. But then in the late 1980s crime rates unexpectedly soared upward again. The new factor in the equation appeared to be the widespread popularity of crack cocaine. Perhaps as many as one-half of all crimes today are drug related.

Since peaking in the early 1990s, crime rates have actually declined (see Figure 4–1). Law enforcement officials attribute recent successes in crime-fighting to police "crackdowns," more aggressive "community policing," and longer prison sentences for repeat offenders, including "three strikes you're out" laws. (All are discussed later in this chapter.) In support of this claim, they observe that the greatest reductions in crime have occurred in the nation's largest cities, especially those such as New York that have adopted tougher law enforcement practices. However, while overall crime rates are down, juvenile crime is on the rise. So it is by no means certain that crime rates will not rise again in future years.

Juvenile Crime. While adult crime rates appear to be moderating, juvenile crime has surged upward in recent years. Indeed, murders committed by juveniles have tripled in the last decade. Yet *the juvenile system is not designed for deterrence.* Children are not held personally responsible for their actions, in the belief that they do not possess the ability to understand the nature or consequences of their behavior or its rightness or wrongness. Yet juvenile crime, most of which is committed by 15- to 17-year-olds, accounts for about 20 percent of the nation's overall crime rate. Offenders under 18 years of age are usually processed in a separate juvenile court

FIGURE 4–1   **Violent Crime Rate**

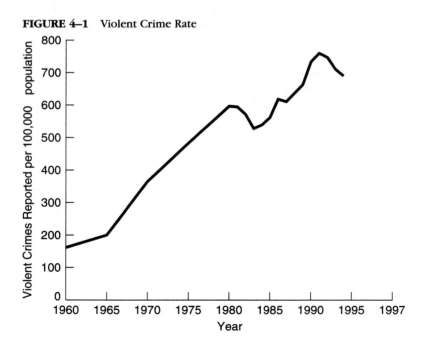

system, regardless of the seriousness of their crime. Only about 2 percent of all young violent offenders are tried as adults.[1]

Juvenile courts rarely impose serious punishment. Available data suggests that about 13 percent of juveniles charged with *violent* crimes are sent to adult court; 16 percent are sent to juvenile detentions centers; and the remaining 71 percent are either dismissed, placed on probation, given suspended sentences, or sent home under supervision of a parent.[2] Very few juveniles who are sentenced to detention facilities stay there very long. Even those convicted of murder cannot be kept in detention facilities beyond the age of 21. Moreover the names of juveniles arrested, charged, or convicted are withheld from publication or broadcast, eliminating whatever social stigma might be associated with their crimes. Their juvenile criminal records are expunged when they become adults, so that they can begin adulthood with "clean" records.

Not surprisingly these policies toward juvenile crime do *not* enjoy widespread support among the American people.[3]

Q. "In your view should juveniles who commit violent crimes be treated the same as adults or should they be given more lenient treatment in a juvenile court?"

Treated same as adults	68%
Given more lenient treatment	13%
Depends	16%
Don't know	3%

Q. "In most places, there are criminal justice programs that treat juveniles differently than adults who commit the same crimes. These programs emphasize protecting and rehabilitating juveniles rather than punishing them. How successful would you say these programs have been at controlling juvenile crime?"

Very successful	1%
Moderately successful	24%
Not very successful	49%
Not successful at all	23%

Whatever the merits of the juvenile system in the treatment of young children, it is clear that the absence of deterrence contributes to criminal behavior among older youths—15-, 16-, and 17-year-olds. Indeed these years are among the most crime-prone ages. Currently some state legislatures are considering reforms of the juvenile system, including more detention facilities, "boot camps" with intensive disciplinary training, and the transfer of older youths who commit violent crimes to the adult justice system.

Victimization.   FBI official crime rates understate the real amount of crime. Many crimes are not reported to the police and therefore cannot be counted in the official rate. In an effort to learn the real amount of crime in the nation, the U.S. Justice Department regularly surveys a national sample, asking people whether they have been a victim of a crime during the past year.[4] These surveys reveal that the victimization rate is many times greater than the official crime rate. The number of forcible rapes as well as burglaries, assaults, and robberies are twice the number reported to police. Only auto theft and murder statistics are reasonably accurate, indicating that most people call the police when their car is stolen or someone is murdered.

Why do people fail to report crime to the police? The most common reason given by interviewees is the belief that the police cannot be effective in dealing with the crime. Other reasons include the feeling that the crime is "a private matter" or that the victim does not want to harm the offender. Fear of reprisal is mentioned much less frequently, usually in cases of assault and family crimes.

About 6 million Americans, or 3 percent of the population, are victims of violent crime each year. This figure applies only to victimizations that take place in a single year. The percentage of persons victimized sometime during their lifetime is much higher. For example, Americans have a 1 in 10,000 chance of being murdered in any one year. But they have a 1 in 133 chance of *ever* becoming a murder victim.[5]

Nonserious Crimes.   The FBI's Uniform Crime Reports do not count so-called "nonserious" crimes, including drug violations, prostitution and sex crimes, gambling, fraud and forgery, driving while intoxicated, and liquor law violations. These crimes vastly outnumber the FBI's indexed "serious crimes." There are five times as many arrests for nonserious as for serious crimes. However, these "nonserious" crimes are often devastating to their victims.

CRIME AND DETERRENCE

The deterrence strategy in criminal justice policy focuses on punishment—its certainty, swiftness, and severity. The effectiveness of deterrence depends on:

- The *certainty* that a crime will be followed by costly punishment. Justice must be sure.
- The *swiftness* of the punishment following the crime. Long delays between crime and punishment break the link in the mind of the criminal between the criminal act and its consequences. And a potential wrongdoer must believe that the costs of a crime will occur within a meaningful time frame, not in a distant, unknowable future. Justice must be swift.
- The *severity* of the punishment. Punishment that is perceived as no more costly than the ordinary hazards of life on the streets, which the potential criminal faces anyhow, will not deter. Punishment must clearly outweigh whatever benefits might be derived from a life of crime in the minds of potential criminals. Punishment must be severe.

These criteria for an effective deterrent policy are ranked in the order of their probable importance. That is, it is most important that punishment for crime be certain. The severity of punishment is probably less important than its swiftness or certainty.

But the current system of criminal justice in America is *not* a serious deterrent to crime. Punishment for crime is neither certain, swift, nor severe. We will argue that the criminal justice system itself, by failing to deter crime, is principally responsible for the fact that *crime in the United States is more common than in any other advanced industrial nation of the world.*

Social Heterogeneity.   Of course, there are many other conflicting theories of crime in America. For example, it is sometimes argued that this nation's high crime rate is a product of its social heterogeneity—the multiethnic, multiracial character of the American population. Low levels of crime in European countries, Japan, and China are often attributed to their homogeneous populations and shared cultures. Blacks in the United States are both victims and perpetrators of crime far more frequently than whites. Whereas blacks constitute only 12.6 percent of the population, they account for 31 percent of all persons arrested for serious crime.[6] The murder victimization rate for black males is more than seven times greater than for white males (see Table 4–2). A larger segment of the black population is in the young crime-prone age (15 and 24 years), and these youths are more likely to live outside husband-wife families. It is argued that the streets of the nation's black inner cities produce a subculture that encourages crime.

Socialization and Control.   Yet another explanation of rising crime focuses on the erosion of social institutions—families, schools, churches, communities—that help to control behavior. These are the institutions that transmit values to children and observe and socially censure impermissible behavior among adults. When ties to family, church, and community are loosened or nonexistent, individuals are less constrained by social mores. Older juveniles turn to peer groups, including gangs, for status and recognition. Defiance of authority, including arrest and detention, and

TABLE 4-2   Murder: Victims, Motives, Weapons

	Victims (Murder Rate, 1992)	Motives (Percent, 1993)		Weapons (Percent, 1993)	
Total	9.1	Felonies, total	19.1	Guns, total	69.6
		Bribery	9.9	Handguns	56.9
White		Narcotics	5.5	Stabbing	12.7
Male	9.0	Sex offense	0.7	Blunt object	4.4
Female	2.8	Other	3.6	Strangulation	1.9
Black		Arguments, total	30.8	Beating	5.0
Male	67.5	Other motives	21.7	Arson	0.9
Female	13.1	Unknown	27.7	Other	5.5

Source: *Statistical Abstract of the United States 1995,* p. 202.

other "macho" behaviors become a source of pride among young males. The deterrent effect of the criminal justice system is minimized. In contrast, when family oversight of behavior is close or when young people find status and recognition in school activities, sports or recreation, or church affairs, social mores are reinforced.

Irrational Crime.   It is also argued that crime is irrational—that the criminal does not weigh benefits against potential costs before committing the act. Many acts of violence are committed by persons acting in blind rage—murders and aggravated assaults among family members, for example. Many rapes are acts of violence, inspired by hatred of women, rather than efforts to obtain sexual pleasure. More murders occur in the heat of argument than in the commission of other felonies (see Table 4–2). These are crimes of passion rather than calculated acts. Thus, it is argued, *no* rational policies can be devised to deter these irrational acts.

Innate Aggression.   Some individuals may have personality traits that predispose them to crime. Antisocial temperament, impulsiveness, and aggressiveness may cause some people to lead troubled lives.[7] Young males are especially likely to be temperamentally aggressive and to have short time horizons. They come into conflict with the law as a result of innate aggressive impulses rather than any rational calculation of benefits or costs.

Deterrence versus Liberty.   Finally, we must recognize that the reduction of crime is not the overriding value of American society. Americans cherish individual liberty. Freedom from repression—from unlawful arrests, forced confessions, restrictions on movement, curfews, arbitrary police actions, unlimited searches of homes or seizures of property, punishment without trial, trials without juries, unfair procedures, brutal punishments, and so on—is more important to Americans than freedom from crime. Many authoritarian governments boast of low crime rates and criminal justice systems that ensure certain, swift, and severe punishment, but these governments fail to protect the personal liberties of their citizens. Indeed, given the choice of punishing all of the guilty, even if some innocents are also punished by mistake, or taking care that innocent persons not be punished, even if some guilty people escape, most Americans would choose the second alternative—protecting the innocent.

WHY CRIME PAYS

While we acknowledge that there are multiple explanations for crime, we shall argue that the frequency of crime in America is largely a product of the failure to adopt rational criminal justice policies.

Lack of Certainty.   The best available estimates of the certainty of punishment for serious crime suggests that very few crimes actually result in jail sentences for the perpetrators. About 14 million serious crimes were reported to the police in 1995,

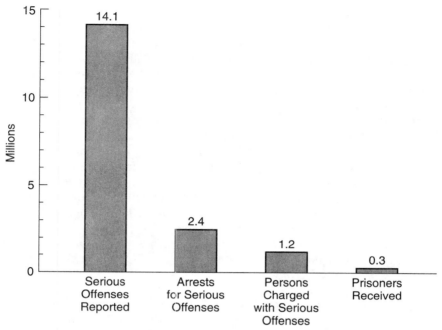

Source: Data from *Statistical Abstract of the United States 1995.*

FIGURE 4–2   Crime and Punishment

but only 2.4 million persons were arrested for these crimes (see Figure 4–2). Some of those arrested were charged with committing more than one crime, but it is estimated that the police "clear" less than 20 percent of reported crimes by arresting the offender. Prosecutors do not charge about half of the persons arrested for serious offenses. Some offenders are handled as juveniles; some are permitted to plead guilty to minor offenses; others are released because witnesses fail to appear or evidence is weak or inadmissible in court. Of the persons charged with serious offenses by prosecutors, fewer than 30 percent receive jail sentences. Convicted felons are three times more likely to receive probation than a prison sentence. Thus, even if punishment could deter crime, our current criminal justice system does *not* ensure punishment for crime.

Lack of Swiftness.   The deterrent effect of a criminal justice system is lost when punishment is so long delayed that it has little relationship to the crime. The bail system, together with trial delays, allow criminal defendants to escape the consequences of their acts for long, indefinite periods of time. Most criminal defendants are free on bail shortly after their arrest; only those accused of the most serious crimes and adjudged to be likely to flee before trial are held in jail without bond. In preliminary hearings held shortly after arrest, judges release most defendants pending trial; even after a trial and a guilty verdict, many defendants are free on bail pending the outcome of lengthy appeals. The Constitution guarantees persons accused of crimes freedom from "excessive bail" (Eighth Amendment), and judges may not hold defendants in jail simply because they think the defendants might commit additional crimes while out on bail.

The court system works very slowly and delays favor the criminal defendant. Defendants request delays in court proceedings to remain free as long as possible. Moreover, they know that witnesses against them will lose interest, move away, grow tired of the hassle, and even forget key facts, if only the case can be postponed long enough. Some criminal cases are delayed for years.

Justice delayed destroys the deterrent effect, especially in the minds of youthful offenders, who are "present oriented" rather than "future oriented." Inner-city youths, with no real prospects for the future anyhow, concentrate their attention on today rather than years into the future. In their limited time frame of reference, they may consider the benefits of their criminal acts to be immediate, while the costs are so far in the future that they have no real meaning. Or the costs may be estimated to be only the arrest itself and a night in jail before release on bail. For deterrence to work, the perceived costs of crime must be greater than the perceived benefits in *the minds of potential wrongdoers*.

The Question of Severity.   More people are imprisoned today in America than at any previous time. Not only are there more inmates in the nation's prisons, but also the proportion of the nation's population behind bars is the highest in recent history. (In 1970, 87 of every 100,000 persons was a federal or state prisoner, compared with 325 in 1995.)[8] This increase in the prison population suggests that the court system is *not* becoming any more lenient over time.

Early Releases.   However, prison overcrowding leads to the early release of many prisoners. The deterrent effect of severe sentences is lost, of course, when criminals know that they will not serve their full sentences. Violent criminals on the average serve only half of their sentences, and nonviolent offenders less than one-third of their sentences (see Figure 4–3).

Incapacitation.   Do prison sentences reduce crime? It is clear that removing habitual offenders from the streets reduces the crimes they commit outside the prison walls for the duration of their sentences. Theoretically, long sentences can reduce crime rates by incapacitating habitual criminals for long periods. But the criminal justice system does not succeed in incapacitating criminals for very long. Indeed, it is estimated that about 20 percent of all violent crimes and 30 percent of property crimes are committed by *persons who would still have been in prison on earlier convictions if they had served their full sentences.*[9]

Recidivism.   Punishment has no discernible effect on the subsequent criminal behavior of persons who have been convicted and imprisoned. An estimated 61 percent of persons admitted to prison are recidivists, that is, persons who have previously served a sentence of incarceration as a juvenile, adult, or both. Of those 39

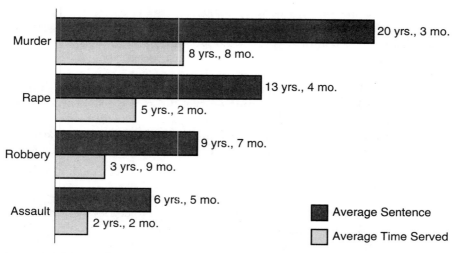

Source: U.S. Bureau of Justice Statistics Sentencing Project Report, 1992.

FIGURE 4–3   Violent Crime Sentences versus Time Served

percent entering prisons without a prior record of incarceration, nearly 60 percent have prior convictions that resulted in probation. Thus, a total of 85 percent of all persons admitted to prison have prior convictions.[10] Clearly the criminal justice system did not "rehabilitate" these people.

POLICE AND LAW ENFORCEMENT

The principal responsibility for law enforcement in America continues to rest with state and local governments. The major federal law enforcement agencies—the FBI and the Drug Enforcement Administration (DEA) in the Department of Justice and the Bureau of Alcohol, Tobacco, and Firearms (ATF) in the Treasury Department— are charged with enforcing federal laws. Today, the role of the federal government in law enforcement is growing, but state and local governments continue to carry the major burdens of police protection, judicial systems, and prison and parole programs. The federal government employs about 120,000 people in all law enforcement activities, compared with more than 1.5 million state and local government law enforcement personnel. Federal prisons contain about 75,000 inmates, compared with over 850,000 in state prisons.

Police Functions.   At least three important functions in society are performed by police: enforcing laws, keeping the peace, and furnishing services. Actually, law enforcement may take up only a small portion of a police officer's daily activity. The service function is far more common—attending accidents, directing traffic, escorting crowds, assisting stranded motorists, and so on. The function of peacekeeping is also very common—breaking up fights, quieting noisy parties, handling domestic or neighborhood quarrels, and the like. It is in this function that police exercise the greatest discretion in the application of the law. In most of these incidents, it is difficult to determine blame, and the police must use personal discretion in handling each case.

The police are on the front line of society's efforts to resolve conflict. Indeed, instead of a legal or law enforcement role, the police are more likely to adopt a peacekeeping role. They are generally lenient in their arrest practices; that is, they use their arrest powers less often than the law allows. Rather than arresting people, the police prefer first to reestablish order. Of course, the decision to be more or less lenient in enforcing the law gives the police a great deal of discretion—they exercise decision-making powers on the streets.

Police Discretion.   What factors influence police decision making? Probably the first factor is the attitude of the other people involved in police encounters. If a person adopts an acquiescent role, displays deference and respect for the police, and conforms to police expectations, he or she is much less likely to be arrested than a person who shows disrespect or uses abusive language.[11] This is not just an arbitrary response. The police learn through training and experience the importance of establishing their authority on the streets.

Police Culture.   The tasks assigned to the police in an urban society would confound highly trained social scientists. Yet only recently have police officers been recruited from colleges and universities. Formal police training emphasizes self-control and caution in dealing with the public, but on-the-job experiences probably reinforce distrust of others. The element of danger in the police officer's job makes him or her naturally suspicious. Police officers see much of the "worst kind" of people, and they see even the "best kind" at their worst. Police forces are semimilitary organizations engaged in rule enforcement. They must be concerned with authority themselves, and they expect others to respect authority. One study neatly summarizes "police culture" in terms of the attitudes that the police bring to the streets:

People cannot be trusted; they are dangerous.

Experience is better than abstract rules.

You must make people respect you.

Everyone hates a cop.

Stronger punishment will deter crime.

The major job of police is to prevent crime.[12]

Community Policing.   Most police activity is "reactive": typically two officers in a patrol car responding to a radio dispatcher who is forwarding reports of incidents. Police agencies frequently evaluate themselves in terms of the number and frequency of patrols, the number of calls responded to, and the elapsed time between the call and the arrival of officers on the scene. But there is little evidence that any of these measures affect crime rates or even citizens' fear of crime or satisfaction with the police.[13]

An alternative strategy is for police to become more "proactive": typically by becoming more visible in the community by walking or bicycling the sidewalks of high crime areas; learning to recognize individuals on the streets and winning their confidence and respect; deterring or scaring away drug dealers, prostitutes, and their customers by a police presence. But this "community policing" is often expensive and potentially more dangerous for police officers.

Police Crackdowns.   Police crackdowns—beefed up police actions against juvenile gangs, prostitutes, and drug traffickers; the frisking of likely suspects on the street for guns and drugs; and arrests for (often ignored) public drinking, graffiti, and vandalism—can reduce crime only if supported by the community as well as prosecutors and judges. Crime rates, even murder rates, have been significantly reduced during periods of police crackdowns in major cities.[14] But these efforts are often sporadic; enthusiasm ebbs as jails fill up and the workload of prosecutors and courts multiplies.

New York City's experience suggests what can be accomplished by stepped up police activity. When police activity was redirected to low-level crimes (for example, graffiti writing, subway turnstyle jumping, underage drinking, street fighting, public urination, low-level prostitution, and drug selling), the effect was to "take back the streets," that is, to make people feel safer in their neighborhoods and thus they begin to walk about again in public spaces. More importantly, the rate of serious crime began to drop, as arrests for minor crimes produced plentiful weapons seizures, as well as the apprehension of many persons wanted for violent felonies. Among the results claimed from this crackdown on "quality of life crimes" was a one-third reduction in the murder rate for the city.[15]

Police Efficiency.   Most crimes are never solved. This is particularly true of property crimes like burglary; these crimes seldom produce eyewitnesses or other useful information. On average across the nation police claim to solve about 14 percent of burglaries; this is their official "clearance rate." Police "clear" only about 50 percent of all violent crimes, and 70 percent of murders (see Table 4–3). Most clearances occur in cases in which the victim and perpetrators know each other.

FEDERALIZING CRIME FIGHTING

Public demands to DO SOMETHING! about crime are heard in Washington as well as state capitols and city halls. The president, senators, Congress members, the attorney general, and other federal officials are politically compelled to respond to these demands by fashioning new and ever-expanding programs of federal involvement in general law enforcement.

TABLE 4-3   Crime and Arrest

	Percent of Crimes Cleared by Arrest
Murder	70.0
Rape	52.1
Robbery	25.6
Aggravated Assault	56.8
Burglary	13.5
Larceny/Theft	19.7

Source: National Center for Policy Analysis, "Crime Pays, But So Does Imprisonment," Dallas: National Center for Policy Analysis, 1992. Calculated from Federal Bureau of Investigation, *Crime in the United States, Uniform Crime Reports,* annual issues (Washington, DC: Government Printing Office).

The Federal Role in Law Enforcement.   Traditionally the federal government's responsibilities were limited to the enforcement of a relatively narrow range of federal criminal laws, including laws dealing with counterfeiting and currency violations; tax evasion, including alcohol, tobacco, and firearm taxes; fraud and embezzlement; robbery or theft of federally insured funds, including banks; interstate criminal activity; murder or assault of a federal official; and federal drug laws. While some federal criminal laws overlapped state laws, most criminal activity—murder, rape, robbery, assault, burglary, theft, auto theft, gambling, sex offenses, and so on—fell under state jurisdiction. Even today most law enforcement activity is undertaken by state and local authorities (see Table 4–4). Over 11 million people are arrested and charged with a crime in the United States each year. But only about 50,000 people are prosecuted for crimes by federal authorities in federal courts.

The U.S. Department of Justice, headed by the attorney general, handles all criminal prosecutions for violation of federal laws. The federal government's principal investigative agencies are the Federal Bureau of Investigation (FBI) and the Drug Enforcement Administration (DEA), both units of the Department of Justice, and the

TABLE 4-4   Criminal Justice Activity by Level of Government

	Federal	State and Local
Full-time Personnel (1,000)		
Law enforcement	88	770
Judicial	51	333
Corrections	24	543
Prisoners		
Number (1,000) present in institutions at end of year (excludes local jails and juvenile detention centers)	79.8	936.9

Source: *Statistical Abstract of the United States 1996,* pp. 212, 219.

Bureau of Alcohol, Tobacco, and Firearms (ATF) in the Treasury Department. Efforts to combine these federal law enforcement agencies have consistently floundered in bureaucratic turf battles.

Crime Fighting from Washington.   The Crime Control Law Enforcement Act of 1994 vastly expanded the federal government's role in crime fighting. The act contains a broad range of new initiatives from Washington:

- Federal grants to cities to place an additional 100,000 police officers on the beat, with an emphasis on community crime prevention. Liberals succeeded in earmarking some grant money for community drug treatment, midnight sports programs, and alternatives to incarceration.
- Federal grants to states for expansion of prison facilities.
- New federal crimes subject to the death penalty, including kidnapping, hostage taking, drive-by shootings, and carjackings. (However, the Supreme Court is unlikely to allow the death penalty to be imposed for any crime other than first-degree murder.)
- Limit death row inmate appeals to one federal habeas corpus petition to be submitted within one year of the final state appeal.

"Three Strikes You're Out."   The most widely publicized provision of the Act mandates life in prison for anyone convicted of a third violent felony. The third violent felony must be prosecuted in federal courts to trigger the mandatory life sentence, but federal judges are instructed to count earlier violent felony convictions in either state or federal courts against the three-strike rule. The argument for the bill centered on the claim that a relatively small number of repeat offenders commit a disproportionate number of crimes. Even if a three-time loser law does not add to deterrence, mandated life sentences will incapacitate these habitual criminals. Opponents argue that this law is too rigid, that judges are better able to decide in individual cases who should be put away for life, and that federal prisons will eventually fill up with geriatric prisoners who are unlikely to commit more crimes. But "three strikes, you're out" is very popular with the American public. A number of states have adopted similar measures and the federal provision is likely to encourage additional states to do so.

CRIME AND GUNS

Many crimes involve the use of guns. The FBI reports that 70 percent of all murders are accomplished with guns[16] (see Table 4–2). Would registering guns, licensing gun owners, or banning handguns altogether, reduce crime?

Gun control legislation is a common policy initiative following highly publicized murders or assassination attempts on prominent figures. The Federal Gun Control Act of 1968 was a response to the assassinations of Senator Robert F. Kennedy and Martin Luther King, Jr., in that year, and efforts to legislate additional restrictions occurred after attempts to assassinate Presidents Gerald Ford and Ronald Reagan. The rationale for restricting gun purchases, licensing gun owners, or banning guns altogether is that fewer crimes would be committed with guns if guns were less readily available. Murders, especially crimes of passion among family members or neighbors, would be reduced, if for no other reason than that it is physically more difficult to kill someone with only a knife, a club, or one's bare hands.

Federal Law.   The Federal Gun Control Act of 1968, as amended, includes the following:

- A ban on interstate and mail-order sales of handguns
- Prohibition of the sale of any firearms to a convicted felon, fugitive, or adjudicated mental defective
- A requirement that all firearms dealers must be licensed by the federal Bureau of Alcohol, Tobacco, and Firearms
- A requirement that manufacturers record by serial number all firearms, and dealers record all sales. (Dealers must require proof of identity and residence of buyers, and buyers must sign a statement certifying their eligibility to purchase.)
- Continued restrictions of private ownership of automatic weapons, military weapons, and other heavy ordinance

Federal regulations also bar the importation of "assault weapons," which are generally defined as automatic weapons.

The Brady Law.   The federal "Brady Law" of 1993 requires a seven-day waiting period for the purchase of a handgun. The national law is named for James S. Brady, former press secretary to President Ronald Reagan, who was severely wounded in the 1981 attempted assassination of the president. Brady and his wife, Sarah, championed the bill for many years before its adoption. Under the law's provisions, handgun dealers must send police agencies a form completed by the buyer (which is already required in most states); police agencies have seven days to make certain the purchaser is not a convicted felon, fugitive, drug addict, or mentally ill person. Supporters believe the law will be a modest step in keeping handguns from dangerous people. Opponents, including the National Rifle Association lobby, believe that the law is an empty political gesture at fighting crime that erodes the Second Amendment right to bear arms.

Gun Ownership.   Gun ownership is widespread in the United States. Estimates vary, but there are probably 200 million firearms in the hands of the nation's 250 million people. Half of all American families admit in public opinion surveys to owning guns. A majority of gun owners say their guns are for hunting and sports; about one-third say the purpose of their gun ownership is self-defense. Interestingly, both those who favor a ban on handguns and those who oppose such a ban cite crime as the reason for their position. Those who want to ban guns say they contribute to crime and violence. Those who oppose a ban feel they need guns for protection against crime and violence.

State Laws.   State laws, and many local ordinances, also govern gun ownership. Handgun laws are common. Most states require that a record of sale be submitted to state or local government agencies; some states require an application and a waiting period before the purchase of a handgun; a few states require a license or a permit to purchase one; most states require a license to carry a "concealed weapon" (hidden gun); while some states prohibit any handgun ownership except by persons licensed by law enforcement officials.

Recently, however, a number of states have relaxed the requirements for law-abiding citizens to obtain a license to carry a concealed weapon. Applicants for licenses in these states are checked for previous felony convictions and usually must show proof of training with a firearm. But licenses are granted without the need to go before a judge or police official and prove a specific need to carry a handgun, as required in many other states.

Gun Laws and Crime.   There is no systematic evidence that gun control laws reduce violent crime. If we compare violent crime rates in jurisdictions with very restrictive gun laws (for example, New York, Massachusetts, New Jersey, Illinois, and the District of Columbia) to those in jurisdictions with very loose controls, we find no differences in rates of violent crime that cannot be attributed to social conditions. Gun laws, including purchase permits, waiting periods, carrying permits, and even complete prohibitions, seem to have no effect on violent crime, or even crimes committed with guns.[17] Indeed, gun laws do not even appear to have any effect on gun ownership. Even the Massachusetts ban on handguns, which calls for a mandatory prison sentence for unlicensed citizens found carrying a firearm, did not reduce gun-related crime.[18] The total number of persons imprisoned for gun crimes was essentially unchanged; however, more persons without criminal records were arrested and charged with gun law violations. Of course, it might be argued that state and local laws are inadequate and only a rigorously enforced federal law could effectively ban handguns. But to date we must conclude that "there is little evidence to show that gun ownership among the population as a whole is, per se, an important cause of criminal violence."[19]

Indeed, some criminologists argue that guns in the hands of law-abiding citizens may reduce violent crime.[20] It is difficult to obtain evidence of "non-events," in this case crimes averted by citizens with weapons or crimes uncommitted by potential offenders fearing confrontation with armed citizens. Proponents of gun control have ready access to data on the number of murders committed with handguns. But there is also some evidence that as many or more crimes against both persons and property are foiled or deterred by gun ownership.

The Right to Bear Arms.   The gun control debate also involves constitutional issues. The Second Amendment to the U.S. Constitution states, "A well regulated militia, being necessary to the security of a free state, the right of the people to keep and bear arms, shall not be infringed." Opponents of gun control view the right to keep and bear arms as an *individual* constitutional right, like the First Amendment freedom of speech or press. Proponents of gun control argue that the Second Amendment protects only the *collective* right of the people to form state militias, that is, the right of the states to maintain National Guard units. Either interpretation can be defended.

Opponents of gun control argue that all rights set forth in the Bill of Rights are interpreted as individual rights. The history surrounding the adoption of the Second Amendment reveals the concern of citizens with the attempt by a despotic government to confiscate their arms and render them helpless to resist tyranny. James Madison writes in *The Federalist,* No. 46, that "the advantage of being armed which the Americans posses over the people of almost every other nation . . . forms a barrier against the enterprise of [tyrannical] ambition." Early American political rhetoric is filled with praise for an armed citizenry able to protect its freedoms with force if necessary. And the "militia" was defined as every adult free male able to carry a weapon. Even early English common law recognized the right of individuals "to have and use arms for self-protection and defense."[21]

Proponents of gun control cite the Supreme Court decision in *United States* v. *Miller* (1939).[22] In this case, the Court considered the constitutionality of the federal National Firearms Act of 1934, which among other things prohibited the transportation of sawed-off shotguns in interstate commerce. The defendant claimed that Congress could not infringe on his right to keep and bear arms. But the Court responded that a sawed-off shotgun had no "relationship to the preservation or efficiency of a well-regulated militia." The clear implication of this decision is that the right to bear arms refers only to a state's right to maintain a militia.

Ethical Conflict.   Perhaps the argument over gun control really has nothing to do with reducing crime or with constitutional interpretations. Instead, two ethics are in conflict. There is the established upper-class liberal ethic of a civilized, educated, well-ordered society that can resolve conflict through laws, courts, and institutions. There is also the individualist ethic stressing one's own responsibility for the protection of family and property in a tough and sometimes dangerous world. These contrasting ethics in America are clearly in conflict over the gun control issue.

THE DRUG WAR

Americans have long harbored ambivalent attitudes toward drug use. Alcohol and tobacco are legal products, although the U.S. Office of the Surgeon General has undertaken campaigns to reduce their use, and the Federal Drug Administration has labeled nicotine an addictive drug. The manufacture, sale, or possession of heroin and cocaine are criminal offenses under both state and federal laws. Marijuana has been "decriminalized" in several states, making its use or possession a misdemeanor comparable to a traffic offense; a majority of states, however, retain criminal sanctions against the possession of marijuana, and its manufacture and sale are still prohibited by federal law. However, popular referenda votes in California and Arizona in 1996 indicate that voters approve of the use of marijuana for therapeutic purposes.

Drug Use.   Overall drug use in the United States today appears to be well below levels of two or three decades ago. This conclusion is drawn from national surveys regularly undertaken by the federal government (see Figure 4–4). But surveys can only report admitted use, and admissions (especially among young people) often reflect current cultural fashions. The percentage of youths ages 12 to 17 admitting drug use doubled from 1992 to 1995, as drugs started to creep back into popular culture and music (see Figure 4–5).

Despite lower levels of overall reported drug use in the nation, the number of emergency room drug admissions as well as drug-induced deaths have risen somewhat.[23] Moreover, heroin, cocaine, and marijuana are available on the streets at lower prices and higher purities than at any time in recent years.[24] The most common interpretation of the combination of poll results reporting reduced drug use, medical reports showing continued drug-induced illnesses and deaths, and law enforcement data showing continued drug availability, is that *casual* use is down but use by *hard-core* addicted persons remains high.

According to the U.S. National Household Survey on Drug Abuse, about 4 percent of the population over 12 years of age are "current users" of marijuana, that is, they have used marijuana in the previous month. About one-third of the population

FIGURE 4–4   Reported Drug Use in the Past Month

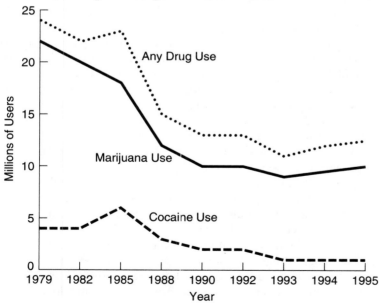

Source: *National Household Survey on Drug Abuse 1995,* U.S. Substance Abuse and Mental Health Services Administration, Washington, DC.

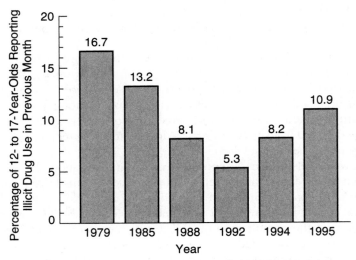

Source: *National Household Survey on Drug Abuse 1995,* U.S. Substance Abuse and Mental Health Services Administration, Washington, DC.

FIGURE 4–5   Reported Teenage Illicit Drug Use

over 12 years of age are reported to have "ever used" marijuana. Current marijuana use is highest (14 percent) among 18- to 25-year-olds, and lowest (2 percent) among persons 35 years of age and older. Available medical evidence on the health effects of marijuana is mixed; conflicting reports have been issued about whether or not it is more or less dangerous than alcohol.

Cocaine use is more limited than marijuana use. Less than one percent of the population over 12 years of age are believed to be "current users." About 10–12 percent of the population is believed to have "ever used" it. Cocaine is not regarded as physically addictive, although the psychological urge to continue its use is strong. It is made from coca leaves and imported into the United States. Originally, its high cost and celebrity use made it favored in upper-class circles. However, cocaine spread rapidly in the streets with the introduction of "crack" in the 1980s. Crack cocaine can be smoked and a single "hit" purchased for a few dollars. The health problems associated with cocaine use are fairly serious, as reported by the National Institute on Drug Abuse. Death, although rare, can occur from a single ingestion. The power of the coca leaf has been known for hundreds of years; Coca-Cola originally contained cocaine, though the drug was removed from the popular drink in 1903.

Heroin use is relatively rare. The Harrison Narcotic Act of 1916 made the manufacture, sale, or possession of heroin in the United States a federal crime.

Various "designer" drugs occasionally appear on the streets. Some are prepared in underground laboratories where hallucinogens, stimulants, and tranquilizers are mixed in various combinations; others are newer formulations that may temporarily baffle law enforcement.

Drugs that are injected intravenously, rather than inhaled, pose additional health dangers. Intravenous injections with contaminated needles are a major contributor to the spread of the HIV-AIDS virus.

Drug Trafficking.   It is very difficult to estimate the total size of the drug market, but $20 to $25 billion per year is a common figure.[25] This would suggest that the drug business is comparable in size to one of the ten largest U.S. industrial corporations. More important, perhaps, drugs produce huge profit margins: a kilo of cocaine purchased in Colombia may cost only $3,600; when sold in the United States, that kilo may retail for $80,000 to $120,000.[26] The price of smuggling a single, easily concealable kilo may run to $15,000. These huge profits allow drug traffickers to corrupt police and government officials as well as private citizens in the United States and other nations.

Interdiction.   Antidrug efforts can be divided into four categories: interdiction, education, enforcement, and treatment. Efforts to seal U.S. borders against the importation of drugs have been frustrated by the sheer volume of smuggling. Each year increasingly large drug shipments are intercepted by the U.S. Drug Enforcement Administration, the U.S. Customs Service, the Coast Guard, and state and local agencies. Yet each year the volume of drugs entering the country seems to increase. Drug "busts" are considered just another cost of business to the traffickers. It is not likely that the use of U.S. military forces to augment other federal agencies can succeed in sealing our borders, and U.S. pressure against Latin American governments to destroy coca crops and assist in interdiction has already resulted in strained relationships. Our neighboring countries wonder why the U.S. government directs its efforts at the suppliers, when the demand for drugs arises within the United States itself. The continued availability of drugs on the nation's streets—drugs at lower prices and higher purities—suggests that interdiction has largely failed.

Education.   Efforts aimed at educating the public about the dangers of drugs have inspired many public and private campaigns, from former First Lady Nancy Reagan's early "Just say no" campaign and Jesse Jackson's "Up with hope, down with dope," to the Advertising Council's TV ads "This is your brain on drugs" and local police-sponsored DARE (drug abuse resistance education) programs.

The decline in overall drug use over several decades is often overlooked in political debates over drug policy. Culturally drug use went from being stylish and liberating to being unfashionable, unwise, and unhealthy. Perhaps educational campaigns contributed to drug use decline, as well as the onset of HIV-AIDS, and the well-publicized drug-related deaths of celebrity athletes and entertainers. The recent rise in reported teenage drug use, however, suggests that educational campaigns may grow stale over time.

Enforcement.   The FBI and state local law enforcement agencies already devote a major portion of their efforts toward combating drugs. An estimated 40 percent of all arrests in the United States are drug related. Federal and state prisons now hold a larger percentage of the nation's population than ever before. Sentences have been lengthened for drug trafficking, and prisons are overcrowded as a direct result of drug-related convictions. Drug testing by government and private employers is increasing, but unless it is random, it is not very useful; some courts have prevented random testing of individuals without their consent.

The U.S. Drug Enforcement Administration (DEA) in the Department of Justice was created by Congress in 1973. Because it has the authority to enforce federal drug laws both in the United States and abroad, DEA officers may go abroad to collect international intelligence and to cooperate with foreign authorities. The U.S. Customs Service has responsibility for stopping the entry of narcotics at U.S. borders. The U.S. Coast Guard cooperates in drug interception. The FBI monitors drug trafficking that contributes to other federal crimes. Surveillance of low-level buying and selling of drugs is usually left to state and local authorities.

Congress created a "drug-czar" position in 1988 (officially the National Drug Control Policy Director) to develop and coordinate antidrug policy in the United States. The national "war on drugs" has included federal funds for prison construction, state and local drug law enforcement activity, and state and local drug treatment programs. But the "war on drugs" in the state and federal law enforcement agencies has directed resources away from investigation and prosecution of property crimes, and even violent crimes, and toward drug offenses.[27] The result is prisons that are now filled with drug offenders; today, over half of the nation's prisoners are incarcerated for drug offenses.

Treatment.   The federal government under the Clinton administration has emphasized drug treatment as a major supplement to enforcement activity. Special "drug courts" and diversion programs developed in the states often give non-violent drug users a choice between entering treatment programs or going to jail. (Washington D.C. Mayor Marion Barry may be the best known example of this approach.) While some users benefit from treatment, the overall success of treatment programs is very poor; most heavy drug users have been through treatment programs more than once. An estimated 60 to 80 percent of heavy cocaine users return to heavy use after treatment.[28]

Although opinion polls show that Americans consistently rank drugs as one of the most important problems confronting the nation, no effective public policies appear likely to be adopted. As a nation the United States is both wealthy and free, two conditions that make it a perfect market for illicit drugs. The costs of truly effective enforcement, both in dollar expenditures and, more importantly, in lost individual liberty, may be more than our society wishes to pay.

Legalization.   The failure of antidrug policies to significantly reduce the drug supply or demand, coupled with the high costs of enforcement and the loss of civil liberties, have caused some observers to propose the legalization of drugs and government control of their production and sale. Prohibition failed earlier in the century to end alcohol consumption, and crime, official corruption, and the enormous cost of futile efforts to stop individuals from drinking eventually forced the nation to end

Prohibition. It is similarly argued that the legalization of drugs would end organized crime's profit monopoly over the drug trade; raise billions of dollars by legally taxing drugs; end the strain on relations with Latin American nations caused by efforts to eradicate drugs; and save additional billions in enforcement costs, which could be used for education and drug treatment.[29] If drugs were legally obtainable under government supervision, it is argued that many of society's current problems would be alleviated: the crime and violence associated with the drug trade, the corruption of public officials, the spread of diseases associated with drug use, and the many infringements of personal liberty associated with antidrug wars.

But even the suggestion of drug legalization offends Americans who believe that it would greatly expand drug use in the country. Cheap, available drugs would greatly increase the numbers of addicted persons, creating a "society of zombies" that would destroy the social fabric of the nation. Cocaine and heroin are far more habit forming than alcohol, and legalization would encourage the development of newer and even more potent and addictive synthetic drugs. Whatever the health costs of drug abuse today, it is argued that legalization would produce public health problems of enormous magnitude.[30] Cocaine is very cheap to produce; the current five- to ten-dollar cost of a "hit" is mostly profit for the dealer; legalization, even with taxation, might produce a fifty-cent "hit." Whatever the damages to society from drug-related crime and efforts to prohibit drugs, the damages from cheap, available drug use would be far greater.

CRIME AND THE COURTS

The development of rational policies in criminal justice is complicated by conflicting values—our commitment to due process of law and our determination to fight crime. Public opinion has long held that the court system is overly concerned with the rights of accused criminals. A majority of Americans believe that the Supreme Court has gone too far in protecting the rights of defendants in criminal cases and that the courts are more concerned with protecting these rights than the rights of victims (see Table 4–5).

Yet although society needs the protection of the police, it is equally important to protect society *from* the police. Arbitrary searches, seizures, and arrests; imprisonment without hearing or trial; forced confessions; beatings and torture; tainted witnesses; excessive punishments; and other human rights violations are all too common throughout the world. The courts function to protect citizens accused of crime as well as to mete out punishment for criminal behavior.

Insufficient Evidence and Dismissal.   About half of all felony arrests result in dismissal of the charges against the defendant. This decision is usually made by the prosecutor (the state's attorney, district attorney, or county prosecutor, as the office is variously designated in the states; or a prosecuting attorney in the U.S. Department of Justice in a federal criminal case). The prosecutor may determine that the

TABLE 4-5   Public Opinion about Crime and Courts

Question: "In general, do you think the courts deal too harshly or not harshly enough with criminals?"[a]

	Too Harshly	Not Harshly Enough	About Right
1972	7	66	16
1975	4	79	10
1985	3	83	8
1990	3	83	9
1995	3	85	8

Question: "Has the Supreme Court gone too far in protecting the rights of defendants in criminal cases?"[b]

Yes	56
No	37
Don't know	7

Question: "Have the laws and the courts become more concerned with protecting the rights of criminals than they are with protecting the rights of victims?"[b]

Yes	70
No	24
Don't know	6

[a] *Gallup Poll Monthly,* various issues.

[b] Gallup Poll, reported in *The American Enterprise,* July/August 1991, p. 78.

offense is not serious or that the offender is not a danger to society or that the resources of the office would be better spent pursuing other cases. But the most common reason for dismissal of the charges is insufficient evidence.

Unreasonable Searches and Seizures.   Individuals are protected by the Fourth Amendment from "unreasonable searches and seizures" of their private "persons, houses, papers, and effects." The amendment lays out specific rules for searches and seizures of evidence: "No warrants shall issue but upon probable cause, supported by Oath or affirmation, and particularly describing the place to be searched, and the persons or things to be seized." Judges cannot issue a warrant just to let the police see if an individual has committed a crime; there must be "probable cause" for such issuance. The indiscriminate searching of whole neighborhoods or groups of people is unconstitutional and is prevented by the Fourth Amendment's requirement that the place to be searched must be specifically described in the warrant. This requirement is meant to prevent "fishing expeditions" into an individual's home and personal effects on the possibility that some evidence of unknown illegal activity might crop up. The only exception is if police officers, in the course of a valid search for a specified item, find other items whose very possession is a crime, for example, illicit drugs.

However, the courts permit the police to undertake many other "reasonable" searches *without* a warrant: searches in connection with a valid arrest, searches to protect the safety of police officers, searches to obtain evidence in the immediate vicinity and in the suspect's control, searches to preserve evidence in danger of being immediately destroyed, and searches with the consent of a suspect. Indeed, most police searches today take place without a warrant under one or another of these conditions. The Supreme Court has also allowed automobile searches and searches of open fields without warrants in many cases. The requirement of "probable cause" has been very loosely defined; even a "partially corroborated anonymous informant's tip" qualifies as probable cause to make a search, seizure, or arrest.[31] And if the police, while making a warranted search or otherwise lawfully on the premises, see evidence of a crime "in plain view," they may seize such evidence without further authorization.[32]

Self-incrimination and Right to Counsel. Freedom from self-incrimination originated in English common law; it was originally designed to prevent persons from being tortured into confessions of guilt. It is also a logical extension of the notion that individuals should not be forced to contribute to their own prosecution, that the burden of proof rests upon the state. The Fifth Amendment protects people from both physical and psychological coercion.[33] It protects not only accused persons at their own trial but also witnesses testifying in trials of others, civil suits, congressional hearings, and so on. Thus, "taking the Fifth" has become a standard phrase in our culture: "I refuse to answer that question on the grounds that it might tend to incriminate me." The protection also means that judges, prosecutors, and juries cannot use the refusal of people to take the stand at their own trial as evidence of guilt. Indeed, a judge or attorney is not even permitted to imply this to a jury, and a judge is obligated to instruct a jury *not* to infer guilt from a defendant's refusal to testify.

The Supreme Court under Justice Earl Warren greatly strengthened the Fifth Amendment protection against self-incrimination and the right to counsel in a series of rulings in the 1960s:

Gideon v. *Wainwright* (1963)—Equal protection under the Fourteenth Amendment requires that free legal counsel be appointed for all indigent defendants in all criminal cases.

Escobedo v. *Illinois* (1964)—Suspects are entitled to confer with counsel as soon as a police investigation focuses on them or once "the process shifts from investigatory to accusatory."

Miranda v. *Arizona* (1966)—Before questioning suspects, a police officer must inform them of all their constitutional rights, including the right to counsel (appointed at no cost to the suspect, if necessary) and the right to remain silent. Although suspects may knowingly waive these rights, the police cannot question anyone who at any point asks for a lawyer or declines "in any manner" to be questioned.

The Exclusionary Rule. Illegally obtained evidence and confessions may not be used in criminal trials. If police find evidence of a crime in an illegal search, or if they elicit statements from suspects without informing them of their rights to remain silent or to have counsel, the evidence or statements produced are not admissible in a trial. This exclusionary rule is one of the more controversial procedural rights that the Supreme Court has extended to criminal defendants. The rule is also unique to the United States: in Great Britain evidence obtained illegally may be used against the accused, although the accused may bring charges against the police for damages.

The rule provides enforcement for the Fourth Amendment guarantee against unreasonable searches and seizures, as well as the Fifth Amendment guarantee against compulsory self-incrimination and the guarantee of counsel. Initially applied only in federal cases, in *Mapp* v. *Ohio* (1961)[34] the Supreme Court extended the exclusionary rule to *all* criminal cases in the United States. A "good faith exception" is made "when law enforcement officers have acted in objective good faith or their transgressions have been minor."[35]

The exclusionary rule is a controversial court policy. Many trial proceedings today are not concerned with the guilt or innocence of the accused but instead focus on possible procedural errors by police or prosecutors. If the defendant's attorney can show that an error was committed, the defendant goes free, regardless of his or her guilt or innocence. Former Supreme Court Justice Felix Frankfurter wrote many years ago, "The history of liberty has largely been the history of procedural safeguards." These safeguards protect us all from the abuse of police powers. But former Chief Justice Warren Burger attacked the exclusionary rule for "the high price it extracts from society—the release of countless guilty criminals."[36] Why should criminals go free because of police misconduct? Why not punish the police directly, perhaps with disciplinary measures imposed by courts that discover procedural errors, instead of letting guilty persons go free? Releasing criminals because of police misconduct punishes society, not the police.

Plea Bargaining.   Most convictions are obtained by guilty pleas. Indeed, about 90 percent of the criminal cases brought to trial are disposed of by guilty pleas before a judge, not trial by jury. The Constitution guarantees defendants a trial by jury (Sixth Amendment), but guilty pleas outnumber jury trials by ten to one.[37]

Plea bargaining, in which the prosecution either reduces the seriousness of the charges, drops some but not all charges, or agrees to recommend lighter penalties in exchange for a guilty plea by the defendant, is very common. Some critics of plea bargaining view it as another form of leniency in the criminal justice system that reduces its deterrent effects. Other critics view plea bargaining as a violation of the Constitution's protection against self-incrimination and guarantee of a fair jury trial. Prosecutors, they say, threaten defendants with serious charges and stiff penalties to force a guilty plea. Still other critics see plea bargaining as an under-the-table process that undermines respect for the criminal justice system.

While the decision to plead guilty or go to trial rests with the defendant, this decision is strongly influenced by the policies of the prosecutor's office. A defendant may plead guilty and accept the certainty of conviction with whatever reduced charges the prosecutor offers and/or accept the prosecutor's pledge to recommend a lighter penalty. Or the defendant may go to trial, confronting serious charges with stiffer penalties, with the hope of being found innocent. However, the possibility of an innocent verdict in a jury trial is only one in six. This apparently strong record of conviction occurs because prosecutors have already dismissed charges in cases in which the evidence is weak or illegally obtained. Thus, most defendants confronting strong cases against them decide to "cop a plea."

It is very fortunate for the nation's court system that most defendants plead guilty. The court system would quickly break down from overload if any substantial proportion of defendants insisted on jury trials.

RICO VERSUS LIBERTY

Many authoritarian governments throughout the world boast of low crime rates and criminal justice systems that mete out swift and severe punishments. How far do we wish to go in restricting individual liberty to fight crime?

Congress passed the Racketeer Influenced and Corrupt Practices (RICO) Act in 1970, following a 1968 presidential campaign in which President Richard Nixon and Independent candidate George C. Wallace made "getting tough on crime" a key issue. RICO was designed to combat organized crime and drug trafficking. Among other provisions, it allows the U.S. Department of Justice to seize the money and property of people suspected of crimes. The popular slogan was "Take the profit out of crime!"

Criminal Forfeiture. Under RICO, federal authorities may seize cash, bank accounts, homes, cars, boats, businesses, and other assets on "probable cause" to believe that the assets were used in criminal activity or were obtained with profits from criminal activity. People may be stopped in an airport terminal, bus station, or street on suspicion of drug trafficking, and have their cash and cars seized by law enforcement agents. Boats and airplanes are also favorite targets of seizure, but RICO also allows the seizure of bank accounts, homes, and businesses.

Assets forfeited to federal law enforcement agencies—FBI, DEA, Customs Service, Treasury and Justice Departments—are usually retained by these agencies (or the profits of selling these assets at auction) and often shared with state and local law enforcement agencies that cooperated in the investigation. Thus, there is a strong bureaucratic incentive for agencies to go after "the profits of crime" and to concentrate on cases likely to result in forfeiture of these assets—primarily drug cases. There is increasing evidence that this incentive has placed drug enforcement ahead of other law enforcement activities in federal, state, and local agencies.

Probable Cause and Burden of Proof in Seizures. RICO permits the government to seize property before any adjudication of guilt. Indeed, a subsequent guilty verdict in a criminal trial is not necessary for the government to retain possession of the property seized. The only requirement is that law enforcement agents have "probable cause" to believe a crime has been committed and that the property seized was used in the crime or purchased with the profits of crime. "Probable cause" is a very loose standard; it includes anonymous tips, "suspicious" behavior, and persons fitting descriptions of classes of criminals.

People whose property is seized under RICO have the burden of appealing to the Justice Department and proving that they are innocent of any crime and, more importantly, that officers had no probable cause to seize their property. The burden of litigation, including hiring an attorney to institute proceedings for the return of the property, falls on the citizen, not on the government. The proceedings are considered a civil suit by an individual against the government, not a criminal case by the government against the individual. Thus, the government need not prove "beyond a reasonable doubt" that the person was involved in criminal activity or the property was used in a crime. Rather the person must prove his or her own innocence and the government's lack of probable cause to seize the property. The probable cause standard allows the government to dispossess people of their property based on hearsay and other "evidence" that would not be admissible in a criminal trial.

Forfeiture laws reach far beyond the profits of crime. RICO allows the government to seize bank accounts, businesses, homes, and property—whether or not they were legitimately acquired—if these assets afforded the accused "a source of influence over criminal enterprise." Thus, bank accounts and legitimate businesses may be seized on the government's assertion that they are covers for illegal activity.

Reform.   Efforts in Congress to reform RICO's forfeiture and seizure provisions have met with strong opposition by the U.S. Department of Justice, the National Association of Attorneys General, the National District Attorney Association, and many state and local law enforcement officials. Moreover, the Supreme Court has been unwilling to intervene, holding instead that government seizure cases are civil cases and that therefore defendants are not entitled to the Fifth Amendment's protection of due process of law afforded to defendants in criminal cases.[38]

PRISONS AND CORRECTIONAL POLICIES

At least four separate theories of crime and punishment compete for preeminence in guiding correctional policies. *Justice:* First, there is the ancient Judeo-Christian idea of holding individuals responsible for their guilty acts and compelling them to pay a debt to society. Retribution is an expression of society's moral outrage, and it lessens the impulse of victims and their families to seek revenge. *Deterrence:* Another philosophy argues that punishment should be sure, speedy, commensurate with the crime, and sufficiently conspicuous to deter others from committing crimes. *Incapacitation:* Still another philosophy in correctional policy is that of protecting the public from lawbreakers or habitual criminals by segregating them behind prison walls. *Rehabilitation:* Finally, there is the theory that criminals are partly or entirely victims of social circumstances beyond their control and that society owes them comprehensive treatment in the form of rehabilitation.

Rising Prison Populations.   Several million Americans are brought to a jail, police station, juvenile home, or prison each year. The vast majority are released within hours or days. There are, however, more than one million inmates in state and federal prisons in the United States. These prisoners are serving time for serious offenses; almost all had a record of crime before they committed the act that led to their current imprisonment. Prison populations have risen dramatically in recent years. Both the total number of prisoners and the incarceration rate (prisoners per 100,000 population) have tripled in 20 years (see Figure 4–6).

Prison Overcrowding.   Higher crime rates and longer sentences create serious overcrowding in prisons. Overcrowding contributes directly to unsanitary and dangerous living conditions and is associated with assaults, rapes, homicides, suicides, and riots. Prison staffs are also placed at risk by overcrowding and the violence it produces.

Federal courts have determined that prison overcrowding is a violation of the U.S. Constitution's Eighth Amendment prohibition against "cruel and unusual punishment." (Simple crowding per se is not unconstitutional; federal courts must also find evidence of its adverse effects.) Virtually all states confront federal court orders to reduce overcrowding at one or more of their prisons or throughout their entire prison system. Most state prison systems are near, at, or over their capacity to house prisoners. Under early release programs, sentences are automatically reduced and

FIGURE 4–6   United States Prison Population 1970–1995

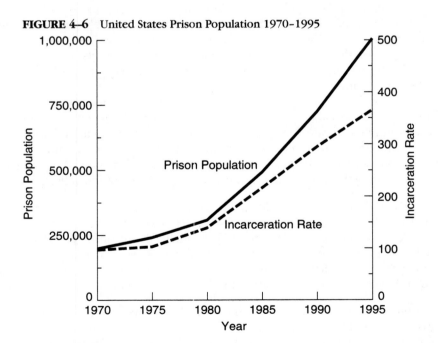

prisoners near the end of their terms are released first. Some states deny early release to certain violent offenders. Nonetheless, violent criminals on the average serve only half of their sentences, and nonviolent offenders less than one-third.

Mandatory Sentencing.   Widespread outrage at these "revolving-door" practices have led citizens and their legislators to enact mandatory minimum prison terms for repeat offenders and determinant sentencing or sentencing guidelines (prescribed specific jail terms for specific criminal offenses). These reforms limit judicial discretion and make punishment policies more explicit. However, these policies also increase prison populations. Unless citizens and legislators are willing to spend tax monies to build more prisons, these policies cannot be implemented.

Failure of Rehabilitation.   If correctional systems could be made to work—that is, actually to rehabilitate prisoners as useful, law-abiding citizens—the benefits to the nation would be enormous. Eighty percent of all felonies are committed by repeat offenders—individuals who have had prior contact with the criminal justice system and were not corrected by it. Reformers generally recommend more education and job training, more and better facilities, smaller prisons, halfway houses where offenders can adjust to civilian life before parole, more parole officers, and greater contact between prisoners and their families and friends. But as criminologist Daniel Glaser points out, "Unfortunately there is no convincing evidence that this investment reduces what criminologists call 'recidivism,' the offenders' return to crime."[39] In short, there is no evidence that people can be rehabilitated, no matter what is done. But prison policies now combine conflicting philosophies in a way that accomplishes none of society's goals. They do not effectively punish or deter individuals from crime. They do not succeed in rehabilitating the criminal. They do not even protect the public by keeping criminals off the streets. Even the maintenance of order within prisons and the protection of the lives of guards and inmates have become serious problems.

Prison life does little to encourage good behavior, as noted by policy analyst John DiIulio, Jr.: "For the most part, the nation's adult and juvenile inmates spend their days in idleness punctuated by meals, violence, and weight lifting. Meaningful educational, vocational, and counseling programs are rare. Strong inmates are permitted to pressure weaker prisoners for sex, drugs, and money. Gangs organized along racial and ethnic lines are often the real 'sovereigns of the cellblock.' "[40]

Failure of Probation.   In addition to the nation's prison population of more than one million, there are three million people currently on probation for serious crimes (See Table 4–6). But probation has been just as ineffective as prison in reducing crime. Even though people placed on probation are considered less dangerous to society than those imprisoned, studies indicate that nearly two-thirds of probationers will be arrested and over one-half will be convicted for a crime committed *while on probation*.

Failure of Parole.   Over two-thirds of all prisoner releases come about by means of parole. Modern penology, with its concern for reform and rehabilitation, appears to favor parole over unconditional releases. The function of parole and

TABLE 4-6   Jail, Prison, Probation, and Parole
Estimated Correctional Population, 1994

Total	5,135,900
Prison	999,808
Jail	483,717
Probation	2,962,166
Parole	690,159

Source: *Bureau of Justice Statistics 1995.*

postrelease supervision is to procure information on the parolees' postprison conduct and to facilitate and graduate the transition between prison and complete freedom. These functions are presumably oriented toward protecting the public and rehabilitating the offender. However, studies of recidivism indicate that up to three-fourths of the persons paroled from prison will be rearrested for serious crimes. There is no difference in this high rate of recidivism between those released under supervised parole and those released unconditionally. Thus, it does not appear that parole succeeds in its objectives.

Prison Costs Reconsidered. Taxpayers are understandably upset with the prospect of spending $50,000 to $75,000 for each new prison bed and $15,000 to $25,000 per year to keep a prisoner behind bars. But if the costs of incarceration are weighed against its benefits, taxpayers may feel better about prison construction and maintenance. A prisoner's "rap sheet" may list only three or four convictions and a dozen arrests. But interviews with offenders suggest that the typical convict has committed hundreds of crimes. Various studies have attempted to estimate the dollars lost to society through the crimes committed by the typical convict in a year.[41] Estimates run from $200,000 to $400,000, which means that a year of crime may be many times more costly to society than a year of incarceration.

Efforts are now underway in many states to lower the cost of prison facilities. Not all prisoners need to be housed in maximum security institutions; nonviolent criminals can be safely housed in less costly minimum security facilities. "Privatization" can also dramatically lower the costs of maintaining prisoners. States and counties can contract with private companies both to build and to maintain prisons at much lower costs than those the government itself requires to perform these functions. Moreover, initial evaluations suggest that conditions in private prisons are much better than in government prisons. Indeed, even prisoners prefer privately run prisons.

CAPITAL PUNISHMENT

Capital punishment has been the topic of a long and heated national debate. Opponents of the death penalty argue that it is cruel and unusual punishment, in violation of the Eighth Amendment of the Constitution. They also argue that the death penalty is applied unequally. A large proportion of those executed have been poor, uneducated, and nonwhite. In contrast, a sense of justice among many Americans demands retribution for heinous crimes—a life for a life. A mere jail sentence for a multiple murderer or rapist-murderer seems unjust compared with the damage inflicted on society and the victims. In most cases, a life sentence means less than ten years in prison under the current parole and probation policies of many states. Convicted murderers have been set free, and some have killed again.

Prohibition on Unfair Application.   Prior to 1972, the death penalty was officially sanctioned by about half of the states as well as by federal law. However, no one had actually suffered the death penalty since 1967 because of numerous legal tangles and direct challenges to the constitutionality of capital punishment.

In *Furman* v. *Georgia* (1972), the Supreme Court ruled that capital punishment as then imposed violated the Eighth Amendment and Fourteenth Amendment prohibitions against cruel and unusual punishment and due process of law.[42] The reasoning in the case is very complex. Only two justices, Brennan and Marshall, declared that capital punishment itself is cruel and unusual. The other justices in the majority felt that death sentences had been applied unfairly: a few individuals were receiving the death penalty for crimes for which many others were receiving much lighter sentences. These justices left open the possibility that capital punishment would be constitutional if it were specified for certain kinds of crime and applied uniformly.

After this decision, a majority of states rewrote their death penalty laws to try to ensure fairness and uniformity of application. Generally, these laws mandate the death penalty for murders committed during rape, robbery, hijacking, or kidnapping; murders of prison guards; murder with torture; and multiple murders. Two trials would be held—one to determine guilt or innocence and another to determine the penalty. At the second trial, evidence of "aggravating" and "mitigating" factors would be presented; if there were aggravating factors but no mitigating factors, the death penalty would be mandatory.

Death Penalty Reinstated.   In a series of cases in 1976 (*Gregg* v. *Georgia, Profitt* v. *Florida, Jurek* v. *Texas*)[43] the Supreme Court finally held that "the punishment of death does *not* invariably violate the Constitution." The Court upheld the death penalty, employing the following rationale: the men who drafted the Bill of Rights accepted death as a common sanction for crime. It is true that the Eighth Amendment prohibition against cruel and unusual punishment must be interpreted in a dynamic fashion, reflecting changing moral values. But the decisions of more than half of the nation's state legislatures to reenact the death penalty since 1972 and the decision of juries to impose the death penalty on hundreds of people under these new laws are evidence that "a large proportion of American society continues to regard it as an appropriate and necessary criminal sanction." Moreover, said the Court, the social purposes of retribution and deterrence justify the use of the death penalty. This ultimate sanction is "an expression of society's moral outrage at particularly offensive conduct." The Court affirmed that *Furman* v. *Georgia* struck down the death penalty only where it was inflicted in "an arbitrary and capricious manner." The Court upheld the death penalty in states where the trial was a two-part proceeding and where, during the second part, the judge or jury was provided with relevant information and standards. The Court upheld the consideration of "aggravating and mitigating circumstances." It also upheld automatic review of all death sentences by state supreme courts to ensure that these sentences were not imposed under the influence of passion or prejudice, that aggravating factors were supported by the evidence, and that the sentence was not disproportionate to the crime. However, the Court disapproved of state laws mandating the death penalty in first degree murder cases, holding that such laws were "unduly harsh and unworkably rigid." The Court has also struck down laws making the death penalty mandatory for a murder committed by a prisoner already serving a life sentence without parole.[44]

Racial Bias. The death penalty has also been challenged as a violation of the Equal Protection Clause of the Fourteenth Amendment because of a racial bias in the application of the punishment. White murderers are just as likely to receive the death penalty as black murderers. However, some statistics show that if the *victim* is white, there is a greater chance that the killer will be sentenced to death than if the victim is black. Nonetheless the Supreme Court has ruled that statistical disparities in the race of victims by itself does not bar the death penalty in all cases. There must be evidence of racial bias against a particular defendant for the Court to reverse a death sentence.[45]

Executions. Today, there are more than two thousand prisoners nationwide on death row, that is, persons convicted and sentenced to death. But only about twenty executions are actually carried out each year. The strategy of death row prisoners and their lawyers, of course, is to delay indefinitely the imposition of the death penalty with endless stays and appeals. So far the strategy has been successful for all but a few luckless murderers. As trial judges and juries continue to impose the death penalty and appellate courts continue to grant stays of execution, the number of prisoners on death row grows. The few who have been executed have averaged ten years of delay between trial and execution.

The writ of habeas corpus is guaranteed in the U.S. Constitution, but how many habeas corpus petitions should a condemned prisoner be allowed to submit? The death penalty, of course, is irreversible, and it must not be imposed if there is any doubt whatsoever about the defendant's guilt. But how many opportunities and resulting delays should death row inmates have to challenge their convictions and sentences? In recent years the Supreme Court has limited habeas corpus petitions in federal courts by prisoners who have already filed claims and lost and who have failed to follow rules of appeal. If new evidence is uncovered after all court appeals have been exhausted, the Supreme Court has indicated that appeal lies with governors' powers of pardon.

Deterrent Value. The death penalty as it is employed today—inflicted on so few after so many years following the crime—has little deterrent effect. Nonetheless, it serves several purposes. It gives prosecutors some leverage in plea bargaining with murder defendants. The defendants may choose to plead guilty in exchange for a life sentence when confronted with the possibility that the prosecutor may win a conviction and the death penalty in a jury trial. More importantly, perhaps, the death penalty is symbolic of the value society places on the lives of innocent victims. It dramatically signifies that society does not excuse or condone the taking of innocent lives. It symbolizes the potential for society's retribution against heinous crime. Public opinion favors the death penalty by three to one. (Only for a few years during the mid-1960s did public opinion appear to oppose the death penalty.) As crime rates increase, large majorities of Americans have come to favor the death penalty.

SUMMARY

Crime is a central problem in our society. We face a conflict between our desire to retain individual freedoms and our desire to ensure the safety of our people.

1. Crime rates have risen unevenly over the past twenty years. After leveling off in the early 1980s because of a decline in the most crime-prone age groups, crime soared upward again with the spread of crack cocaine. The victimization rate is several times greater than the reported crime rate. These statistics suggest that the current system of criminal justice is not a serious deterrent to crime.

2. A rational policy toward crime would endeavor to make its costs far outweigh its benefits and in theory deter potential wrongdoers. Effective deterrence requires that punishment be certain, swift, and severe. However, certainty and swiftness are probably of more importance to deterrence than is severity.

3. But punishment for crime in the United States today is neither certain nor swift. The likelihood of going to jail for any particular crime is probably less than one in a hundred. Speedy trial and punishment are rare; criminal defendants usually succeed in obtaining long delays between arrest and trial, when most are free on bail.

4. The police provide many services to society in addition to law enforcement. Indeed, only a small proportion of their time is spent in fighting crime. It is difficult to demonstrate conclusively that increased police protection reduces the actual amount of crime.

5. Guns are used in a large number of violent crimes. Public policy on gun control varies throughout the nation. However, states with strict gun control laws do not have lower rates of violent crime, or even of gun-related crime, than states without such laws.

6. Public policies toward alcohol and drug use are ambivalent. Although the health dangers of cigarettes, alcohol, marijuana, cocaine, and heroin are widely known, the manufacture, sale, and use of each of these substances are treated differently in law enforcement.

7. The judicial system fails to deter criminal conduct. Court congestion, increased litigation, excessive delays, endless appeals, variation in sentencing, and excessive plea bargaining all combine to detract from deterrence.

8. The exclusionary rule, which prohibits the use of illegally obtained evidence in court, has generated controversy since it was first announced by the Supreme Court in *Mapp* v. *Ohio* in 1961.

9. About half of all serious charges are dismissed by prosecutors before trial. But most convictions are obtained by guilty pleas without jury trials. Plea bargaining is the most common means of resolving criminal cases. Without plea bargaining, the court system would break down from overload.

10. Prison and parole policies have failed to rehabilitate prisoners. Prisons can reduce crime only by incapacitating criminals for periods of time. Most prisoners are recidivists—persons who previously served a sentence of incarceration before being sentenced again. Parolees—persons released by officials for good behavior—are just as likely to commit new crimes as those released after serving full sentences.

11. Capital punishment as currently imposed—on very few persons and after very long delays—is not an effective deterrent.

NOTES

1. U.S. General Accounting Office, *Juvenile Justice* (Washington, DC: Government Printing Office, 1995), p. 2.
2. Data from Virginia as reported in William J. Bennett, John J. DiIulio, Jr., and John P. Walters, *Body Count* (New York: Simon & Schuster, 1996), p. 119.
3. Bureau of Justice Statistics, *Sourcebook of Criminal Justice Statistics 1994*, p. 179.
4. U.S. Department of Justice, *Criminal Victimization in the United States*, published annually (Washington, DC: Bureau of Justice Statistics).
5. U.S. Department of Justice, *The Risk of Violent Crime* (Washington, DC: Bureau of Justice Statistics, 1985).
6. *Statistical Abstract of the United States 1995*, p. 206.
7. James Q. Wilson and Richard J. Herrnstein, *Crime and Human Nature* (New York: Simon & Schuster, 1985).
8. *Statistical Abstract of the United States 1995*, p. 217.
9. John J. DiIulio, Jr., "Punishing Smarter," *Brookings Review* (Summer 1989), 3–12.
10. U.S. Department of Justice, Bureau of Justice Statistics, *Examining Readmission*, February 1985.
11. Stuart A. Sheingold, "Cultural Cleavage and Criminal Justice," *Journal of Politics* (November 1978) 40, 865–897.
12. Peter Manning, "The Police," in *Criminal Justice in America*, ed. Richard Quinney (Boston: Little, Brown, 1974).
13. See Stuart Sheingold, *The Politics of Law and Order* (New York: Layman, 1984).
14. For a summary, see John J. DiIulio, Jr., "Arresting Ideas: Tougher Law Enforcement Is Driving Down Crime," *Policy Review* (Fall 1995), 12–16.
15. William S. Bratlon, "The New City Police Department's Civil Enforcement of Quality of Life Crimes," *Journal of Law and Policy 1995*, pp. 447–464; also cited by William J. Bennett, et al., *Body Count*, op. cit.
16. *Statistical Abstract of the United States 1992*, p. 183, 185.
17. Douglas R. Murray, "Handguns, Gun Control Laws and Firearm Violence," *Social Problems*, 23 (1975); James D. Wright and Peter H. Rossi, *Weapons, Crime, and Violence in America* (Washington, DC: U.S. Department of Justice, National Institute of Justice, 1981).
18. David Rossman, *The Impact of the Mandatory Gun Law in Massachusetts* (Boston: Boston University School of Law, 1979).
19. Wright and Rossi, *Weapons, Crime, and Violence*, p. 540.

20. Gary Kleck, *Point Blank Guns and Violence in America* (New York: Aldine de Gruyter, 1991); Gary Kleck, "The Impact of Gun Control and Gun Ownership Levels on Violence Rates," *Journal of Quantitative Criminology* (1993), pp. 249–287.
21. William Blackstone, *Commentaries of the Laws of England,* Vol. 1, p. 144.
22. *United States* v. *Miller,* 307 U.S. 174 (1939).
23. U.S. Department of Health and Human Services, *Drug Abuse Warning Network 1995;* cited by William J. Bennett et. al, op. cit., pp. 156–158.
24. Office of the National Drug Control Policy, *National Drug Control Strategy* (Washington, DC: Government Printing Office, 1996).
25. *Congressional Quarterly Weekly Report,* June 25, 1988.
26. Ethan A. Nadelmann, "U.S. Drug Policy," *Foreign Policy,* Spring 1988, pp. 83–108.
27. See David W. Rasmussen and Bruce L. Benson, *The Economic Anatomy of the Drug War* (Latham, MD: Rowman and Littlefield, 1994).
28. Various studies cited by William J. Bennett, et al., *Body Count,* pp. 172–180.
29. Ethan A. Nadelmann, "The Case for Legalization," *The Public Interest,* Summer 1988, pp. 3–31.
30. John Kaplan, "Taking Drugs Seriously," *The Public Interest,* Summer 1988, pp. 32–50.
31. *Illinois* v. *Gates,* 462 U.S. 213 (1983).
32. *Arizona* v. *Hicks,* 480 U.S. 321 (1987).
33. *Spano* v. *New York,* 360 U.S. 315 (1959).
34. *Mapp* v. *Ohio,* 367 U.S. 643 (1961).
35. *United States* v. *Leon,* 468 U.S. 897 (1984).
36. Warren Burger, Address on the State of the Judiciary to the American Bar Association, August 10, 1970.
37. U.S. Department of Justice, Bureau of Justice Statistics, *The Prevalence of Guilty Pleas,* December 1984.
38. *Toledo* v. *Pearson Yacht Leasing,* 416 U.S. 663 (1974); *Caplin & Drysdale* v. *U.S.,* 491 U.S. 617 (1989).
39. Daniel Glaser, *Effectiveness of a Prison and Parole System* (New York: Bobbs-Merill, 1969), p. 4.
40. John J. DiIulio, Jr., "Punishing Smarter," *Brookings Review* (Summer 1989), 8.
41. See Richard Abell, "Beyond Willie Horton, The Battle of the Prison Bulge," *Policy Review,* 44 (Winter 1989), 32–35.
42. *Furman* v. *Georgia,* 408 U.S. 238 (1972).
43. 428 U.S. 153 (1976).
44. *Summer* v. *Schman,* 107 S. Ct. 2716 (1987).
45. *McCluskey* v. *Kemp,* 481 U.S. 279 (1987).

BIBLIOGRAPHY

Bennett, William J., John J. DiIulio, Jr., and John P. Walters. *Body Count.* New York: Simon & Schuster, 1996.
Kleck, Gary. *Point Blank: Guns and Violence in America.* New York: Aldine de Gruyter, 1991.
Wilson, James Q. *Thinking About Crime.* 2nd ed. New York: Basic Books, 1984.
Wilson, James Q., and Richard J. Herrnstein. *Crime and Human Nature.* New York: Simon & Schuster, 1985.

5

HEALTH AND WELFARE
The Search for Rational Strategies

Welfare recipients stand in line for the federal cheese giveaway program. (UPI/Corbis–Bettmann)

RATIONALITY AND IRRATIONALITY IN THE WELFARE STATE

When most Americans think of social welfare programs, they think of the poor—the 35 to 40 million people living below the poverty line. But if the money spent each year by the federal government for social welfare were targeted on the poor, each poor person—man, woman, and child—would receive more than $25,000 per year! In other words, if the nation's social welfare spending were directed toward the poor, there would be no poverty in America.

Why does poverty persist in a nation where total social welfare spending is more than four times the amount needed to eliminate poverty? The answer is that the poor are *not* the principal beneficiaries of social welfare spending. Most of it, including the largest programs—Social Security and Medicare—goes to the *non-poor*. Only about one-sixth of federal social welfare spending is "means-tested," that is, distributed to recipients based on their low-income or poverty status. The middle class, not the poor, is the major beneficiary of the nation's social welfare spending.

"Entitlements."   Entitlements are government benefits for which Congress has set eligibility criteria—age, income, retirement, disability, unemployment, and so forth. Everyone who meets the criteria is "entitled" to the benefit.

Most of the nation's major entitlement programs were launched either in the New Deal years of the 1930s under President Franklin D. Roosevelt (Social Security, Unemployment Compensation, Aid to Families with Dependent Children [AFDC], and Aid to Aged, Blind, and Disabled, now called Supplemental Security Income or SSI) or the Great Society years of the 1960s under President Lyndon B. Johnson (food stamps, Medicare, Medicaid).

Today nearly one-third of the population of the United States is "entitled" to some form of government benefit. *Social insurance* entitlements may be claimed by persons regardless of their income or wealth. Entitlement to Social Security and Medicare is determined by *age,* not income or poverty. Entitlement to unemployment compensation benefits is determined by employment status. Federal employee and veterans' retirement benefits are based on previous government or military service. These non-means-tested programs account for the largest number of recipients of government benefits. In contrast, *public assistance* programs (including cash welfare assistance, Medicaid, food stamps, and so forth) are means-tested: benefits are limited to low-income recipients (see Table 5–1). Because many programs overlap, with individuals receiving more than one type of entitlement benefit, it is not really possible to know exactly the total number of people receiving government assistance. But it is clear that government entitlements go to a very large segment of our society.

Entitlement Spending.   Entitlement spending accounts for nearly 60 percent of all federal government spending (see Figure 9–5 in Chapter 9). Most entitlement payments do *not* go to the poor. The largest shares of entitlement spending—Social Security, Medicare, veterans' and federal retirement—go to retirees. These three

TABLE 5-1   Major Federal Entitlement Programs

Social Insurance Programs (No Means Test for Entitlement to Benefits)	Beneficiaries (Millions)
Social Security	
Total	42.9
Retirement	29.9
Survivors	7.4
Disabled	5.6
Medicare	
Total	36.9
Unemployment Compensation	
Total	7.9

Public Assistance Programs (Means-Tested Entitlement)	Beneficiaries (Millions)
Cash Aid	
Temporary Assistance for Needy Families (formerly AFDC)	14.0
SSI	6.3
General assistance	0.9
Income tax credit	37.8
Medical Care	
Medicaid	35.0
Maternal and Child Health Services	11.6
Food Benefits	
Food stamps	2.6
School lunches	25.6
Women, infants, children	6.9
Nutrition program for elderly	2.1
Housing Benefits	
Total	4.1
Education Aid	
Stafford Loans	3.8
Pell Grants	3.8
Head Start	0.7
Work study	0.8
Educational opportunity grants	0.9
Job Training	
Total	1.8
Energy Assistance	
Total	6.1

Source: *Statistical Abstract of the United States 1996,* pp. 117, 186, 371, 375, 382, 383.

programs alone account for two-thirds of all entitlement payments. Payments to the poor—welfare and Medicaid—account for less than one-third of federal entitlement spending. As we shall see in Chapter 9, "Economic Policy," the federal government's chronic deficits, and resulting heavy debt burdens on future generations, cannot be reduced without reining in entitlement spending.

Rational Strategies, Irrational Results.   It is not really possible in this chapter to describe all the problems of the poor in America or all the difficulties in developing rational social welfare policies. But it is possible to describe the general design of alternative strategies to deal with welfare and health in America, to observe how these strategies have been implemented in public policy, and to outline some of the obstacles to a rational approach to social welfare problems.

POVERTY IN AMERICA

A rational approach to policymaking requires a clear definition of the problem. But political conflict over the nature and extent of poverty in America is a major obstacle to a rational approach to social welfare policy.

Proponents of programs for the poor frequently make high estimates of that population. They view the problem of poverty as persistent, even in an affluent society; they contend that many millions of people suffer from hunger, exposure, and remedial illness. Their definition of the problem virtually mandates immediate and massive public welfare programs.

In contrast, others minimize the number of poor in America. They believe that the poor are considerably better off than the middle class of fifty years ago and even wealthy by the standards of most other societies in the world. They believe government welfare programs cause poverty, destroy family life and rob the poor of incentives to work, save, and assume responsibility for their own well-being. They deny that anyone needs to suffer from hunger, exposure, or remedial illness if they use the services and facilities available to them.

How Many Poor?   How much poverty really exists in America? According to the U.S. Bureau of the Census, there were about 38 million poor people in the United States in 1995, or approximately 14 percent of the population. This official estimate of poverty includes all those Americans whose annual cash income falls below that which is required to maintain a decent standard of living. The dollar amount of the "poverty line" is flexible to take into account the effect of inflation; the amount rises each year with the rate of inflation. In 1995 the poverty line for a family of four was approximately $15,000 per year (see Table 5–2). The median income for all families for the nation that year was $39,000.[1]

Liberal Criticism.   This official definition of poverty has many critics. Some liberal critics believe that poverty is underestimated because (1) the official definition includes cash income from welfare and social security, and without this gov-

TABLE 5-2   Poverty in America

Poverty definition 1995 for family of four	$15,000
Number of poor	38 million
Poverty percentage of total population	14.0
Race (% poor)	
White	11.2
Black	30.6
Hispanic	30.7
Age (% poor)	
Under 18	21.8
Over 65	11.7
Family (% poor)	
Married couple	9.1
Female householder, no husband	38.6
Female householder, no husband, children under 18	52.9

Source: U.S. Bureau of the Census, *Current Population Reports.*

ernment assistance, the number of poor would be much higher, perhaps 25 percent of the total population; (2) the official definition does not count the many "near poor"; there are 40 million Americans, or more than 18 percent of the population, living below 125 percent of the poverty level; (3) the official definition does not take into account regional differences in the cost of living, climate, or accepted styles of living; and (4) the official definition does not consider what people *think* they need to live adequately.

Conservative Criticism.   Some conservative critics also challenge the official definition of poverty: (1) it does not consider the value of family assets; people (usually older) who own their own mortgage-free homes, furniture, and automobiles may have current incomes below the poverty line yet not suffer hardship; (2) there are many families and individuals who are officially counted as poor but who do not think of themselves as such—students, for example, who deliberately postpone earning an income to secure an education; (3) many persons (poor and nonpoor) underreport their real income, which leads to overestimates of the number of poor; and (4) more importantly, the official definition of poverty excludes "in-kind" (non-cash) benefits given to the poor by governments, for example, food stamps, free medical care, public housing, and school lunches. If these benefits were costed out (calculated as cash income), there may be only half as many poor people as shown in official statistics. This figure might be thought of as the "net poverty" rate, which refers to people who remain poor even after counting their in-kind government benefits. The net poverty rate is shown together with the official poverty rate in Figure 5–1.

Latent Poverty.   How many people would be poor if we did not have government Social Security and welfare programs? What percentage of the population can be thought of as "latent poor," that is, persons who would be poor without the

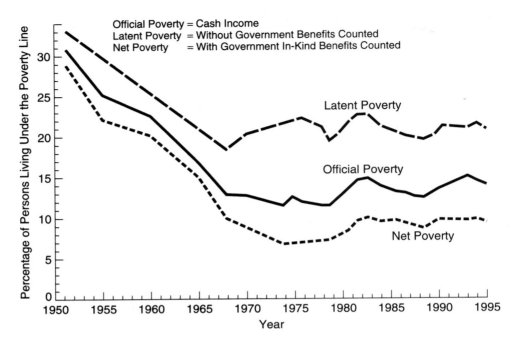

Sources: 1950 to 1980 from *Losing Ground: American Social Policy 1950–1980* by Charles Murray. 1981 to 1995 from U.S. Bureau of the Census, *Current Population Reports.*

FIGURE 5–1   Three Definitions of Poverty

assistance they receive from federal programs? Charles Murray, a social scientist, refers to the latent poverty figure as "the most damning statistic," because it counts the number of people in our society who are economically dependent and cannot stand on their own.[2] Latent poverty has been growing since the late 1960s, as more and more people became dependent on government Social Security and welfare payments (see Figure 5–1). Latent poverty was estimated to be around 23 percent in 1992, well above the 14.5 percent in official poverty.

WHO ARE THE POOR?

Poverty occurs in many kinds of families and all races and ethnic groups. However, some groups experience poverty in proportions greater than the national average.

Family Structure.   Poverty is most common among female-headed families. The incidence of poverty among these families in 1995 was 39 percent, compared to only 9 percent for married couples (see Table 5–2). For female-headed families with children under 18 poverty exceeds 50 percent. These women and their children make up more than two-thirds of all the persons living in poverty in the United States. These figures describe "the feminization of poverty" in America. Clearly, poverty is closely related to family structure. Today the disintegration of the traditional husband-wife family is the single most influential factor contributing to poverty.

Race. Blacks experience poverty in much greater proportions than whites. Over the years the poverty rate among blacks in the United States has been more than three times higher than that among whites. Poverty among Hispanics is also significantly greater than among whites.

The relationship between race and family structure is a controversial topic. About 46 percent of all black families in the United States in 1994 were headed by females, compared with about 14 percent of all white families. More than 50 percent of all black female-headed families live in poverty.

These facts are not in dispute, but their implications have generated controversial debate. Senator Daniel Patrick Moynihan (D.-N.Y.) ran into a firestorm of criticism when he suggested as far back as 1965 that the disintegration of black family life was a major cause of poverty. Although Moynihan argued that black families had been victimized by slavery and segregation, his views were interpreted by critics as racist.

Age. The aged in the United States experience *less* poverty than the nonaged. The aged are not poor, despite the popularity of the phrase "the poor and the aged." The poverty rate for persons over sixty-five years of age is well below the national average. Moreover, the aged are much wealthier than the nonaged. They are more likely than younger people to own homes with paid-up mortgages. A large portion of their medical expenses are paid by Medicare. With fewer expenses, the aged, even with relatively smaller cash incomes, experience poverty in a different fashion than a young mother with children. The lowering of the poverty rate among the aged is a relatively recent occurrence. Continuing increases in Social Security benefits over the years are largely responsible for this singular "victory" in the war against poverty.

Wealth. Wealth is the net worth of all one's possessions—home value minus mortgage, auto value minus loan, business value minus debts, plus bank accounts, other savings, stocks and bonds, and real estate. All calculations of poverty consider *income,* not *wealth.* It is possible for people to have considerable wealth (for example, to own a mortgage-free home and a loan-free automobile and have savings and investments) yet fall within the official definition of poverty because their current cash income is low. Indeed, the elderly on the average are twice as wealthy as the rest of the population and ten times wealthier than young adults.[3]

Temporary versus Persistent Poverty. Most poverty is temporary, and most welfare dependency is relatively brief, lasting less than 3 years. Tracing poor families over time presents a different picture of the nature of poverty and welfare from the "snapshot" view taken in any one year. For example, we know that over the last decade 11 to 15 percent of the nation's population had been officially classified as poor in any one year (see Figure 5–1). However, over a decade as many as 25 percent of the nation's population may have fallen below the poverty line at one time or another.[4] Only some poverty is persistent: about 6 percent of the population remains in poverty for more than five years. This means that most of the people who experience poverty in their lives do so for only a short period of time.

However, the persistently poor place a disproportionate burden on welfare resources. Less than half of the people on welfare rolls at any one time are persistently poor, that is, likely to remain on welfare for five or more years. Thus, for most welfare recipients, welfare payments are a relatively short-term aid that helps them over life's difficult times. But for others, welfare is a more permanent part of their lives.

Policy Implications.   What implications do these observations about welfare dynamics have for public policy? First, for most people poverty is only a temporary occurrence in their lives. It is associated with divorce or separation, job loss, illness or disability, or some other misfortune. Conceivably, in the absence of government welfare programs, some people might remain married who now separate or divorce, knowing that welfare would cushion the financial impact of their decision; and some people may leave an unsatisfactory job knowing that they can rely on welfare. But it is reasonable to assume that most of the temporary poverty in America is not a product of any structural characteristic of American society, including government welfare programs. For the temporarily poor, welfare is short-term assistance, and welfare programs are more akin to insurance—tiding people over the difficult events of life.

For the persistently poor, welfare is not a temporary expedient but a way of life. Many of the persistently poor are single, young women who came onto welfare rolls following the birth of their first child. If the welfare system itself is the cause of poverty, its effects are most likely to be observed among these people. It is important to remember that most spells of welfare dependency are relatively short. This suggests that a brief experience with the welfare system does not necessarily create long-term dependency. However, significant numbers of welfare recipients are persistently poor and dependent. It is by no means certain that the welfare system itself causes this long-term dependence. But a pattern of continuous welfare dependence may indeed be a product of attitudinal and behavioral characteristics toward family, work, and education, which are caused in part by welfare policy itself.

WHY ARE THE POOR POOR?

Inasmuch as policymakers cannot even agree on the definition of poverty, it comes as no surprise that they cannot agree on its causes. Yet rationality in public policymaking requires some agreement on the causes of social problems.

Low Productivity.   Many economists explain poverty in terms of *human capital theory*. The poor are poor because their economic productivity is low. They do not have the human capital—the knowledge, skills, training, work habits, abilities—

to sell to employers in a free market. Absence from the labor force is the largest single source of poverty. Over two-thirds of the poor are children, mothers of small children, or aged or disabled people, all of whom cannot reasonably be expected to find employment. No improvement in the general economy is likely to affect these people directly. Since the private economy has no role for them, they are largely the responsibility of government. The poorly educated and unskilled are also at a disadvantage in a free labor market. The demand for their labor is low, employment is often temporary, and wage rates are low.

Economic Stagnation.   Economists also recognize that some poverty results from inadequate aggregate demand. Serious recessions with increases in unemployment raise the proportion of the population living below the poverty line. (Note the increases in the poverty percentages reported for the 1982–1983 and 1991–1992 economic recessions in Figure 5–1.) According to this view, the most effective antipoverty policy is to assure continued economic growth and employment opportunity. Historically, the greatest reductions in poverty have occurred during prosperous times.

Discrimination.   Discrimination plays a role in poverty that is largely unaccounted for by economic theory. We have already observed that blacks are more than three times more likely to experience poverty than whites. It is true that some of the income differences between blacks and whites are a product of educational differences. However, blacks earn less than whites even at the same educational level. If the free market operated without interference by discrimination, we would expect little or no difference in income between blacks and whites with the same education.

Culture of Poverty.   Yet another explanation focuses on a "culture of poverty." According to this notion, poverty is a "way of life," which is learned by the poor. The culture of poverty involves not just a low income but also indifference, alienation, apathy, and irresponsibility. This culture fosters a lack of self-discipline to work hard, to plan and save for the future, and to get ahead. It also encourages family instability, immediate gratification, and "present-orientedness" instead of "future-orientedness." All of these attitudes prevent the poor from taking advantage of the opportunities available to them. Even cash payments do not change the way of life of these hardcore poor very much. According to this theory, additional money will be spent quickly for nonessential or frivolous items.
     Opponents of this idea argue that it diverts attention from the conditions of poverty that *foster* family instability, present-orientedness, and other ways of life of the poor. The question is really whether a lack of money creates a culture of poverty or vice versa. Reformers are likely to focus on the condition of poverty as the fundamental cause of the social pathologies that afflict the poor.

Disintegrating Family Structure.   Poverty is closely associated with family structure. As we have seen, poverty is greatest among female-headed households and least among husband-wife households. Family structure affects the income of both black and white families.[5]

	1994 Median Income
White	
Married couple families	$45,555
Female-headed household, no husband present	$22,605
Black	
Married couple families	$40,432
Female-headed household, no husband present	$14,650

It may be fashionable in some circles to view husband-wife families as traditional or even antiquated and to redefine *family* as any household with more than one person. But no worse advice could be given to the poor.

Trends in family composition in the United States are not reassuring. Husband-wife families have declined from 87.5 percent of all families in 1960 to 79.2 percent in 1990, and these families are projected to decline to 75 percent of all households by 2000. Female-headed households with no husband present increased from 6.8 percent of all households in 1960 to 16.5 percent in 1990, and they are projected to rise to 20 percent in 2000.[6]

Births to Single Women.   Of all age groups, children are most likely to be poor; more than 20 percent of America's children live in poverty. Disintegrating family structure explains most of this: Only 12 percent of children living with married parents live in poverty, whereas 66 percent of those living with single mothers do so.[7] Rises in the numbers and percentages of births to single women promise the continuation of child poverty in the United States. Major increases over the last twenty years in births to unmarried women have occurred among both blacks and whites, but rates among blacks have been especially high (see Figure 5–2).

The "Truly Disadvantaged."   The nation's largest cities have become the principal location of virtually all of the social problems confronting our society—poverty, homelessness, racial tension, drug abuse, delinquency, and crime. These problems are made worse by their concentration in large cities. Yet the concentration of social ills in cities is a relatively recent occurrence; as late as 1970, there were higher rates of poverty in rural America than in the cities.

Why has the "inner city" become the locus of social problems? Some observers argue that changes in the labor market from industrial goods-producing jobs to professional, financial, and technical service-producing jobs have increasingly divided the labor market into low-wage and high-wage sectors.[8] The decline in manufacturing jobs, together with a shift in remaining manufacturing jobs and commercial (sales) jobs to the suburbs, has left inner-city residents with fewer and lower paying job opportunities. The rise in joblessness in the inner cities has in turn increased the concentration of poor people, added to the number of poor single-parent families, and increased welfare dependency.

At the same time, inner-city neighborhoods have experienced an out-migration

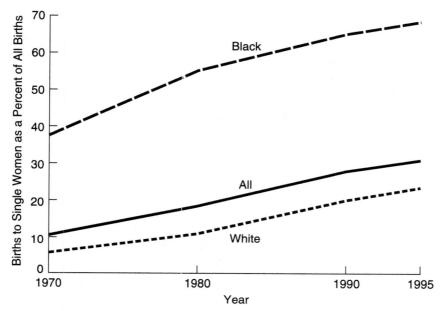

FIGURE 5–2   Births to Single Women

of working-class and middle-class families. Previously these families invested their income and time in their neighborhoods, patronizing local churches, stores, schools, and community organizations. Their presence in the community provided "role models" for youth. But their out-migration has decreased contact between the classes, leaving the poorest Americans isolated and "truly disadvantaged." Inner-city residents now lack not only nearby jobs, but also access to job information and social learning through working role models. Neighborhoods that have few legitimate employment opportunities, inadequate job information networks, and poor schools not only weaken the traditional work ethic, but also give rise to illegal income-producing activities in the streets—drugs, crime, prostitution. A jobless family living in a neighborhood where these ills are concentrated is influenced by the behaviors, beliefs, and perceptions of the people around them. These "concentration effects" make things worse.

   Capitalist Exploitation.   Finally, we might consider a Marxist explanation of poverty in a capitalist society. Typically, Marxists argue that poverty is maintained by the ruling class to serve their self-interest. The poor are available to do society's dirty work, to take jobs that are physically dirty or dangerous, temporary, dead-end, and underpaid. The poor buy old, used, and defective merchandise that others do not want. They are often punished and accused of wrongdoing as a means of upholding societal norms. For example, the poor are called lazy because society values hardworking, industrious people. Poverty allows those in the middle and upper classes to maintain their higher status in society. The poor allow others to improve their position in society by providing a market for legal (and illegal) business activities in the slums. The poor help fill the ranks of the "army of the unemployed," who function to keep wage rates low by threatening to take the jobs of striking workers. If we accept this Marxist explanation, public policy in a capitalist society will be designed to maintain poverty. Welfare programs will not be designed to alleviate or end poverty but rather to "regulate" the poor.[9] In other words, welfare policy will be designed to avoid rioting, violence, or revolution, yet guarantee a continuation of poverty.

THE PREVENTIVE STRATEGY: SOCIAL SECURITY

The administration of President Franklin D. Roosevelt brought conscious attempts by the federal government to develop rational programs to achieve societal goals. In the most important piece of legislation of the New Deal, the Social Security Act of 1935, the federal government undertook to establish the basic framework for welfare policies at the federal, state, and local levels and, more importantly, to set forth a strategy for dealing with poverty. The Depression convinced the national leadership and a great many citizens that poverty could result from forces over which the individual had no control—loss of job, old age, death of the family breadwinner, or physical disability. One solution was to require individuals to purchase insurance against their own indigency resulting from any of these misfortunes.

Social Insurance. The social insurance concept devised by the New Deal planners was designed to prevent poverty resulting from uncontrollable forces. Social insurance was based on the same notion as private insurance—sharing risks and setting aside money for a rainy day. Social insurance was not to be charity or public assistance; it was to be preventive. It relied on the individual's compulsory contribution to his or her own protection. In contrast, public assistance is only alleviative and relies on general tax revenues from all taxpayers. Indeed, when the Roosevelt administration presented the social insurance plan to Congress in the Social Security Act of 1935, it contended that it would eventually abolish the need for any public assistance program because individuals would be compelled to protect themselves against poverty.

OASDI. The key feature of the Social Security Act of 1935 is the Old Age Survivor's Disability and Insurance (OASDI) program, generally known as Social Security.* This is a compulsory social insurance program financed by regular deductions from earnings, which gives individuals a legal right to benefits in the event of certain occurrences that cause a reduction of their income: old age, death of the head of

---

* The original Social Security Act of 1935 did not include disability insurance; this was added by amendment in 1950. Health insurance for the aged—Medicare—was added by amendment in 1965; this is discussed later in the chapter.

household, or permanent disability. OASDI now covers about nine out of every ten workers in the United States, including the self-employed. The only large group outside its coverage are federal employees, who have their own retirement system. Both employees (through payroll deductions) and employers pay equal amounts into the Federal Insurance Contributions Act (FICA) toward the employees' insurance.

Retirement Benefits. Upon retirement, an insured worker is entitled to monthly benefit payments based on age at retirement and the amount earned during his or her working years. In 1972 Congress ordered automatic cost-of-living adjustments (COLAs) indexed to inflation. The formula for calculating COLAs increases benefits faster than actual cost-of-living for the elderly.

Survivor and Disability Benefits. OASDI also provides benefit payments to survivors of an insured worker, including a spouse if there are dependent children. But if there are no dependent children, benefits will not begin until the spouse reaches retirement age. OASDI provides benefit payments to persons who suffer permanent and total disabilities that prevent them from working for more than 1 year.

Unemployment Compensation. A second important feature of the Social Security Act of 1935 was that it induced states to enact unemployment compensation programs through the imposition of the payroll tax on all employers. A federal unemployment tax is levied on the payroll of employers of four or more workers, but employers paying into state insurance programs that meet federal standards may use these state payments to offset most of their federal unemployment tax. In other words, the federal government threatens to undertake an unemployment compensation program and tax if the states do not do so themselves. This federal program succeeded in inducing all fifty states to establish such programs. However, the federal standards are flexible and the states have considerable freedom in shaping their own programs. In all cases, unemployed workers must report in person and show that they are willing and able to work in order to receive unemployment compensation benefits. In practice, this means that unemployed workers must register with the U.S. Employment Service (usually located in the same building as the state unemployment compensation office) as a condition of receiving their unemployment checks. States cannot deny workers benefits for refusing to work as strikebreakers or for rates lower than prevailing rates. But basic decisions concerning the amount of benefits, eligibility, and the length of time that benefits can be drawn are largely left to the states.

EVALUATION: INTENDED AND UNINTENDED CONSEQUENCES OF SOCIAL SECURITY

The framers of the Social Security Act of 1935 created a "trust fund" with the expectation that a reserve would be built up from social insurance premiums from working people. The reserve would earn interest, and the interest and principal would be used in later years to pay benefits. Benefits for an individual would be in proportion to his or her contributions. General tax revenues would not be used at all. It was intended that the system would resemble the financing of private insurance, but it turned out not to work that way at all.

The "Trust Fund."   The social insurance system is now financed on a pay-as-you-go, rather than a reserve system. Today, the income from all social insurance premiums (taxes) pays for current Social Security benefits. Today, this generation of workers is paying for the benefits of the last generation, and it is hoped that this generation's benefits will be financed by the next generation of workers. Social Security "trust fund" revenues are now lumped together with general tax revenues in the federal budget.

The Social Security "Surplus."   In 1983 a National Commission on Social Security Reform, appointed by President Reagan and made up of equal numbers of Democrats and Republicans, recommended increases in Social Security taxes to build a reserve for large numbers of baby-boom generation retirees expected after the year 2000. Congress raised the Social Security tax, and the trust fund began to build a "surplus." That is, income from the Social Security tax currently exceeds payments to beneficiaries. The surplus is officially used to purchase U.S. government bonds.

However, Social Security taxes are shown in the federal budget as current revenues (see Chapter 10), and current revenues offset all current expenditures of the federal government. The federal government runs high deficits each year: current federal spending regularly exceeds current federal revenues by $100 to $200 *billion* or more per year. The Social Security "surplus" hides additional deficits in overall federal spending, and the use of the trust fund to purchase federal government bonds helps Washington in its deficit financing. In short, the "trust fund surplus" is merely an accounting gimmick; current Social Security taxes are being used to finance current spending, and future retirement benefits will have to be paid from future revenues.

The Generational Compact.   Taxing current workers to pay benefits to current retirees may be viewed as a compact between generations. Each generation of workers in effect agrees to pay benefits to an earlier generation of retirees, in the hope that the next generation will pay for their own retirement. But low birthrates (reducing the number of workers), longer life spans (increasing the number of retirees), and very generous benefits are straining workers' ability to pay. The generational compact is likely to break as American workers are called on to pay higher payroll taxes to support a larger aged population.

The Dependency Ratio.   Since current workers must pay for the benefits of current retirees and other beneficiaries, the dependency ratio becomes an important component of evaluating the future of Social Security. The dependency ratio for Social Security is the number of recipients as a percentage of the number of contributing workers. Americans are living longer, thereby increasing the dependency ratio.

A child born in 1935, when the Social Security system was created, could expect to live only to age sixty-one, four years *less* than the retirement age of sixty-five. The life expectancy of a child born in 1980 is seventy-four years, nine years *beyond* the retirement age. In the early years of Social Security, there were ten workers supporting each retiree—a dependency ratio of 10 to 1. But today, as the U.S. population grows older—because of lower birthrates and longer life spans—there are only three workers for each retiree, and by 2010 the dependency will rise to two workers for each retiree.

Tax Burdens.   Congress has gradually increased the Social Security payroll tax from 3 percent combined employee and employer contributions to 15.3 percent combined contribution today. The maximum employee contribution has grown from $30 to over $5,000 since the beginning of the program. The Social Security tax is now *the second-largest source of federal revenue.*

Generous COLAs.   Currently Social Security annual COLAs (cost of living adjustments) are based on the consumer price index (CPI), which estimates the cost of all consumer items each year. There are serious problems with the use of the CPI to provide annual values in Social Security benefits. First of all, cost estimates in the CPI include home buying, mortgage interest, child rearing, and other costs that many retirees do not confront. Most *workers* do not have the same protection against inflation as retirees; that is, average wage rates do not always match the increases in cost of living. Over the years, the COLAs have improved the economic well-being of Social Security recipients relative to American workers. Secondly, the CPI has been shown to *over*estimate rises in the real cost of living. (It does so by ignoring quality improvements in goods as well as shifts of consumers to cheaper products and discount stores when prices rise.) Overestimates in the CPI result in more generous COLAs each year.

Wealthy Retirees.   Social Security benefits are paid to all eligible retirees, regardless of whatever other income they may receive. There is no means test for benefits. The result is that large numbers of affluent Americans receive government checks each month. Of course, they paid into Social Security during their working years and they can claim these checks as a legal "entitlement" under the insurance principle. But currently their benefits far exceed their previous payments.

Since the aged experience less poverty than today's workers (see Table 5–2) and possess considerably more wealth, Social Security benefits constitute a "negative" redistribution of income, that is, a transfer of income from poorer to richer people. The elderly are generally better off than the people supporting them.

SOCIAL SECURITY REFORM?

Without significant reform, Social Security will become so burdensome to working taxpayers in the next century that retirees are unlikely to receive their scheduled benefits. The "baby boom" from 1945 to 1960 produced a large generation of people who crowded schools and colleges in the 1960s and 1970s and encountered stiff competition for jobs in the 1980s. The baby boom generation will be retiring beginning in 2010. Changes in lifestyle—less smoking, more exercise, better weight control—as well as medical advances, may increase the aged population even more.

It is unrealistic to believe that working Americans in the next century will consent to paying more than 50 percent of their current incomes to support retirees. The "generational compact" is likely to break before younger workers today reach retirement age. Indeed, many younger people, for good reason, have lost their confidence in the Social Security system to support them in their old age.

The "Third Rail" of American Politics.   Social Security is the most expensive program in the federal budget but also the most politically sacrosanct. Politicians regularly call it the "third rail" of American politics—touch it and die.

Senior citizens are the most politically powerful age group in the population. They constitute 28 percent of the voting-age population, but more important, because of their high turnout rates, they constitute nearly one-third of the voters on election day. Moreover, seniors are well represented in Washington; the American Association of Retired Persons (AARP) is the nation's single largest organized interest group, with more than 30 million members. Most seniors, and their lobbyists in Washington, adamantly oppose any Social Security reforms that might reduce future benefits.

Reform Proposals.   In theory, Congress could reform Social Security by limiting COLAs to the true increases in the cost of living for retirees, or by introducing means tests to deny benefits to high-income retirees, or by increasing the age at which Social Security benefits begin. But politically these reforms are very unlikely.

Yet another proposed reform is to allow the Social Security trust fund to invest in the private stock market with the expectation that stock values will increase over time. But this would mean shifting funds away from federal government bonds, thus adding to annual federal deficit figures. Moreover, it would mean that a government agency, presumably the Social Security Administration, would be making private investment decisions for Americans. Perhaps the nation's workers would prefer a plan that allows them to deposit part of their payroll tax into an individual retirement account to buy securities of their own choosing. But such a plan would expose individuals to the risk of bad investment decisions.

THE ALLEVIATIVE STRATEGY: PUBLIC ASSISTANCE

The Social Security and unemployment compensation programs were based on the insurance strategy for preventing poverty, but in the Social Security Act of 1935 the federal government also undertook to help the states provide public assistance to certain needy people. This strategy was designed to alleviate the conditions of poverty. The original idea was to provide a minimum level of subsistence to certain categories of needy adults—the aged, blind, and disabled—and to provide for the care of dependent children.

Supplemental Security Income. Supplemental Security Income (SSI) is a means-tested, federally administered income assistance program that provides monthly cash payments to needy elderly (65 or older), blind, and disabled people. A loose definition of "disability"—including alcoholism, drug abuse, and attention deficiency among children—has led to a rapid growth in the number of SSI beneficiaries.

Medicaid. Medicaid is a joint federal-state program that provides health services to low-income Americans. Most Medicaid spending goes to the elderly and nonelderly disabled people. Women and children receiving public assistance benefits automatically qualify for Medicaid, as does anyone who gets cash assistance under SSI. States can also offer Medicaid to the "medically needy"—those who face crushing medical costs but whose income or assets are too high to qualify for SSI or Temporary Assistance for Needy Families (formerly AFDC), including pregnant women and young children not receiving other aid. Medicaid also pays for long-term nursing home care, but only after beneficiaries have used up virtually all of their savings and income.

Food Stamps. The food stamp program provides low-income households with coupons that they can redeem for enough food to provide a minimal, nutritious diet. The program is overseen by the federal government, but is administered by the states.

Temporary Assistance for Needy Families. Today the largest cash assistance program is a federal block grant to the states for needy families with dependent children. A result of welfare reform legislation passed by Congress in 1996 and signed by President Clinton, this program replaces Aid to Families with Dependent Children (AFDC). Its major provisions include the following:

Federal funding. Money distributed to each state based on its previous federal funding for AFDC and related programs. Financial incentives will be provided to states that reduce their out-of-wedlock births, beginning in fiscal 1998.

State funding. To receive their full share of federal welfare funds, states will have to spend at least 75 percent of the state funds they previously spent on AFDC and related programs. States will lose one dollar in federal funding for each dollar they fall short of this requirement.

Work requirements. Adults receiving welfare benefits will be required to begin working within two years of receiving aid. States may exempt from this work requirement a parent of a child 12 months of age or younger. States will be required to have at least 50 percent of their welfare caseload engaged in work by 2002.

Restrictions on aid. Federal funds cannot be used for adults who have *received welfare for more than five years,* although state and local funds could be used. States can exempt up to 20 percent of their caseload from this time limit. States can also opt to impose a shorter time limit on benefits. None of the funds can be used for adults who do not work *after receiving welfare for two years*. In addition, states will have the option to (1) deny welfare assistance to children born to welfare recipients, or (2) deny welfare to unwed parents under age 18 unless they live with an adult and attend school.

Medicaid. States will be required to continue to offer Medicaid coverage for one year to welfare recipients who lose their welfare benefits because of increased earnings.

Immigrants. Federal welfare funds are denied to illegal immigrants, as well as to most legal immigrants until they become citizens.

EVALUATION: CONFLICTING VALUES AND STRATEGIES IN PUBLIC ASSISTANCE

Developing a rational strategy to assist the poor is hampered by the clash of values over individual responsibility and social compassion. As Harvard sociologist David Ellwood explains,

> Welfare brings some of our most precious values—involving autonomy, responsibility, work, family, community and compassion—into conflict. We want to help those who are not making it but in so doing, we seem to cheapen the efforts of those who are struggling hard just to get by. We want to offer financial support to those with low incomes, but if we do we reduce the pressure on them and their incentive to work. We want to help people who are not able to help themselves but then we worry that people will not bother to help themselves. We recognize the insecurity of single-parent families but, in helping them, we appear to be promoting or supporting their formation.[10]

The social insurance programs that largely serve the middle class (Social Security, Medicare, unemployment compensation) are politically popular and enjoy the support of large numbers of politically active beneficiaries. But public assistance programs that largely serve the poor (cash aid, SSI, food stamps, Medicaid) are far less popular and are surrounded by many controversies.

Public Policy as a Cause of Poverty?   Can the government itself create poverty by fashioning social welfare programs and policies that destroy incentives to work, encourage families to break up, and condemn the poor to social dependency? Can the social welfare system sentence many people to a life of poverty who would otherwise form families, take low-paying jobs, and perhaps with hard work and perseverance gradually pull themselves and their children into the mainstream of American life?

Losing the War on Poverty.   Poverty in America steadily declined from 1950, when about 30 percent of the population was officially poor, to 1970, when about 11 percent of the population was poor. During this period of progress toward the elimination of poverty, government welfare programs were minimal. There were small AFDC programs for women with children who lived alone; eligibility was restricted and welfare authorities checked to see if an employable male lived on the premises. There were also federal payments for the aged, blind, and disabled poor. Welfare rolls were modest; only about 1 to 2 percent of American families received AFDC payments.

With the addition of many Great Society welfare programs, the downward trend in poverty ended. Indeed, the numbers and proportion of the population living in poverty began to move upward in the 1970s and early 1980s (see Figure 5–1). This was a period in which AFDC payments were significantly increased and eligibility rules were relaxed. The food stamp program was initiated in 1965 and became a major new welfare benefit. Medicaid was initiated in the same year and by the late 1970s became the costliest of all welfare programs. Federal aid to the aged, blind, and disabled were merged into a new SSI program (Supplement Security Income), which quadrupled in numbers of recipients.

Poverty increased in the 1970s and 1980s despite a reasonably healthy economy. Discrimination did not become significantly worse during this period; the civil rights laws enacted in the 1960s were opening many new opportunities for blacks. Finally, poverty was reduced among the aged because of generous increases in Social Security benefits. The greatest increases in poverty occurred in families headed by *working-age* persons. In short, it is difficult to find alternative explanations for the rise in poverty. Policymakers became obliged to consider the possibility that policy changes—new welfare programs, expanded benefits, and relaxed eligibility requirements—contributed to increased poverty.

Work Disincentives.   The effect of generous welfare benefits and relaxed eligibility requirements on employment has been argued for centuries. Surveys show that the poor prefer work over welfare, but welfare payments may produce subtle effects on the behavior of the poor. People unwilling to take minimum-wage jobs may never acquire the work habits required to move into better-paying jobs later in their lives. Welfare may even help to create a dependent and defeatist subculture, lowering personal self-esteem and contributing to joblessness, illegitimacy, and broken families.

Disincentives to work are magnified by the "pyramiding effect" of separate public assistance and social service programs. A family on the welfare rolls is generally entitled to participate in the food stamp program, to receive health care through Medicaid, to gain access to free or low-rent public housing, to receive free lunches in public schools, and to receive a variety of other social and educational benefits at little or no cost to themselves. These benefits and services available to the poor are not counted as income, yet the nonpoor must pay for similar services out of their own earnings. If a family head on welfare takes a job, he or she not only loses welfare assistance but, more importantly perhaps, becomes ineligible for food stamps, Medicaid, public housing, and many other social services. Thus, only a fairly well-paying job would justify going off the welfare rolls.

Social Dependency.   The nonworking poor pose the greatest challenge to welfare policy. Nonworking poor (families headed by persons who do not work) make up nearly half of the poverty population, and they remain poor over prolonged periods of time. The traditional American solution to social problems is to create job opportunities and provide the education and training required to take advantage of these opportunities. But the nonworking poor, mainly nonelderly female-headed families, are largely unaffected by job programs or employment conditions. Although the nonworking poor often express a desire to work, they often reject menial minimum-wage jobs and give up trying to manage the logistics of finding transportation, setting up child care, and getting to the job every day. They would prefer work to welfare, but they are unwilling to encounter the practical difficulties of the job market.

Family Effects.   There is little doubt that social dependency and family structure are closely related. As noted earlier, poverty is much more frequent among female-headed households with no husband present than among husband-wife households. As births to unmarried women rise, poverty and social dependency increase. (In 1970, only 11 percent of births were to unmarried women; by 1995 this figure had risen to 31 percent of all births and 69 percent of minority births.) The troubling question is whether welfare policy simply ameliorates some of the hardships confronting unmarried mothers and their children, or whether it contributes to social dependency by mitigating the consequences of unmarried motherhood.

WELFARE REFORM

A consensus grew over the years that long-term social dependency had to be addressed in welfare policy. The fact that most nonpoor mothers work convinced many liberals that welfare mothers had no special claim to stay at home with their children. And many conservatives acknowledged that some transitional assistance—education, job training, continued health care, and day care for children—might be necessary to move welfare mothers into the workforce.

Family Support Act.   A Family Support Act passed by Congress in 1988 required states to

- Develop a federal job-training program (JOBS) for most adults receiving AFDC payments; AFDC recipients not exempt because of age, illness, or disability may be required to participate
- Provide child care for JOBS participants
- Furnish transitional child care and Medicaid for twelve months after a participant leaves AFDC to take a job
- Strengthen its child-support enforcement programs

However, the states were slow to implement the program. Neither the federal government nor the states fully funded the JOBS or child-care provisions of the act, and a recession in 1991 increased welfare rolls beyond expectations. More importantly, moving people from welfare rolls to private employment proved to be more costly than simply providing welfare assistance.

No state "workfare" program required all welfare recipients to take jobs. Most programs allowed mothers with preschool children to opt out altogether. Moreover, state and local welfare bureaucracies generally resisted reform. Some opposition was philosophical, calling it "slavefare"; other barriers arose in providing the necessary funds for casework supervision, realistic job training, and effective job placement.

The Welfare Reform Battle.   Like earlier welfare reform efforts, the Clinton administration proposed to "empower people with the education, training, child care they need for up to two years, so they can break the cycle of dependency." However, Clinton proposed to go one important step further: "After two years, require those who can work to go to work, either in the private sector or in community service."[11] But a two-year limit to welfare payments was viewed as "punitive" by many liberal groups, even with education, training, child care, and continuing Medicaid benefits.

Although President Clinton had once promised "to end welfare as we know it," it was the Republican-controlled Congress elected in 1994 that proceeded to do so. The Republican-sponsored welfare reform bill ended the 60-year-old federal "entitlement" for low-income families with children—the venerable AFDC program. In its place the Republicans devised a "devolution" of responsibility to the states through federal block grants—Temporary Assistance to Needy Families—lump sum allocations to the states for cash welfare payments with benefits and eligibility requirements decided by the states. Conservatives in Congress imposed tough-minded "strings" to state aid, including a two-year limit on continuing cash benefits and a five-year lifetime limit; a "family cap" that would deny additional cash benefit to women already on welfare who bear more children; the denial of cash welfare to unwed parents under 18 years of age unless they live with an adult and attend school; and the denial of federally funded public assistance to illegal immigrants as well as legal immigrants who have not become citizens.

Democrats in Congress obtained some modifications to these requirements, as well as guarantees that states would not reduce their welfare funding below previous years' AFDC spending; exemptions from time limits and work requirements for some portion of welfare recipients; and community service alternatives to work requirements.

President Clinton vetoed the first welfare reform bill passed by Congress in early 1996, but as the presidential election neared, he reversed himself and signed the welfare reform act establishing the Temporary Assistance to Needy Families program (described earlier). The final program compromised many of the key issues: the family cap and school and adult supervision for teenage mothers was left to the states to decide; states were obliged to spend at least 75 percent of the funds previously spent on AFDC; states can exempt up to 20 percent of welfare recipients from time limits and work requirements. Food stamps, SSI, and Medicaid were continued as federal "entitlements." President Clinton promised to "improve" welfare reform, by eliminating restrictions on immigrant aid, making community service an alternative to work requirements, and so on. But continuing GOP control of Congress promises strong opposition to any efforts to "undo" welfare reform.

Prospects for Success.   While nearly everyone agrees that getting people off of welfare rolls and onto payrolls is the main goal of reform, there are major obstacles to the achievement of this goal. First of all, a substantial portion (perhaps 25 to 40 percent) of long-term welfare recipients have handicaps—physical disabilities, chronic illnesses, learning disabilities, alcohol or drug abuse problems—that prevent them from holding a full-time job. Many long-term recipients have no work experience (perhaps 40 percent) and two-thirds of them did not graduate from high school. Almost half have three or more children, making day-care arrangements a major obstacle. It is unlikely that any counseling, education, job training, or job placement programs advocated by liberals could ever succeed in getting these people into productive employment. Policymakers argue whether or not there are 5 million jobs available to unskilled mothers, but even if there are such jobs available, they would be low-paying, minimum-wage jobs that would not lift them out of poverty.[12]

Yet welfare rolls across the nation have begun to decline. (After peaking in 1994 at over 14 million, the number of AFDC recipients declined to about 12 million in 1996.[13]) This decline began *before* Congress passed the welfare reform law, and it may simply reflect the nation's improved economy. But it may also reflect the welfare reform efforts that some states had initiated before Congress acted. If so, then nationwide welfare reform may turn out to be successful.

HOMELESSNESS AND PUBLIC POLICY

For a pitiful few in America, sickness, hardship, and abandonment have risen dramatically in recent years. These few are the nation's homeless "street people," suffering exposure, alcoholism, drug abuse, and chronic mental illness while wandering the streets of the nation's larger cities. No one knows the total number of homeless, but the best systematic estimate is 250,000 to 350,000.[14] In most large cities, street people are the most visible social welfare problem.

The issue of homelessness has become so politicized that an accurate assessment of the problem and a rational strategy for dealing with it have become virtually impossible.[15] The term *homeless* is used to describe many different situations. There are the street people who sleep in subways, bus stations, parks, or the streets. Some of them are temporarily traveling in search of work; some have left home for a few days or are youthful runaways; others have roamed the streets for months or years. There are the sheltered homeless who obtain housing in shelters operated by local governments or private charities. As the number of shelters has grown in recent years, the number of sheltered homeless has also grown. But most of the sheltered homeless come from other housing, not the streets. These are people who have been recently evicted from rental units or have previously lived with family or friends. They often include families with children; the street homeless are virtually all single persons.

The ranks of the street homeless expand and contract with the seasons. The homeless are difficult subjects for systematic interviewing; many do not wish to admit to alcoholism, drug dependence, or mental illness. The television networks sensationalize the topic, exaggerate the number of homeless, and incorrectly portray them as middle-class families victimized by economic misfortune.

Who Are the Homeless?   Serious studies indicate that close to half of the street homeless are chronic alcohol and drug abusers and an additional one-fourth to one-third are mentally ill.[16] The drug abusers, especially "crack" cocaine users, are the fastest growing groups among the homeless. Moreover, the alcohol and drug abusers and mentally ill are likely to remain on the streets for long periods of time. Among the 15 to 25 percent of the homeless who are neither mentally ill nor dependent on alcohol or drugs, homelessness is more likely to be temporary.

Public Policy as a Cause of Homelessness.   The current plight of the homeless is primarily a result of various "reforms" in public policy, notably the "deinstitutionalization" of care for the mentally ill, the "decriminalization" of vagrancy and public intoxication, newly recognized rights to refuse treatment, and the renewal of central cities and the elimination of low-rent apartments and cheap hotels.

Deinstitutionalization.   Deinstitutionalization was a reform advanced by mental health care professionals and social welfare activists in the 1960s and 1970s to release chronic mental patients from state-run mental hospitals. It was widely recognized that aside from drugs, no psychiatric therapies have much success among the long-term mentally ill. Drug therapies can be administered on an outpatient basis; they usually do not require hospitalization. So it was argued that no one could be rightfully kept in a mental institution against his or her will; people who had committed no crimes and who posed no danger to others should be released. Federal and state monies for mental health were to be directed toward community mental health facilities that would treat the mentally ill on a voluntary outpatient basis. The nation's mental hospitals were emptied of all but the most dangerous patients. The population of mental hospitals declined by more than 80 percent between 1960 and 1980.[17]

Decriminalization.   Vagrancy (homelessness) and public intoxication are no longer crimes. Involuntary confinement has been abolished for the mentally ill and for substance abusers, unless a person is adjudged in court to be "a danger to himself or others," which means a person must commit a serious act of violence before the courts will intervene. For many homeless this means the freedom to "die with their rights on." The homeless are victimized by cold, exposure, hunger, the availability of alcohol and illegal drugs, and violent street crimes perpetrated against them, in addition to the ravages of their illness itself.

The Failure of Community Care.   Community-based care is largely irrelevant to the plight of the chronic mentally ill and alcohol and drug abusers in the streets. Most are "uncooperative"; they are isolated from society; they have no family members or doctors or counselors to turn to for help. For them, community care is a Salvation Army meal and cot; a night in a city-run refuge for the homeless; or a ride to the city hospital psychiatric ward for a brief period of "observation," after which they must be released again to the streets. The nation's vast social welfare system provides little help. They lose their Social Security, welfare, and disability checks because they have no permanent address. They cannot handle forms, appointments, or interviews; the welfare bureaucracy is intimidating. Welfare workers seldom provide the aggressive care management and mental health care that these people need.

Housing Policy.   Thus, for most of the homeless, their problems are far more intractable than the availability of low-cost housing. Nonetheless, government policies in many cities create shortages of such housing. Rent controls assist a few older middle-class families who occupied apartments when controls were imposed, but controls discourage new housing construction and thus guarantee housing shortages and inflated rents within a few years of their imposition. Urban renewal destroys low-rent apartments as well as single-room-occupancy (SRO) hotels and "flophouses." Building and housing codes make it economically more advantageous for owners to abandon buildings than to rent them at low rates. Contrary to common political rhetoric, homelessness is *not* a result of cuts in public housing. Occupied public housing units expanded from 1.2 to 1.4 million from 1980 to 1990, and the number of households receiving housing assistance doubled.[18]

HEALTH CARE IN AMERICA

There is no better illustration of the dilemmas of rational policymaking in America than in the field of health. Again, the first obstacle to rationalism is in defining the problem. Is our goal to have *good health*—that is, whether we live at all (infant mortality), how well we live (days lost to sickness), and how long we live (life spans and adult mortality)? Or is our goal to have *good medical care*—frequent visits to the doctor, well-equipped and accessible hospitals, and equal access to medical care by rich and poor alike?

Perhaps the first lesson in health policy is understanding that good medical care does not necessarily mean good health. Good health correlates best with factors over which doctors and hospitals have no control: heredity, lifestyle (smoking, eating, drinking, exercise, worry), and the physical environment (sewage disposal, water quality, conditions of work, and so forth). Most of the bad things that happen to people's health are beyond the reach of doctors and hospitals. In the long run, infant mortality, sickness and disease, and life span are affected very little by the quality of medical care. If you want a long, healthy life, choose parents who have lived a long, healthy life, and then do all the things your mother always told you to do:

don't smoke, don't drink, get lots of exercise and rest, don't overeat, relax, and don't worry.

Leading Causes of Death.   Historically, most of the reductions in infant and adult death rates have resulted from public health and sanitation, including immunization against smallpox, clean public water supply, sanitary sewage disposal, improved diets, and increased standards of living. Many of the leading causes of death today (see Table 5–3), including heart disease, stroke, cirrhosis of the liver, accidents, and suicides, are closely linked to personal habits and lifestyles and are beyond the reach of medicine.

The overall death rate in the United States (the number of deaths per 100,000 people) continues to decline. Considerable progress is being made by the nation in reducing death rates for many of the major killers—heart disease, stroke, pneumonia, diabetes, and emphysema. However, the cancer death rate continues to rise despite increased medical spending.

Access to Medical Care.   Americans now generally view access to medical care as a right. No one should be denied medical care or suffer pain or remedial illness for lack of financial resources. There is widespread agreement on this ethical principle. The tough questions arise when we seek rational strategies to implement it.

Medicaid: Health Care as Welfare.   Medicaid is the federal government's largest single welfare program for the poor. Its costs now exceed the costs of all other public assistance programs—including family assistance, SSI, and the food stamp program. Medicaid was begun in 1965 and grew quickly into the nation's largest welfare program.

Medicaid is a combined federal and state program. The states exercise fairly

TABLE 5-3   Leading Causes of Death[a]

	1960	1970	1980	1990	1995
All Causes	954.7	945.3	883.4	866.3	880.0
Heart disease	369.0	362.0	334.3	289.0	288.4
Stroke (cerebrovascular)	108.0	101.9	80.5	57.9	58.2
Cancer	149.2	162.8	181.9	201.7	205.6
Accidents	52.3	56.4	48.4	37.3	35.1
Pneumonia	37.3	30.9	26.7	31.3	39.2
Diabetes	16.7	18.9	15.5	19.5	20.9
Suicide	10.6	11.6	12.5	12.3	12.1
Homicide	4.7	8.3	9.4	10.2	10.1
AIDS	—	—	—	9.6	14.5

[a] Deaths per 100,000 population per year.

Source: *Statistical Abstract of the United States 1996,* p. 96.

broad administrative powers and carry almost half of the financial burden. Medicaid is a welfare program designed for needy persons: no prior contributions are required, monies come from general tax revenues, and most recipients are already on welfare rolls. Although states differ in their eligibility requirements, they must cover all people receiving federally funded public assistance payments. In addition, a majority extend coverage to other "medically needy"—individuals who do not qualify for public assistance but whose incomes are low enough to qualify as needy. About half of the states extend Medicaid to families whose head is receiving unemployment compensation.

States also help set benefits. All states are required by the federal government to provide inpatient and outpatient hospital care, physicians' services, family planning, laboratory services and X-rays, and nursing and home health care. They must also develop an early and periodic screening, diagnosis, and treatment program for all children under Medicaid. However, states themselves generally decide on the rate of reimbursement to hospitals and physicians. Low rates can discourage hospitals and physicians from providing good care. To make up for low payments, they may schedule too many patients in too short a time, prescribe unnecessary tests and procedures designed to make treatment more expensive, or shift costs incurred in treating Medicaid patients to more affluent patients with private insurance.

Medicare: Health Care as Government Insurance.   Medicare, like Medicaid, was enacted in 1965 as an amendment to the nation's basic Social Security Act. Medicare provides prepaid hospital insurance and low-cost voluntary medical insurance for the aged, directly under federal administration. Medicare includes HI— a compulsory basic health insurance plan covering hospital costs for the aged, which is financed out of payroll taxes collected under the Social Security system— and SMI—a voluntary, supplemental medical insurance program that will pay 80 percent of "allowable" charges for physicians' services and other medical expenses, financed in part by contributions from the aged and in part by general tax revenues.

Only *aged* persons are covered by Medicare provisions. Eligibility is not dependent on income; all aged persons eligible for Social Security are also eligible for Medicare. No physical examination is required and preexisting conditions are covered. The costs of SMI are so low to the beneficiaries that participation by the elderly is almost universal.

Both the HI and SMI provisions of Medicare require patients to pay small initial charges or "deductibles." The purpose is to discourage unnecessary hospital or physician care. HI generally pays the full charges for the first sixty days of hospitalization each year after a deductible charge equivalent to one day's stay; but many doctors charge higher rates than allowable under SMI. Indeed, it is estimated that only about half of the doctors in the nation accept SMI allowable payments as payment in full. Many doctors bill Medicare patients for charges above the allowable SMI payments. Medicare does not pay for prescription drugs, eyeglasses, hearing aids, or routine physical examinations.

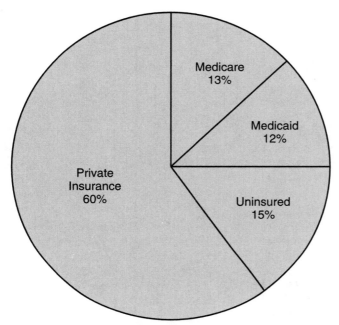

Source: *Statistical Abstract of the United States 1996,* p. 120.

FIGURE 5–3   Health Insurance Coverage

Private Health Insurance.   Approximately 85 percent of the population of the United States is covered by either private or government health insurance (see Figure 5–3). But about 15 percent of the population has no medical insurance. Most of the uninsured are working Americans and their families—people who are not poor enough to qualify for Medicaid nor old enough to qualify for Medicare.

EVALUATION: HEALTH CARE ACCESS AND COSTS

The United States spends more of its resources on health care than any other advanced industrialized nation, yet it ranks well below other nations in key measures of the health of its people. The United States spends more than 12 percent of its GNP for health care, compared to only about 6 percent for Japan and Great Britain and 8 percent for Germany (see Figure 5–4). Yet life expectancy in the United States is lower, and the infant death rate is higher, than in these nations. The United States offers the most advanced and sophisticated medical care in the world, attracting patients from countries that rank ahead of us in these common health measures. The United States is the locus of the most advanced medical research in the world, drawing researchers from all over the world. This apparent paradox—the highest quality

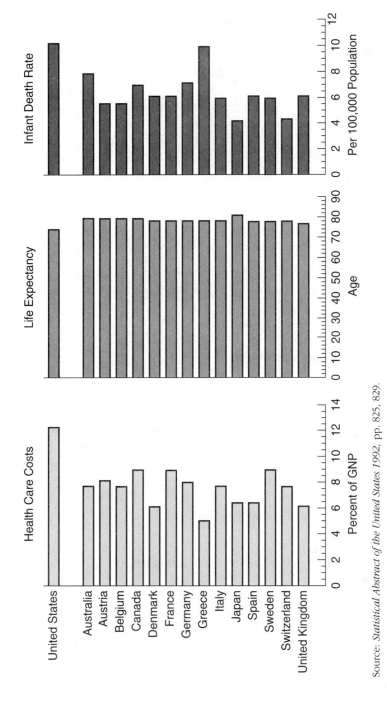

Source: *Statistical Abstract of the United States 1992*, pp. 825, 829.

FIGURE 5–4 Health Care Costs and Benefits: A Cross-national Comparison

medical care, combined with poor health statistics for the general public—suggest that our nation's health care problems center more on access to care, education, and prevention of health problems than on the quality of care available.

Access to Health Care.   While Medicare covers the aged and Medicaid covers the poor, many working Americans and their dependents have no health insurance. These people may postpone or go without needed medical care or be denied medical care by hospitals and physicians except in emergencies. Confronted with serious illness they may be obliged to impoverish themselves to become eligible for Medicaid. Their unpaid medical bills must be absorbed by hospitals or shifted to paying patients and their insurance companies. Many uninsured people work for small businesses or are self-employed or unemployed.

Nursing-Home Care.   As the number and proportion of the elderly population grow in the United States (80 years and over is the fastest-growing age group in the nation), the need for long-term nursing-home care grows. Medicare does not pay for long-term care or catastrophic illness. It covers only the first 60 days of hospitalization and nursing-home care for 100 days only if the patient is sent there from a hospital. Medicaid assistance to the needy is paid to nursing-home patients, but middle-class people cannot qualify for Medicaid without first "spending down" their savings. Long-term nursing-home care threatens their assets and their children's inheritance. Private insurance policies covering long-term care are said to be too expensive. So senior citizen groups have lobbied heavily for long-term nursing-home care to be paid for by taxpayers under Medicare.

No Constraints on Costs.   No system of health care can provide as much as people will use without restraint. Each individual, believing his or her health and life are at stake, will want the most thorough diagnostic testing, the most constant care, the most advanced treatment. And doctors have no strong incentive to try to save on costs; they want the most advanced diagnostic and treatment facilities available for their patients. Under conditions of uncertainty in a medical situation—and there is always some uncertainty—physicians can always think of one more thing that might be done—one more consultation, one more test, one more therapeutic approach. The patient wants the best, and the doctor wants it too. Any tendency for doctors to limit testing and treatment is countered by the threat of malpractice suits; it is always easier to order one more test or procedure than to risk the chance that failure to do so will some day be cause for a court suit. So both patients and doctors push up the costs of health care, particularly when public or private insurance pays.

Third-party Payers.   There is little cost constraint on patients and physicians when they know "third-party payers" will foot the bill. Both private insurers and the government have undertaken various efforts to control costs. Their cost-control regulations and restrictions have created a mountain of paperwork for physicians and hospitals and created frustrations and anger among both care-givers and patients. And these efforts have not had much success in limiting overall medical costs.

Health Care Inflation. The costs of health care in the United States have risen much faster than prices in general. Medical costs have tripled over the last ten years. The nation's total medical bill is more than 12 percent of the gross national product (see Figure 5–5).

Certainly third-party payment by government and private insurance has contributed to this inflation, but there are other causes as well. Advances in medical technology have produced elaborate and expensive equipment. Hospitals that have made heavy financial investment in this equipment must use it as often as possible. Physicians trained in highly specialized techniques and procedures wish to use them. The threat of malpractice suits forces doctors to practice "defensive medi-

FIGURE 5–5   The Growth of Health Care Costs

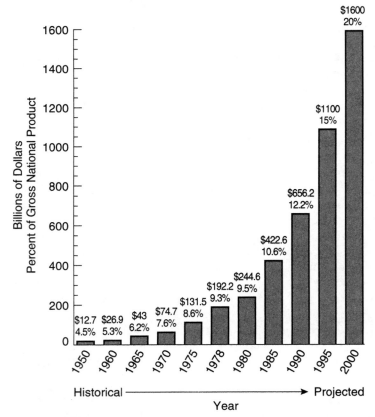

Source: *Statistical Abstract of the United States 1996.* Projection by Congressional Budget Office, in *Congressional Quarterly Weekly Report,* March 13, 1993, p. 596.

cine"—to order multiple tests and consultations to guard against even the most remote medical possibilities. The system encourages the provision of unnecessary tests and services.

Coping with Medical Costs.   Various efforts have been made to counter rising costs. Private insurers have negotiated discounts with groups of physicians and with hospitals (so-called "preferred provider organizations") and have implemented rules to guide physicians about when patients should and should not receive costly diagnostic and therapeutic procedures (so-called "managed care"). The government has replaced payments to hospitals under Medicare based on costs incurred, with payment of fixed fees based on primary and secondary diagnoses at the time of admission (the diagnosis-related group, or DRG system). Government and private insurers have encouraged the expansion of health maintenance organizations (HMOs) that promise to provide a stipulated list of services to patients for a fixed fee and that are able to provide care at lower total costs than can other providers.

These efforts, however, create a great deal of paperwork for physicians and hospitals and often frustrate and anger both care-givers and patients. Doctors and hospitals argue that the administrative costs imposed by these cost-control measures far exceed whatever savings are achieved.

HEALTH CARE REFORM STRATEGIES

Health care reform centers on two central problems: controlling costs and expanding access. These problems are related: expanding access to Americans who are currently uninsured and closing gaps in coverage require increases in costs, even while the central thrust of reform is to bring down overall health care costs.

Health care reform strategies generally fall into three categories: 1) single-payer plans that call for the federal government to impose health insurance taxes and directly administer health benefits for everyone; 2) universal health insurance plans that require employers to pay all or most of the cost of their employees' insurance and offer government subsidies for the poor, uninsured, and some small businesses; and 3) open access plans that do not mandate coverage for everyone but require insurance companies to accept all applicants and the government to expand Medicaid to cover the uninsured and low-income workers.

Single-payer Plans.   Liberals have pressed for a Canadian-style health care system in which the government would provide health insurance for all Americans in a single national plan paid for by increases in taxes. In effect, a single-payer plan would expand Medicare, now available to only the aged, to everyone. The plan boasts of simplicity, savings in administrative costs over multiple insurers, and direct federal control over prices to be paid for hospital and physician services and drugs. Single-payer universal coverage would require major new taxes.

Employer-based Plans.   Others have endorsed universal coverage through employer-based insurance for most workers combined with government subsidies to pay the insurance costs for people living below the poverty line and to assist others in purchasing insurance.

Some employer-based plans offer employers a "play or pay" choice—either offer government-approved insurance plans to their employees (with the employer paying 80 percent or more of the costs), or face a payroll tax that would be used to fund health insurance for people outside of employer-based plans. These plans generally recognize that the federal government itself will have to provide or pay for health insurance for large numbers of unemployed and uninsured Americans. This requires significant increases in taxes.

Clinton's Failed National Health Care Plan.   In 1992 a committee headed by First Lady Hillary Rodham Clinton proposed a comprehensive plan to restructure completely the nation's health care system. The Clinton health plan was incorporated into a very complex, 1,342-page bill that would have reorganized the entire health care industry in America—nearly one-sixth of the nation's economy. Its key elements included the following:

- Government-sponsored "health alliances" throughout the country to pool the mandated insurance premiums of firms and individuals to purchase health care from HMOs, hospitals, physicians' groups, nursing homes, and so on.
- Mandated employer-paid health insurance for workers and their dependents (80 percent of costs, with a cap of 7.9 percent of payroll).
- Mandated "comprehensive" benefits, including prescription drugs, mental health and substance abuse treatment, childhood immunization, dental coverage, eyeglasses for children, and all pregnancy-related services, including abortion.
- Health insurance for all citizens and legal residents. Government subsidies would be provided for small employers and persons not covered by employer-mandated insurance.
- Cost containment by a national health board that would set an overall health care budget and allocate totals to health alliances around the country.

The Clinton plan failed to pass Congress for a variety of reasons. The choice of a rational-comprehensive plan that would have restructured one-sixth of the economy, as opposed to more modest incremental reforms, may have been the initial mistake. The complex plan caused a great deal of public confusion and enabled opponents—notably the health insurance industry with its effective "Harry and Louise" television ads—to raise fears about the effects of the plan on consumers. Liberals in Congress, who favored a Canadian-style government health care system paid for by tax increases, were only lukewarm supporters of the president's plan. Republicans were able to brand the president's bill as a "government takeover" of health care. The president was unwilling to consider more modest reforms. After months of debate, public opinion polls showed a majority of Americans were opposed to Clinton's plan.

Open Access Plans.   Conservatives have worried over proposals that call for the federal government to take over the nation's health care system. They argue that most Americans are satisfied with their health insurance. They do not believe the system is in "crisis," and they believe that current problems in health care can be remedied with modest reforms. Open access plans do not guarantee universal coverage but rather guarantee insurance to anyone who wishes to purchase it. No one would be forced to buy insurance, and employers would not be mandated to provide it for their employees. Minimum wage employees not covered by an insurance plan might be permitted to buy into Medicaid coverage at reduced rates. Insurance costs for basic coverage for both individuals and employers might be made tax deductible. (Currently, individuals receive no deduction.) Costs might be lowered by mandating the adoption of uniform reimbursement forms, and more importantly, by reforming medical malpractice laws and limiting damages for "pain and suffering."

Kennedy-Kassebaum Act.   Some modest reforms were enacted in 1996 in the Kennedy-Kassebaum Act, named for its bipartisan sponsorship by liberal Democratic Senator Edward M. Kennedy and moderate Republican Senator Nancy Kassebaum. This act guarantees the "portability" of health insurance—allowing workers to maintain their insurance coverage if they lose or change jobs. Their new employer's health insurance company cannot deny them insurance for "preexisting conditions."

The Interest Group Challenges.   Rational reform strategies confront the reality of interest group politics, and interest group battles over the details of health care reform have been intense. Virtually everyone has a financial stake in the nation's health care system.

- Employers, especially small businesses, are fearful of added costs of government mandated insurance.
- Physicians strongly oppose price controls and treatment guidelines, as well as programs that take away a patient's choice of physician.
- Psychiatrists, psychologists, mental health and drug abuse counselors, physical therapists, chiropractors, optometrists, and dentists all want their own services to be covered.
- Drug companies want to see prescription drugs paid for, but they vigorously oppose price controls on drugs.
- Hospitals want all patients to be insured but oppose government payment schedules.
- Health maintenance organizations and preferred provider organizations expected to gain from reform.
- Medical specialists and medical technology manufacturers may lose under proposals to monitor care.

- The powerful senior citizens lobby wants added benefits, including coverage for drugs, eyeglasses, dental care, and nursing homes, but it fears folding Medicare into a large health care system.
- Veterans groups want to retain separate Veterans Administration (VA) hospitals and medical services.
- Opponents of abortion rights are prepared to do battle to keep national coverage from including such procedures, whereas many supporters of abortion rights argue that it should be included.

SUMMARY

A rational approach to social welfare policy requires a clear definition of objectives, the development of alternative strategies for achieving them, and a careful comparison and weighing of the costs and benefits of each. But there are seemingly insurmountable problems in developing a completely rational policy:

1. Contrasting definitions of poverty constitute one obstacle to rational policy-making. Official government sources define poverty in terms of minimum dollar amounts required for subsistence. In recent years 12 to 14 percent of the population has remained below the official poverty line.

2. Latent poverty refers to people who would fall below the poverty line in the absence of government assistance. Latent poverty has also risen over the past 25 years, as more people have become dependent on government.

3. Contrasting explanations of poverty also make it difficult to formulate a rational policy. Is poverty a product of a lack of knowledge, skills, and training? Or recession and unemployment? Or a culture of poverty? Certainly the disintegration of the traditional husband-wife family is closely associated with poverty. How can the government devise a rational policy to keep families together, or at least not encourage them to dissolve?

4. Government welfare policies themselves may be a significant cause of poverty. Poverty in America had steadily declined before the development of Great Society programs, the relaxation of eligibility requirements for welfare assistance, and the rapid increase of welfare expenditures in the 1970s. To what extent do government programs themselves encourage social dependency and harm the long-term prospects of the poor?

5. The social insurance concept was designed as a preventive strategy to insure people against indigence arising from old age, death of a family breadwinner, or physical disability. But the Social Security "trust fund" idea remains in name only. Today each generation of workers is expected to pay the benefits for each generation of retirees. Yet after the year 2000 the dependency ratio will rise to a point where it will become increasingly difficult for workers to support the large number of Social Security recipients.

6. The federal government also pursues an alleviative strategy in assisting the poor with a variety of direct cash and in-kind benefit programs. The SSI program provides direct federal cash payments to the aged, blind, and disabled. As a welfare

program, SSI is paid from general tax revenues, and recipients must prove their need. The federal government also provides assistance to the states for cash family assistance. The largest in-kind welfare programs are the federal food stamp and Medicaid programs.

7. "Rational" strategies sometimes produce unintended consequences. De-institutionalization of the mentally ill and decriminalization of public intoxication produced many homeless people. It is often difficult to reach these people through conventional welfare programs.

8. The paramount objective in national health policy has never been clearly defined. Is it *good health,* as defined by lower death rates, less illness, and longer life? Or is it *access to good medical care?* If good health is the objective, preventive efforts to change people's personal habits and lifestyles are more likely to improve health than anything else.

9. Medicare for the aged and Medicaid for the poor, together with private and employer-provided insurance, guarantee access to health care for about 85 percent of the population. But about 15 percent, including many workers and their families, have no health insurance; many other Americans worry about loss of insurance with unemployment or job changes.

10. The United States devotes more resources to health care than other advanced democracies, yet it ranks well below other nations in common measures of the health of its citizens. Health care cost inflation is increasingly burdensome for both government and private employers.

11. Health care reform centers on two conflicting goals—expanding access to all Americans while containing costs. The Clinton administration tried to completely restructure the nation's health care system rather than make modest, incremental reforms. But comprehensive, rational reform is threatened by the multiple demands of interest groups.

NOTES

1. U.S. Bureau of the Census, *Statistical Abstract of the United States 1996* (Washington, DC, U.S. Government Printing Office, 1996).
2. Charles Murray, *Losing Ground* (New York: Basic Books, 1984).
3. *Statistical Abstract of the United States 1993,* p. 477.
4. Greg J. Duncan, *Years of Poverty, Years of Plenty* (Ann Arbor, MI: Institute of Social Research, 1984).
5. *Statistical Abstract of the United States 1996,* p. 468.
6. *Statistical Abstract of the United States 1992,* p. 52; projections by Senator Daniel Patrick Moynihan, "Family and Nation," Godkin Lectures, Harvard University, 1985.
7. U.S. Bureau of the Census, *Current Population Reports,* no. 181, p. 60.
8. See William Julius Wilson, *The Truly Disadvantaged* (Chicago: University of Chicago Press, 1987).
9. Francis Fox Piven and Richard A. Cloward, *Regulating the Poor: The Functions of Public Welfare* (New York: Vintage Books, 1971.)
10. David Ellwood, *Poor Support: Poverty in the American Family* (New York: Basic Books 1988), p. 6.
11. Bill Clinton and Al Gore, *Putting People First* (New York: Times Books, 1992), p. 165.

12. Estimates by U.S. Department of Health and Human Services and the Urban Institute. Reported in *U.S. News and World Report,* January 16, 1995, pp. 30–40.
13. *New York Times,* February 2, 1997, p.12.
14. Peter H. Rossi, *Down and Out in America* (Chicago: University of Chicago Press, 1989).
15. Robert C. Ellickson, "The Homelessness Muddle," *The Public Interest,* Spring 1990, pp. 45–60.
16. As reported in a 27-city survey by the U.S. Conference of Mayors. See *U.S. News and World Report,* January 15, 1990, pp. 27–29.
17. *Newsweek,* January 6, 1985, p. 16.
18. *Statistical Abstract of the United States 1992,* p. 724.

BIBLIOGRAPHY

JENCKS, CHRISTOPHER, and PAUL E. PETERSON. *The Urban Underclass.* Washington, DC: Brookings Institution, 1991.
KELSO, WILLIAM A. *Poverty and the Underclass.* New York: New York University Press, 1994.
LEVITAN, SAR A. *Programs in Aid of the Poor.* 6th ed. Baltimore: Johns Hopkins University Press, 1991.
MACMANUS, SUSAN. *Young Versus Old.* Boulder: Westview Press, 1996.
MARMOR, THEODORE, R., JERRY L. MASHAW, and PHILIP L. HARVEY. *America's Misunderstood Welfare State.* New York: Basic Books, 1990.
MEAD, LAWRENCE M. *The New Politics of Poverty.* New York: Basic Books, 1992.
MURRAY, CHARLES. *Losing Ground.* New York: Basic Books, 1984.
WILSON, WILLIAM J. *The Truly Disadvantaged.* Chicago: University of Chicago Press, 1987.

6

EDUCATION
The Group Struggle

A teacher sparks an interest in reading at a Cardinal Spellman Center Head Start class. (Jacques Chenet/Woodfin Camp & Associates)

MULTIPLE GOALS IN EDUCATIONAL POLICY

Perhaps the most widely recommended "solution" to the problems that confront American society is more and better schooling. If there ever was a time when schools were expected only to combat ignorance and illiteracy, that time is far behind us. Today, schools are expected to do many things: resolve racial conflict and build an integrated society; inspire patriotism and good citizenship; provide values, aspirations, and a sense of identity to disadvantaged children; offer various forms of recreation and mass entertainment (football games, bands, choruses, cheerleading, and the like); reduce conflict in society by teaching children to get along well with others and to adjust to group living; reduce the highway accident toll by teaching students to be good drivers; fight disease and poor health through physical education, health training, and even medical treatment; eliminate unemployment and poverty by teaching job skills; end malnutrition and hunger through school lunch and milk programs; fight drug abuse and educate children about sex; and act as custodians for teenagers who have no interest in education but whom we do not permit either to work or to roam the streets unsupervised. In other words, nearly all the nation's problems are reflected in demands placed on the nation's schools. And, of course, these demands are frequently conflicting.

Educational policy affects a wide variety of interests and stimulates a great deal of interest group activity. We will describe the major interests involved in federal educational policy and examine the constitutional provisions and court policies dealing with religion in the public schools. We will observe how both racial and religious group interests are mobilized in educational policymaking, and we will see the importance of resolving group conflict in the development of educational policy. We will also describe the structure of educational decision making and the resulting multiple points of group access in a fragmented federal-state-local educational system. We will examine the broad categories of group interests—teachers, taxpayers, school board members, school administrators, and parents—involved in educational policy at the local level. Finally, we will discuss the governing and financing of public higher education—the nation's investment in state colleges and universities.

Today about 50 million pupils attend grade school and high school in America—about 44 million of which attend public schools and about 6 million attend private schools. About 15 million students are enrolled in institutions of higher education—community colleges, colleges, and universities.

BATTLING OVER THE BASICS

Citizens' groups with an interest in education—parents, taxpayers, and employers—have confronted professional educators—school administrators, state education officials, and teachers' unions—over the vital question of what should be taught in public schools. Public sentiment is strongly in favor of teaching the basic "three Rs" ("reading, 'riting, and 'rithmetic"), enforcing minimum standards with tests, and even testing teachers themselves for their mastery of all the basics. Parents are less enthusiastic than professional educators about emotional growth, "getting along with others," self expression and self-image, cultural enrichment, and various "innovative" programs of education.

The SAT Score Controversy.   For many years critics of modern public education cited declining scores on standardized tests, particularly the Scholastic Aptitude Test (SAT), required by many colleges and universities, as evidence of the failure of the schools to teach basic reading and mathematics skills. The SAT scores declined significantly during the 1960s and 1970s, even as per pupil educational spending was rising and federal aid to education was initiated (see Figure 6–1). Critics charged that the nation was pouring money into a failed educational system; they pressed their case for a return to the basics.

However, professional educators argued that declining SAT scores were really a function of how many students took the test. During the years of declining scores, increasing numbers and proportions were taking the test—students who never aspired to college in the past whose test scores did not match those of the earlier, smaller group of college-bound test-takers.

"Recentering" SAT Scores.   Indeed, in 1996, the College Board, sponsors of the SAT, decided to "recenter" the scores in recognition of the fact that national averages were unlikely to ever recover to the 500 mark. (Under the scoring system in effect since the 1940s, students over the past 30 years regularly averaged in the 420s on

FIGURE 6–1   Average SAT Score Trends

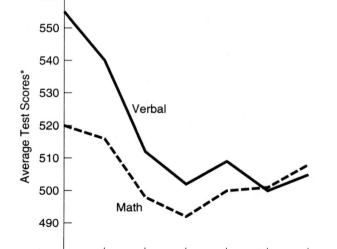

* Scores for all years "recentered" on 1996 scale for comparison.

the verbal and in the 470s on the mathematical tests.) Critics charged that this artificial boost in scores was designed by educators to make American students appear better prepared and, thereby, to deflect criticism of the schools. Now it is possible to miss a few questions and still score a perfect 800; more than 500 students a year now register a perfect 1600 combined verbal and math scores.

Cross-national Comparisons. It is also possible to measure educational performance by comparing scores of American students with those of students of other nations on common school subjects, notably math and science. The results of one such study, involving 500,000 13-year-old students in 41 countries, are shown in Table 6–1. The performance of the U.S. students can best be described as mediocre. In the countries with top-performing students, education appears to have a higher cultural priority, that is, education is highly valued in the family and society generally. Moreover, in all of the top-performing nations, educational standards and testing are determined at the national level rather than by states and school districts as in the United States. These international comparisons appear to support efforts in the United States to develop national standards and national testing. But educational groups in the states, as well as conservative groups fearing a "federal takeover" of American education, generally resist the imposition of national standards.

A Nation at Risk. The decline in SAT scores ended in the 1980s. A "back to basics" citizens' reform movement in education was given impetus by an influential 1983 report by the National Commission on Excellence in Education entitled "A Nation at Risk."[1]

> Our nation is at risk. . . . If an unfriendly foreign power had attempted to impose on America the mediocre educational performance that exists today, we might well have viewed it as an act of war.

The commission's recommendations set the agenda for educational policy debate. Among the many recommendations were these:

- A minimum high school curriculum of four years of English, three years of mathematics, three years of social science, and one-half year of computer science
- Four to six years of foreign language study beginning in the elementary grades
- Standardized tests for achievement for all of these subjects
- More homework, a seven-hour school day, and a 200- to 220-day school year
- Reliable grades and standardized tests for promotion and graduation
- "Performance-based" salaries for teachers and rewards for "superior" teaching

Testing. Many state legislatures responded to the commission's report and the demand for greater achievement in basic skills by requiring minimum competence testing (MCT examinations) in the schools. These tests may be used as diagnostic tools to determine the need for remedial education, or minimum scores may be required for promotion or graduation. Currently, about half of the states require

TABLE 6-1   Cross-national Comparisons of Student Performance in Math and Science

Math

Top Five	Score
1 Singapore	643
2 South Korea	607
3 Japan	605
4 Hong Kong	588
5 Belgium	565

Somewhere in the Middle	
13 France	538
18 Canada	527
23 Germany	509
25 England	506
28 United States	500

Bottom Five	
37 Portugal	454
38 Iran	428
39 Kuwait	392
40 Colombia	385
42 South Africa	354

Science

Top Five	Score
1 Singapore	607
2 Czech Republic	574
3 Japan	571
4 South Korea	565
5 Bulgaria	565

Somewhere in the middle	
10 England	552
17 United States	534
18 Germany	531
18 Canada	531
28 France	498

Bottom Five	
37 Iran	470
38 Cyprus	463
39 Kuwait	430
40 Colombia	411
41 South Africa	326

Note: scoring on a scale of 200 to 800

Source: Third International Mathematics and Science Study, as reported in *New York Times,* November 21, 1996.

students to pass a minimum competency test to receive a high school diploma. These tests usually require performance at an eighth- or ninth-grade level.

Professional educators have been less enthusiastic about testing than citizen groups and state legislators. Educators contend that MCT leads to narrow "test-taking" education rather than broad preparation for life. That is, it requires teachers to devote more time to coaching students on how to pass an exam rather than preparing them for productive lives after graduation.

But the most serious opposition to MCT has come from minority group leaders who charge that the tests are racially biased. Average scores of black students are frequently lower than those of white students, and larger percentages of black students are held back from promotion and graduation by testing than are white students. Some black leaders charge that racial bias in the examination itself, as well as racial isolation in the school, contribute to black-white differences in exam scores. Denying a disproportionate number of black students a diploma because of the schools' failure to teach basics may be viewed as a form of discrimination. However, to date federal courts have declined to rule that MCT itself is discriminatory, as long as sufficient time and opportunity have been provided for all students to prepare for the examination.

Testing Teachers.   Professional education groups have also opposed teacher competency tests, arguing that standardized tests cannot really measure competency in the classroom. The National Education Association has opposed all testing of teachers; the American Federation of Teachers is willing to accept competency testing only for new teachers. Today, only a few states have adopted teacher competency tests, but the results have been disquieting. Large numbers of experienced teachers have failed the tests; black teachers have failed more often than white teachers, raising again the issue of racial fairness in testing.

THE EDUCATIONAL GROUPS

Interest group activity in education involves a wide array of racial, religious, labor, and civil rights organizations, as well as citizens' and educational groups.

Citizens versus Professionals.   Many disputes over education pit citizens' groups against professional educators. Citizens' groups assert that schools are public institutions that should be governed by the local citizenry through their elected representatives. This was the original concept in American public education developed in the nineteenth century. But as school issues became more complex, the knowledge of citizen school boards seemed insufficient to cope with the many problems confronting the schools—teaching innovations, curricular changes, multi-million-dollar building programs, special education programs, and so forth. In the twentieth century, the school superintendent and his or her administrative assistants came to exercise more and more control over day-to-day operations of the schools. Theoretically, the superintendent only implements the policies of the board, but in practice he or she has assumed much of the policymaking in education. The superintendent is a full-time administrator, receiving direct advice from attorneys, architects, accountants, and educational consultants, and generally setting the agenda for school board meetings.

The resulting "professionalism" in education tangles directly with the democratic notion of the people's control of the school. There are few meetings of local school boards that do not involve at least some tug-of-war between board members and the superintendent. Professional educators often support the idea that "politics" should be kept out of education; this means that elected school board members should not interfere in educational decisions. But school board members and interested citizens generally believe that popular control of education is a vital component of democracy. Schools should be responsive to community needs and desires. Frequently, citizen criticism has focused on the schools' failure to teach basic skills—reading, writing, and arithmetic. These issues have in turn raised the underlying question—who should govern our schools, professional educators or interested citizens?

Professional Educators.   Professional educators can be divided into at least three distinct groups. Numerically, the largest group (2.5 million) is comprised of schoolteachers. But perhaps the most powerful group is that of professional school administrators, particularly the superintendents of schools. A third group consists of the faculties of teachers' colleges and departments of education at universities. This last group often interacts with the state departments of education, diffuses educational innovations and ideologies to each generation of teachers, and influences requirements for teacher certification within the states.

Teachers' Unions.   Most of the nation's teachers are organized into either the older and larger National Education Association (NEA), with about 2 million members, or the smaller but more militant American Federation of Teachers (AFT). The NEA maintains a large Washington office and makes substantial campaign contributions to political candidates. The AFT has a smaller membership, concentrated in big-city school districts, but as an affiliate of the AFL-CIO it can call on assistance from organized labor. State and district chapters of both unions have achieved collective bargaining status in most states and large urban school districts. The chapters have shut down schools to force concessions by superintendents, board members, and taxpayers not only in salaries and benefits but also in classroom conditions, school discipline, and other educational matters. Both educational groups lobby Congress as well as the White House and other parts of the executive branch, particularly the Department of Education (DOE). Indeed, the DOE was created in 1979 largely because of President Carter's campaign pledge to educational groups to create a separate education department.

Voters and Taxpayers.   School politics at the community level differ from one community to another, but it is possible to identify a number of political groups that appear on the scene almost everywhere. There is, first, the small band of voters who turn out for school elections. On the average, only about 25 to 35 percent of eligible voters bother to cast ballots in school elections. Voter turnout at school bond and tax elections also demonstrates no groundswell of public interest in school affairs. Perhaps even more interesting is the finding that the larger the voter turnout in a school referendum, the more likely the *defeat* of educational proposals. In general, the best way to defeat a school bond referendum is to have a large turnout. Proponents of educational expenditures are better advised not to work for a large turnout but for a better-informed and more educationally oriented electorate.

School Boards.   School board members constitute another important group of actors in local school politics. They are selected largely from among concerned parents (often with ties to schoolteachers or administrators), as well as among local civic leaders. There is some evidence that people who are interested in education and have some knowledge of what the schools are doing tend to support education more than do the less informed citizens.

Racial and Religious Groups.   Because of the frequent involvement of racial and religious issues in education, such groups as the National Association for the Advancement of Colored People (NAACP), National Catholic Education Conference, the American Jewish Congress, Americans United for the Separation of Church and State, and the American Civil Liberties Union all become involved in educational policy. These well-established national organizations have long led the battles in federal courts over segregation and other racial issues in the schools (see Chapter 3), prayer and Bible reading in the schools, and public financing of religious schools (see below).

Community-based religious groups are often active on behalf of the restoration of traditional moral values in local schools. Among the well-publicized issues of concern in these community battles are sex education courses that imply approval of premarital sex, the distribution of contraceptives in schools, and the teaching of evolution and the exclusion of "creationism."

THE FEDERAL GOVERNMENT'S ROLE IN EDUCATION

Traditionally, education in the United States was a community responsibility. But over the years, state governments have assumed major responsibility for public education. The federal government remains largely an interested spectator in the area of educational policy. While the U.S. Supreme Court has taken the lead in guaranteeing racial equality in education and separating religion from public schools, the U.S. Congress has never assumed any significant share of the costs of education. State and local taxpayers have always borne over 90 percent of the costs of public elementary and secondary education; the federal share has never exceeded 10 percent (see Table 6–2). Similarly, federal expenditures for higher education have never exceeded 15 percent of the total costs.

Nonetheless the federal government's interest in education is a long-standing

TABLE 6-2   Sources of Funds for Public Education in the United States

	Percentage of School Expenditures by Source		
	1980	1990	1995
Elementary and Secondary			
Federal	9.2	6.3	7.0
State	49.1	48.3	47.8
Local	41.7	45.4	44.2
Higher Education			
Federal	15.2	12.3	12.2
State	31.4	27.5	24.1
Local	2.7	2.6	2.6
Tuition	20.4	24.3	26.5
Gifts, grants, other	30.3	35.9	34.6

Source: *Statistical Abstract of the United States 1996*, pp. 170, 185.

one. In the famous Northwest Ordinance of 1787, Congress offered land grants for public schools in the new territories and gave succeeding generations words to be forever etched on grammar school cornerstones: "Religion, morality, and knowledge, being necessary to good government and the happiness of mankind, schools and the means for education should ever be encouraged." The earliest democrats believed that the safest repository of the ultimate powers of society was the people themselves. If the people made mistakes, the remedy was not to remove power from their hands but to help them in forming their judgment through education. If the common people were to be granted the right to vote, they must be educated for the task. This meant that public education had to be universal, free, and compulsory. Compulsory education began in Massachusetts in 1852 and was eventually adopted by Mississippi in 1918.

Early Federal Aid.   In 1862 the Morrill Land Grant Act provided grants of federal land to each state for the establishment of colleges specializing in agricultural and mechanical arts. These became known as land-grant colleges. In 1867 Congress established a U.S. Office of Education; in 1979, a separate, cabinet-level Department of Education was created. The Smith-Hughes Act of 1917 set up the first program of federal grants-in-aid to promote vocational education, enabling schools to provide training in agriculture, home economics, trades, and industries. In the National School Lunch and Milk programs, begun in 1946, federal grants and commodity donations were made for nonprofit lunches and milk served in public and private schools. In the Federal Impacted Areas Aid program, begun in 1950, federal aid was authorized for "federally impacted" areas of the nation. These are areas in which federal activities create a substantial increase in school enrollments or a reduction in taxable resources because of a federally owned property. In response to the Soviet Union's success in launching the first satellite into space in 1957, Congress became concerned that the American educational system might not be keeping abreast of advances being made in other nations, particularly in science and technology. In the National Defense Education Act of 1958, Congress provided financial aid to states and public school districts to improve instruction in science, mathematics, and foreign languages. Congress also established a system of loans to undergraduates, fellowships to graduate students, and funds to colleges—all in an effort to improve the training of teachers in America.

ESEA.   The Elementary and Secondary Education Act (ESEA) of 1965 established the single largest federal aid to education programs. "Poverty-impacted" schools were the principal beneficiaries of ESEA, receiving instructional materials and educational research and training. Title I of ESEA (now referred to as Chapter 1) provided federal financial assistance to "local educational agencies serving areas with concentrations of children from low-income families" for programs "which contribute particularly to meeting the special needs of educationally deprived children."

Educational Block Grants.   Early in the Reagan administration, the Education Consolidation and Improvement Act of 1981 consolidated ESEA and other federal educational grant programs into single block grants for states and communities. The purpose was to give states and local school districts greater discretion over the use of federal educational aid. Chapter 1 educational aid was retained, but greater flexibility in its use was given to local school officials.

Head Start.   The most popular federal educational aid program is Head Start, which emerged from President Lyndon B. Johnson's "War on Poverty" in the 1960s to provide special preschool preparation to disadvantaged children before they enter kindergarten or first grade. Over the years it has enjoyed great popularity among parents, members of Congress, and both Republican and Democratic presidents. However, despite an avalanche of research by professional educators seeking to prove the value of the program, the results can only be described as mixed at best. Much of the value of Head Start preparation disappears after a few years of schooling; disadvantaged pupils who attended Head Start do not perform much better in middle school than disadvantaged pupils who did not attend. Nevertheless, Head Start remains politically very popular.

Federal Aid and Educational Quality.   It is difficult to demonstrate that federal aid programs improve the quality of education in America. Indeed, during the years in which federal aid was increasing, student achievement scores were declining (see Figure 6–1). In the report "A Nation at Risk," the National Commission on Excellence in Education reaffirmed that "state and local government officials, including school board members and governors, and legislators, have *the primary responsibility* for funding and governing the schools." Raising the educational achievement levels of America's youth depends less on how much is spent than on how it is spent.

EDUCATIONAL REFORM AND PARENTAL CHOICE

Anxiety over education in America has lessened somewhat since the 1983 report "A Nation at Risk." Although opinion polls indicate that voters rank education at or near the top of their list of priorities, educational reform has moved very slowly. Perhaps the stimulus to reform has abated because SAT scores are no longer declining, or because states and school districts have made some modest advances in imposing performance standards and testing, or because the U.S. economy is currently performing well in the global marketplace. Certainly continuing federal budget deficits (see Chapter 9) pose a major obstacle to increased federal spending for education. But perhaps interest group conflict over the direction of reform is also a major obstacle to educational progress.

"Goals 2000."   Bill Clinton was widely praised for his educational policies as governor of Arkansas, including the introduction of pupil and teacher testing (despite opposition of the state teachers' union). As president, Clinton's principal educational initiative has been Goals 2000: Educate America Act. This act was designed to advance a series of national educational goals first developed in a series of "educational summits" that involved President Bush and the nation's governors:

- Every child must start school ready to learn.
- The high school graduation rate will be increased to at least 90 percent.
- U.S. students will become first in the world in mathematics and science achievement.
- Every adult American will become literate.
- Every school in the United States will be free of drugs and violence and will offer a disciplined environment conducive to learning.

But it is not altogether clear how these goals are to be achieved. The act specifically denies the federal government "control" over curriculum, instruction, and the allocation of state and local educational resources. But federal grants were to be offered to encourage states to adopt national standards and tests to monitor progress toward these goals.

Clinton Initiatives.   President Clinton proclaimed that education would be given a high priority in his second term in the White House. He continued his support for national testing and proposed additional federal funds for school construction. He also proposed a combination of tax credits and deductions for college tuition, with a special emphasis on the first two years of college. Yet Clinton's proposals, like the earlier Goals 2000, raise the issue of who will set national academic standards and how will state progress toward the standards be measured. Many professional educators oppose achievement measures that focus on test performance. Many liberals worry that disadvantaged students will be held to the same national standards regardless of how effective their schools are. Many conservatives charge that the program threatens a federal takeover of education in America—traditionally a community responsibility. These conflicts, together with budget restraints, continue to limit the federal government's role in education.

What Works?   Social science research suggests that educational performance is enhanced when the schools are perceived by children to be extensions or substitutes for their family.[2] Academic achievement and graduation rates improve for all students, but especially for students from disadvantaged backgrounds, in schools where there is a high expectation of achievement, an orderly and disciplined environment for learning, an emphasis on basic skills, frequent monitoring of students' progress, and teacher-parent interaction and agreement on values and norms. When parents choose schools for their children, as in the case of private and Catholic schools, these values are strengthened.[3]

Parental Choice.   "Choice" is currently a key word in the movement to reform American education. Parental choice among schools and the resulting competition among schools for enrollment is said to improve academic achievement and graduation rates as well as increase parental satisfaction and teachers' morale. Principals and teachers are encouraged to work directly with parents to set clear goals, develop specialized curricula, impose discipline, and demand more from the students. Choice plans are said to do more than just benefit the parents who have the knowledge to choose schools wisely for their children. They also send a message to educators to structure their schools to give parents what they want for their children or risk losing enrollment and funding.[4]

Charter Schools.   One way to implement parental choice is the "charter" school. Community educational groups sign a "charter" with their school district or state educational authority to establish their own school. They receive waivers from most state and school district regulations to enable them to be more innovative; in exchange for this flexibility they promise to show specific student achievement. In 1991 Minnesota was the first state to permit charter schools, and about a dozen states have followed suit; but so far relatively few charter schools have been established.

Magnet Schools.   Another common reform proposal is the "magnet school." High schools might choose to specialize, some emphasizing math and science, others the fine arts, others business, and still others vocational training. Some schools might be "adopted" by business, professional organizations, or universities. Magnet schools, with reputations for quality and specialized instruction, are frequently recommended for inner-city areas in order to attract white pupils and reduce racial isolation.

Privatized Public Schools.   A more radical version of the charter school is the privately contracted public school, where a private profit-making corporation contracts with the school district to provide schooling for its pupils, thus replacing the public schools. Private firms usually promise to provide pupil education at a lower cost to school districts than the districts regularly incur in providing schools themselves. The private firms make their profits from cost savings in instructional delivery and program management. And they usually promise to produce better results—higher test scores, fewer dropouts, and more employable graduates. So far only limited experiments have taken place throughout the country.

But privatization is bitterly opposed by public school administrators, public school teachers, and especially teachers' unions. They argue that profit-making entrepreneurs do not have the community's best interest at heart, that private firms teach only test-taking skills at the expense of broader educational goals, and that there is no hard evidence so far that private firms can produce better educational results.

Educational Vouchers. An even more controversial version of parental choice involves educational vouchers that would be given to parents to spend at any school they choose, public or private. State governments would redeem the vouchers submitted by schools by paying specified amounts—perhaps the equivalent of the state's per pupil educational spending (the U.S. average was more than $5,500 in 1995). All public and private schools would compete equally for students, and state education funds would flow to those schools that enrolled more students. Competition would encourage all schools to satisfy parental demands for excellence. Racial or religious or ethnic discrimination would be strictly prohibited in any private or public school receiving vouchers. Providing vouchers for private school education would be most effective for children from poor or disadvantage homes. These children currently do not have the same options as children from more affluent homes of fleeing the public schools and enrolling in private academies.

Yet there is strong opposition to the voucher idea, especially from professional school administrators and state educational agencies. They argue that giving parents the right to move their children from school to school disrupts educational planning and threatens the viability of schools that are perceived as inferior. It may lead to a stratification of schools into popular schools that would attract the best students, and the less popular schools that would be left with the task of educating students whose parents were unaware or uninterested in their children's education. Other opponents of choice plans fear that public education might be undermined if the choice available to parents includes the option of sending their children to private, church-related schools. Public education groups are fearful that vouchers will divert public money from public to private schools. As governor of Arkansas, Bill Clinton endorsed the notion of choice, but only *within* the public school system.[5]

California Votes to Reject Vouchers. The educational choice movement was dealt a major setback in 1993 when California voters soundly defeated a citizens' initiative known as Proposition 174, Parental Choice in Education. Professional educators, teachers' unions, and liberal groups joined together to mount an expensive, highly publicized campaign to defeat the measure. Proposition 174 promised to "empower parents" by granting each schoolchild a "scholarship" (voucher) equal to about one-half of the average amount of state and local government aid per pupil in California (about $2,600). The money was to be paid directly to the schools in which parents chose to enroll their children. Either public or private schools could qualify as "independently scholarship-redeeming schools"; schools that discriminated on the basis of race, ethnicity, color, or national origin would not be eligible.

Opposition groups, including the powerful California Teachers Association, argued that the proposal would create "a two-tier system of schools, one for the haves, one for the have-nots." They portrayed vouchers as "an entitlement program offering wealthy families a private-school subsidy for their children, paid for by the taxpayers," noting that there was no means test for the vouchers. About 10 percent of California's schoolchildren were in private schools already; their parents would enjoy an immediate windfall benefit from the program. Opponents warned that public education would suffer grievously if both money and gifted students were removed from public schools. Although only half of the costs of educating a public school student would go into a voucher, it was argued that public schools would face financial difficulties from the implementation of the program. The initial costs of vouchers for pupils already attending private schools posed a major financial problem. No one could accurately estimate how many pupils would eventually transfer from public to private schools. Finally, opponents made inroads in the electorate by warning that taxpayers' money would go to religious schools and by noting that the content of instruction and credentials of teachers were unregulated in the proposal.

BATTLES OVER SCHOOL FINANCES

Spending for education varies enormously across the United States. Nationwide about $5,500 per year is spent on the public education of each child.[6] Yet national averages can obscure as much as they reveal about the record of the states in public education. In 1995 for example, public school expenditures for each pupil ranged from $3,431 in Utah to $9,206 in New Jersey. (See Table 12–1 in Chapter 12 for a ranking of the states in educational spending per pupil.) Why is it that some states spend more than twice as much on the education of each child as other states? Economic resources are an important determinant of a state's willingness and ability to provide educational services. Most of the variation among states in educational spending can be explained by differences among them in economic resources (see Figure 12–1 in Chapter 12 for a view of the relationship between personal income and educational spending in the states).

Inequalities among School Districts.   Another issue in the struggle over public education is that of distributing the benefits and costs of education equitably. Most school revenues are derived from *local* property taxes. In every state except Hawaii, local school boards must raise money from property taxes to finance their schools. This means that communities that do *not* have much taxable property cannot finance their schools as well as communities that are blessed with great wealth. Frequently, wealthy communities can provide better education for their children at *lower* tax rates than poor communities can provide at *higher* tax rates, simply because of disparities in the value of taxable property from one community to the next.

School Inequalities as a Constitutional Issue.   Do disparities among school districts within a state deny "equal protection of laws" guaranteed by the Fourteenth Amendment of the U.S. Constitution and similar guarantees found in most state constitutions? The U.S. Supreme Court ruled that disparities in financial resources among school districts in a state, and resulting inequalities in educational spending per pupil across a state, do *not* violate the Equal Protection Clause of the Fourteenth Amendment. There is no duty under the U.S. Constitution for a state to equalize educational resources within the state.[7]

However, in recent years *state courts* have increasingly intervened in school financing to insure equality among school districts based on their own interpretation of *state* constitutional provisions. Beginning with an early California state supreme court decision requiring that state funds be used to help equalize resources among the state's school districts,[8] many state courts have pressured their legislatures to come up with equalization plans in state school grants to overcome disparities in property tax revenues among school districts. State court equalization orders are generally based on *state* constitutional provisions guaranteeing equality. To achieve equity in school funding among communities, an increasing number of state courts are ordering their legislatures to substitute state general revenues for local property taxes.

PUBLIC POLICY AND HIGHER EDUCATION

State governments have been involved in higher education since the colonial era. State governments in the Northeast frequently made contributions to private colleges in their states, a practice that continues today. The first state university to be chartered by a state legislature was the University of Georgia in 1794. Before the Civil War, northeastern states relied exclusively on private colleges, and the southern states assumed the leadership in public higher education. The antebellum curricula at southern state universities, however, resembled the rigid classical studies of the early private colleges—Greek and Latin, history, philosophy, and literature.

Growth of Public Universities.   It was not until the Morrill Land Grant Act of 1862 that public higher education began to make major strides in the states. Interestingly, the eastern states were slow to respond to the opportunity afforded by the Morrill Act to develop public universities. The southern states were economically depressed in the post–Civil War period, and leadership in public higher education passed to the midwestern states. The philosophy of the Morrill Act emphasized agricultural and mechanical studies rather than the classical curricula of eastern colleges, and the movement for "A and M" education spread rapidly in the agricultural states. The early groups of midwestern state universities were closely tied to agricultural education, including agricultural extension services. State universities also took the responsibility for the training of public school teachers in colleges of education. The state universities introduced a broad range of modern subjects in the university curricula—business administration, agriculture, home economics, education, engineering. It was not until the 1960s that the eastern states began to emphasize public higher education, as evidenced by the development of the huge, multicampus State University of New York.

Today, public higher education enrolls three-fourths of the nation's college and university students (see Table 6–3). Perhaps more importantly, the nation's leading state universities can challenge the best private institutions in academic excellence. The University of California at Berkeley and the University of Michigan are deservedly ranked with Harvard, Yale, Princeton, Stanford, and Chicago.

Federal Aid.   Federal aid to colleges and universities has come in a variety of forms. Yet overall the federal share of higher education remains under 10 percent. State governments carry the major burden of higher education in America through their support of state colleges and universities.

Historically, the Morrill Act of 1862 provided the groundwork for federal assistance to higher education. In 1890 Congress activated several federal grants to support the operations of the land-grant colleges, and this aid, although very modest, continues to the present. The GI bills following World War II and the Korean War (enacted in 1944 and 1952, respectively) were not, strictly speaking, aid-to-education bills but rather a form of assistance to veterans to help them adjust to civilian life. Nevertheless, these bills had a great impact on higher education because of the millions of veterans who were able to enroll in college. Congress continues to provide educational benefits to veterans but at reduced levels from the wartime GI bills. The National Defense Education Act of 1958 also affected higher education by assisting students, particularly in science, mathematics, and modern foreign languages.

Today, the federal government directly assists many colleges and universities through grants and loans for construction and improvement of facilities; and it sup-

TABLE 6-3   Higher Education in America

	1970	1980	1990	1994
Institutions				
Four-year colleges and universities	1,665	1,957	2,141	2,190
Two-year colleges	891	1,274	1,418	1,442
Faculty (thousands)	573	846	824	825
Enrollment (thousands)				
Total	8,581	12,097	13,457	14,305
Four-year colleges and universities	6,290	7,571	8,374	8,739
Two-year colleges	1,630	4,526	5,083	5,566
Public	5,800	9,457	10,515	11,189
Private	2,120	2,640	2,942	3,116
Graduate	1,031	1,343	1,518	1,688
Undergraduate	7,376	10,475	11,666	12,329

Source: *Statistical Abstract of the United States 1996*, p. 183.

ports the U.S. Military Academy (West Point), U.S. Naval Academy (Annapolis), U.S. Air Force Academy (Colorado Springs), U.S. Coast Guard Academy, U.S. Merchant Marine Academy, Gallaudet College, and Howard University.

Student Assistance.   The principal source of federal aid for higher education comes to colleges and universities from various forms of student assistance. Basic Educational Opportunity Grants (commonly called Pell Grants for their chief sponsor, U.S. Senator Claiborne Pell) provide college students in good standing with grants based on what their families could be expected to pay. A guaranteed student loan program (Stafford Loans) encourages private banks to make loans to college students by guaranteeing federal repayment if the students default. Many of these loans are now made directly to students by the federal government through colleges and universities, eliminating the middle role of banks. The average loan is about $3,000. Repayment usually does not begin until after the student graduates or leaves college. A Perkins Loan program extends this guarantee to students from very low-income families. A Supplemental Educational Opportunity Grant program allows students to borrow from the financial aid offices of their own universities. Finally, the College Work-Study program uses federal funds to allow colleges and universities to employ students part time while they go to school.

Most of these federal subsidies go to middle-class students and their families. These programs are politically popular, although no administration can provide as much funding for them as students demand. The default rate is approaching 15 percent of all loans, a figure that would quickly bankrupt the nation's private credit industry. (The foreclosure rate on home mortgages is about 1 percent.) The U.S. Department of Education has been slow to find a remedy for these defaults.

The Clinton administration initiated a $1,500 income tax credit applicable to the cost of the first two years of college. The amount is roughly the cost of tuition at a community college. (Initially Clinton proposed that students receiving the credit be required to maintain a B average, but the prospect of grade inflation by professors pressured to keep students financially afloat, together with the prospect of the Internal Revenue Service monitoring grades, defeated this provision.) President Clinton argued that the tuition tax credit would offer middle-class family tax relief and encourage education. Opponents argued that the proposal would encourage colleges to raise tuition thus offsetting the aid, and that the lost federal revenues would be better spent by increasing Pell Grants, student loans, and work-study opportunities.

Federal Research Support.   Federal support for scientific research has also had an important impact on higher education. In 1950 Congress established the National Science Foundation (NSF) to promote scientific research and education. The NSF has provided fellowships for graduate education in the sciences, and supported many specific scientific research projects, and supported the construction and maintenance of scientific centers. In 1965 Congress established a National Endowment for the Arts and a National Endowment for the Humanities but funded these fields at only a tiny fraction of the amount given to NSF. In addition to NSF, many other federal agencies have granted research contracts to universities for specific projects. Thus, with federal support, research has become a very big item in university life.

GROUPS IN HIGHER EDUCATION

There are many influential groups in public higher education—aside from the governors and legislators who must vote the funds each year.

Trustees.   First, there are the boards of trustees (often called regents) that govern public colleges and universities. Their authority varies from state to state, but in nearly every state they are expected not only to set broad policy directions in higher education but also to insulate higher education from direct political involvement of governors and legislators. Prominent citizens who are appointed to these boards are expected to champion higher education with the public and the legislature.

Presidents.   Another key group in higher education is made up of university and college presidents and their top administrative assistants. Generally, university presidents are the chief spokespersons for higher education, and they must convince the public, the regents, the governor, and the legislature of the value of state colleges and universities. The president's crucial role is to maintain support for higher education in the state; he or she frequently delegates administrative responsibilities for the internal operation of the university to the vice presidents and deans. Support for higher education among the public and its representatives can be affected by a broad spectrum of university activities, some of which are not directly related to the pursuit of knowledge. A winning football team can stimulate legislative enthusiasm and gain appropriations for a new classroom building. University service-oriented research—developing new crops or feeds, assessing the state's mineral resources, advising state and local government agencies on administrative problems, analyzing the state economy, advising local school authorities, and so forth—may help to convince the public of the practical benefits of knowledge. University faculties may be interested in advanced research and the education of future Ph.D.s, but legislators and their constituents are more interested in the quality and effectiveness of undergraduate teaching.

Faculty.   The faculties of the nation's 3,500 colleges and universities traditionally identified themselves as professionals with strong attachments to their institutions. The historic pattern of college and university governance included faculty participation in policymaking—not only academic requirements but also budgeting, personnel, building programs, and so forth. But governance by faculty committee has proven cumbersome, unwieldy, and time-consuming in an era of large-scale enrollments, multimillion-dollar budgets, and increases in the size and complexity of academic administration. Increasingly, concepts of public accountability, academic management, cost control, and centralized budgeting and purchasing have transferred power in colleges and universities from faculties to professional academic administrators.

Unions.   The traditional organization of faculties has been the American Association of University Professors (AAUP); historically, this group confined itself to publishing data on salaries and officially censuring colleges or universities that violate longstanding notions of academic freedom or tenure. (Tenure is the tradition by which a faculty member who has demonstrated his or her competence by service in a college or university position for three to seven years cannot thereafter be dismissed except for "cause"—serious infraction of established rules or dereliction of duty, to be proved in an open hearing.) In recent years, the American Federation of Teachers (AFT) succeeded in convincing some faculty members that traditional patterns of individual bargaining over salaries, teaching load, and working conditions in colleges and universities should be replaced by collective bargaining in the manner of unionized labor. The growth of the AFT has spurred the AAUP on many campuses to assume a more militant attitude on behalf of faculty interests. The AAUP remains the largest faculty organization in the nation, but most of the nation's faculties are not affiliated with either the AAUP or the AFT.

Students.   The nation's 15 million students are the most numerous yet least influential of the groups directly involved in higher education. Students can be compared to other consumer groups in society, which are generally less well organized than the groups that provide goods and services. American student political activism has been sporadic and generally directed toward broad national issues. Most students view their condition in life as a short-term one; organizing for effective group action requires a commitment of time and energy that most students are unwilling to subtract from their studies and social life. Nonetheless, students' complaints are often filtered through parents to state legislators or university officials.

READING, WRITING, AND RELIGION

The First Amendment of the Constitution of the United States contains two important guarantees of religious freedom: (1) "Congress shall make no law respecting an establishment of religion . . ." and (2) "or prohibiting the free exercise thereof." The due process clause of the Fourteenth Amendment made these guarantees of religious liberty applicable to the states and their subdivisions as well as to Congress.

"Free Exercise."   Most of the debate over religion in the public schools centers on the "no establishment" clause of the First Amendment rather than the "free exercise" clause. However, it was respect for the "free exercise" clause that caused the Supreme Court in 1925 to declare unconstitutional an attempt by a state to prohibit private and parochial schools and to force all children to attend public schools. In the words of the Supreme Court, "The fundamental theory of liberty upon which all governments in this Union repose excludes any general power of the state to standardize its children by forcing them to accept instruction from public teachers

only. The child is not the mere creature of the state."[9] It is this decision that protects the entire structure of private religious schools in this nation.

"No Establishment."   A great deal of religious conflict in America has centered on the meaning of the "no establishment" clause, and the public schools have been the principal scene of this conflict. One interpretation of the clause holds that it does not prevent the government from aiding religious schools or encouraging religious beliefs in the public schools as long as it does not discriminate against any particular religion. Another interpretation is that the clause creates a "wall of separation" between church and state in America to prevent the government from directly aiding religious schools or encouraging religious beliefs in any way.

Government Aid to Church-related Schools.   The question of how much government aid can go to church schools and for what purposes is still largely unresolved. Proponents of public aid for church schools argue that these schools render a valuable public service by instructing millions of children who would have to be instructed by the state, at great expense, if the church schools were to close. There seem to be many precedents for public support of religious institutions: church property has always been exempt from taxation, church contributions are deductible from federal income taxes, federal funds have been appropriated for the construction of hospitals operated by religious organizations, chaplains are provided in the armed forces as well as in Congress, veterans' programs permit veterans to use their educational subsidies to finance college educations at church-related universities, and so on.

Opponents of aid to church schools argue that free public schools are available to the parents of all children regardless of religious denomination. If religious parents are not content with the type of school that the state provides, they should expect to pay for the operation of religious schools. The state is under no obligation to finance their religious preferences. Opponents also argue that it is unfair to compel taxpayers to support religion directly or indirectly. The diversion of any substantial amount of public funds to church schools would weaken the public school system. The public schools bring together children of different religious backgrounds and by so doing supposedly encourage tolerance and understanding. In contrast, church-related schools segregate children of different backgrounds, and it is not in the public interest to encourage such segregation. And so the dispute continues.

The "Wall of Separation."   Those favoring government aid to church-related schools frequently refer to the language found in several cases decided by the Supreme Court, which appears to support the idea that government can *in a limited fashion* support the activities of church-related schools.[10] In *Everson* v. *Board of Education* (1947), the Supreme Court upheld bus transportation for parochial school children at public expense on the grounds that the "wall of separation between church and state does not prohibit the state from adopting a general program which helps *all* children." Interestingly in this case, even though the Court permitted the expenditure of public funds to assist children going to and from parochial schools, it voiced the opinion that the "no establishment" clause of the First Amendment should constitute a "wall of separation" between church and state. In the words of the Court,

> Neither a state nor the federal government can set up a church. Neither can pass laws which aid one religion, aid all religions, or prefer one religion over another. Neither can force nor influence a person to go to or to remain away from church against his will, or force him to profess a belief or disbelief in any religion. No person can be punished for entertaining or professing religious beliefs or disbeliefs, for church attendance or nonattendance. No tax in any amount, large or small, can be levied to support any religious activities or institutions, whatever they may be called, or whatever form they may adopt to teach or practice religion. Neither a state nor the federal government can, openly or secretly, participate in the affairs of any religious organizations or groups, and vice versa.[11]

So the *Everson* case can be cited by those interests that support the allocation of public funds for assistance to children in parochial schools, as well as those interests that oppose any public support, direct or indirect, of religion.

Avoiding "Excessive Entanglement."   One of the most important Supreme Court decisions in the history of church-state relations in America came in 1971 in the case of *Lemon* v. *Kurtzman*.[12] The Supreme Court held that it was unconstitutional for a state (Pennsylvania) to pay the costs of teachers' salaries or instructional materials in parochial schools. The Court acknowledged that it had previously approved the provision of state textbooks and bus transportation directly to parochial school children. But it held that state payments to parochial schools involved "excessive entanglement between government and religion" and violated both the "no establishment" and "free exercise" clauses of the First Amendment. State payments to religious schools, the Court said, would require excessive government controls and surveillance to ensure that funds were used only for secular instruction. Moreover, the Court expressed the fear that state aid to parochial schools would create "political divisions along religious lines . . . one of the principal evils against which the First Amendment was intended to protect." However, in *Roemer* v. *Maryland* (1976) the Court upheld general public grants of money to church-related colleges: "Religious institutions need not be quarantined from public benefits which are neutrally available to all."[13]

Prayer in Public Schools.   Religious conflict also focuses on the question of prayer and Bible-reading ceremonies in public schools. A few years ago the practice of opening the school day with such ceremonies was widespread in American public schools. Usually the prayer was a Protestant rendition of the Lord's Prayer and the reading was from the King James version of the Bible. To avoid the denominational aspects of the ceremonies, the New York State Board of Regents substituted a nondenominational prayer, which it required to be said aloud in each class in the presence of a teacher at the beginning of each school day: "Almighty God, we acknowledge our dependence upon Thee, and we beg Thy blessings upon us, our parents, our teachers, and our country."

New York argued that this prayer did not violate the "no establishment" clause because it was denominationally neutral and because students' participation was voluntary. However, in *Engle* v. *Vitale* (1962), the Supreme Court stated that "the constitutional prohibition against laws respecting an establishment of a religion must at least mean in this country it is no part of the business of government to compose official prayers for any group of the American people to recite as part of a religious program carried on by government." The Court pointed out that making prayer voluntary did not free it from the prohibitions of the "no establishment" clause; that clause prevented the establishment of a religious ceremony by a government agency, regardless of whether the ceremony was voluntary or not:

> Neither the fact that the prayer may be denominationally neutral, nor the fact that its observance on the part of the students is voluntary can serve to free it from the limitations of the establishment clause, as it might from the free exercise clause, of the First Amendment, both of which are operative against the states by virtue of the Fourteenth Amendment. . . . The establishment clause, unlike the free exercise clause, does not depend on any showing of direct governmental compulsion and is violated by the enactment of laws which establish an official religion whether those laws operate directly to coerce nonobserving individuals or not.[14]

One year later, in the case of *Abbington Township* v. *Schempp*, the Court considered the constitutionality of Bible-reading ceremonies in the public schools.[15] Here again, even though the children were not required to participate, the Court found that Bible reading as an opening exercise in the schools was a religious ceremony. The Court went to some trouble in its opinion to point out that it was not "throwing the Bible out of the schools," for it specifically stated that the study of the Bible or of religion, when presented as part of a secular program of education, did not violate the First Amendment, but religious *ceremonies* involving Bible reading or prayer, established by a state or school district, did so.

State efforts to encourage "voluntary prayer" in public schools have also been struck down by the Supreme Court as unconstitutional. When the state of Alabama authorized a period of silence for "meditation or voluntary prayer" in public schools, the Court ruled that this was an "establishment of religion." The Court said that the law had no secular purpose, that it conveyed "a message of state endorsement and promotion of prayer," and that its real intent was to encourage prayer in public schools.[16] In a stinging dissenting opinion, Chief Justice Warren Burger noted that the Supreme Court itself opened its session with a prayer, that both houses of Congress opened every session with prayers led by official chaplains paid by the government. "To suggest that a moment of silence statute that includes the word *prayer* unconstitutionally endorses religion, manifests not neutrality but hostility toward religion."

SUMMARY

Let us summarize educational policy issues with particular reference to group conflicts involved:

1. American education reflects all of the conflicting demands of society. Schools are expected to address themselves to virtually all of the nation's problems,

from racial conflict to drug abuse to highway accidents. They are also supposed to raise the verbal and mathematical performance levels of students to better equip the nation's workforce in a competitive global economy. Various interests give different priorities to these diverse and sometimes conflicting goals.

2. In recent years, citizen groups, parents, taxpayers, and employers have inspired a back-to-basics movement in the schools, emphasizing reading, writing, and mathematical performance and calling for frequent testing of students' skills and the improvement of teachers' competency. Professional educators—school administrators, state education officials, and teachers' unions—have tended to resist test-oriented reforms, emphasizing instead the education of the whole child.

3. Conflict between citizens and professional educators is reflected in arguments over "professionalism" versus "responsiveness" in public schools. Parents, taxpayers, and locally elected school board members tend to emphasize responsiveness to citizens' demands; school superintendents and state education agencies tend to emphasize professional administration of the schools. Teachers' unions, notably state and local chapters of the NEA and AFT, represent still another group interest in education—organized teachers.

4. Professional educational groups and teachers' unions have long lobbied in Washington for increased federal financing of education. Federal aid to education grew with the Elementary and Secondary Education Act of 1965, but the federal share of educational spending never exceeded 10 percent. State and local governments continue to bear the major burden of educational finance. The creation of a cabinet-level Department of Education in 1977 also reflected the influence of professional educators.

5. There is little direct evidence that increased funding for schools improves the educational performance of students. Citizen groups and independent study commissions, as well as the Reagan and Bush administrations, emphasized reforms in education rather than increased federal spending. President Clinton has supported national testing of schoolchildren (generally opposed by professional educators) as well as increased federal spending on education (universally supported by professional educators).

6. Current reforms in education center on choice plans. Choice would empower parents and end the monopoly of public school administrators. But plans that allow parents to choose private over public schools threaten America's traditional reliance on public education. Choice *within* public school systems is somewhat less controversial, and various states are experimenting with charter and magnet schools.

7. Public higher education in the states involves many diverse groups—governors, legislators, regents, college and university presidents, and faculties. State governments, through their support of state colleges and universities, bear the major burden of higher education in the United States. Federal support for research, plus various student loan programs, are an important contribution to higher education. Yet federal support amounts to less than 10 percent of total higher education spending.

8. Religious groups, private school interests, and public school defenders frequently battle over the place of religion in education. The U.S. Supreme Court has become the referee in the group struggle over religion and education. The Court must interpret the meaning of the "no establishment" clause of the First Amendment

of the Constitution as it affects government aid to church-related schools and prayer in the public schools.

NOTES

1. National Commission on Excellence in Education, *A Nation at Risk* (Washington, DC: U.S. Government Printing Office, 1983).
2. See James S. Coleman, Thomas Hoffer, and Sally Kilgore, *High School Achievement* (New York: Basic Books, 1982); John E. Chubb and Terry M. Moe, *Politics, Markets, and America's Schools* (Washington, DC: Brookings Institution, 1990); Chester E. Finn, Jr., *We Must Take Charge: Our Schools and Our Future* (New York: Free Press, 1991).
3. James S. Coleman and Thomas Hoffer, *Public and Private High Schools* (New York: Basic Books, 1987).
4. See John E. Chubb and Terry M. Moe, "Politics, Markets, and the Organization of Schools," *American Political Science Review* 82 (December 1988), 1065–1087.
5. Bill Clinton and Al Gore, *Putting People First* (New York: Times Books, 1992), p. 86.
6. *Statistical Abstract of the United States 1996.*
7. *Rodriquez* v. *San Antonio Independent School District,* 411 U.S. 1 (1973).
8. *Serrano* v. *Priest,* 5 Cal. 584 (1971).
9. *Pierce* v. *The Society of Sisters,* 268 U.S. 510 (1925).
10. *Cochran* v. *Board of Education,* 281 U.S. 370 (1930).
11. *Everson* v. *Board of Education,* 330 U.S. 1 (1947).
12. *Lemon* v. *Kurtzman,* 403 U.S. 602 (1971).
13. *Roemer* v. *Maryland,* 415 U.S. 382 (1976).
14. *Engle* v. *Vitale,* 370 U.S. 421 (1962).
15. *Abbington Township* v. *Schempp,* 374 203 (1963).
16. *Wallace* v. *Jaffree,* June 4, 1985.

BIBLIOGRAPHY

Bloom, Allan D. *The Closing of the American Mind.* New York: Simon & Schuster, 1987.

Chubb, John E., and Terry M. Moe. *Politics, Markets, and America's Schools.* Washington, DC: Brookings Institution, 1990.

Coleman, James S., and Thomas Hoffer. *Public and Private High Schools.* New York: Basic Books, 1987.

Kozol, Jonathan. *Savage Inequalities.* New York: Crown, 1991.

Marshall, Ray, and Marc Tucker. *Thinking for a Living: Education and the Wealth of Nations.* New York: Basic Books, 1992.

National Commission on Excellence in Education. *A Nation at Risk.* Washington, DC: U.S. Government Printing Office, 1983.

7

ENVIRONMENTAL POLICY
Externalities and Interests

A truck empties trash at a landfill. (Draper Aden Associates)

PUBLIC CHOICE AND THE ENVIRONMENT

All human activity produces waste. Environmentalists, the mass media, politicians, and bureaucrats may portray pollution as a "moral evil," but in fact it is a cost of production. We can no more "stop polluting" than we can halt our natural body functions. As soon as we come to understand that we cannot outlaw pollution and come to see pollution as a cost of human activity, we can begin to devise creative environmental policies.

Environmental Externalities. Public choice theory views pollution as a "problem" when it is not a cost to its producer—that is, when producers can ignore the costs of their pollution and shift them onto others or society in general. An "externality" occurs when one individual, firm, or government undertakes an activity that imposes unwanted costs on others. A manufacturing firm or local government that discharges waste into a river shifts its own costs to individuals, firms, or local governments downstream, who must forego using the river for recreation and water supply or else undertake the costs of cleaning it up themselves. A coal-burning electricity-generating plant that discharges waste into the air shifts its costs to others, who must endure irritating smog. By shifting these costs to others, polluting firms lower their production costs, which allows them to lower their prices to customers and/or increase their own profits. Polluting governments have lower costs of disposing their community's waste, which allows them to lower taxes for their own citizens. As long as these costs of production can be shifted to others, polluting individuals, firms, and governments have no incentive to minimize waste or develop alternative techniques of production. And because the prices charged by polluting firms and governments are lower than they would otherwise be, people are encouraged to buy more of their goods and services, thus adding even more to pollution.

Costs of Regulation. Environmental policies are costly. These costs are often ignored when environmental regulations are considered. Direct spending by business and government for pollution abatement and control has grown rapidly over recent years (see Table 7–1) and today exceeds $100 billion per year. Yet governments themselves—federal, state, and local governments combined—pay less than one-quarter of the environmental bill. Businesses and consumers pay over three-quarters of the environmental bill. Governments can shift the costs of their policies onto private individuals and firms by enacting regulations requiring pollution control. A government's own budget is unaffected by these regulations, but the costs are

TABLE 7–1   Spending for Pollution Abatement and Control

	1975	1980	1993
Total ($ billions)	$28.4	$51.5	109.0
Percent government	24.3	21.8	24.7

Source: *Statistical Abstract of the United States 1996*, p. 239.

paid by society. Indeed, as environmental costs multiply for American businesses, the costs of their products rise in world markets. Unless other nations impose similar costs on their businesses, U.S. firms face a competitive disadvantage. In other words, pollution is a global issue, not only because air and water pollution flows across national boundaries, but also because polluting nations can "free-ride" on the environmental safeguards of other nations.

Benefits in Relation to Costs.   Public choice theory requires that environmental policies be evaluated in terms of their net benefits to society; that is, the costs of environmental policies should not exceed their benefits to society. It is much less costly to reduce the first 50 to 75 percent of any environmental pollutant or hazard than to eliminate all (100 percent) of it (see Figure 7–1). As any pollutant or hazard is reduced, the cost of further reductions rises and the net benefits to society of additional reductions decline. As the limit of zero pollution or zero environmental risk is approached, additional benefits are minuscule but additional costs are astronomical. Ignoring these economic realities simply wastes the resources of society, lowers our standard of living, and in the long run impairs our ability to deal effectively with any societal problem, including environmental protection.

Risk Assessment.   Life is full of risks. Environmental policy responds to popularly perceived risks—threats to life or health arising from air or water pollution, solid and hazardous wastes, toxic substances, nuclear energy, pesticides, and so on. The complete elimination of risk (zero risk) is impossible, and efforts to approach zero risk impose enormous costs on society. Any rational approach to risk policy recognizes that some level of risk will always accompany human activity; and that

FIGURE 7–1   Cost-Benefit Ratio in Environmental Protection

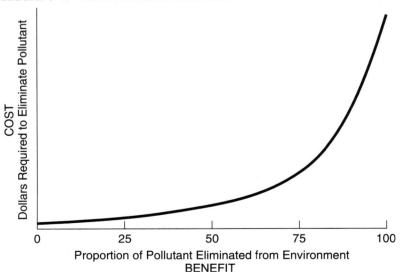

governments should compare the relative costs of dealing with different types and levels of risk. Policymakers should assess risks against a common benchmark, such as the cost per life saved, and then choose to devote societal resources to efforts likely to achieve maximum risk reduction at minimum cost (see Table 7–2).

But such a rational approach—sometimes referred to as comparative risk assessment—is rare in environmental policymaking. One problem is the scientific uncertainty of risk calculations. Many risk calculations are made from animal experimentation, using extraordinarily heavy doses or exposures to various substances, and then extrapolating to the human condition. These calculations almost always *over*estimate risks to humans. When publicized, this research produces a "carcinogen of the month." But perhaps the most serious problem in comparative risk assessment is the divergence between scientific calculations of risk and popular perceptions of risk. Well-publicized yet minimal risks attract the attention of policymakers and drive environmental policy, while more serious unpublicized risks are ignored. Indeed, even the U.S. Environmental Protection Agency (EPA) has acknowledged that its programs' priorities are largely *un*related to rankings of risk.[1] Finally, many environmentalists argue that comparative risk assessment is morally unacceptable. They contend that any level of risk which can be reduced should be, regardless of cost, because no price can be placed on a human life. A related argument is that no price can be placed on the preservation of trees, plants, animals, forests, open spaces, scenic views, and so forth.

Bureaucratic Incentives.   Bureaucrats in various agencies, including the EPA, have many incentives to overestimate risks and impose excessive regulatory costs on society. Bureaucrats know that they will face intense criticism for failing to anticipate a risk that actually results in death—whether from a new toxic substance, a radiation leak, or an airframe design—but they face only minor grumbling about the

TABLE 7–2   Simple Risk Assessment Ratios

Deaths per Million People per Year		Cost of Avoiding One Death (in Millions of 1990 Dollars)	
Airline crash (1 trip)	1	Aircraft cabin fire protection	0.1
Drunk driving	50	Seatbelts on cars	0.1
Serving as police officer	220	Seatbelts on buses	0.7
Skydiving	2,000	Collision avoidance systems on aircraft	1.5
Cigarette smoking (one pack per day)	3,000	Eliminating asbestos from buildings	111.0
		Compliance with EPA regulation on dichloropropane in drinking water	653
		Compliance with EPA regulation on atrazine in drinking water	92,069

Source: U.S. Office of Management and Budget, reprinted in *Governing,* April, 1994, p. 63.

costs of regulations dealing with the risk. When in doubt, and there is always some doubt about scientific evidence, bureaucrats naturally turn toward regulation. EPA Director Carol Browner observed that "There are just times when science doesn't give up the answer" and therefore EPA should proceed to regulate a substance until it is proved to be safe.[2]

Command and Control.   Traditionally, environmental policy has relied on centralized and uniform controls—administrative or legislative rules and regulations that require the use of pollution control devices or that apply rigid emission standards to specified pollution sites and sources. But this "command and control" approach has failed to create the necessary incentives for individuals, private firms, and local governments to clean up the environment. First, the bureaucrats or legislators who impose specific regulations lack detailed knowledge of production processes and alternative methods of pollution abatement. Moreover, individuals, firms, or local governments that do succeed in reducing pollution increase their risk of being targeted by the regulators for even tougher (and much more costly) emission standards. This creates a disincentive to innovate in pollution control—a disincentive that magnifies inefficiencies over time. Finally, specific regulations give polluters an incentive to meet the requirements of the law or regulation but not actually to reduce pollution.

Market Incentives.   When government action is necessary to curb environmental externalities, public choice theorists argue that it is better to establish *private economic incentives* to reduce pollution than to rely on centralized, uniform, and specific regulations. Market-based approaches that provide flexibility, encourage innovation, and support economic growth are more cost effective in achieving environmental goals than regulations devised in Washington. These approaches may involve setting overall pollution limits, while permitting industries, utilities, and state and local governments to determine how to meet these limits. They may also involve permitting specific pollution sources—factories, refineries, utilities, governments—to trade allowable emissions among themselves to achieve the most efficient use of the emissions. Yet to date environmental policy in the United States relies principally on centralized command and control, with the EPA accumulating vast power over virtually every segment of economic activity in the nation.

ENVIRONMENTAL EXTERNALITIES

The air and water in the United States are far cleaner today than in previous decades. This is true despite growth in population and even greater growth in waste products. Nonetheless, genuine concern for environmental externalities centers on the disposal of solid waste (especially hazardous wastes), water pollution, and air pollution.

TABLE 7-3   Growth in Solid Wastes

	1960	1970	1980	1985	1990	1995
Gross waste (millions of tons)	87.50	120.50	142.60	164.40	195.70	209.10
Waste per person per day (lbs)	2.65	3.22	3.43	3.77	4.30	4.40

Source: *Statistical Abstract of the United States 1996*, p. 237.

Solid Waste Disposal

Every American produces about 4.4 pounds of solid waste per day (see Table 7–3). The annual load of waste dumped on the environment includes 48 billion cans, 26 billion bottles and jars, 2 billion disposable razors, 16 billion disposable diapers, and 4 million automobiles and trucks. The nation spends billions of dollars annually on hauling all this away from homes and businesses. Over time, the types of solid wastes disposed of as municipal garbage have changed, with plastic and paper replacing metal in the municipal garbage pail.

There are essentially three methods of disposing of solid wastes—landfills, incineration, and recycling. Modern landfills have nearly everywhere replaced town dumps. Landfills are usually lined with clay so that potentially toxic wastes do not seep into the water system. Even so, hazardous wastes are separated from those that are not hazardous and handled separately. Given a reasonable site, there is nothing especially wrong with a landfill that contains no hazardous wastes. However, landfill sites need to meet strict standards and people do not want landfills near their residences. These conditions combine to make it difficult to develop new landfills. Some communities today resort to paying to use another community's landfill—often hundreds of miles from where the garbage originated—but no one thinks of this as a long-term solution.

Contrary to popular rhetoric, there is no "landfill crisis"; the nation is not "running out of land." However, both government agencies and private waste disposal firms are being stymied by the powerful, organized NIMBYs ("not in my back yard"). Landfill sites are plentiful but local opposition is always strong. Timid politicians cannot confront the NIMBYs, so they end up overusing old landfills or trying to ship their garbage elsewhere.

Another alternative is to burn the garbage. Modern incinerators are special plants, usually equipped with machinery to separate the garbage into different types, with scrubbers to reduce air pollution from the burning and often with electrical generators powered by heat from the garbage fire. Garbage is put through a shredder to promote even burning; metal is separated out by magnets, and the garbage is passed over screens that separate it further. At this point about half the garbage has been removed and hauled to a landfill. The remaining garbage is shredded still further into what is called fluff, or perhaps it is compressed into pellets or briquets. This material is then burned, usually at another site and perhaps together with coal, to produce electricity. The ash is handled by the public utility as it would handle any other ash, which often means selling it to towns to use on roads. One problem with this method is the substances emitted from the chimney of the incinerator or the utility that is burning the garbage. Another problem: because the garbage separated during the screening phase still has to be disposed of, the need for landfill sites is only reduced, not eliminated.

A third method of reducing the amount of solid waste is recycling. Recycling is the conversion of wastes into useful products. Most of the time, waste cannot be recycled into the same product it was originally but rather into some other form. Newspapers are recycled into cardboard, insulation, animal bedding, and cat litter, but in an exception to the general rule, some is recycled into newsprint.

Overall, about 24 percent of all solid waste in the United States is recovered for reuse.[3] This is a notable improvement over the mere 7 percent that was recycled 25 years ago. Some materials lend themselves fairly well to recycling (e.g., 38 percent of aluminum cans, 35 percent of paper products), but other materials do not (e.g., 5 percent of plastics). At present there is more material available for recycling than plants can effectively use; millions of tons of recycled newspapers are either piled up as excess inventory in paper mills or dumped or burned. Nonetheless, recycling does have a modest effect in reducing the load on incinerators and landfills.

Hazardous Waste

Hazardous wastes are those that pose a significant threat to public health or the environment because of their "quantity, concentration, or physical, chemical, or infectious characteristics."[4] The Resource Conservation and Recovery Act of 1976 gave the EPA the authority to determine which substances are hazardous, and the EPA has so classified several hundred substances. Releases of more than a specified amount must be reported to the National Response Center. Substances are considered hazardous if they easily catch fire, are corrosive, or react easily with other chemicals. Many substances are declared toxic by the EPA because massive daily doses administered to laboratory animals cause cancers to develop. Toxic chemical releases must also be reported annually, and extremely hazardous substances require emergency planning. Thus far the United States has avoided any toxic releases comparable to the accident in Bhopal, India, which killed almost 3,000 people. However, smaller toxic releases have caused death and injury.

Nuclear wastes create special problems. These are the wastes from nuclear fission reactors and nuclear weapons plants. Some have been in existence for 50 years. Because the waste is radioactive and some of it stays radioactive for thousands of years, it has proven very difficult to dispose of. Current plans to store some wastes in deep, stable, underground sites have run into local opposition. Most nuclear waste in the United States is stored at the site where it was generated, pending some long-term plan for handling it.

Hazardous wastes from old sites also constitute an environmental problem. These wastes need to be moved to more secure landfills. Otherwise, they can affect the health of people living near the waste site, often by seeping into the water supply. The EPA is committed to cleaning up such sites under the Superfund laws of 1980 and 1986. As a first step, they have developed a National Priorities List of sites that need attention, based on a hazard ranking system. The EPA has listed more than 1,200 hazardous waste sites, but only about 40 (3 percent) have undergone full cleanup to date.

Water Pollution

Debris and sludge, organic wastes, and chemical effluents are the three major types of water pollutants. These pollutants come from (1) domestic sewage, (2) industrial waste, (3) agricultural runoff of fertilizers and pesticides, and (4) "natural" processes, including silt deposits and sedimentation, which may be increased by nearby construction. A common standard for measuring water pollution is biochemical oxygen demand (BOD), which identifies the amount of oxygen consumed by wastes. This measure, however, does not consider chemical substances that may be toxic to humans or fish. It is estimated that domestic sewage accounts for 30 percent of BOD, and industrial and agricultural wastes for 70 percent.

Primary sewage treatment—which uses screens and settling chambers, where filth falls out of the water as sludge—is fairly common. Secondary sewage treatment is designed to remove organic wastes, usually by trickling water through a bed of rocks 3 to 10 feet deep, where bacteria consume the organic matter. Remaining germs are killed by chlorination. Tertiary sewage treatment uses mechanical and chemical filtration processes to remove almost all contaminants from water. Many northeastern cities, including New York, dump sewage sludge into the ocean after only primary treatment or no treatment at all. Although federal law prohibits dumping raw sewage into the ocean, it has proven difficult to secure compliance from coastal cities. Federal water pollution abatement goals call for the establishment of secondary treatment in all American communities. In most industrial plants, tertiary treatment ultimately will be required to deal with the flow of chemical pollutants. But tertiary treatment is expensive; it costs two or three times as much to build and operate a tertiary sewage treatment plant as it does a secondary plant. Even today, however, one-third of all Americans live in communities where their sewage gets nothing but primary treatment.

Phosphates are major water pollutants that overstimulate plant life in water, which in turn kills fish. Phosphates run off from fertilized farm land. Farming is the major source of water pollution in the United States.

Waterfronts and seashores are natural resources. The growing numbers of waterfront homes, amusement centers, marinas, and pleasure boats are altering the environment of the nation's coastal areas. Marshes and estuaries at the water's edge are essential to the production of seafood and shellfish, yet they are steadily shrinking with the growth of residential-commercial-industrial development. Oil spills are unsightly. Although pollution is much greater in Europe than in America, America's coastal areas still require protection. Federal law makes petroleum companies liable for the cleanup costs of oil spills and outlaws flushing of raw sewage from boat toilets. The *EXXON Valdez* oil spill in Alaska in 1989 focused attention on the environmental risks of transporting billions of barrels of foreign and domestic oil each year in the United States.

The federal government has provided financial assistance to states and cities to build sewage treatment plants ever since the 1930s. Efforts to establish national standards for water quality began in the 1960s and culminated in the Water Pollution Control Act of 1972. This act set "national goals" for elimination of all the discharge of *all* pollutants into navigable waters; it required industries and municipalities to install "the best available technology"; it gave the EPA authority to initiate legal actions against pollution caused by firms and governments; it increased federal funds available to municipalities for the construction of sewage treatment plants.

The EPA is authorized by the Safe Drinking Water Act of 1974 to set minimum standards for water quality throughout the nation. The EPA does not set a zero standard for fecal bacteria or phosphate or other pollutants; to do so would commit the nation to astronomical cost projections for "clean" water and would never be possible to attain anyway. The EPA has considerable power to raise or lower standards, and hence to increase or reduce costs.

Water quality in the United States has improved significantly over the last two decades (see Table 7–4). The problem, of course, is that removing *all* pollutants is neither cost effective nor possible. There is a law of diminishing returns at work in environmental efforts that tells us that removing the last 1 percent of pollution is more costly than removing the first 99 percent. Setting unrealistic standards for clean air and clean water is self-defeating.

Air Pollution

The air we breathe is about one-fifth oxygen and a little less than four-fifths nitrogen, with traces of other gases, water vapor, and the waste products we put into it. Most air pollution is caused by the gasoline-powered internal combustion engines of cars, trucks, and buses. Motor vehicles account for more than 56 percent of the total polluting material sent into the atmosphere every year (see Figure 7–2). The largest industrial polluters are petroleum refineries, smelters (aluminum, copper, lead, and zinc), and iron foundries. Electrical power plants also contribute to total air pollutants by burning coal or oil for electric power. Heating is also a major source of pollution; homes, apartments, and offices use coal, gas, and oil for heat. Another source of pollution is the incineration of garbage, trash, metal, glass, and other refuse by both governments and industries.

TABLE 7-4   Improvements in Water Quality

Pollutant (Standard)	1975	1980	1985	1990	1995
Fecal coliform bacteria (above 200 cells per 100 mL)	36	31	28	26	28
Dissolved oxygen (allow 5 mg per liter)	5	5	3	2	1
Phosphorus (above 1 mg per liter)	5	4	3	3	4
Lead (above 50 micrograms per liter)	NA	5	0	0	0

Figures are violations rates—the proportion of measures that violate the EPA standards.

Source: *Statistical Abstract of the United States 1996*, p. 233.

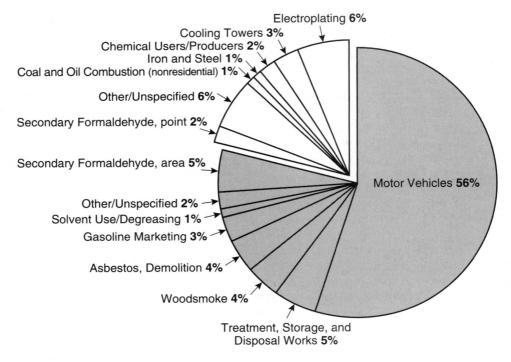

Electroplating **6%**
Cooling Towers **3%**
Chemical Users/Producers **2%**
Iron and Steel **1%**
Coal and Oil Combustion (nonresidential) **1%**

Other/Unspecified **6%**

Secondary Formaldehyde, point **2%**

Secondary Formaldehyde, area **5%**

Other/Unspecified **2%**
Solvent Use/Degreasing **1%**
Gasoline Marketing **3%**

Asbestos, Demolition **4%**

Woodsmoke **4%**

Treatment, Storage, and
Disposal Works **5%**

Motor Vehicles **56%**

(Does not add to 100% due to rounding)

☐ **Area Sources 80%**
Cars, homes, and businesses

☐ **Point Sources 20%**
Large industrial facilities

Source: Environmental Protection Agency.

FIGURE 7–2   Sources of Air Pollution

Air pollutants fall into two major types: particles and gases. The particles include ashes; soot; and lead, the unburnable additive in gasoline. Often the brilliant red sunsets we admire are caused by large particles in the air. Less obvious but more damaging are the gases: (1) sulfur dioxide, which in combination with moisture can form sulfuric acid; (2) hydrocarbons—any combination of hydrogen and carbon; (3) nitrogen oxide, which can combine with hydrocarbons and the sun's ultraviolet rays to form smog; and (4) carbon monoxide, which is produced when gasoline is burned.

It is difficult at the present time to assess the full impact of air pollution on health. We know that when the smog or pollution count rises in a particular city there are more deaths due to emphysema than would normally have been expected. In the streets of certain cities at certain hours of heavy traffic, carbon monoxide can deprive the body of oxygen; people exposed to it may exhibit drowsiness, headache, poor vision, impaired coordination, and reduced capacity to reason. Nitrogen oxide irritates the eyes, nose, throat, and respiratory system; it damages plants, buildings, and statues. Finally, urban residents have been found to be twice as likely to contract lung cancer as rural residents.

However, it is known that smoking is much more hazardous than the worst air pollution. As one expert testified, "If you want to pass all of these regulations because smog stinks, or because it burns your eyes, or because it blocks your view of the mountains, OK—fine. But if you are trying to pass all of these regulations because smog is a health hazard—forget it—because it is not."[5]

The air we breathe is significantly cleaner today than 25 years ago. All major air pollution emissions are declining (see Table 7–5). Federal clean air legislation (described later in this chapter) is generally credited with causing these improvements.

INTEREST GROUP EFFECTS

Americans live longer and healthier lives today than at any time in their country's history. Life expectancy at birth is now seventy-five years, up four full years since 1970. Concentrations of pesticides in human tissue have fallen 75 percent in those same years, and lead concentrations in the blood have fallen 40 percent. Cancer deaths are up slightly but not because of environmental hazards: The National Cancer Institute estimates that only 2 percent of all cancer deaths can be attributed to environmental sources. The primary causes of premature death are what they have always been: smoking, diets rich in fat and lean in fiber, lack of exercise, and alcohol abuse. Yet public opinion generally perceives the environment as increasingly contaminated and dangerous and this perception drives public policy.

Interest Group Economics. Organized environmental interests must recruit memberships and contributions (see Table 7–6). They must justify their activities by publicizing and dramatizing environmental threats. When Greenpeace boats disrupt a U.S. Navy exercise, they are attracting the publicity required for a successful direct

TABLE 7-5   Decline in Air Pollution Emissions

	1970	1980	1990	1995
Sulfur dioxides	31.2	25.9	22.4	21.1
Nitrogen dioxides	20.6	23.3	23.0	22.6
Carbon monoxide	128.1	115.6	100.6	98.0
Particulate matter	13.0	7.1	3.8	3.7
Lead	0.22	0.07	0.06	0.05

Figures are millions of metric tons.

Source: *Statistical Abstract of the United States 1996,* p. 234.

TABLE 7-6   The Environmentalists Ranked by Estimated Annual Budget

1. National Wildlife Federation	6. Natural Resources Defense Council
2. Greenpeace	7. Environmental Defense Fund
3. National Audubon Society	8. Defenders of Wildlife
4. Sierra Club	9. Friends of the Earth
5. Wilderness Society	10. Environmental Action

Source: *Congressional Quarterly Weekly Report,* January 20, 1990, p. 146.

mail fund-raising drive. The mass media, especially the television networks, welcome stories that capture and hold audiences' attention. Stories are chosen for their emotional impact, and threats to personal life and safety satisfy the need for drama in the news. Statistics that indicate negligible risks or scientific testimony that minimizes threats or presents ambiguous findings, do not make good news stories. Politicians wish to be perceived as acting aggressively to protect citizens from any risk, however minor. Politicians want to be seen as "clean" defenders of the pristine wilderness. And government bureaucrats understand that the greater the public fear of environmental threat, the easier it is to justify expanded powers and budgets.

Shaping Public Opinion.   Interest group activity and media coverage of environmental threats have succeeded in convincing most Americans that environment pollution is getting worse. Evidence that the nation's air and water are measurably cleaner in the 1990s than in the 1970s is ignored. Catastrophic predictions of impending environmental doom create a climate of opinion that precludes rational discussion of the benefits and costs of environmental policies. Opinion polls report that 74 percent of Americans agree with this statement: "Protecting the environment is so important that requirements and standards cannot be too high and continued environmental improvements must be made *regardless of cost.*"[6] If taken seriously, such an attitude would prevent either scientific or economic considerations from guiding policy. Environmentalism threatens to become a moral crusade that dismisses science and economics as irrelevant or even wicked. In such a climate of opinion, moral absolutism replaces rational public policy.

Serious and reliable scientific information on environmental questions is difficult to find on television. Scientists give poor interviews; they use technical language, cite statistics, speak of complexities and uncertainties, and seldom see issues as one-sided. In contrast, environmental activists simplify and dramatize issues and exaggerate environmental threats. The public itself appears to tolerate familiar and common risks to health and safety more easily than the unknown and unfamiliar risks of environmental contaminates. For example, individuals easily tolerate very great risks when they can choose to avoid them, such as skiing and mountain climbing, and risks that are familiar to them, such as smoking. But people appear unwilling to tolerate even minor risks, when they are involuntarily exposed to them, for example, nuclear radioactivity, and when the risks have long-delayed or unknown effects, for example, chemicals and insecticides.

Interest Group Politics.   Everyone is opposed to pollution. It is difficult publicly to oppose clean air or clean water laws—who wants to stand up for dirt? Thus the environmentalists begin with a psychological and political advantage: they are "clean" and their opponents are "dirty." The news media, Congress, and executive agencies can be moved to support environmental protection measures with little consideration of their costs—in job loss, price increases, unmet consumer demands, increased dependence on foreign sources of energy. Industry—notably the electric power companies, oil and gas companies, chemical companies, automakers, and coal companies—must fight a rearguard action, continually seeking delays, amendments, and adjustments in federal standards. They must endeavor to point out the increased costs to society of unreasonably high standards in environmental protection legislation. But industry is suspect; the environmentalists can charge that industry opposition to environmental protection is motivated by greed for higher profits. And the charge is partially true, although most of the cost of antipollution efforts is passed on to the consumer in the form of higher prices.

The environmentalists are generally upper-middle-class or upper-class individuals whose income and wealth are secure. Their aesthetic preferences for a no-growth, clean, unpolluted environment take precedence over jobs and income, which new industries can produce. Workers and small businesspeople whose jobs or income depend on energy production, oil refining, forestry, mining, smelting, or manufacturing are unlikely to be ardent environmentalists. But there is a psychological impulse in all of us to preserve scenic beauty, protect wildlife, and conserve natural resources. It is easy to perceive industry and technology as the villain, and "man against technology" has a humanistic appeal.

NIMBY Power.   Environmental groups have powerful allies in the nation's NIMBYs—local residents who feel inconvenienced or threatened by specific projects. Even people who otherwise recognize the general need for new commercial or industrial developments, highways, airports, power plants, pipelines, or waste disposal sites, nonetheless voice the protest "not in my back yard," earning them the NIMBY label. Although they may constitute only a small group in a community, they become very active participants in policymaking—meeting, organizing, petitioning, parading, and demonstrating. NIMBYs are frequently the most powerful interests opposing specific developmental projects and are found nearly everywhere. They frequently take up environmental interests, using environmental arguments to protect their own property investments.

Radical Environmentalism.   At the extreme fringe of the environmental movement one finds strong opposition to economic development, to scientific advancement, and even to humanity. According to the Club of Rome (a radical environmental organization), "The real enemy, then, is humanity itself."[7] The "green" movement is international, with well-organized interest groups and even political parties in western European nations. Its program to "Save the Planet" includes the deindustrialization of Western nations; reduction of the human population; elimination of all uses of fossil fuels, including automobiles; the elimination of nuclear power; an end to cattle raising, logging, land clearance, and so on; and the transfer of existing wealth from the industrialized nations to underdeveloped countries.[8]

SCIENCE VERSUS ENVIRONMENTALISM

A rational public choice approach to environmental issues requires careful evaluation of all of the scientific facts about environmental risks, so that they may be weighed against the costs of their reduction. But environmental interest groups must rally public opinion and pressure political officeholders to action. To do so, they are tempted to select some scientific facts and ignore others and to cite scientists who agree with their position (even when they may be a tiny minority in the scientific community) and ignore those who disagree or who say not enough research has been done to provide answers. To the scientific community, public opinion polls are useless; only evidence counts. To the environmental movement, public opinion polls are all-important.

Global Warming. Gloomy predictions about catastrophic warming of the Earth's surface have been issued by the media and environmental interest groups in support of massive new regulatory efforts. This global warming is theorized to be a result of emissions of carbon dioxide and other gases that trap the sun's heat in the atmosphere. As carbon dioxide increases in the atmosphere as a result of increased human activity, more heat is trapped. Deforestation contributes to increased carbon dioxide by removing trees, which absorb carbon dioxide and produce oxygen. The dire predictions of greenhouse effects include droughts and crop destruction, melting of the polar ice caps, and ocean flooding. These predictions have become widely believed; people now blame any heat wave on the "greenhouse effect." New environmental regulations and increased powers for the EPA are justified by reference to "global warming."

It is true, of course, that the Earth's atmosphere creates a greenhouse effect; if not, temperatures on the Earth's surface would be like those on the moon—unbearably cold (−270°F) at night and unbearably hot (+212°F) during the day. The greenhouse gases, including carbon dioxide, moderate the Earth's surface temperature. And it is true that carbon dioxide is increasing in the atmosphere, an increase of about 25 percent since the beginning of the Industrial Revolution in 1850. It is also true that various computer simulations of the effect of increased dioxides in the atmosphere have predicted future increases of 1 to 8 degrees in the average 57°F temperature on the Earth. But average temperatures on the Earth's surface have increased less than 0.5 degree since the Industrial Revolution over the past hundred years.[9] Ocean temperatures have remained constant since the first reasonably accurate measurement at the beginning of the twentieth century,[10] and sophisticated satellite measurement of global temperatures over the past 10 years fails to show any significant warming.[11] The last ice age, when average temperatures were 9 degrees cooler, ended 15,000 years ago; the Earth's temperature changes very, very slowly. Warming estimates by computer simulations are very unreliable; they range from 1 degree (not significant) to 8 degrees (significant only if it occurs rapidly).

Few scientists believe that greenhouse warming can be detected in normal climatic variations from year to year. (In the 1970s environmentalists seized on a modest worldwide temperature drop to warn of the threat of global *cooling*—"a new ice age must now stand alongside nuclear war as a likely source of wholesale death and misery for mankind."[12]) There is ample historical evidence of wide variations in temperature. When the Vikings discovered Greenland it was indeed green at that time, not covered with glacial ice as it is today. Science does not claim to know what caused the prehistoric ice ages or the Earth's subsequent warming, but we are certain that these periods were not due to industrialization or the burning of fossil fuels.

Carbon dioxide is produced from the respiration of all living things, as well as from decaying vegetation and burning of fossil fuels. Human activity accounts for about half of the production of carbon dioxide. Hydrocarbons also contribute to the greenhouse effect; these are produced by growing plants, especially evergreens (causing the blue haze of the Great Smoky Mountains), and are found in industrial and automobile emissions. Methane, another greenhouse gas, is produced by rotting vegetation and the flatulence of cows.

Whatever the merits of reducing fossil fuel emissions—such as those from auto exhaust, burning coal, electric energy plants—predictions of catastrophic warming of the earth are based more on speculation than reality. Nonetheless, popular belief in "global warming" strengthens the influence of environmental interests and bureaucrats calling for drastic restrictions on emissions.

The Rio Treaty to "Save the Planet."   Environmentalists argue that "drastic action" is required now to avert "catastrophic" global warming. Vice President Al Gore is a leading exponent of the view that governments cannot afford to wait until the scientific evidence demonstrates global warming, but rather governments must immediately impose a system of "global environmental regulations" in order to "save the planet."[13] Inasmuch as Third World nations are just beginning to industrialize, they pose the greatest threat of new sources of global pollution. But the industrialized nations are responsible for "undermining the Earth's life support system" (the United States is usually singled out as the primary culprit), and therefore they must compensate poorer nations in exchange for their pledge not to add to global pollution. The international environmental agenda includes massive transfers of wealth from industrialized nations to less developed countries.

The Rio Treaty incorporates these ideas. It is a product of the "Earth Summit," officially the United Nations Conference on Environment and Development held in Rio de Janeiro, Brazil, in 1992. It was attended by 178 nations as well as hundreds of environmental interest groups, officially sanctioned as "nongovernmental organizations." The conference produced a Global Climate Change Treaty, signed by President Bush and ratified by the U.S. Senate, which declares, among other things, that "lack of scientific certainty shall not be used as a reason for postponing cost-effective measures to prevent environmental degradation"! The statement is, of course, a contradiction: without scientific information, it is impossible to determine cost effectiveness. There was very little involvement of scientists at the Rio meeting. On the contrary, a group of 250 of the world's leading scientists, including 27 Nobel Prize winners, issued an appeal to world leaders in response to the Rio Treaty:

> We are worried, at the dawn of the twenty-first century, of the emergence of an irrational ideology, which is opposed to scientific and industrial progress and impedes economic and social development. . . . Humanity has always progressed by harnessing nature to its needs and not the reverse. . . . The greatest evils which stalk our Earth are ignorance and oppression, and not science, technology, and industry.[14]

Notwithstanding the great uncertainties surrounding "global warming," several recent United Nations–sponsored meetings have called for drastic actions to curtail carbon dioxide emission, including a legally binding treaty to force nations to keep emissions at 1990 levels beyond the year 2000.

Acid Rain.   All water has some acid content. Rainwater is normally slightly acid, as is the water in lakes and streams. Acidity is higher in some regions and bodies of water than in others. An increase in acidity can change the vegetation and wildlife of lakes and streams. Indeed, if acidity increased to the levels of residential swimming pools, most forms of animal life would be lost. The effect of nitric acid, which is found in most crop fertilizers, is to promote plant growth in water. Excessive growth of algae in water fed from fertilized land can choke out fish.

The term *acid rain* refers to increases over the normal acidity of rainwater attributable to emissions from motor vehicles, electric power plants, and other industries. Rainwater in certain parts of the northeastern United States and Canada is slightly more acidic than rainwater elsewhere. (Acidity and alkalinity are measured on a pH scale from 0 to 14.0, with 7.0 being neutral. Average rainwater pH is 5.0; rainwater in affected areas has been measured at 4.2.) It is widely speculated that this increase in acidity is a product of sulfur and nitrogen emissions from coal-burning power plants. But lakes and streams are *not* "dying from acid rain." Indeed, it is difficult to demonstrate that any adverse effects occur to streams or lakes or forests or human health from acidity in rainwater.

Environmental groups and the mass media have largely ignored serious studies of the effects of rainwater acidity. A massive ten-year, $500 million study, the National Acid Precipitation Assessment Project (NAPAP), was the most comprehensive study ever conducted on a single environmental issue. It concluded that (1) there is no evidence that acid rain has affected American forests except for damage to red spruce at high elevations in the eastern mountains; (2) there is no evidence of acid rain damage to crops; (3) there is no evidence of human health risks from acid rain to healthy individuals, but it could pose a risk to asthmatics, people with heart and lung disease, and the elderly; and (4) overall, less than 5 percent of the nation's lakes and 10 percent of its streams have elevated acid levels.[15] The NAPAP report concluded that acid rain is not a serious environmental issue, and that "an expensive crash program to accelerate the current rate of reduction of acid rain is not justified." Nonetheless, President Bush and Congress chose to ignore the NAPAP report and enact many new, costly regulations designed to reduce acid rain in the Clean Air Act of 1990.

The Ozone Hole.   Ozone is a gas similar to oxygen. Some chemicals in automobile exhaust can catalyze oxygen in the air to break down into ozone, which is a principle ingredient in smog. It makes the air hazy or even brown. In heavy concentrations in some cities and under certain weather conditions, it can cause eye and lung irritation. Some cities declare a "smog alert" when ozone levels become too high. Persons with respiratory diseases, the elderly, and children are advised to stay indoors to avoid inflammation of the lungs. There is no question that ozone production is an "externality."

A more recent, widely publicized story is that ozone levels in the upper atmosphere are declining. Ozone in the upper atmosphere is believed to reflect some of the sun's ultraviolet light and prevent it from reaching the earth. Ultraviolet light can contribute to skin cancer. Fluorocarbons (including freon in air conditioners) breaks down ozone into ordinary oxygen. So the theory has been advanced that the release of fluorocarbons is creating an "ozone hole" in the atmosphere, allowing more ultraviolet light to reach earth and cause more skin cancer.

Although it is true that fluorocarbons break down ozone, it is not clear whether they contribute to a decline in ozone levels in the upper atmosphere or not, or indeed whether ozone in the upper atmosphere is in fact declining. An "ozone hole" is reported to exist during the Antarctic summer. A modest reduction in sunbathing would be many thousand times more effective in reducing skin cancer than eliminating flurocarbons. Yet belief in the catastrophic effects of an "ozone hole" drives environmental policy.

Radon.   Trace amounts of uranium are found in virtually all forms of rock and soil. (Indeed, the age of materials can be estimated by the radioactive dating.) The decay of this uranium produces a radioactive isotope in the air, popularly referred to as "radon." Occasionally air that has been trapped underground for long periods registers higher levels of radon than surface air. The air in most residential basements registers higher radon levels than surface air. This phenomenon has given rise to a radon scare—fear of the health effects of "the silent killer," that is, air with higher than average radiation levels. The only scientific evidence in support of this fear was derived from the higher cancer rates exhibited by uranium miners, who experienced long-term exposure to air with the highest radioactivity levels ever recorded. Nonetheless, in the 1980s, the EPA set radon standards for homes that, if implemented, would have required millions of American homeowners to install costly ventilation equipment. Fortunately, EPA decided not to actively enforce its standards for radon, fearing a public backlash against senseless regulations.

THE NUCLEAR INDUSTRY MELTDOWN

Nuclear power is the cleanest and safest form of energy available. But the political struggle over nuclear power has all but destroyed early hopes that nuclear power could reduce U.S. dependence on fossil fuels. Nuclear power now provides about 18 percent of the nation's total electricity. Many early studies recommended that the United States strive for 50 percent nuclear electric generation by 1990. But under current policies it is unlikely that nuclear power will ever be able to supply any more energy than it does today. The nuclear industry itself is in a state of "meltdown" and the cause of the meltdown is political, not technological.

In its developmental stages, nuclear power was a government monopoly. The Atomic Energy Act of 1946 created the Atomic Energy Commission (AEC), which established civilian rather than military control over nuclear energy. The AEC was responsible for the research, development, and production of nuclear weapons, as well as the development of the peaceful uses of nuclear energy. The AEC contracted with the Westinghouse Corporation to build a reactor and with the Duquesne Light Company to operate the world's first nuclear power plant at Shippingport, Pennsylvania, in 1957. Under the Atomic Energy Act of 1954 the AEC granted permits to build, and licenses to operate, nuclear plants; the AEC also retained control over nuclear fuel.

The AEC promoted the growth of the nuclear industry for over twenty years. By the late 1970s there were seventy nuclear power plants licensed to operate and eighty-five construction permits issued. But opponents of nuclear power succeeded in the Energy Reorganization Act of 1974 in separating the nuclear regulatory function from the research and development function. Today a separate agency, the Nuclear Regulatory Commission (NRC), regulates all aspects of nuclear power. Only about 100 nuclear power plants are operating in the United States today. Many planned plants were canceled, and no new plants have been started in more than two decades.

Nuclear power has long been under attack by a wide assortment of "no-nuke" groups. The core opposition is found among environmental activist groups. But fear plays the most important role in nuclear politics. The mushroom cloud image of the devastation of Japanese cities at the end of World War II is still with us. The mass media cannot resist dramatic accounts of nuclear accidents. The public is captivated by the "China syndrome" story—an overheated nuclear core melts down the containing vessels and the plant itself and releases radioactivity that kills millions.

Nuclear power offers a means of generating electricity without discharging any pollutants into the air or water. It is the cleanest form of energy production. It does not diminish the world's supply of oil, gas, or coal. However, used reactor fuel remains radioactive for hundreds of years and there are potential problems in burying this radioactive waste. Spent fuel is now piling up in storage areas in specially designed pools of water at nuclear power sites. When these existing storage places are filled to capacity, spent fuel will have to be transported somewhere else, adding to new complaints about the dangers of radioactive waste. There are many technical alternatives in dealing with waste, but there is no political consensus about which alternative to choose.

The nuclear power industry in the United States has a 50-year record of safety. No one has ever died or been seriously harmed by radioactivity from a nuclear power plant in the United States.[16] This record includes more than 100 nuclear power plants operated in the United States and hundreds of nuclear-powered surface and submarine ships operated by the U.S. Navy; in contrast, coal mine deaths average more than 200 per year.[17] Despite sensational media coverage, the failure of the nuclear reactor at Three Mile Island, Pennsylvania, in 1979 did not result in injury to anyone or cause damage beyond the plant. There are more than 300 nuclear power plants operating outside of the United States. France generates 65 percent of its electricity by nuclear means. The worst nuclear accident in history occurred at Chernobyl in the Ukraine in 1986; it resulted in 31 deaths from radiation.

Zero risk is an impossible standard, and the costs of efforts to approach zero risk are astronomical. Under popular pressure to achieve near-zero risk, the NRC has imposed licensing requirements that now make nuclear plants the most expensive means of generating electricity. No new nuclear plants have been proposed in nearly two decades, and private utilities have canceled dozens of planned nuclear plants. The nation's largest nuclear plant complex, the Washington Public Power Service, was forced into bankruptcy. Indeed, the existing nuclear power industry in the United States may be driven to extinction by ever-increasing costs of near-zero risk regulatory policy. The stated policy of the national government may be to keep open the nuclear power option, but the actual effect of nuclear regulatory policy is to foreclose that option.

POLITICIANS AND BUREAUCRATS: REGULATING THE ENVIRONMENT

Federal environmental policymaking began in earnest in the 1970s with the creation of the Environmental Protection Agency (EPA) and the passage of clean air and water acts. Potentially, the EPA is the most powerful and far-reaching bureaucracy in Washington today, with legal authority over any activity in the nation that affects the air, water, or ground.

The Environmental Protection Agency.   The EPA was created in an executive order by President Richard Nixon in 1970 to reorganize the federal bureaucracy to consolidate responsibility for (1) water pollution, (2) air pollution, (3) solid waste management, (4) radiation control, and (5) hazardous and toxic substance control. The EPA is a regulatory agency with power to establish and enforce policy.

The National Environmental Protection Act.   In 1970 Congress created the Council on Environmental Quality (CEQ), to advise the President and Congress on environmental matters. The CEQ is an advisory agency. However, the act requires all federal agencies as well as state, local, and private organizations receiving federal monies to file lengthy "environmental impact statements." If the CEQ wants to delay or obstruct a project, it can ask for endless revisions, changes, or additions in the statement. The CEQ cannot by itself halt a project, but it can conduct public hearings for the press, pressure other governmental agencies, and make recommendations to the President. The courts have ruled that the requirement for an environmental impact statement is judicially enforceable.

The Clean Air Act of 1970.   The Clean Air Act of 1970 authorized the EPA to identify air pollutants that cause a health threat and to establish and enforce standards of emission. The EPA began by focusing on automobile emissions, requiring the installation of pollution equipment on all new cars. The EPA ordered lead removed from auto fuel and engines redesigned for lead-free gasoline. It also ordered the installation of emission controls in automobiles. More radical solutions advanced by the EPA (for example, to halt driving in certain cities) were blocked by courts and Congress. The EPA was even more aggressive in pursuing stationary sources of air pollution with requirements for "smoke-stack scrubbers," low-sulfur coal, and other very costly devices. Industry opposition led to some relaxation of these requirements in the Clean Air Act Amendments of 1977.

The Water Pollution Control Act of 1972.   This act stiffened early antipollution laws, but set an unrealistic goal: "that the discharge of pollutants into the navigable waters be eliminated by 1985." After a flood of lawsuits the EPA was forced to abandon the zero-discharge standard. Forcing municipal governments to clean up their discharges proved more difficult than forcing industry to do so. Many municipalities remain in violation of federal water quality standards.

Endangered Species Act of 1973.   This legislation authorizes the U.S. Fish and Wildlife Service to designate endangered species for federal protection and to regulate activities in their "critical habitat." Initially the law was widely praised as at least partially responsible for the survival of nationally symbolic species such as the bald eagle; but increasingly the law has been used to prevent landowners from using their property in order to protect obscure varieties of rodents, birds, and insects. Today more than 1,000 species are on the endangered species list and there is virtually no land in the United States on which an endangered species does *not* live. The U.S. Fish and Wildlife Service has the potential to control any land in the nation under the Endangered Species Act.

Wetlands.   In 1975 a federal court ruled that the Clean Water Act of 1972 also applied to "wetlands" adjacent to navigable waters. This gave the EPA control over millions of acres of land, estimated to be the equivalent of Ohio, Indiana, and Illinois combined. The result has been a bureaucratic nightmare for owners of land that is classified as wetlands.

Resource Conservation and Recovery Act of 1976.   The act authorizes EPA to oversee the nation's solid waste removal and disposal, including the regulation of landfills, incinerators, industrial waste, hazardous waste, and recycling programs.

Toxic Substances Control Act of 1976.   The Toxic Substances Control Act authorized the EPA to designate hazardous and toxic substances and to establish standards for their release into the environment.

The Comprehensive Environmental Response Act of 1980.   The Comprehensive Environmental Response Act established a "Superfund" for cleaning up old toxic and hazardous waste sites. Out of 20,000 potential sites, the EPA has placed more than 1,200 on its National Priority List. The act specifies that EPA oversee the cleanup of these sites assessing costs to the parties responsible for the pollution. If these parties cannot be found or have no money, then the government's Superfund is to be used. But over the years, clean-up efforts have been seriously hampered by EPA's overly rigid site orders (for example, dirt must be cleaned to the point where it can be safely eaten daily by small children),[18] lengthy lawsuits against previous owners and users (including little league teams) that divert funds to legal fees, and complicated negotiations with local government over the cleanup of old landfill sites. EPA also enforces "retroactive liability," holding owners liable for waste dumped legally before the law was enacted in 1980. Under current EPA policies, full cleanup of all hazardous waste sites on the National Priority List would cost many billions of dollars, far more than presidents or Congresses are likely to appropriate.

Clean Air Act of 1990.   The Clean Air Act Amendments of 1990 enacted many new regulations aimed at a variety of perceived threats to the environment:

> *Acid rain.* Sulfur dioxide emissions must be cut from 20 to 10 million tons annually, and nitrogen oxide emissions must be cut by 2 million tons. Midwestern coal-burning utilities must burn low-sulphur coal and install added smoke-scrubbing equipment at increased costs to their consumers.
> *Ozone hole.* Production of chlorofluorocarbons and hydrochlorofluorocarbons (aerosol sprays, insulating materials) is outlawed, and new regulations are placed on chemicals used in air conditioners and refrigerators.
> *Urban smog.* Additional mandated pollution control equipment is required on new automobiles. Oil companies must produce cleaner-burning fuel. There is also a special requirement that automobile companies produce an experimental fleet of cars to be sold in southern California.
> *Toxic air pollutants.* New definitions and regulations govern more than 200 substances as "toxic air pollutants" released into the air from a wide variety of sources, from gas stations to dry cleaners. The EPA is given authority to require all of these sources to install "the best available control technology" and to provide "an ample margin of safety" for nearby residents.

It is difficult to estimate the overall cost to society of these tighter standards. (The Bush administration claimed they would cost only $16 billion a year, but the

Business Roundtable, made up of chief executives of the nation's largest industries, estimated the costs to exceed $100 billion.) It is even more difficult to estimate the benefits to society of additional reductions in air pollutants. Perhaps cleaner air will improve health and reduce medical costs, but no reliable estimate can be made of the amount of these benefits, if any.

ALTERNATIVE SOLUTIONS

Economists view pollution as a cost of production, a cost that producers may try to externalize to others. Once we view pollution in this fashion, it becomes possible to envision a variety of market-based environmental policies that hold much more promise of success than centralized governmental commands and regulations. If more attention is given to the generation of pollution rather than its control, if pollution becomes a cost to its producers, it will be reduced through the ordinary operations of a free market economy.

Property Rights and "Takings."   Public choice theory seeks solutions to externalities, including pollution, through the proper determination of the rights and responsibilities of property ownership. The U.S. Constitution (Fifth Amendment) states clearly: "nor shall private property be taken for public use without just compensation." Taking land for highways, streets, and public buildings, even when the owners do not wish to sell, is known as *eminent domain*. Governments must go to court and show that the land is needed for legitimate public purposes; the court will then establish a fair price "just compensation," based on testimony from the owner, the government, and impartial appraisers. Eminent domain is a constitutional protection to American citizens against arbitrary government seizure of their land.

But what if government does not "take" ownership of the property, but instead restricts the owner's use of it through regulation? Environmental regulations may reduce the value of the property to the owner. Should the owner be compensated for loss of uses? Courts have always recognized that governments can make laws to protect the health, safety, and general welfare of its citizens. Owners of property have never been entitled to any compensation for obeying laws with a clear public purpose.

However, the U.S. Supreme Court has held that a regulation that denies a property owner *all* economically beneficial use of land (e.g., a state coastal zone management regulation preventing *any* construction on a beach lot) was a "taking" that required just compensation to the owner in order to be constitutional.[19] The Takings Clause of the Constitution's Fifth Amendment was designed to protect private property from unjust taking by government. Its purpose is "to bar Government from forcing some people alone to bear public burdens which, in all fairness and justice, should be borne by the public as a whole."[20] If society wants open spaces, wildlife preserves, environmental havens, or other amenities, *all* citizens should pay for them, not just the owners of particular properties.

The question remains, however, how far can government go in environmental regulation without compensating property owners? Depriving landowners of *all* beneficial uses of their land without compensation is clearly unconstitutional. But what if their use of their land is devalued by 50 percent or 25 percent? Are governments constitutionally required to compensate them in proportion to their losses? In the past, federal courts have ruled that "mere diminution" in the value of property is not a "taking" within the meaning of the Fifth Amendment and hence does not require the government to compensate landowners. However, in recent years both Congress and the federal courts, as well as some states, have undertaken to reconsider "how far" government can go in depriving property owners of valued uses of their land. Increasingly, regulatory devaluations of 50 percent or more are becoming highly suspect, and property owners have a reasonable chance of recovering compensation from governments.

Regulatory Problems.   The current "command and control" approach to environmental policy is inefficient. Pollution abatement practices are many and varied; the best practice depends on circumstances that can vary from one plant to another. The cost of reducing pollution varies enormously; some sources can reduce pollution cheaply, while some can do so only at great cost. A centralized government bureaucracy in Washington cannot efficiently supervise practices in every location in the nation. And uniform nationwide regulations discourage innovation. New pollution abatement methods are discouraged by government rules requiring older methods.

Pollution Taxes.   A more effective alternative is pollution taxation. Taxes on pollutants, imposed on those who generate them, would provide economic incentives for individuals, firms, and local governments to find the cheapest and most effective method to limit pollution. A tax on each firm that generates pollution, based on the amount and type of pollution generated, would substitute economic incentives for pollution abatement for central directories of politicized bureaucracies. By imposing a per unit tax on the emission of pollutants, such as sulfur dioxide, any feasible amount of abatement can be achieved depending on the level of the tax. Each polluter would be given the information and motivation to reduce pollution as cheaply and efficiently as possible in order to reduce the tax. Those who do so would be rewarded with lower taxes and higher profits. Those who do not would be obliged to pass the tax on to customers in the form of higher prices. Consumers would be given an incentive to reduce their use of high-pollution products and search for alternatives. By shifting environmental policy away from centralized bureaucratic control and toward decentralized market incentives, it would be possible to increase environmental quality while at the same time promoting economic growth.

Tradable Emission Allowances.   A positive development in recent environmental policy proposals has been the greater attention given to tradable emission allowances. The total emission allowances reflect the overall goal of the environmental policy, for example, a cap of 10 million tons of sulfur dioxide emissions. Emission allowances would be distributed to existing utilities, refineries, and other sources of pollution. Plant owners would be free to buy or sell these allowances among themselves. Thus, emission rates among individual plants would vary, but overall emissions would be held at the target level. Tradable allowances reduce the overall costs of compliance by allowing flexibility. They encourage innovation in technology; innovative plants can sell their excess allowances at a profit. Plants that could reduce emissions only at a very high cost to their customers could purchase emission allowances and continue operations. Bureaucratic enforcement would be kept to a minimum, simply measuring emissions rather than dictating plant operations.

Waste Charges.   Another effective alternative is charging businesses and households by the amount of garbage collected. Governments rarely reflect the true costs of garbage collection and landfill operations in their pricing of services. Direct charges based on the volume of garbage collected would inspire businesses and households to buy less unnecessary packaging and to undertake recycling efforts voluntarily.

Economic Growth.   Policies that retard economic growth are usually counterproductive to environmental protection. The world's worst polluters are underdeveloped nations. As income increases, people make greater efforts to improve environmental quality. Market economies are more successful at environmental protection than socialist economies. The socialist economies of Eastern Europe produced severe environmental degradation because there were no market incentives guiding production.

SUMMARY

Public choice theory views environmental pollution as an externality of human activity. Individuals, firms, and governments frequently impose unwanted costs on others. The environment, especially air and water, is a common pool resource: access is unrestricted; there are no clearly defined property rights to it; no one has the individual responsibility of caring for it; individuals, firms, and governments tend to use it to carry off waste materials, thus generating unwanted costs or externalities on everyone else. The government has a legitimate interest in managing environmental externalities. Public choice theory offers valuable guidelines in dealing with them.

1. Economic growth is not incompatible with environmental protection. On the contrary, increases in wealth and advances in technology provide the best hope for a cleaner environment.

2. Effective pollution control and risk reduction must be balanced against its costs. Environmental policies whose costs exceed benefits will impair society's ability to deal effectively with environmental problems.

3. The costs of removing additional environmental pollutants and risks rise as we approach zero tolerance. Total elimination of pollutants from air, water, or ground involves astronomical costs and wastes the resources of society.

4. Rational determination of benefits and costs requires scientific evidence. The deliberate rejection of scientific evidence on environmental issues, and the ideological or emotional inspiration to act even in the absence of scientific information, renders cost-effective policymaking impossible.

5. Traditional command and control approaches to environmental protection are less effective than market incentives. Legislatures and bureaucrats that endeavor to devise laws and regulations to reduce pollution are less effective than individuals, firms, and local governments with strong market incentives to reduce pollution in a cost-effective manner.

6. The air and water in the United States are measurably cleaner today than in 1970, when the first major environmental policies were enacted. Improvements in air and water quality have occurred despite growth in the population and growth in waste products.

7. Nonetheless, most Americans believe that pollution is growing worse. Interest group activity and media coverage of environmental "crises," together with economic prosperity and the end of the Cold War, have pushed environmental issues to the forefront of American politics. Predictions of global doom create a climate of opinion that precludes rational analyses of the benefits and costs of environmental policies.

8. Current policy initiatives focus on sulfur dioxide and nitrogen oxide from coal-burning utilities, emissions of ozone and carbon monoxide from automobiles and stationary sources, and toxic air pollutants released from a wide variety of sources.

9. The U.S. Constitution prohibits the "taking" of private property for public use without "just compensation." Current regulatory policy places the burden of environmental protection on landowners, limiting their use of land but not compensating them for their losses.

10. If firms were taxed on the basis of the pollutants they emit, a strong market incentive would be created for a reduction in pollution. A pollution tax would capture the externalities and force producers and consumers to incorporate the full environmental costs of products in the price. It would encourage polluters to find ways themselves to reduce pollution rather than simply comply with government regulations. Waste charges would encourage consumers to reduce their use of waste-producing goods.

NOTES

1. U.S. Environmental Protection Agency, *Unfinished Business: A Comparative Assessment of Environmental Problems* (Washington, DC: EPA, 1987).
2. As quoted in *Governing* (February 1995), 49.
3. *Statistical Abstract of the United States 1996*, p. 237.
4. Resource Conservation and Recovery Act, PL 94–580, Section 4001 (1976).
5. Quote from Richard J. Lescoe, M.D., former director of the California Lung Association, in *World Research Ink* (November/December 1979), 10.
6. *New York Times,* April 27, 1990.

7. Club of Rome, *The First Global Revolution* (New York: Pantheon Books, 1991), p. 115.
8. Christopher Manes, *Green Rage* (Boston: Little, Brown, 1990).
9. Hugh W. Ellsaesser et al, "Global Climate Trends as Revealed by Recorded Data," *Review of Geophysics,* 24 (November 1986), 745–792.
10. Patrick J. Michaels and David E. Stooksbury, "Global Warning: A Reduced Threat?" *Bulletin of the American Meteorological Society,* 23 (October 1992), 1563–1577.
11. Roy W. Spence and John R. Christy, "Precise Monitoring of Global Temperature Trends from Satellites," *Science,* 247 (March 1990), 1558–1562.
12. Nigel Calder, "In the Grip of a New Ice Age," *International Wildlife,* July 1975; cited by Dixie Lee Ray, *Environmental Overkill* (Washington, DC: Regnery Gateway, 1993), p. 15.
13. Al Gore, *Earth in the Balance* (Boston: Houghton Mifflin, 1992).
14. "The Heidelberg Appeal," *Wall Street Journal,* June 1, 1992, p. 1.
15. National Acid Precipitation Assessment Project, *The Causes and Effects of Acidic Deposition* (Washington, DC: U.S. Government Printing Office, 1990).
16. For an excellent, unbiased discussion of nuclear safety, see Harold W. Lewis, "The Safety of Fission Reactors," *Scientific American,* 242 (March 1980), 53–65.
17. Herbert Inhaber, "Risk with Energy from Conventional and Nonconventional Sources," *Science,* February 23, 1979, pp. 700–718.
18. See *Governing,* April, 1994, p. 62.
19. *Lucas* v. *South Carolina Coastal Council,* 112 Sup. Ct. 2886 (1992).
20. *Dolan* v. *City of Tigard* (1994).

BIBLIOGRAPHY

BLOCK, BEN and HAROLD LYONS. *Apocalypse Not: Science, Economics, and Environmentalism.* Washington, DC: CATO Institute, 1993.
GORE, AL. *Earth in the Balance.* Boston: Houghton Mifflin, 1992.
PORTNEY, KENT E. *Controversial Issues in Environmental Policy.* Newbury Park, CA: Sage Publications, 1992.
RAY, DIXIE LEE. *Environmental Overkill.* Washington, DC: Regnery Gateway, 1993.
SINGER, S. FRED, ED. *Global Climate Change: Human and Natural Influences.* New York: Paragon House, 1989.
WILDAVSKY, AARON. *Searching for Safety.* New Brunswick, NJ: Transaction Publishers, 1988.

8

DEFENSE POLICY
Strategies for Serious Games

President Clinton greets a soldier during an executive visit to troops deployed in Bosnia. (Reuters/Win McNamee/Archive Photos)

NATIONAL SECURITY AS A SERIOUS GAME

Game theory provides an interesting way of thinking about defense policy. Defense policies of major world powers are interdependent. Each nation must adjust its own defense policies to reflect not only its own national objectives but also its expectations of what other powers may do. Outcomes depend on the combination of choices made in world capitals. Moreover, it is not unreasonable to assume that nations strive for rationality in defense policymaking. Nations choose defense strategies (policies) that are designed to achieve an optimum payoff even after considering all their opponents' possible strategies. Thus, national defense policymaking conforms to basic game theory notions. Our use of game theory is limited, however, to suggesting interesting questions, posing dilemmas, and providing a vocabulary for dealing with policymaking in a competitive, interdependent world.

A rational approach to the formulation of defense policy begins with a careful assessment of the range of threats to the nation and its interests. Once major threats have been identified, the next step is to develop strategies designed to counter them and protect the nation's interests. Once strategies have been devised, defense policymaking must determine the appropriate forces (military units, personnel, weapons, training, readiness, and so forth) required to implement them. Finally, budgets must be calculated to finance the required force levels. Thus, a rational game plan proceeds from

Threat Assessments

to

Strategies

to

Force Levels

to

Budget Requests

Of course, differences and uncertainties arise at each step in this process—differing assessments of the nature and magnitude of the threats facing the nation, the right strategies to confront these threats, the force levels necessary to implement the strategies, and the funds required to provide these forces.

CONFRONTING NUCLEAR THREATS

For more than 40 years, following the end of World War II in 1945, the United States and the former Union of Soviet Socialist Republics (USSR) confronted each other in a superpower struggle as intense an any in the history of nations. Indeed, nuclear weaponry made the Cold War more dangerous than any national confrontation in the past. The nuclear arsenals of the United States and the former USSR threatened a human holocaust. Yet paradoxically, the very destructiveness of nuclear weapons caused leaders on both sides to exercise extreme caution in their relations with each other. Scores of wars, large and small, were fought by different nations during the Cold War years, yet American and Soviet troops never engaged in direct combat against each other.

Deterrence.   To maintain nuclear peace, the United States relied primarily on the policy of deterrence. Deterrence is based on the notion that a nation can dissuade a rational enemy from attacking by maintaining the capacity to destroy the enemy's society even after the nation has suffered a well-executed surprise attack by the enemy. It assumes that the worst may happen—a surprise first strike against our own nuclear forces. It emphasizes second-strike capability—the ability of a nation's forces to survive a surprise attack by the enemy and then to inflict an unacceptable level of destruction on the enemy's homeland in retaliation. Deterrence is really a psychological defense against attack; no effective physical defenses against a ballistic missile attack exist even today.

The strategy of deterrence maintains peace through fear of retaliation. It is based on the rational self-interest of national leaders. It does not depend on their love of peace or fear of God or sense of humanity. If America loses its deterrent—its ability to threaten retaliation—then peace would rest on the fragile hope that our potential enemies would be merciful, kind, and compassionate. No national leader can afford to take such a risk.

Strategic Weapons.   To implement the deterrent strategy, the United States relied on a TRIAD of weapons systems: land-based missiles (ICBMs), submarine-launched missiles (SLBMs), and manned bombers. Each "leg" of the TRIAD was supposed to be an independent, survivable, second-strike force. Thus, each leg posed separate and unique problems for an enemy in devising a way to destroy the U.S. second-strike deterrent.

The United States built Minuteman ICBMs in the early 1960s. About half of the Minuteman force carried multiple independently targeted reentry vehicles (MIRVs); nuclear warheads that separate from the missile itself can be accurately directed to separate targets. The Soviets developed a very large missile in 1975, the SS-18, that is capable of carrying ten very destructive (1 megaton) and very accurate MIRV warheads. The SS-18 gave the Soviet Union "hard-target kill" capability—the ability to destroy Minuteman missiles in their silos. In response the United States developed the MX missile; it is smaller than the SS-18 yet capable of carrying ten accurate MIRV warheads. The MX partially restored the strategic imbalance created by the SS-18. However, Congress refused to buy more than fifty MXs because they were vulnerable to attack. For over a decade, Congress and the Defense Department debated various plans to make land-based missiles survivable. Research went forward on a small ICBM, labeled the Midgetman, that would launch a single missile from a mobile vehicle that could move about the countryside, making it difficult for an enemy to target it successfully. But the end of the Cold War led President George Bush to cancel the Midgetman project.

The second leg of the TRIAD was the intercontinental bomber. Manned bombers can survive a first strike if they are in the air. Given adequate warning (knowledge that the enemy has fired its ICBMs or SLBMs), a significant percentage of bombers on alert status can get off the ground before incoming missiles arrive. Unlike missiles, manned bombers can be called back if the alert is an error; they can be redirected to other targets in flight, and they can be used in conventional non-nuclear war if needed.

The U.S. intercontinental manned bomber force was composed mainly of aged, slow, and large B-52s. The development of cruise missiles in the 1970s helped to extend the deterrent capabilities of the B-52. Cruise missiles are small, air-breathing, subsonic, low-flying guided missiles that can be launched from aircraft (ALCMs) or from surface ships or submerged submarines (Tomahawk cruise missiles). Equipping the B-52s with ALCMs gave them "standoff" capability—the ability to attack targets from a distance without flying over the heaviest enemy air defenses.

A more advanced manned bomber, the B-1, was developed and tested in the mid-1970s as a replacement for the aging B-52s. The B-1 is a small, intercontinental, supersonic bomber, designed for low-altitude penetration of modern air defenses. One hundred of the aircraft were built in the 1980s. Today, successful penetration of enemy air defenses requires highly sophisticated aircraft employing the most advanced "stealth" (radar-evading) technology. Stealth technology refers to airframe design and construction materials that minimize the aircraft's reflection on radar screens. Although no aircraft can be invisible, a very small radar "signature," or "blip," may go undetected in background clutter, or make accurate tracking and targeting by enemy surface-to-air missiles very difficult. Beginning in the late 1970s, the United States made rapid strides in secret research. A stealth fighter, the F117A, was built and deployed with little public attention. In 1989 the Air Force rolled out its first stealth bomber, the B-2, with its revolutionary flying wing. The end of the Cold War, combined with the high cost of the new bomber, inspired President Clinton to halt production of the B-2 at 20 aircraft.

The third leg of the TRIAD is the submarine-launched ballistic missile (SLBM) force. It is the most "survivable" force and therefore, the best second-strike component of the TRIAD. Most defense analysts believe that antisubmarine warfare capability is not now, nor will it be in the foreseeable future, capable of destroying a significant portion of our SLBM force on a surprise first strike. The first SLBM-carrying submarines (SSBNs) went to sea in 1960. The current Trident submarine program is now replacing earlier SSBNs with the newer, quieter boats, each with 24 launch tubes. A total of 18 Trident submarines carrying a total of 432 SLBMs will become America's principle nuclear deterrent force in the future.

ARMS CONTROL GAMES

The United States and the Soviet Union engaged in negotiations over strategic arms for many years. They began in 1970 under President Richard Nixon and his national security advisor, Henry Kissinger, and were originally labeled the Strategic Arms Limitation Talks (SALT).

SALT I.   SALT I in 1972 was a milestone in that it marked the first effort by the superpowers to limit strategic nuclear weapons. It consisted of a formal treaty halting further development of antiballistic missile systems (ABMs) and an executive agreement placing numerical limits on offensive missiles. The ABM treaty reflected the theory that the populations of each nation should remain undefended from a ballistic missile attack in order to hold them hostage against a first strike by either nation. Under the offensive arms agreement, each side was frozen at the total number of offensive missiles completed or under construction at the time.

SALT II.   After seven more years of difficult negotiations, the United States and the Soviet Union signed the lengthy and complicated SALT II treaty in 1979. It set an overall limit on "strategic nuclear launch vehicles"—ICBMs, SLBMs, and bombers with cruise missiles—at 2,250 for each side. It also limited the number of missiles that could have multiple warheads (MIRVs). When the Soviet Union invaded Afghanistan, President Carter withdrew the SALT II treaty from Senate consideration. However, Carter, and later President Reagan, announced that the United States would abide by the provisions of the unratified SALT II treaty as long as the USSR did so too.

START.   In negotiations with the Soviets, the Reagan administration established three central principles of arms control—*reductions, equality,* and *verification.* The new goal was to be reductions in missiles and warheads, not merely limitations on future numbers and types of weapons, as in previous SALT talks. To symbolize this new direction, President Reagan renamed the negotiations the Strategic Arms Reductions Talks, or START.

INF Treaty.   The Intermediate-range Nuclear Forces (INF) Treaty in 1987 was the first agreement between the nuclear powers that actually resulted in the reduction of nuclear weapons. It eliminated an entire class of nuclear weapons—missiles with an intermediate range between 300 and 3,800 miles. It was the first treaty that resulted in equal levels (zero) of arms for the United States and the USSR. To reach an equal level, the Soviets were required to destroy more missiles and warheads than the United States. Finally, INF was the first treaty to provide for on-site inspection for verification. The proportion of each side's nuclear weapons covered by the INF Treaty was small, but it set the pattern for future arms control agreements in its provisions for reductions, equality, and verification.

START I.   The long-awaited agreement on long-range strategic nuclear weapons was finally signed in Moscow in 1991 by presidents George Bush and Mikhail Gorbachev. The START I Treaty reduced the total number of deployed strategic nuclear delivery systems (ICBMs, SLBMs, and manned bombers) to no more than 1,600, a 30 percent reduction from the SALT II level. The total number of strategic nuclear warheads were reduced to no more than 6,000, a reduction of nearly 50 percent. Verification included on-site and short-notice inspections, as well as "national technical means" (satellite surveillance). Since the collapse of the USSR, the Russian Republic, the Ukraine, Bylorusse, and Kazakstan—those nations in which Soviet nuclear missiles were located—all pledged to abide by the START I agreement.

START II.   The end of the Cold War was confirmed by the far-reaching START II agreement between President George Bush and Russian President Boris Yeltsin. This agreement caps over twenty years of nuclear arms control negotiations by promising to eliminate the threat of a first-strike nuclear attack by either side. Its most important provision is the agreement to eliminate all multiwarhead (MIRV) land-based missiles by the year 2003. It also calls for the reduction of overall strategic warheads to 3,500, slashing the nuclear arsenals of both nations by more than two-thirds from Cold War levels (see Figure 8–1).

POST–COLD WAR NUCLEAR DETERRENCE AND DEFENSE

Democratic developments in Russia have radically changed our assessment of the intentions of its leaders, but their nuclear capabilities remain awesome. The United States has been assured that the rational and responsible leaders remain in command and control of this enormous destructive force and that strategic nuclear weapons will be dismantled on schedule in accord with the START treaties. However, defense policymakers in both the Bush and Clinton administrations have urged the continued maintenance of sufficient strategic nuclear forces to deter nuclear attack or intimidation by any leadership groups that might someday come into control of the awesome arsenal of the former Soviet Union.

FIGURE 8–1   Strategic Nuclear Arms under START Treaties

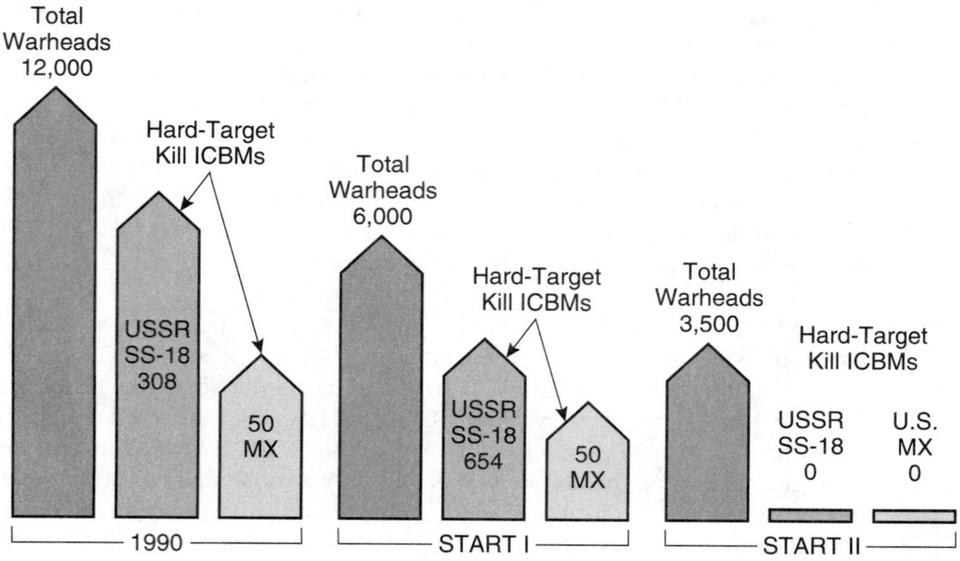

Minimal Deterrence.   The end of the Cold War has produced a radical reevaluation of the forces required for deterrence. Overall strategic nuclear forces will drop by two-thirds from Cold War levels by 2003. American nuclear warhead production has been brought to a halt. All MIRV ICBMs are being eliminated from the arsenals of both nations. For the United States this means the dismantling of 50 MX missiles and the conversion of 500 MIRV Minuteman IIIs into single-warhead missiles. All older Minuteman IIs are being dismantled, and the Midgetman mobile missile program has been canceled. All U.S. strategic bombers have been taken off of alert status. Most remaining B-52 and B-1 bombers are being reconfigured to carry conventional (nonnuclear) weapons. The B-2 bomber program has been capped at only 20 aircraft. Only the Trident submarine program is relatively unaffected by the cuts in strategic weaponry (see Table 8–1).

Nondeterrable Threats.   But even as the threat of a large-scale nuclear attack recedes, the threats arising from "nondeterrable" sources are increasing. Today, the principal nondeterrable nuclear threats are estimated to be (1) missiles launched by a terrorist nation, (2) unauthorized missile launches by elements within the former Soviet Union during periods of internal crises and turmoil, and (3) accidental missile launches. Global nuclear and ballistic missile proliferation steadily increases over time the likelihood of these types of threats. Terrorist, unauthorized, and accidental launches are considered "nondeterrable" because the threat of nuclear retaliation is largely meaningless.

The Spread of Mass Terror Weapons.   The threat of mass terror weapons—nuclear, chemical, or biological, especially those carried by medium- or long-range missiles—is likely to increase dramatically in the next century. Iraq, Iran, and Libya,

TABLE 8-1   U.S. Strategic Forces

	1990	2003 (START II)	
ICBMs			
Minuteman II	450	0	
Minuteman III	500	500	(single warhead)
Peacekeeper (MX)	50	0	
SSBNs			
Trident submarines	12	18	
(SLBMs)	288	432	
Poseidon submarines	22	0	
(SLBMs)	352	0	
Aircraft			
B-52 G&H	210	100	
B-1 B	96	95	
B-2	—	20	
Nuclear warheads	11,766	3,500	

for example, are all likely to acquire mass terror weapons and long-range delivery systems in the absence of any action by the United States to prevent them from doing so. North Korea is already reported to possess nuclear weapons and to be developing long-range missiles to carry them.

Ballistic Missile Defenses—"Star Wars."   For a half century, since the terrible nuclear blasts of Hiroshima and Nagasaki in Japan in 1945, the world has avoided nuclear war. Peace has been maintained by deterrence—by the threat of devastating nuclear attacks that would be launched in retaliation to an enemy first strike. But in 1983 President Reagan urged that instead of deterring war through fear of retaliation, we should seek a technological defense against nuclear missiles, one that would eventually render them "impotent and obsolete."[1] Reagan's Strategic Defense Initiative (SDI), dubbed "Star Wars" by the media, was a research program designed to explore ways of destroying enemy nuclear missiles in space before they could reach their targets. Destroying a missile or warhead in flight is a challenging technical feat, comparable to "hitting a bullet with a bullet." SDI included research on laser beams, satellite surveillance, computerized battle-management systems, and "smart" and "brilliant" weapon systems.

The success of the Patriot antiballistic missile in destroying short-range Iraqi Scud missiles during the Gulf War demonstrated that enemy missiles could be intercepted in flight. The Patriot is a ground-based "tactical" weapon designed to protect specific military targets. It cannot protect the entire population of the United States, but the Patriot silenced critics who had claimed that successful interception of an incoming missile was impossible.

The Future of Ballistic Missile Defenses.   Opposition to SDI has continued in Congress. As a Reagan-era initiative, partisanship tends to cloud the debate. In 1993 President Clinton announced the termination of the separate SDI organization, but he assured the nation that research would continue on ground-based ballistic missile defenses. Research on *space-based* interceptors was redirected toward *ground-based* systems. Republicans have pressed for the deployment of a "thin" anti-missile defense system that would protect U.S. territory against a small-scale nuclear, chemical or biological weapons attack—the kind of attack that might be launched by terrorist nations such as Iran, Iraq, Libya, or North Korea, or a rogue Russian military unit. But the Clinton administration has postponed indefinitely all plans to deploy missile defenses to protect the U.S. population.

NATO AND EUROPEAN SECURITY

The preservation of democracy in Western Europe has been the centerpiece of U.S. foreign and military policy for most of the twentieth century. The United States fought in two world wars to preserve democracy in Europe.

Origins of NATO.   In response to aggressive Soviet moves in Europe after World War II, the United States, Canada, Belgium, Britain, Denmark, France, Iceland, Italy, Luxembourg, the Netherlands, Norway, and Portugal joined in the North Atlantic Treaty Organization (NATO). Each nation pledged that "an armed attack against one . . . shall be considered an attack against them all." Greece and Turkey joined in 1952 and West Germany in 1955. To give this pledge credibility, a joint NATO military command was established with a U.S. commanding officer (the first was General of the Army Dwight D. Eisenhower). After the formation of NATO, the Soviets made no further advances in Western Europe. The Soviets themselves, in response to NATO, drew up a comparable treaty among their own Eastern European satellite nations—the Warsaw Pact. It included Poland, Hungary, Czechoslovakia, Romania, Bulgaria, and the German Democratic Republic (the former East Germany).

Cold War Games.   Confronted with overwhelming Soviet and Warsaw Pact superiority in conventional forces—troops, tanks, armored personnel carriers, artillery, and combat aircraft—NATO was forced to rely on the threat of nuclear weapons to deter Soviet aggression. A "flexible response" strategy envisioned that NATO's conventional forces would try to halt an initial Soviet thrust until reserves from the United States and other European nations could be brought into the battle. But if Soviet forces overran NATO defenses, the NATO command would be authorized to use battlefield nuclear weapons against Soviet armored columns and troop concentrations. Note that this strategy implied NATO's "first use" of tactical *nuclear* weapons against Soviet *conventional* weapons.

Collapse of Communism in Eastern Europe.   The dramatic collapse of the communist governments of Eastern Europe in 1989—Poland, Hungary, Romania, Bulgaria, and East Germany—vastly reduced the threat of a military attack on Western Europe. The dismantling of communist governments came about as a direct result of President Michail Gorbachev's decision to renounce the use of Soviet military force to keep them in power. For over forty years, the communist governments of Eastern Europe were supported by Soviet tanks; bloody Soviet military operations put down civilian uprisings in Hungary in 1956 and Czechoslovakia in 1968. The threat of Soviet military intervention crushed the Solidarity movement in Poland in 1981, yet that same movement became the government of Poland in 1989. Any effort today by a Russian leader to reimpose control over Eastern European nations would probably result in widespread bloodshed.

Germany United.   The collapse of the Berlin Wall in 1989 and the formal unification of Germany in 1990 rearranged the balance of military power in central Europe. Today Germany is the strongest military power in Europe. It remains a member of NATO.

Collapse of the Warsaw Pact and the USSR.   The Warsaw Pact collapsed following the ouster of communist governments in the Eastern European nations and was officially dissolved in 1991. Its former members requested the withdrawal of Russian troops from their territory; the Russian government complied, although withdrawals were slowed by economic conditions in that nation.

At the same time strong independence movements emerged in the republics of the USSR. Lithuania, Estonia, and Latvia—Baltic Sea nations that had been forcibly incorporated into the Soviet Union in 1939—led the way to independence in 1991. Soon all fifteen republics declared their independence, and the Union of Soviet Socialist Republics officially ceased to exist after December 31, 1991. Russian President Boris Yeltsin took over the offices of former Soviet Union President Mikhail Gorbachev. The red flag with its banner and sickle atop the Kremlin was replaced by the flag of the Russian Republic.

Stability in Russia and Eastern Europe.   A historic opportunity exists in Russia for the successful transition to a stable democracy and a prosperous market economy. Despite the pain that these reforms cause in the short run, they are the only path to a democratic, prosperous Russia.

If Russia, Ukraine, and the other new republics make a full transition to democracy and capitalism, the twenty-first century promises much more peace and prosperity for the peoples of the world than the twentieth century. But if they fail, the United States and other Western nations will be confronted with many dangers. For example,

- Continuing economic deterioration in Russia may undermine the weak traditions of democracy. The specter of a "Weimar Russia," in which initial advances toward democracy fail and an authoritarian leader emerges, haunts Europeans who remember the failure of the brief Weimar democracy in Germany before the rise of Hitler.
- The collapse of the democratic movement may usher in an authoritarian nationalistic, militaristic Russian regime. Such a regime may seek to reassert its control of the new independent republics or even reassert dominance in Poland and other Eastern European nations.
- Continuing differences among the republics of the former Soviet Union and the rekindling of ancient hatreds among national ethnic groups may result in armed conflict. With nuclear weapons, the potential for disaster is far greater than in Bosnia or other regions of the world that have experienced ethnic conflicts.
- A breakdown of nuclear command and control may result in the sale of nuclear weapons to terrorists or terrorist regimes.

The United States in NATO.   The residual threat to Western Europe posed by Russian forces, even under a hostile regime, is very weak. The Russian military, over 4 million strong as late as 1990, is now down to less than 2 million, a number that is smaller than the forces of the European NATO countries, exclusive of U.S. forces. Moreover, Russian military morale is reported to be low and equipment in disrepair. Even if an anti-Western regime were to emerge in Moscow, considerable time would be required to reconstitute a Russian force capable of threatening Western Europe.

The United States Is Continuing Its Political Commitments to NATO.   The total withdrawal of U.S. military forces would probably mean an end to the NATO alliance. The United States has already reduced its "forward presence" in Europe by over half. Proponents of a continued U.S. military presence in Europe argue that it provides reassurance and stability as democracy emerges in Eastern Europe; they note that both our old allies and new friends in Europe have urged the United States to remain involved in European security. Opponents counter that the Western European nations are now quite capable of shouldering the burden of their own security.

NATO Expansion.   Despite Russian objections, NATO extended its membership eastward in 1997 by admitting Poland, Hungary, and the Czech Republic. These nations had long petitioned for membership in NATO, hoping to acquire the protection of the alliance against any renewal of Russian expansionism. Russian President Boris Yeltsin urged the United States and NATO not to expand eastward; he argued that nationalist and communist parties in Russia might gain public support if NATO expanded, at the expense of democratic forces. But proponents of NATO expansion argued successfully that a historic opportunity existed to solidify freedom and democracy in Eastern Europe by admitting those nations to NATO. Russia was reassured that it would be "consulted" on NATO policies, but was given no veto powers over these policies or no guarantee that other Eastern European nations might also be admitted to NATO in the future.

NATO in Bosnia.   Traditionally, NATO forces were never deployed outside of Western Europe. Should NATO consider using its forces for peacekeeping outside of the territory of members nations? NATO troops were deployed to Bosnia in 1995 to halt ethnic conflict raging among Serbs, Croats, and Muslims in the former province of Yugoslavia. U.S. aircraft and ground troops participated in this first excursion of NATO forces outside of Western Europe. But Eastern Europe is rife with ethnic conflict, and it is not clear what U.S. national security interests justify exposing American troops to the dangers of intervention.

POST–COLD WAR REGIONAL THREATS

For over four decades the Soviet threat drove American defense policy, force planning, training, strategy and tactics, weapons research and procurement, troop deployments, and defense budgeting. The fundamental change in the world balance of power has inspired a complete reexamination of defense policy over the last few years. While policymakers agree on the need for a thorough reevaluation of defense policy, they do not always agree on the right forces for the future.

Regional Threats.   The most likely threats today are those posed by regional aggressors. Saddam Hussein's Iraq is the model of new regional threat. Today U.S. military force levels are structured on the experience of defeating Iraq in the Gulf War.

- *Iraq.* Saddam Hussein's million-man army with its 5,000 tanks was reduced to one-third of its size in the Gulf War. The UN-sponsored economic blockade of

Iraq has hampered that nation's efforts to rebuild these conventional forces to their former size. However, Iraq continues to harbor Scud missiles and continues its efforts to acquire weapons of mass destruction—nuclear, chemical, and biological.

- *Iran*. Iran possesses a million-man army and it has been shopping for both conventional weapons and nuclear components in world arms markets. China and the former Soviet Union have supplied it with surface-to-surface missiles. Iran has also acquired a submarine force for operations in the Persian Gulf and a sizable air force. Iran supports terrorist groups throughout the Middle East and provides a beacon for violent Islamic fundamentalism. The Israelis consider Iran to be the principal threat to peace and stability in the region.
- *Syria*. Syria's military forces are impressive, with more than 700,000 soldiers and 4,000 tanks. Syria remains officially at war with Israel, and its troops occupy most of Lebanon.
- *Libya*. Muummar Khadafy's military forces are not a major threat, yet Libya remains a major base for worldwide terrorist activity.
- *North Korea*. North Korea remains the most authoritarian and militarist regime in the world. It devotes a very large proportion of its economy and population to its military. It supports a one million-man army with 4,000 tanks, a large air force, and a large submarine force. North Korea's nuclear weapons program is very advanced. Its "Great Leader," Kim Il-Sung, never renounced his intention to reunify Korea by force. His son, "Dear Leader" Kim Jong III, has replaced his father. In recognition of South Korea's burgeoning economy and progressive strengthening of its armed forces, the United States has undertaken a gradual reduction of American ground forces in South Korea. However, some U.S. ground forces are likely to remain near the border to deter invasion by North Korea. South Korea's army is only about half as large as that of North Korea; in the event of war, the United States would need to provide immediate air combat support.
- *China*. The People's Republic of China now possesses the world's largest armed forces—more than 3 million soldiers, nearly 10,000 tanks, and more than 4,000 combat aircraft. China has ICBMs with multiheaded nuclear warheads capable of reaching the United States. China has always asserted that Taiwan is a province of China (as has the government of the Republic of China in Taiwan); Beijing continues to declare unification a goal. It has stated a preference for peaceful reunification, but the threat of force has always been present. The Beijing government's policies toward Hong Kong, the former British colony incorporated into the People's Republic of China in 1997, will signal China's future course. Beijing continues to voice support for market reforms of its economy, but it acted with brutal force to suppress the democracy movement in Tiananmen Square in 1989.

Terrorism.   The threat of terrorism creates two military requirements. The first is the ability to punish nations that sponsor terrorism and to dissuade other nations from continuing their support of terrorism. In 1986 the United States struck at Libya in a limited air attack in response to various Libyan-supported acts of terrorism around the world. In 1993 the United States struck Iraq's intelligence center in Baghdad in response to a foiled plot to assassinate former President George Bush. These types of operations are carried out by conventional military forces. A second requirement is the ability to take direct action against terrorists to capture or kill them or to free their hostages. These operations are carried out by highly trained, specially equipped special operations forces.

Unanticipated Threats.   The United States anticipated very few of the dozens of crises that required the use of military force over the past decade. Few would have forecast that U.S. troops would be engaged in combat in Grenada in 1984, Panama in 1990, or even the Persian Gulf in 1991. General Colin Powell has tried to convince Congress that "The real threat is the unknown, the uncertain. In a very real sense, the primary threat to our security is instability and [being] unprepared to handle a crisis or war that no one expected or predicted."[2] But it is difficult to convince taxpayers or their elected representatives to prepare for the unknown.

WHEN TO USE MILITARY FORCE?

All modern presidents have acknowledged that the most agonizing decisions they have made were to send U.S. military forces into combat. These decisions cost lives. The American people are willing to send their sons and daughters into danger—and even to see some of them wounded or killed—but *only* if a president convinces them that the outcome "is worth dying for." A president must be able to explain why they lost their lives and to justify their sacrifice.

To Protect Vital Interests.   The U.S. military learned many bitter lessons in its long, bloody experience in Vietnam. Among those lessons:

- The United States should commit its military forces only in support of vital national interests.
- If military forces are committed, they must have clearly defined military objectives—the destruction of enemy forces and/or the capture of enemy-held territory.
- Any commitment of U.S. forces must be of sufficient strength to ensure overwhelming and decisive victory with the fewest possible casualties.
- Before committing U.S. military forces, there must be some reasonable assurances that the effort has the support of the American people and their representatives in Congress.
- The commitment of U.S. military forces should be a last resort, after political, economic, and diplomatic efforts have proven ineffective.

These guidelines for the use of military force are widely supported within the U.S. military itself.[3] Contrary to Hollywood stereotypes, military leaders are extremely reluctant to go to war when no vital interest of the United States is at stake, where there are no clear-cut military objectives, without the support of Congress or the American people, or without sufficient force to achieve speedy and decisive victory with minimal casualties. They are wary of seeing their troops placed in danger merely to advance diplomatic goals, or to engage in "peacekeeping," to "stabilize governments," or to "show the flag." They are reluctant to undertake humanitarian missions while being shot at. They do not like to risk their soldiers' lives under "rules of engagement" that limit their ability to defend themselves.

In Support of Important Political Objectives.   In contrast to military leaders, political leaders and diplomats often reflect the view that "war is a continuation of politics by other means"—a view commonly attributed to nineteenth-century German theorist of war Karl von Clausewitz. Military force may be used to protect interests that are important but not necessarily vital. Otherwise, the United States would be rendered largely impotent in world affairs. A diplomat's ability to achieve a satisfactory result often depends on the expressed or implied threat of military force. The distinguished international political theorist Hans Morgenthau wrote: "Since military strength is the obvious measure of a nation's power, its demonstration serves to impress others with that nation's power."[4]

Currently American military forces must be prepared to carry out a variety of missions in addition to the conduct of conventional war:

- Demonstrating U.S. resolve in crisis situations.
- Demonstrating U.S. support for democratic governments.
- Protecting U.S. citizens living abroad.
- Striking at terrorist targets to deter or retaliate.
- Peacemaking among warring factions or nations.
- Peacekeeping where hostile factions or nations have accepted a peace agreement.
- Providing humanitarian aid often under warlike conditions.

In pursuit of such objectives, recent U.S. presidents have sent troops to Lebanon in 1982 to stabilize the government (Reagan), to Grenada in 1983 to rescue American medical students and restore democratic government (Reagan), to Panama in 1989 to oust drug-trafficking General Manuel Antonio Noriega from power and to protect U.S. citizens (Bush), to Somalia in 1992–1993 to provide emergency humanitarian aid (Bush and Clinton), to Haiti in 1994 to restore constitutional government (Clinton), and to Bosnia in 1995–1996 for peacekeeping among warring ethnic factions (see Table 8–2).

Proponents of these more flexible uses of U.S. military forces usually deny any intent to be the "world's policeman." Rather, they argue that each situation must be judged independently on its own merits—weighing the importance of U.S. goals against expected costs. No military operation is without risk, but some risks may be worth taking to advance important political interests even though these interests may not be deemed "vital" to the United States. The media, particularly television, play an influential role in pressuring the president to use military force. Pictures of

TABLE 8-2   Major Deployments of U.S. Military Forces since World War II

Year	Area	President
1950–53	Korea	Truman
1958	Lebanon	Eisenhower
1961–64	Vietnam	Kennedy
1962	Cuban waters	Kennedy
1965–73	Vietnam	Johnson, Nixon
1965	Dominican Republic	Johnson
1970	Laos	Nixon
1970	Cambodia	Nixon
1975	Cambodia	Ford
1980	Iran	Carter
1982–83	Lebanon	Reagan
1983	Grenada	Reagan
1989	Panama	Bush
1990–91	Persian Gulf	Bush
1992–93	Somalia	Bush, Clinton
1994–95	Haiti	Clinton
1995–96	Bosnia	Clinton

torture and killing, starvation and death, and devastation and destruction from around the world provide a powerful emotional stimulus to U.S. military intervention. Generally a president can count on an initial "rally 'round the flag" surge in popular support for a military action, despite overall poor public knowledge of international politics. But if casualties mount during an operation, if no victory or end appears in sight, then press coverage of body bags coming home, military funeral services, and bereaved families create pressure on a president to end U.S. involvement. Unless the U.S. military can produce speedy and decisive results with few casualties, public support for military intervention wavers and critical voices in Congress arise.

DETERMINING MILITARY FORCE LEVELS

Overall military force levels in the United States are threat-driven, that is, determined by the size and nature of the perceived threats to national security. It is true that particular weapons systems or base openings or closings may be driven by political forces such as the influence of defense contractors in Congress or the power of a member of Congress from a district heavily affected by defense spending. And not everyone in the White House and Congress, or even the Defense Department, agrees on the precise nature of the threats confronting the United States now or in the future. Yet defense policy planning and the "sizing" of U.S. military forces begins with an assessment of the threats confronting the nation.

Iraqi-equivalent Major Regional Threats. Today U.S. military force levels are designed to confront major regional threats. The military forces required by the United States are based on the notion of an "Iraqi-equivalent" regional threat—the military forces required by the United States to defeat Iraq speedily and decisively in the Gulf War. But current planning also envisions the possibility that a second aggressor might decide to challenge the United States somewhere else in the world while our forces were involved in an Iraqi-equivalent war. For example, if U.S. forces were involved in the Persian Gulf against Iraq or Iran, North Korea might decide to take advantage of the situation and launch an invasion of South Korea. The United States currently plans to maintain sufficient additional U.S. forces to "fight and win two nearly simultaneous major regional conflicts." The ambiguous wording—"nearly simultaneous"—recognizes that the United States may not be able to airlift and sealift sufficient forces to fight and win two regional wars at the same time. American forces will be obliged to hold one aggressor (principally with air power) while defeating the other; once one aggressor is defeated, the United States can then redeploy sufficient forces to defeat a second aggressor.

Future Force Levels. The revised threat assessment rationalized deep cuts in military forces and defense budgets in the Clinton administration. The Army is reduced to 10 active combat divisions and the Air Force to 12 fighter wings. (A U.S. Army division includes 15,000 to 18,000 troops; an Air Force fighter wing includes approximately 72 combat aircraft.) The Navy deploys 12 carrier battle groups (a carrier battle group typically includes one aircraft carrier with 75 to 85 aircraft, plus defending cruisers, destroyers, frigates, attack submarines, and support ships). The Marine Corps retains all three of its Marine expeditionary forces (each MEF includes one Marine division, one Marine air wing, and supporting services) (see Table 8–3).

Criticism. While most defense experts agree on the assessment of the threat—the need to prepare to fight and win two major regional conflicts simultaneously—many believe that the Clinton administration's projected force levels are inadequate for these tasks. Opponents contend that the reduced numbers of Army

TABLE 8-3   Post–Cold War Military Force Levels

	End of Cold War 1990	Clinton Review 1998
Active duty personnel (in millions)	2.1	1.4
Army divisions	18	10
Navy carrier battle groups	15	12
Marine expeditionary forces	3	3
Air Force fighter wings	24	12

Source: Office of the Secretary of Defense, *Quadrennial Defense Review*, May 19, 1997.

and Air Force combat units and the limited transport and support services available to the military are inadequate for two major regional conflicts. Casualties can be kept low only when overwhelming military force is employed quickly and decisively, as in Operation Desert Storm. Lives are lost when minimal forces are sent into combat, when they have inadequate air combat support, or when they are extended over too broad a front. Potential regional foes—for example, Iran and North Korea—deploy modern heavy armor and artillery forces. The United States benefited from a six-month buildup of its heavy forces in the Gulf region before Operation Desert Storm began; such a period of preparation is unlikely in a future conflict. Commitments of U.S. troops to peacekeeping and humanitarian missions divert resources, training, and morale away from war-fighting. These commitments further erode the ability of the United States to confront multiple regional aggressors.

Post–Cold War Defense Spending.   The U.S. investment in national defense during the long Cold War succeeded in its most vital objective—deterring nuclear war. It also maintained the peace and security of Western Europe, which had experienced two world wars in the first half of the twentieth century. The achievement of these objectives of the U.S. national defense policy led to a welcome yet paradoxical result—a lessening of the threat to national security and a reduction in national defense needs (see Figure 8–2). American defense spending has steadily declined in real dollars since 1986, and it is projected to decline to less than 15

FIGURE 8–2   Trends in Defense Spending

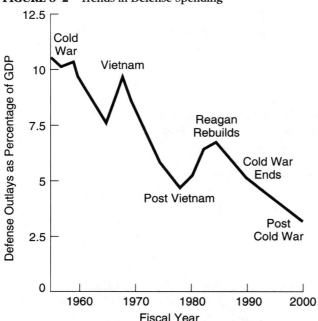

percent of federal spending and less than 3 percent of the nation's GNP. These are levels roughly comparable to those that prevailed before Pearl Harbor was attacked in 1941.

THE USE OF FORCE: THE GULF WAR

Too often political leaders send military forces into hostile regions with no clear military mission. Military forces are designed to destroy enemy forces and capture enemy territory. When given other vague or ill-defined missions—"peacekeeping," "stabilizing governments," "sending diplomatic signals," and so on—military forces are misused.

Saddam Hussein's Invasion of Kuwait.   Saddam Hussein's August 2, 1990, invasion of Kuwait was apparently designed to restore his military prestige after a long and indecisive war against Iran; to secure additional oil revenues to finance the continued buildup of Iraqi military power; and to intimidate (and perhaps invade) Saudi Arabia and the Gulf states, thereby securing control over a major share of the world's oil reserves. On paper, Iraq possessed the fourth-largest military force in the world, with 1 million troops, battle-hardened from eight years of war with Iran. In addition Iraq had deadly chemical weapons, which it had previously used against Iran and its own Kurdish population.[5]

The Iraqi invasion met with a surprisingly swift response by the United Nations, with Security Council resolutions condemning the invasion, demanding an immediate withdrawal, and imposing a trade embargo and economic sanctions. President George Bush immediately set to work to stitch together a coalition military force that would eventually include thirty nations.

Clear Political and Military Objectives.   Early in the crisis President Bush committed U.S. forces in the Gulf region to the military defense of Saudi Arabia in Operation Desert Shield. The president feared that Saddam Hussein would order his troops to continue their offensive into the Arabian peninsula and force Saudia Arabia and the other Gulf states to submit to his domination. The president described the early U.S. military deployment as "defensive." But he soon became convinced that neither diplomacy nor an economic blockade would dislodge Saddam from Kuwait; that Saddam would use the added oil resources to continue his military buildup, including the acquisition of nuclear weapons; and that his aggression, if unpunished, would intimidate other Gulf nations and cede political leadership in the region to the ruthless autocrat.

President Bush formulated clear strategic objectives for his military commanders, ordering them to prepare an "offensive" plan that would (1) force the immediate and unconditional withdrawal of Iraqi forces from Kuwait, (2) destroy Saddam Hussein's nuclear and chemical weapons facilities, and (3) ensure that Iraqi military forces would no longer be capable of posing a threat to the region.

Overwhelming and Decisive Military Force.   The top U.S. military commanders—including the Chairman of the Joint Chiefs of Staff, General Colin Powell, and the commander in the field, General Norman Schwarzkopf—had been field officers in Vietnam, and they were resolved not to repeat the mistakes of that war. They were reluctant to go into battle without the full support of the American people. If ordered to fight, they wanted to employ overwhelming and decisive military force; they wanted to avoid gradual escalation, protracted conflict, target limitations, and political interference in the conduct of the war. Accordingly, they presented the President with a plan that called for a very large military buildup. More than 500,000 U.S. military personnel were sent to the Gulf region, including elements of six Army divisions and two Marine divisions, with, 1,900 tanks, 930 artillery pieces, 500 attack helicopters, and more than 1,000 combat aircraft. Coalition forces also included British and French heavy armored units and Egyptian, Syrian, Saudi, and other Arab forces.

Debating the Use of Force.   When President Bush announced this massive buildup of forces on November 8, however, he immediately faced a barrage of criticism at home for abandoning his earlier defensive posture. Senator Sam Nunn, respected chair of the Senate Armed Forces Committee, opened hearings that urged the President to continue economic sanctions and avoid the heavy casualties that a land war was expected to produce. But Bush was convinced that sanctions would not work, that Saddam would hold out for years, and that eventually the political coalition backing the embargo would break up. He believed that Saddam would become an increasingly powerful opponent who would soon dominate the Arab world and Mideast oil reserves. Moreover, unless stopped quickly, Saddam would soon acquire nuclear weapons.

On November 29, 1990, Secretary of State James Baker won the support of UN Security Council members, including the Soviet Union (with China abstaining), for a resolution authorizing coalition forces to "use all necessary means" against Iraq unless it withdrew from Kuwait by January 15. Following a lengthy debate in Congress, on January 12 President Bush won a similar resolution in the House (250–183) and the Senate (52–47).

Operation Desert Storm.   From Baghdad, CNN reporters Bernard Shaw and Peter Arnett were startled on the night of January 16 when Operation Desert Storm began with an air attack on key installations in the city. Iraqi forces were also surprised, despite the prompt timing of the attack. Saddam had assured them that the United States lacked the resolve to fight and that even if war broke out, U.S. public opinion would force a settlement as casualties rose.

The success of the coalition air force was spectacular. More than 110,000 combat missions were flown with only 39 aircraft losses, none in air combat. Most Iraqi aircraft were compelled to stay on the ground, as runway and control facilities were destroyed; 38 Iraqi planes were shot down in combat, and 140 escaped to Iran. Strategic targets—including nuclear facilities, chemical warfare plants, command centers, and military communications—were repeatedly attacked. "Smart" weapons performed superbly. American TV audiences saw videotapes of laser-guided bombs entering the doors and air shafts of enemy bunkers. Civilian damage was lower than in any previous air war. After five weeks of air war, intelligence estimated that nearly half the Iraqi tanks and artillery in the field had been destroyed, demoralized troops were hiding in deep shelters, and the battlefield had been isolated and prepared for ground operations.

General Schwarzkopf's plan for the ground war emphasized deception and maneuver. He wanted the Iraqis to believe that the main attack would come directly against Kuwait's southern border and would be supported by a Marine landing on the coast. While Iraqi forces prepared for attacks from the south and the east coasts, Schwarzkopf sent heavily armed columns in a "Hail Mary" play—a wide sweep to the west, outflanking and cutting off Iraqi forces in the battle area. The Iraqi forces, blinded by air attack and obliged to stay in their bunkers, were not able to know about or respond to the flanking attack. On the night of February 24, the ground attack began. Marines breached ditches and mine fields and raced directly to the Kuwait airport. Army helicopter air assaults lunged deep into Iraq; armored columns raced northward across the desert to outflank Iraqi forces and than attack them from the west; a surge in air attacks kept Iraqi forces holed up in their bunkers. Iraqi troops surrendered in droves, highways from Kuwait city became a massive junkyard of Iraqi vehicles, and Iraqi forces that tried to fight were quickly destroyed. After one hundred hours of ground fighting, President Bush ordered a ceasefire.

Results of the War.   The United States achieved a decisive military victory quickly and with remarkably few casualties. The president resisted calls to expand the original objectives of war and go on to capture Baghdad, to destroy the Iraqi economy, to encourage Iraq's disintegration as a nation, or to kill Saddam, although it was expected that defeat would lead to his ouster. Although the war left many political issues unresolved, it was the most decisive military outcome the United States had achieved since the end of World War II. President Bush chose to declare victory and celebrate the return of American troops.

But the results of the war were mixed. In retrospect, the president's decision to end the war after only one hundred hours of ground operations appears to have been premature. Not all of his original objectives had been fully accomplished. Units of Saddam's elite Republican Guard, which would have been surrounded and destroyed with another's day's fighting, escaped back to Baghdad. With these surviving forces, Saddam maintained his cruel grip on the country and proceeded to attack his regime's opponents brutally, especially the Kurdish minority in northern Iraq. Later investigations revealed that his nuclear weapons facilities had not been completely destroyed. And finally, Saddam's continuation in power appeared to mock the sacrifices in lives exacted by the war.

Lessons of the Gulf War.   The Gulf War taught the nation a number of lessons about the effective use of military power:[6]

- The rapid employment of overwhelming forces is both politically and militarily superior to gradual escalation and employment of minimum force. The use of overwhelming force reduces total casualties and achieves an earlier and more decisive victory.
- The nation's political leadership is vastly more effective when it concentrates on developing and maintaining foreign and domestic political support for a war while leaving the planning and execution of military operations to the military leadership.
- A rapid conclusion of hostilities ensures that public support will not erode over time and that protracted combat and a steady stream of casualties will not fuel antiwar sentiments.
- Military force can capture territory and destroy enemy forces, but it cannot guarantee peace. Even a military-weakened Saddam Hussein remains a threat to stability in the Middle East.

Perhaps the most important lesson, however, is that the end of the Cold War does not mean that the United States no longer requires military power.

SUMMARY

Decisions about defense policy in Washington and in other capitals are interdependent—strategies, force levels, and spending decisions depend on perceived threats posed by other major powers. Game theory provides a way of thinking rationally about decision making in competitive, interdependent situations.

1. Deterrence strategy seeks to prevent nuclear war by making the consequences of a nuclear attack unacceptable to a rational enemy. Deterrence emphasizes *second-strike* capability—the ability of a nation's forces to survive an attack and inflict unacceptable levels of destruction on the attacker in retaliation.

2. To implement its deterrence strategy, the United States maintained a TRIAD of strategic forces—land-based missiles, submarine-launched missiles, and manned bombers. Submarine-based missiles remain the most survivable of nuclear deterrent forces.

3. The end of the Cold War has resulted in a decline in overall strategic nuclear forces by two-thirds. The START agreements slash total nuclear warheads on both sides and require the elimination of all land-based MIRV missiles. The resulting force levels on both sides will virtually eliminate the possibility of launching a rational first strike.

4. Current strategic debate focus on nondeterrable threats—missiles launched by a terrorist nation, unauthorized missile launches by elements within the former Soviet Union, and accidental missile launches. Global nuclear proliferation increases the likelihood of these threats. President Ronald Reagan began a large-scale research

program, the Strategic Defense Initiative (SDI), or "Star Wars," to develop a capability to intercept and destroy incoming ballistic missiles. The SDI organization has been terminated, but research continues on ground-based ballistic missile defenses. No decision has been made to deploy anti-missile defense to protect U.S. populations.

5. The preservation of democracy in Western Europe has been a central goal of U.S. policy throughout the twentieth century. In the NATO alliance the United States and Western European nations pledge that an armed attack against one will be considered an armed attack against all. A joint NATO military command is designated to implement this pledge.

6. The collapse of communist governments in Eastern Europe, the unification of Germany, and the dissolution of the Soviet Union have greatly diminished the threat to European security. These developments allowed the number of U.S. troops stationed in Europe to be reduced by over one-half. Today important questions confront NATO, notably whether or not to admit newly democratic nations of Eastern Europe and whether to deploy its troops on missions outside of Western Europe.

7. Post–Cold War U.S. defense policy is driven primarily by the threats posed by potential regional aggressors. Terrorism, as well as the need to respond to unanticipated crises, also influences defense policy.

8. In the bottom-up review, U.S. military force levels are designed to confront two nearly simultaneous, major, Iraqi-equivalent regional conflicts. This threat assessment is said to justify drastic reductions in Army and Air Force combat units. Navy and Marine combat units, traditionally designed for regional wars, face less drastic cuts. The end of the Cold War has brought projected defense spending to less than 15 percent of total federal spending and less than 3 percent of GNP.

9. The U.S. has never adopted clear policy guidelines regarding when to use military force. Most military leaders argue that troops should be used only to protect vital national interests, with clearly defined military objectives, and with the support of Congress and the American people. Furthermore, military force should only be used with sufficient force to achieve speedy and decisive victory with minimum casualties, and only as a last resort.

10. In contrast, many political and diplomatic leaders argue that troops may be used in support of important political objectives and humanitarian goals. These may include demonstrating U.S. resolve in crisis situations, U.S. support for democratic governments, peacemaking among warring factions or nations, peacekeeping where hostile parties have agreed to a settlement, and the provision of humanitarian aid.

NOTES

1. President Ronald Reagan, *The President's Strategic Defense Initiative*, The White House, January 3, 1985.
2. General Colin Powell, Testimony Before the Budget Committee of the U.S. Senate, February 1992.

3. See Caspar W. Weinberger, "The Uses of Military Force," *Defense* (Arlington, VA: American Forces Information Survey, 1985).
4. Han Morganthau, *Politics Among Nations* (New York: Knopf, 1973), p. 27.
5. *The Military Balance 1991–92* (London: International Institute for Strategic Studies, 1991).
6. See Harry G. Summers, Jr., *On Strategy II: A Critical Analysis of the Gulf War* (New York: Dell, 1992).

BIBLIOGRAPHY

DILLER, DANIEL C., ED. *Russia and the Independent States*. Washington, DC: CQ Press, 1992.
The Military Balance. London: International Institute for Strategic Studies, annually.
Office of the Secretary of Defense, *The Bottom-Up Review*. Washington, DC: U.S. Department of Defense, 1993.
SNOW, DONALD M. *Distant Thunder*. New York: St. Martins Press, 1992.
SNOW, DONALD M. *National Security*. 2nd ed. New York: St. Martins Press, 1991.
SPANIER, JOHN. *Games Nations Play*. 8th ed. Washington, DC: CQ Press, 1992.
SUMMERS, HARRY G., JR. *On Strategy II: A Critical Analysis of the Gulf War*. New York: Dell, 1992.

9

ECONOMIC POLICY
Incrementalism at Work

Former White House Chief of Staff Leon Panetta, right, and Budget Director Franklin Raines, share a laugh while meeting reporters in the White House briefing room. (Wilfredo Lee/AP/Wide World Photos)

INCREMENTALISM IN FISCAL AND MONETARY POLICY

Government economic policy is exercised primarily through its *fiscal policies*—its decisions about taxing, spending, and deficit levels—and its *monetary policies*—its decisions about the money supply and interest rates. Fiscal policy is determined largely in the annual preparation of the federal budget by the president and the Office of Management and Budget and in the annual consideration by Congress of appropriations bills and revisions of the tax laws. These decisions determine overall federal spending levels, as well as spending priorities among federal programs; together with tax policy decisions (see Chapter 10), these spending decisions determine the size of the federal government's annual deficits. (Federal expenditures have exceeded federal revenues every year since 1960.) Monetary policy is determined by the independent Federal Reserve Board—"the Fed"—which can expand or contract the money supply through its oversight of the nation's banks.

If economic policymaking were completely rational, it would be closely tied to a coherent economic theory. The goals of economic policy are widely shared: growth in economic output and standards of living, full and productive employment of the nation's workforce, and stable prices with low inflation. But a variety of economic theories compete for preeminence as ways to achieve these goals. From time to time, national economic policy has been guided by different theories; or worse, it has been guided by conflicting theories simultaneously.

In practice, fiscal and monetary policies are made *incrementally*; that is, decisionmakers concentrate their attention on modest changes—increases or decreases—in existing taxing, spending, and deficit levels as well as the money supply and interest rates. Incrementalism is especially pervasive in annual federal budget making. Budget makers do not reconsider the value of all existing programs each year or even pay much attention to previously established expenditure levels. Rather last year's expenditures are usually considered as a base of spending for each program, and active consideration of budget proposals focuses on new items and increases over last year's base.

Incrementalism describes the process of economic policymaking, and it also provides very good short-term predictions of government policies. Last year's expenditure level for any government program is the best predictor of next year's expenditure level. Incrementalism is also an explanatory theory—it helps to explain why government programs, policies, and expenditures persist and grow over time, long after their value to society has diminished or ended altogether. But before examining incrementalism in government policymaking, let us consider some of the leading rational theories that compete as guides to economic policy.

ECONOMIC THEORIES AS POLICY GUIDES

Macroeconomic theories, when applied to the government's influence on the economy, focus on aggregate amounts of spending, taxes, borrowing, and money. Macroeconomic theories try both to explain economic cycles and to prescribe government policies to counter inflation and recession.

Classical Theory.   Classical economists generally view a market economy as a self-adjusting mechanism that will achieve an equilibrium of full employment, maximum productivity, and stable prices if left alone by the government. The price mechanism will adjust the decisions of millions of Americans to bring into balance the supply and demand of goods and labor. Regarding recessions, if workers are temporarily unemployed because the supply for workers exceeds the demand, wages (the price of labor) will fall; eventually it will again become profitable for businesses to have more workers at lower wages and thus end unemployment. Similarly, if the demand for goods (automobiles, houses, clothing, kitchenware, and so forth) falls, business inventories will rise and businesspeople will reduce prices (often through rebates, sales, etc.) until demand picks up again. Regarding inflation, general increases in prices will reduce demand and automatically bring it back into line with supply unless the government interferes. In short, classical economic theory relies on the free movement of prices to counter both recession and inflation.

Keynesian Theory.   But the Great Depression of the 1930s shattered popular confidence in classical economics. During that decade, the average unemployment rate was 18 percent, rising to 25 percent in the worst year, 1933. But even in 1936, seven years after the great stock market crash in 1929, unemployment was still 18 percent of the workforce, raising questions about the ability of the market to stabilize itself and ensure high employment and productivity.

According to the British economist John Maynard Keynes, economic instability was a product of fluctuations in demand. Both unemployment and lower wages reduced the demand for goods; businesses cut production and laid off more workers to adjust for lower demand for their goods; but cuts and layoffs further reduced demand and accelerated the downward spiral. Keynesian theory suggested that the economy could fall into a recession and stay there. Only government could take the necessary countercyclical steps to expand demand by spending more money itself and lowering taxes. Of course, the government cannot add to aggregate demand if it balances the budget. Rather, during a recession it must incur deficits to add to total demand, spending more than it receives in revenue. To counter inflationary trends, the government should take just the opposite steps.

"We Are All Keynesians."   Keynesian ideas dominated policymaking for nearly half a century. Countercyclical policies were written into the Employment Act of 1946, specifically pledging the federal government "to promote maximum employment production and purchasing power" through its aggregate to taxing and spending. The act created the Council of Economic Advisors to "develop and recommend to the president national economic policies" and required the president to submit to Congress an annual economic report assessing the state of the economy. While arguments continued over whether policy should tilt toward fighting recession or fighting inflation, by 1970 President Richard Nixon announced that "we are all Keynesians."

Yet while most economists endorsed government deficits to counter recessions, it became increasingly clear that politicians were unable to end deficit spending after the recession was over. Politicians were more fearful of unemployment than inflation, and since Keynesian theory portrayed these events as opposite ends of a seesaw, politicians were given a rationale for continued deficit spending. More importantly, by removing the moral strictures against deficits, politicians were encouraged to indulge the current generation of voters and shift the cost to future generations.

Supply-side Economics.   Supply-side economists argue that attention to long-term economic growth is more important than short-term manipulation of demand. Economic growth, which requires an expansion in the productive capacity of society, increases the overall supply of goods and services and thereby holds down prices. Inflation is reduced or ended altogether. More importantly, everyone's standard of living is improved with the availability of more goods and services at stable prices. Economic growth even increases government revenues over the long run.

Most supply-side economists believe that the free market is better equipped than government to bring about lower prices and more supplies of what people need and want. Government, they argue, is the problem, not the solution. Government taxing, spending, and monetary policies have promoted immediate consumption instead of investment in the future. High taxes penalize hard work, creativity, investment, and savings. The government should provide tax incentives to encourage investment and savings; tax rates should be lowered to encourage work and enterprise. Overall government spending should be held in check; if possible, the governmental proportion of the GNP should be reduced over time. Government regulations should be minimized to increase productivity and growth. Overall, the government should act to stimulate production and supply rather than demand and consumption.

Economic policy in the 1980s under President Reagan reflected these supply-side views. According to Reagan, the most important cause of the nation's economic problems—inflation, unemployment, low productivity, low investment—was the government itself. Upon taking office the Reagan administration (1) cut the rate of growth in federal domestic spending, (2) reduced income taxes and, lowered the top marginal tax rates, and (3) slowed the growth of government regulations. The economy registered strong growth during the Reagan years (see Figure 9–1). But the Reagan administration failed to cut government spending; on the contrary, government spending continued to increase during the Reagan years, although the rate of growth was slowed. Tax cuts did not result in greatly increased revenues, as predicted by some supply-side economists. Government spending was not slowed sufficiently to offset these lost revenues, and defense spending was increased. The result was *the largest series of annual federal budget deficits in history* and a staggering explosion of the national debt from $1 to $4 trillion during the Reagan-Bush years.

Clinton and Enterprise Economics.   The recession of the early 1990s, coupled with continuing budget deficits, fueled Bill Clinton's campaign for the presidency. Clinton publicly ridiculed the supply-side notion of the Reagan-Bush years, calling it "failed trickle-down" economics. Instead, Clinton appeared to embrace neoliberal "enterprise economics" that stresses the government's responsibility to stimulate eco-

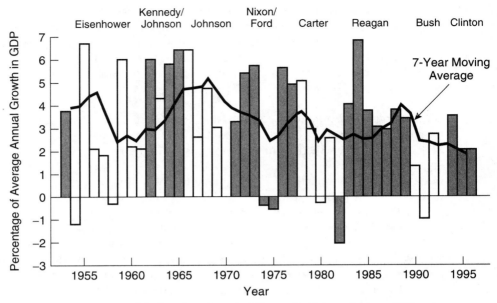

Source: *Economic Report of the President,* Council of Economic Advisers, February 1996.

FIGURE 9–1   Economic Growth over Time

nomic growth. Enterprise economics argues that the federal government must take the leading role in improving America's competitive position in the global economy. Since 1970, the average weekly and hourly wages of workers have declined in real (inflation-adjusted) dollars. In other words, the average worker has less purchasing power today than a generation ago. (Average real family income has risen only because more family members are working, but each worker is earning less.) Moreover, there is greater inequality in the distribution of family income than in 1970, that is, a greater differentiation between high-income and low-income families.

Enterprise economics claims to reject both the conservative supply-side emphasis on stimulating private investment capital and the liberal Keynesian emphasis on stimulating demand. Instead, it calls for government "investment" (spending) in (1) "human capital"—education and skill training of workers; (2) technology—especially communications and transportation; and (3) infrastructure—roads, bridges, ports, airports, and so on. The Clinton administration has backed away from industrial policy—targeting government grants and subsidies to specific emerging industries—fearing that government subsidies to specific industries would make interest group politics the driving force in the economy. Instead government "investments" are to be directed at resources common to all economic activities.[1]

Monetarist Economics.   Keynesian theory recommended not only increased government spending, reduced taxes, and larger deficits during recessions but also an expansion of the money supply. Expanding the supply of money, by easing bank reserve requirements and lowering bank interest rates, was expected to add to demand. Similarly, during inflationary periods, the government was supposed to tighten the supply of money by increasing bank reserve requirements and increasing interest rates. Thus, by increasing or decreasing the overall supply of money, the government could "fine-tune" the economy.

The independent Federal Reserve Board, commonly called "the Fed," can expand or contract the money supply through its oversight of the operation of banks participating in the Federal Reserve System. The Fed is headed by a seven-person board of governors, appointed by the president for overlapping terms of fourteen years. By controlling the amount of money banks can lend, the Fed can regulate the money supply and influence interest rates.

However, monetarist economic theory contends that economic stability can be achieved only by holding the rate of monetary growth to the same rate as the economy itself. Led by the Nobel Prize-winning economist Milton Friedman, monetarists challenge the view that manipulating the money supply can effectively influence economic activity. They argue that over the long run real income is a function of actual economic output. Increasing the supply of money faster than output only creates inflation. The value of each dollar declines because there is more money to buy the same amount of goods. Government manipulation of the money supply can only produce short-term economic effects. Monetarists believe that high interest rates are a product of investors' fears of continued inflation. As soon as investors come to believe that the Fed will stick to noninflationary policies, interest rates will come down. In short, monetarists believe that government tinkering with the money supply is the problem, not the solution.

INCREMENTALISM AND GOVERNMENT SPENDING

Government spending has grown dramatically in all modern presidential administrations, regardless of their professed beliefs in economic theories. The expenditures of all governments in the United States—the federal government, together with fifty state governments and over 83 local governments—grew from $480 billion in 1959 to over $2.5 *trillion* in 1995 (see Table 9–1). This means that governments spend an amount equivalent to 35 percent of the nation's gross domestic product (GDP)—the sum of all of the goods and services produced in the United States in a year. Today the federal government alone spends well over $1.6 trillion dollars each year, more than 20 percent of the nation's GDP.

Incrementalism in Budget Making.   The incremental model of policymaking is particularly well suited to assist in understanding the budgeting process and the growth of government spending. Budgeting is incremental because decision makers generally consider last year's expenditures as a base and limit active consideration of budget proposals to new items or requested increases over the base. Thus, the attention of presidents, members of Congress, governors, legislators, mayors, and

TABLE 9-1   The Growth of Government Spending

	ALL GOVERNMENT SPENDING			FEDERAL GOVERNMENT SPENDING	
	GDP Billions	Billions	Percent of GDP	Billions	Percent of GDP
1959	480.2	131.9	27.5	92.1	19.2
1965	671.0	185.8	27.6	118.2	17.6
1970	985.4	311.2	31.6	195.6	19.8
1975	1,509.8	530.6	35.2	332.3	22.0
1980	2,644.1	861.0	32.6	590.9	22.3
1985	3,967.7	1,342.2	33.8	946.4	23.8
1992	5,868.6	2,068.6	35.2	1,381.8	23.5
1995	7,254	2,539	35.0	1,538.9	22.5
1998*	8,313	N.A.	N.A.	1,687.5	20.3

* Projections based on President's fiscal 1998 budget.

Source: *Economic Report of the President 1997.* Washington, DC: U.S. Government Printing Office, 1997.

councils is focused on a narrow range of increases or decreases in a budget. A budget is almost never reviewed as a whole every year, in the sense of reconsidering the value of all existing programs. Departments are seldom required to defend or explain budget requests that do not exceed current appropriations; only requested *increases* in appropriations require explanation.

Budget decisions are made incrementally because policymakers do not have the time, energy, or information to review every dollar of every budget request every year. Nor do they wish to refight annually every political battle over the establishment of programs. Reformers have proposed the "zero-based" budget to force agencies to justify every penny requested, not just requested increases. In theory, zero-based budgeting would eliminate unnecessary spending protected by incrementalism. But in practice, it requires so much wasted effort in justifying already accepted programs each year that executive agencies and legislative committees grow tired of the effort and return to incrementalism.

Bureaucratic Expansionism.   Both bureaucrats and the legislators who decide on their budgets are personally interested in expanding government budgets.[2] Bureaucrats are interested in increasing the amount of money they can spend and the number of employees under their supervision. Legislators want to increase the resources over which they have jurisdiction and enhance the government's capacity to deal with their own constituents. Interest groups also want to increase the size of government programs that benefit their own members. Benefits are visible and concentrated. Costs, even though they may exceed the benefits, are diffused among all of the nation's taxpayers.

Fragmented Decision Making. In theory, the Office of Management and Budget (OMB) in the executive branch and the Congressional Budget Office (CBO) in the legislative branch are supposed to bring together budget requests and fit them into a coherent whole, while at the same time relating them to revenue estimates. But it is very difficult for the president, and almost impossible for Congress, to view the total policy impact of a budget. The fragmented character of the budgetary process helps to secure political agreement on the budget as well as reduce the burden of calculation. If each congressional subcommittee challenged the result of the others, conflict might be so great that no budget would ever be passed. It is much easier to agree on a small increase or decrease to a single program than it is to compare the worth of one program to that of all the others. However, to counter fragmentation in the federal budget, Congress established not only the CBO but also House and Senate budget committees to examine the budget as a whole (see the following section). It is interesting to note that their purpose is to try to overcome fragmentation in federal budget making.

Nonprogrammatic Decision Making. Reformers frequently call for "program budgeting"—the allocation of funds by program area with careful calculation of the costs and benefits of specific policy options. But decision makers seldom evaluate whole programs and almost never eliminate programs altogether. Wildavsky points out that some political functions are served by *non*program budgeting:

> Agreement comes much readily when the items can be treated in dollars instead of basic differences in policy. Calculating budgets in monetary increments facilitates bargaining and logrolling. It becomes possible to swap an increase here for a decrease there or for an increase elsewhere without always having to consider the ultimate desirability of the programs blatantly in competition.[3]

"UNCONTROLLABLE" GOVERNMENT SPENDING

Government budgeting is incremental in part because of "uncontrollables" in the federal budget. These are items determined by past policies of Congress and represent commitments in future federal budgets. Most federal spending is "uncontrollable," that is, based on previous decisions of Congress and not easily changed in the annual budget making. Sources of uncontrollable spending include the following:

Entitlement Programs. Federal programs that provide classes of people with a legally enforceable right to benefits are called "entitlement" programs, and they account for over half of all federal spending, including Social Security, welfare, Medicare and Medicaid, food stamps, federal employees' retirement, and veterans' benefits. Entitlements now constitute nearly 60 percent of all federal spending (see Figure 5–1 "Entitlement Spending in the Federal Budget" in Chapter 5). These entitlements are benefits that past Congresses have pledged the federal government to pay. Entitlements are not really uncontrollable. Congress can always amend the basic laws that established them; but this is politically difficult and might be regarded by voters as a failure of trust.

Indexing of Benefits.   One reason that spending increases each year is that Congress has authorized automatic increases in benefits tied to increases in prices. Benefits are "indexed" to the Consumer Price Index under Social Security, SSI, food stamps, and veterans' pensions. This indexing pushes up the cost of entitlement programs each year, even when the number of recipients stays the same. Indexing, of course, runs counter to federal efforts to restrain inflation. Moreover the Consumer Price Index generally overestimates real increases in the cost of living.

Increasing Costs of In-kind Benefits.   Rises in the cost of major in-kind (noncash) benefits, particularly medical costs of Medicaid and Medicare, also guarantee growth in federal spending. These in-kind benefit programs have risen faster in cost than cash benefit programs.

Interest on the National Debt.   Interest payments have grown rapidly as a percentage of all federal spending. The federal government has a long history of deficits. Only one year in the past thirty has the government balanced the budget. The result is a national debt over $6 *trillion*. Each year the deficit increases, interest payments go up. Interest payments also rise with increases in interest rates. Interest payments are now more than 14 percent of total federal spending.

Backdoor Spending.   Some federal spending does not appear on the budget. For example, spending by the postal service is not included in the federal budget. No clear rule explains why some agencies are in the budget and others are not. But "off-budget" agencies have the same economic effects as other government agencies. Another form of backdoor spending is found in government-guaranteed loans. Initially government guarantees for loans—FHA housing, guaranteed student loans, veterans' loans, and so forth—do not require federal money. The government merely promises to repay the loan if the borrower fails to do so. Yet these loans create an obligation against the government.

CHANGING BUDGET PRIORITIES: CHALLENGING INCREMENTALISM

Incrementalism may help to explain the process of budgetary decision making, but it appears unable to explain major changes in budgetary priorities over time. Incrementalism views public policy as a continuation of past government activities, with only incremental modifications from year to year. Yet increments add up over time: some programs, like Social Security and Medicare, expand over the years, taking ever larger shares of federal spending; other programs, like national defense, gradually contract as a share of federal spending.

Revolutions in spending patterns are not anticipated by incremental theory.

Nonetheless, the United States experienced a revolution in spending priorities during the 1970s. In a single decade America's national priorities in defense and social welfare were reversed. In 1965 national defense expenditures accounted for 43 percent of the federal budget, while Social Security and welfare expenditures combined accounted for only 22 percent (see Table 9–2). While the mass media focused on the war in Vietnam and on Watergate, these national priorities were reversed. By 1975, only a decade later, defense accounted for only 26 percent of the federal budget, while Social Security and welfare expenditures had grown to 35 percent. This reversal of national priorities occurred during both Democratic (Johnson) and Republican (Nixon and Ford) administrations in Washington *and* during the nation's longest war. In short, what we thought we knew about the effects of politics and war on social welfare spending turned out to be wrong.

Federal budget outlays over two decades for major programs are shown in Table 9–2 in both dollars and percentages of the total federal budget. Note how spending for national defense has declined very rapidly as a percentage of total federal spending. The Reagan defense buildup of the 1980s only expanded defense spending to about 27 percent of total federal spending, well below early Cold War levels under presidents Eisenhower, Kennedy, and Johnson. The end of the Cold War precipitated a rapid decline in defense spending (see Chapter 8). These trends defy traditional incremental expectations.

Today Social Security is the largest single item in the budget. Medicare (for the aged) and Medicaid (for the poor) are the fastest-growing items in the budget. The growth of these health care programs can hardly be described as incremental.

THE BURDENS OF GOVERNMENT DEBT

Decades of annual deficits—over forty years in which the federal government has spent more than it received in revenues—has driven up the accumulated debt of the United States government to over $6 *trillion* dollars. The national debt now exceeds $16,000 for every man, woman, and child in the nation, or more than $60,000 for every one of America's 66 million families.

This debt is owed mostly to American banks and financial institutions and private citizens who buy Treasury bonds. Only about 13 percent is owed to foreign banks, firms, and individuals. As old debt comes due, the Treasury Department sells new bonds to pay off the old; that is, it continues to "roll over" or "float" the debt. The debt today is smaller as a percentage of the GDP than at some periods in U.S. history (see Figure 9–2). Indeed, in order to pay the costs of fighting World War II, the U.S. government ran up a debt of 110 percent of GDP; the current debt is the highest in history in dollar terms but only about 70 percent of the GDP. This suggests that the debt is still manageable because of the size and strength of the U.S. economy.

The ability to float such a huge debt depends on public confidence in the U.S. government—confidence that it will continue to pay interest on its debt, that it will pay off the principal of bond issues when they come due, and that the value of the bonds will not decline over time because of inflation.

TABLE 9-2   Federal Budget Priorities over the Years

BILLIONS OF DOLLARS								
Function	1960	1965	1970	1975	1980	1985	1991	1998[a]
National defense	45.9	49.6	81.7	86.5	134.0	252.7	273.3	259.4
Income security[b]	3.7	9.1	15.6	50.2	86.5	128.2	170.8	247.5
Social Security	4.3	16.4	30.3	64.7	118.5	188.6	269.0	384.3
Medicare	—	—	6.2	12.7	32.1	65.8	104.5	207.1
Health[c]	0.8	1.8	5.9	12.9	23.2	33.5	71.2	138.2
Agriculture	3.3	4.8	5.2	3.0	8.8	25.6	15.2	12.3
Natural resources	1.0	2.1	3.1	7.3	13.9	13.4	18.6	22.3
Energy	0.5	0.7	1.0	2.9	10.2	5.7	1.7	2.3
Veterans' benefits	5.4	5.1	8.7	16.6	21.2	26.3	31.3	41.0
Interest on debt	8.3	10.4	14.4	23.2	52.5	129.4	194.5	249.9
All other[d]	9.0	15.3	23.5	52.3	90.0	68.1	172.9	163.7
Total	92.2	118.3	195.6	332.3	590.9	912.8	1,323.0	1,687.5

PERCENTAGE DISTRIBUTION								
Function	1960	1965	1970	1975	1980	1985	1991	1998
National defense	55.8	43.0	41.8	26.0	22.7	26.7	20.6	15.3
Income security[b]	4.5	7.9	8.0	15.1	14.6	13.5	12.9	14.6
Social Security	5.2	14.2	15.5	19.5	20.1	19.9	20.3	22.8
Medicare	0.0	0.0	3.2	3.8	5.4	7.0	7.9	12.2
Health[c]	0.9	1.5	3.0	3.9	3.9	3.5	5.4	8.1
Agriculture	4.0	4.2	2.7	0.9	1.5	2.7	1.1	0.7
Natural resources	1.2	1.8	1.6	2.2	2.4	1.4	1.4	1.3
Energy	0.6	0.6	0.5	0.9	1.7	0.6	0.1	0.1
Veterans' benefits	6.6	4.4	4.4	5.0	3.6	2.8	2.4	2.4
Interest on debt	10.1	9.0	7.4	7.0	8.9	13.7	14.7	14.8
All other[d]	11.0	13.3	12.0	15.7	15.3	8.2	13.2	9.7
Total	100.0	100.0	100.0	100.0	100.0	100.0	100.0	100.0

[a] Estimates.

[b] This includes public assistance, food stamps, railroad and government employee retirement benefits, and unemployment compensation.

[c] This includes Medicaid, health research, and occupational health and safety.

[d] This includes international affairs, science, space, transportation, education, commerce, community development, justice, and general government.

Sources: *Statistical Abstract of the United States 1992* and *The Budget of the United States Government—Fiscal Year 1998*.

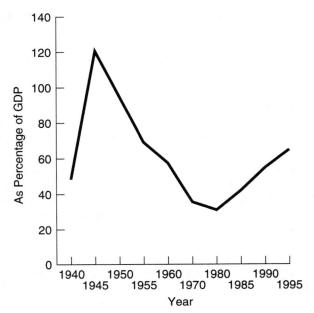

Source: *Budget of the United States Government 1997.*

FIGURE 9–2   **Federal Debt as a Percentage of GDP**

Burdening Future Generations.   Interest payments on the national debt come from current taxes and so divert money away from all other government programs. Even if the federal government manages to balance its current annual budgets, interest payments on the total debt already incurred will remain obligations of the children and grandchildren of the current generation of taxpayers. In short, today's high spending and low taxing are shifting the burden of debt from the current generation to future generations.

Slowing Economic Growth.   The huge federal debt, and the need to sell even more government bonds each year to cover annual increases in the debt (new deficits), requires the Treasury Department to borrow large amounts of money each year. This money is diverted from the private sector, where it would otherwise be available as loans to establish new businesses; to expand old ones; to modernize industrial plants and equipment; and to finance the purchase of homes, cars, appliances, and other credit items for consumers. In other words, the federal government's borrowing "crowds out" capital markets. The less capital available in the private sector, the slower the economy grows.

Limiting Policy Initiatives.   Continuing government deficits and the increasing costs of interest payments limit the president's and Congress's ability to deal with other problems confronting the nation. Any new spending initiatives for health, schools, research, or infrastructure add to federal deficits and by so doing slow economic growth. Thus, if the federal government tries to stimulate the economy by increasing its spending, it simultaneously increases already burdensome deficits, takes more money away from the private sector, and thereby threatens to undo whatever stimulative effect was intended.

Default and Hyperinflation.   No one expects the United States ever to default on its debt—that is, to refuse to pay interest or principal when it comes due—although other debt-ridden nations have done so in the past and many threaten to do so today. But there is always the possibility that a future administration in Washington might "monetarize" the debt, that is, simply print currency and use it to pay off bondholders. Of course, this currency would flood the nation and soon become worthless. Hyperinflation would leave U.S. bondholders with worthless money. These financial disasters—default or hyperinflation—are unlikely, but the existence of a high federal deficit means that they are not unthinkable.

Dealing with Deficits.   The simple and responsible solution to the federal deficit is to have the president and Congress prepare and pass only balanced budgets. But that solution has eluded policymakers for over four decades. Neither presidents nor Congress, Democrats nor Republicans, have been willing to reduce expenditures or raise taxes to balance budgets. American politics has reached a level of irresponsibility at which calls for a balanced budget are considered "naive" and "unrealistic." So Washington searches for politically painless remedies.

The Balanced Budget Constitutional Amendment.   Constitutions govern government. Presumably, if the people wish to discipline their government they can do so by amending the Constitution to restrict the actions of officials. Popular opinion (see Figure 9–3) has long favored a constitutional amendment to obligate the president to submit and the Congress to pass only *balanced* federal budgets. (Most proposals for an amendment include escape clauses for wars and national emergencies or for deficits approved by a two-thirds vote of both houses of Congress.) In 1995, the House of Representatives by a vote of 300 to 132 passed an amendment to the

FIGURE 9–3   Public Opinion on a Balanced Budget
Amendment

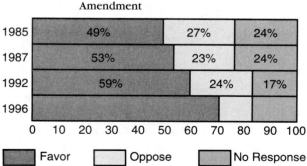

Constitution requiring a balanced budget by 2002 (or the second year after ratification, whichever is later). But the amendment failed by a single vote in the U.S. Senate to get the necessary two-thirds majority that would have sent it to the states for ratification. President Clinton and most Democrats in Congress opposed the amendment. One of the strongest lobbying groups opposing the amendment was the American Association of Retired Persons, which feared that a balanced budget might mean less generous Social Security payments.

Tax Increases and Deficits.   In theory a balanced federal budget could be achieved by either cutting spending or increasing taxes. Since cutting spending, especially entitlements, has proven to be politically impossible, presidents and Congress have turned to raising taxes (see Chapter 10, "Tax Policy"). In 1990, President Bush was forced to retract his campaign pledge "Read my lips! No new taxes!" and agree to an increase in the top marginal income tax rate from 28 to 31 percent in a budget agreement with a Democrat-controlled Congress. But revenues from the tax increases were washed away in a sea of red ink, and Bush suffered the wrath of the voters in the 1992 presidential election.

Clinton's plan to reduce deficits centered on major tax increases for upper-income Americans. Clinton won a narrow victory in Congress in 1993, raising the top marginal income tax rate from 31 to 39.6 percent; the corporate rate was raised from 34 to 35 percent; the gasoline tax was raised from four to eight cents per gallon; and Social Security beneficiaries were obliged to pay income taxes on 85 percent of their benefits, up from 50 percent.

Annual federal deficits have declined in size during the Clinton presidency (see Figure 9–4). Yet they remain more than $100 billion per year. Budget projections for future years forecast a return to annual deficits of $200 billion a year or more as entitlement spending continues to grow.

Deficits and Entitlements.   Entitlement programs account for well over half of all federal spending (see Figure 9–5). Virtually everyone who has examined the federal government's budget—economists, politicians, and private citizens—understands that "capping entitlements" is the only way to slow the growth of federal spending. The problem is the political gridlock that has arisen over what programs will be reduced or capped.

Note that most entitlement payments do not go to the poor. The largest share of entitlements—Social Security, Medicare, veterans' and federal retirement—goes to retirees. These three programs alone account for more than two-thirds of all entitlement payments and 41 percent of all federal expenditures. Payments to the poor and unemployed—welfare, Medicaid, and unemployment insurance—account for less than one-third of federal entitlement spending, and 18 percent of all federal expenditures.

The Politics of Deficits.   Despite all the pious rhetoric about the need to "balance the budget," deficit financing appeals to politicians. It allows them to provide high levels of government benefits while avoiding the onerous task of raising taxes.

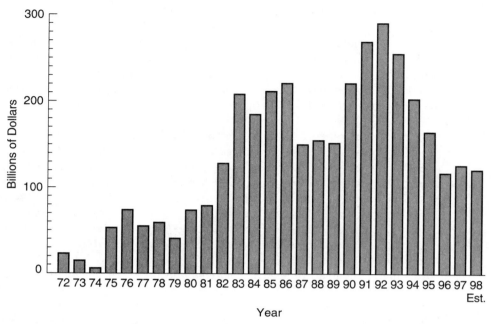

Sources: *Statistical Abstract of the United States; Budget of the United States Government 1998.*

FIGURE 9–4   Annual Federal Deficits

To be sure, the burden of future interest payments is shifted to young people and future generations. But today's elected politicians know they will be long gone before these burdens are fully realized; their time frame is the next election. Also, politicians are reluctant to cross swords with politically active older voters, the principal beneficiaries of entitlement programs.

THE FORMAL BUDGETARY PROCESS

The president, through the Office of Management and Budget (OMB), located in the Executive Office, has the key responsibility for budget preparation. In addition to this major task, the OMB has related responsibilities for improving the organization and management of the executive agencies, for coordinating the extensive statistical services of the federal government, and for analyzing and reviewing proposed legislation to determine its effect of administration and finance.

The Constitution gives the president no formal powers over taxing and spending. Constitutionally all the president can do is "make recommendations" to Congress. It is difficult to imagine that prior to 1921 the president played no direct role in the budget process. The secretary of the Treasury compiled the estimates of the individual agencies, and these were sent, without revision, to Congress for its consideration. It was not until the Budget and Accounting Act of 1921 that the president

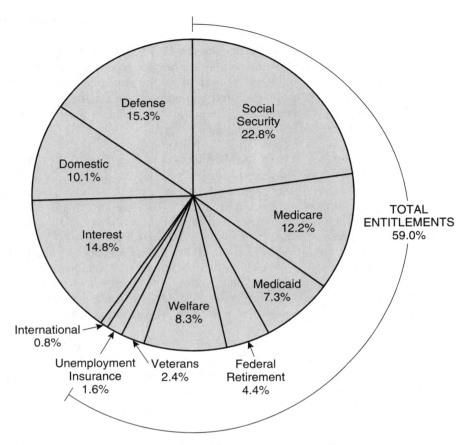

Source: *Budget of the United States Government 1998.*

FIGURE 9–5   Entitlement Spending in the Federal Budget

acquired responsibility for budget formulation and thus developed a means of directly influencing spending policy.

OMB—Preparing the Presidential Budget.   Preparation of the fiscal budget
starts more than a year before the beginning of the fiscal year for which it is intended. After preliminary consultation with the executive agencies and in accord
with presidential policy, the OMB develops targets or ceilings within which the
agencies are encouraged to build their requests. This work begins a full sixteen to
eighteen months before the beginning of the fiscal year for which the budget is being prepared. (In other words, work would begin in January 1997 on the budget for
the fiscal year beginning October 1, 1998, and ending September 30, 1999.) Budgets
are named for the fiscal year in which they end, so this example describes the work
on *The Budget of the United States Government, Fiscal Year 1999,* or more simply,
"FY99."

Budget materials and instructions go to the agencies with the request that the forms be completed and returned to the OMB. This request is followed by about three months' arduous work by agency-employed budget officers, department heads, and the grass-roots bureaucracy in Washington and out in the field. Budget officials at the bureau level check requests from the smaller units, compare them with the previous years' estimates, hold conferences, and make adjustments. The process of checking, reviewing, modifying, and discussing is repeated on a larger scale at the department level.

The heads of agencies are expected to submit their completed requests to the OMB by mid-September or early October. Occasionally a schedule of "over ceiling" items (requests above the suggested ceilings) will be included.

With the requests of the spending agencies at hand, the OMB begins its own budget review. Hearings are given each agency. Top agency officials support their requests as convincingly as possible. On rare occasions dissatisfied agencies may ask the budget director to take their cases to the president.

In December, the president and the OMB director will devote time to the document, which by now is approaching its final stages of assembly. They and their staffs will "blue-pencil," revise, and make last-minute changes as well as prepare the president's message, which accompanies the budget to Congress. After the budget is in legislative hands, the president may recommend further alterations as needs dictate.

Although the completed document includes a revenue plan with general estimates for taxes and other income, it is primarily an expenditure budget. Revenue and tax policy staff work centers in the Treasury Department and not in the OMB. In late January the president presents *The Budget of the United States Government* for the fiscal year beginning October 1 to Congress (see Figure 9–6).

House and Senate Budget Committees.   In an effort to consider the budget as a whole, Congress has established House and Senate budget committees and a Congressional Budget Office (CBO) to review the president's budget after its submission to Congress. These committees draft a first budget resolution (due May 15) setting forth target goals to guide committee actions on specific appropriation and revenue measures. If appropriations measures exceed the targets in the budget resolution, it comes back to the floor in a reconciliation measure. A second budget resolution (due September 15) sets binding budget figures for committees and subcommittees considering appropriations. In practice, however, these two budget resolutions have been folded into a single measure because Congress does not want to reargue the same issues.

Appropriations Acts.   Congressional approval of each year's spending is usually divided into thirteen separate appropriations bills, each covering separate broad categories of spending. These appropriations bills are drawn up by the House and Senate appropriations committees and their specialized subcommittees. Indeed, House appropriations subcommittees function as overseers of the agencies included

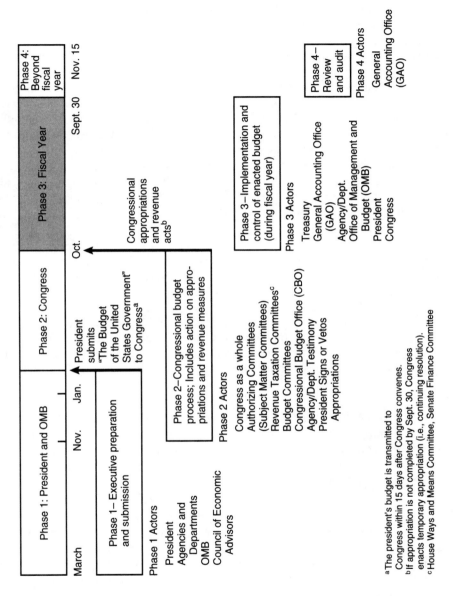

Phase 1: President and OMB	Phase 2: Congress	Phase 3: Fiscal Year	Phase 4: Beyond fiscal year

March   Nov.   Jan.   Oct.   Sept. 30   Nov. 15

Phase 1 – Executive preparation and submission

President submits "The Budget of the United States Government" to Congress[a]

Congressional appropriations and revenue acts[b]

Phase 3 – Implementation and control of enacted budget (during fiscal year)

Phase 4 – Review and audit

Phase 1 Actors

President
Agencies and
   Departments
OMB
Council of Economic
   Advisors

Phase 2 – Congressional budget process; Includes action on appropriations and revenue measures

Phase 2 Actors

Congress as a whole
Authorizing Committees
  (Subject Matter Committees)
Revenue Taxation Committees[c]
Budget Committees
Congressional Budget Office (CBO)
Agency/Dept. Testimony
President Signs or Vetos
  Appropriations

Phase 3 Actors

Treasury
General Accounting Office
  (GAO)
Agency/Dept.
Office of Management and
  Budget (OMB)
President
Congress

Phase 4 Actors

General
Accounting Office
(GAO)

[a] The president's budget is transmitted to Congress within 15 days after Congress convenes.
[b] If appropriation is not completed by Sept. 30, Congress enacts temporary appropriation (i.e., continuing resolution).
[c] House Ways and Means Committee, Senate Finance Committee

FIGURE 9–6 Major Steps in the Budget Process

in their appropriations bill. The appropriations committees must stay within overall totals set forth in the budget resolutions adopted by Congress.

An *appropriations* act provides money for spending, and no funds can be spent without it. An *authorization* is an act of Congress establishing a government program and defining the amount of money that it may spend. Authorizations may be for several years. However, the authorization does not actually provide the money that has been authorized; only an appropriations act can do that. Appropriations acts are almost always for a single fiscal year. Congress has its own rule that does not allow appropriations for programs that have not been authorized. However, appropriations frequently provide less money for programs than earlier authorizations.

Appropriations acts include both obligational *authority* and *outlays.* An obligation of authority permits a government agency to enter into contracts calling for payments into future years (new obligated authority). Outlays are to be spent in the fiscal year for which they are appropriated.

Appropriations Committees.   Considerations of specific appropriations measures are functions of the appropriations committees in both houses. Committee work in the House of Representatives is usually more thorough than it is in the Senate; the committee in the Senate tends to be a "court of appeal" for agencies opposed to House action. Each committee, moreover, has about ten largely independent subcommittees to review the requests of a particular agency or a group of related functions. Specific appropriations bills are taken up by the subcommittees in hearings. Departmental officers answer questions on the conduct of their programs and defend their requests for the next fiscal year; lobbyists and other witnesses testify.

Revenue Acts.   The House Committee on Ways and Means and the Senate Finance Committee are the major instruments of Congress for consideration of *taxing* measures. Through long history and jealous pride they have maintained formal independence of the appropriations committees, further fragmenting legislative consideration of the budget.

Presidential Veto.   In terms of aggregate amounts, Congress does not regularly make great changes in the executive budget. It is more likely to shift money among programs and projects. The budget is approved by Congress in the form of appropriations bills, usually thirteen of them, each ordinarily providing for several departments and agencies. The number of revenue measures is smaller. As with other bills that are passed by Congress, the president has ten days to approve or veto appropriations legislation.

Continuing Resolutions and "Shutdowns."   All appropriations acts *should* be passed by both houses and signed by the president into law before October 1, the date of the start of the fiscal year. However, it is rare for Congress to meet this deadline, so the government usually finds itself beginning a new fiscal year without a budget. Constitutionally, any U.S. government agency for which Congress does not pass an appropriations act may not draw money from the Treasury and thus is obliged to shut down. To get around this problem, Congress usually adopts a "continuing resolution" that authorizes government agencies to keep spending money for a specified period at the same level as in the previous fiscal year.

A continuing resolution is supposed to grant additional time for Congress to pass, and the president to sign, appropriations acts. But occasionally this process has broken down in the heat of political combat over the budget. The time period specified in a continuing resolution has expired without agreement on appropriations acts or even on a new continuing resolution. Shutdowns occurred during the bitter battle between President Bill Clinton and the Republican-controlled Congress over the Fiscal Year 1996 budget. In theory, the absence of either appropriations acts or a continuing resolution should cause the entire federal government to "shut down," that is, to cease all operations and expenditures for lack of funds. But in practice, such shutdowns have been only partial, affecting only "nonessential" government employees and causing relatively little disruption.

The Line-Item Veto.   For many years, presidents, both Democratic and Republican, petitioned Congress to give them the line-item veto—the ability to veto some provisions of a bill while accepting other provisions. The lack of presidential line-item veto power was especially frustrating when dealing with appropriations bills because the president could not veto specific pork-barrel provisions from major spending bills for defense, education, housing, welfare, and so on. Finally, in 1996 Congress granted the president authority to "cancel" spending items in any appropriation act, any new entitlement, or any limited tax benefit. Such cancellation would take effect immediately unless blocked by a special "disapproval bill" passed by Congress. The president could veto the disapproval bill, and a two-thirds vote of both houses would be required to override the veto.

Potentially, this veto shifts enormous power to the president. A president could use it to threaten individual lawmakers with cancellation of their pet spending projects if they fail to support the president on certain legislation. Opponents of the line-item veto challenge its constitutionality, arguing that it transfers legislative power—granted by the Constitution only to Congress—to the president.

SUMMARY

Government economic policy is made primarily through fiscal policies—decisions about taxing, spending, and deficits levels—and monetary policy—decisions about money supply and interest rates. Although a variety of macroeconomic theories compete to guide economic policy, in practice, fiscal and monetary policy decisions tend to be made incrementally. Incrementalism not only describes the process of economic policymaking but also explains why government policies, programs, and expenditure levels persist and grow over time.

1. Keynesian economic theory recommends government manipulation of aggregate demand by raising spending, lowering taxes, and incurring debt during recessions and pursuing the opposite policies during inflations. But supply-side economists view these traditional countercyclical taxing and spending policies as "the failed policies of the past," which produce inflation, high interest rates, and a stagnant economy. They argue that high government taxing and spending levels promote immediate consumption instead of investment in the future and penalize hard work, creativity, and saving. President Reagan's Program for Economic Recovery slowed the rate of growth of government domestic spending and reduced personal income tax rates. But a temporary surge in defense spending and continuing growth in entitlement spending created the largest deficits in peacetime history.

2. In his presidential campaign Bill Clinton labeled Reagan and Bush policies as "failed trickle-down" economics. He spoke of a new "enterprise economics" that stresses the government's responsibility to stimulate economic growth through "investment" (spending) for "human capital, technology, and infrastructure." But deficits curtailed Clinton's spending plans. In 1993 he pushed a major tax increase through Congress that succeeded in reducing the size of the government's annual deficits.

3. Government spending has grown in all modern presidential administrations. Today the federal government spends the equivalent of 23 percent of the nation's GDP, and all governments combined—federal, state, and local—spend about 35 percent.

4. The budgetary process itself is incremental, fragmented, and nonprogrammatic. Policymakers generally consider last year's expenditure as a base and focus their attention on a narrow range of increases. Evaluating the desirability of every public program every year might create politically insoluble conflict as well as exhaust the energies of budget makers.

5. The range of decisions available to policymakers in the development of an annual budget is really quite small. "Uncontrollable" items account for over two-thirds of the federal budget. Entitlement programs, with automatic annual increases in benefits and with increasing costs of in-kind benefits, account for most of the "uncontrollable" increases in federal spending.

6. Today, entitlement programs account for more than half of all federal spending. Social Security is the largest single item in the federal budget. Defense spending, which was once the largest share of all federal spending, is now much less than spending for social programs. This shift in national priorities occurred between 1965 and 1975, during both a Democratic and a Republican administration and during the nation's longest war. This reversal of federal budget priorities raises questions about whether budgeting is truly incremental.

7. Decades of annual federal deficits have resulted in the accumulation of a national debt in excess of $5 trillion dollars. This debt burdens future generations with heavy interest payments, currently 15 percent of the federal budget; it slows economic growth and limits policy initiatives in all areas of government concern.

8. Despite a great deal of rhetoric about the need to balance the budget, deficits continue and debt accumulates. "Deficit reduction plans," budget "summits," and tax increases have all failed to limit the growth of federal spending.

9. Limiting or capping entitlement programs is required to reduce deficits, but politicians are unwilling to confront the beneficiaries of these programs. It is easier to pass on the burdens to future generations.

NOTES

1. See Will Marshall and Martin Schram, eds., *Mandate for Change* (New York: Berkley Books, 1993).
2. William A. Niskanen, *Bureaucracy and Representative Government* (Chicago: Aldine, 1971).
3. Aaron Wildavsky, *The New Politics of the Budgetary Process* (Boston: Scott, Foresman, 1988), p. 136.

BIBLIOGRAPHY

KETTL, DONALD F. *Deficit Politics*. New York: Macmillan, 1992.

LIEBERMAN, CARL. *Making Economic Policy*. Englewood Cliffs, NJ: Prentice Hall, 1991.

MARSHALL, WILL, and MARTIN SCHRAM. *Mandate for Change*. New York: Berkley Books, 1993.

SAMUELSON, ROBERT. *The Good Life and Its Discontents: The American Dream in an Age of Entitlement*. New York: Times Books, 1996.

SHUMAN, HOWARD E. *The Politics of the Budget*. 3rd ed. Englewood Cliffs, NJ: Prentice Hall, 1992.

WILDAVSKY, AARON. *The New Politics of the Budgetary Process*. 2nd ed. New York: HarperCollins, 1992.

10

TAX POLICY
Battling the Special Interests

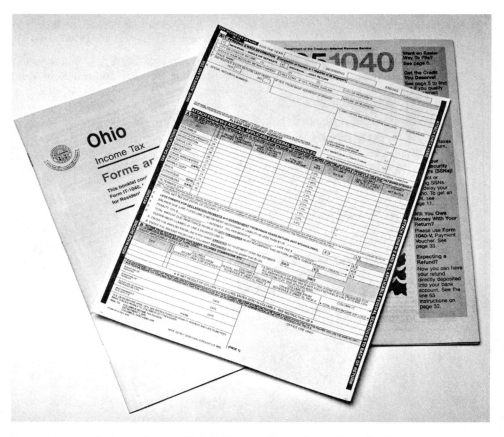

Federal, state, and city tax forms. (Mark C. Burnett/Photo Researchers, Inc.)

INTEREST GROUPS AND TAX POLICY

The interplay of interest groups in policymaking is often praised as "pluralism." Political scientist Robert A. Dahl, for example, proclaimed the "central guiding thread of American constitutional development" to be "the evolution of a political system in which all the active and legitimate groups in the population can make themselves heard at some critical stage in the process of decision."[1] Public policy is portrayed by interest group theory as the equilibrium in the struggle between interest groups (see Chapter 2). While this equilibrium is not the same as majority preference, it is considered by pluralists to be the best possible approximation of the public interest in a large and diverse society.

But what if only a small proportion of the American people are organized into politically effective interest groups? What if the interest group system represents well-organized, economically powerful producer groups, who actively seek immediate tangible benefits from the government? What if the interest group system leaves out a majority of Americans, particularly the less-organized, economically dispersed consumers and taxpayers, who wish for broad policy goals such as fairness, simplicity, and general economic well-being?

There is no better illustration of the influence of organized interest groups in policymaking than national tax policy. Every economics textbook tells us that the public interest is best served by a tax system that is universal, simple, and fair and that promotes economic growth and well-being. But the federal tax system is very nearly the opposite: it is complex, unfair, and nonuniversal. About *one-half* of all personal income in the United States escapes taxation through various exemptions, deductions, and special treatments in tax laws. Tax laws treat different types of income differently. They penalize work, savings, and investment and divert capital investment into nonproductive tax shelters and an illegal underground economy.

The unfairness, complexity, and inefficiency of the tax laws can be attributed largely to organized interest groups. The nation's elected policymakers are fully aware of this. Dan Rostenkowski, former chair of the House Ways and Means Committee, which writes the nation's tax laws, once admitted,

> We gave oil companies breaks to fuel our oil industry. We gave real estate incentives to build more housing. We sharpened our technology with research and development credits. We gave tax breaks to encourage people to save. We pile one tax benefit on top of another—each one backed with good intention.
> Unfortunately it didn't take too long before those with the best accountants and lawyers figured out how to beat the system . . . and the cost of government was shifted to families like those in my neighborhood who don't have the guile to play the game of hide-and-seek with the IRS. . . .
> In the end tax reform comes down to a struggle between the narrow interests of the few—and the broad interests of working American families.[2]

Yet the special interests do not *always* win in tax policy. In a dramatic turnabout in the Tax Reform Act of 1986, the special interests suffered a rare defeat. Republican President Ronald Reagan and a Democratically-controlled Congress joined together in a sweeping reform of the nation's tax laws.

Interest groups, however, do not abandon the field of battle after a defeat. Rather they remain in the fray, first to minimize the costs of their defeat and then later to launch counterattacks to restore their privileges, exemptions, and special treatments. They know that the general public's passion for reform wanes over time and that public inattentiveness to the details of public policy is their greatest ally.

In this chapter we will first outline the current federal tax system, then review some of the underlying issues that drive tax politics, and finally examine the influence of the special interests in shaping tax policy. We will describe how reform was accomplished over the opposition of the special interests in the Tax Reform Act of 1986 and then how these reforms were whittled away in subsequent tax policy decisions.

THE FEDERAL TAX SYSTEM

The federal government derives its revenues from a variety of sources—the individual income tax; Social Security payroll deductions; the corporate income tax; excise taxes on gasoline, liquor, tobacco, telephones, air travel, and other consumer items; estate and gift taxes; custom duties and a wide variety of charges and fees (see Figure 10–1). And inasmuch as total revenues from taxes and fees consistently fail to match total spending, the federal government is obliged to borrow additional money each year (see "The Burdens of Government Debt" in Chapter 9).

Individual Income Taxes. More than 100 years ago, Supreme Court Justice Stephen J. Field, in striking down as unconstitutional a progressive income tax enacted by Congress, predicted that such a tax would lead to class wars: "Our political contests will become a war of the poor against the rich, a war constantly growing in intensity and bitterness."[3] But populist sentiment in the early twentieth century—the anger of midwestern farmers toward eastern rail tycoons and the beliefs of impoverished southerners that they would never have incomes high enough to pay an income tax—helped secure the passage of the Sixteenth Amendment to the U.S. Constitution. The federal income tax that was passed by Congress in 1914 had a top rate of 7 percent; less than 1 percent of the population had incomes high enough to be taxed. Today the top rate is 39.6 percent (actually over 42 percent when mandated phase-outs of deductions are calculated); about half of the population pays income taxes.

Today the personal income tax is the federal government's largest single source of revenue. Personal income is taxed at five separate rates—15, 28, 31, 36, and 39.6 percent. These rates apply progressively to levels of income, or "brackets", that are indexed annually to reflect inflation. (In 1996, for married taxpayers filing jointly, the first $41,200 was taxed at 15 percent; income between $41,200 and $99,600 was taxed at 28 percent; income between $99,600 and $151,750 was taxed at 31 percent; income between $151,750 and $271,050 was taxed at 36 percent; and income over $271,050 was taxed at 39.6 percent.) The phaseout of personal exemptions for high-income taxpayers actually pushes the top marginal rate over 42 percent.

The federal income tax is automatically deducted from the paychecks of all employees except farm and domestic workers. This withholding system is the backbone of the income tax. There is no withholding of nonwage income, but taxpayers

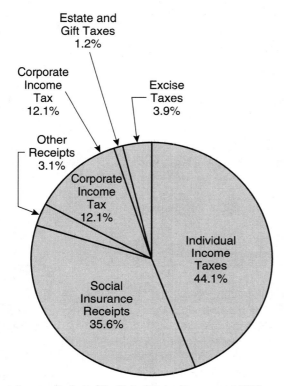

Estate and
Gift Taxes
1.2%

Corporate
Income
Tax
12.1%

Excise
Taxes
3.9%

Other
Receipts
3.1%

Corporate
Income
Tax
12.1%

Individual
Income
Taxes
44.1%

Social
Insurance
Receipts
35.6%

Source: *Budget of the United States Government 1998.*

FIGURE 10–1   Sources of Federal Revenue

with such income must file a Declaration of Estimated Taxes and pay this estimate in quarterly installments. Before April 15 of each year, all income-earning Americans must report their taxable income to the Internal Revenue Service on its Form 1040.

Americans are usually surprised to learn that half of all personal income is *not* taxed. To understand why, we must know how the tax laws distinguish between *adjusted gross income* (which is an individual's total money income minus expenses incurred in earning it) and *taxable income* (that part of adjusted gross income subject to taxation). Federal tax rates apply only to taxable income. Federal tax laws allow many reductions in adjusted gross income in the calculation of taxable income.

Tax expenditures is a term meant to identify tax revenues that are lost to the federal government because of exemptions, deductions, and special treatments in tax laws. Table 10–1 lists the major tax expenditures in federal tax law. There is a continual struggle between proponents of special tax exemptions to achieve social goals and those who believe that the tax laws should be simplified and social goals met by direct expenditures.

Low-income working families pay no personal income taxes, although Social Security taxes are deducted from their paychecks. A combination of the personal deduction ($2,550 for each family member in 1996) and the standardized deduction

TABLE 10-1   Major "Tax Expenditures" in Federal Tax Policy

Personal exemption and standardized deduction
Deductibility of mortgage interest on owner-occupied homes
Deductibility of property taxes on first and second homes
Deferral of capital gains on home sales
Deductibility of charitable contributions
Credit for child-care expenses
Exclusion of employer contributions to pension plans and medical insurance
Exclusion of Social Security benefits
Exclusion of interest on public-purpose state and local bonds
Deductibility of state and local income taxes
Exclusion of income earned abroad
Accelerated depreciation of machinery, equipment, and structures
Medical expenses over 7.5 percent of income
Tax credits for children (added in 1997)
Tax credits for two years of college (added in 1997)

($4,000 for a single taxpayer and $6,700 for a married couple in 1996) ensures that families with incomes under $15,000 pay no income taxes. Moreover, these families are also entitled to an earned income tax credit—a direct payment (maximum of $3,500 in 1996) to low-income taxpayers who file for it.

Upper-income taxpayers usually itemize their deductions. About 75 percent of all taxpayers take the standardized deduction; the 25 percent who itemize are middle- and upper-income taxpayers who have deductions exceeding the standardized amount. But an alternative minimum tax (AMT) is designed to ensure that taxpayers who claim numerous deductions pay a minimum tax. The AMT applies a 26 percent rate (28 percent over $175,000) to a taxpayer's income, subject to very few exclusions.

Corporate Income Taxes.   The corporate income tax provides only about 12 percent of the federal government's total income. The Tax Reform Act of 1986 reduced the top corporate income tax from 46 to 34 percent. However, prior to this act, corporations had many ways of reducing their taxable income, often to zero. The result was that many very large and profitable corporations paid little or no taxes. Some of the most notorious of these corporate tax breaks were modified or eliminated in the Tax Reform Act of 1986. Congress raised the corporate income tax rate to 35 percent in 1993.

Who pays the corporate income tax? Economists differ over whether this tax is "shifted" to consumers or whether corporations and their stockholders bear its burden. The evidence on the *incidence*—that is, who actually bears the burden—of the corporate income tax is inconclusive.[4]

Religious, charitable, and educational organizations, as well as labor unions, are exempt from corporate income taxes, except for income they may derive from "unrelated business activity."

Social Security Taxes.   The second-largest and fastest-growing source of federal revenue is social insurance taxes, which now provide 36 percent of the federal government's income. Social insurance taxes include Social Security (OASDI, or Old Age Survivors and Disability Insurance) and Medicare (HI, or Health Insurance). Employers pay half of these taxes directly and withhold half from employees' wages. Over the years Social Security taxes rose incrementally in two ways: a gradual increase in the combined employer-employee tax rate (percent) and a gradual increase in the maximum earnings base of the tax (see Table 10–2). Today the OASDI tax (12.4 percent) and the HI tax (2.90 percent) are differentiated, with proceeds going to separate OASDI and HI "trust funds" in the federal treasury. The OASDI tax is limited to the first $62,700 (in 1996) in wage income; wages above that amount as well as nonwage income (profits, interest, dividends, rents, and so forth) are not subject to this tax. Thus, the OASDI tax is "regressive"—that is, it captures a larger share of the income of lower-income Americans than of higher-income Americans. In contrast, the HI tax applies to all income.

The taxes collected under Social Security are earmarked (by Social Security number) for the account of each taxpayer. Workers, therefore, feel that they are receiving benefits as a right rather than as a gift of the government. However, benefits are only slightly related to the earning record of the individual worker; there are both minimum and maximum benefit levels, which prevent benefits from corresponding to payments. Indeed, for current recipients of Social Security, less than 15 percent of the benefits can be attributed to their prior contributions. Current taxpayers are paying more than 85 percent of the benefits being received by current retirees.

Today a majority of taxpayers pay more in Social Security taxes than in income taxes. Indeed, combined employer and employee Social Security taxes now amount to nearly $9,500 annually at the top of the wage base. If we assume that the employer's share of the tax actually comes out of wages that would otherwise be paid to the employee, over 75 percent of all taxpayers pay more in Social Security taxes than income taxes.

TABLE 10-2   Social Security Taxes

	Combined Employee-Employer Tax Rate OASDI and HI	Maximum Wage Base OASDI
1937	2.0%	$ 3,000
1950	3.0	3,000
1960	6.0	4,800
1970	9.6	7,800
1980	12.26	25,900
1985	14.10	39,600
1996	15.3	62,700

Source: *Statistical Abstract of the United States 1996.*

Estate and Gift Taxes.   Taxes on property left to heirs is one of the oldest forms of taxation in the world. Federal estate taxes now begin on estates of $600,000 (scheduled to rise to 1 million) and levy a tax of 37 to 55 percent on amounts above this level. Because taxes at death could be easily avoided by simply giving estates to heirs while still alive, a federal gift tax is also levied. There is an annual exclusion of $10,000 in gifts per donee.

Excise Taxes and Custom Duties.   Federal taxes on liquor, tobacco, gasoline, telephones, air travel, and other so-called luxury items account for only about 1 to 2 percent of total federal revenue. Customs taxes on imports provide another 1 to 2 percent of total federal revenue.

TAXATION, FAIRNESS, AND GROWTH

The goal of any tax system is not only to raise sufficient revenue for the government to perform its assigned tasks, but also to do so simply, efficiently, and fairly, and in a way that does not impair economic growth. The argument on behalf of tax reform is that the federal tax system fails to meet *any* of these criteria:

- Tax forms are so complex that a majority of taxpayers hire professional tax preparers; an army of accountants and lawyers make their living from the tax code.
- Tax laws are unfair in treating various sources of income differently; the many exemptions, deductions, and special treatments are perceived as loopholes that allow the privileged to escape fair taxation.
- Tax laws encourage tax avoidance, directing investment away from productive uses and into inefficient tax shelters; whenever people make decisions about savings and investment based on tax laws instead of most productive use, the whole economy suffers.
- Tax laws encourage cheating and reduce trust in government; they encourage the growth of an underground economy, transactions that are never reported on tax forms.
- High marginal tax rates discourage work and investment; economic growth is diminished when individuals face tax rates of 50 percent or more (combined federal, state, and local taxes) on additional income they receive from additional work, savings, or investments.

But the goals of fairness, simplicity, and economic growth are frequently lost in the clash of special interests. Various interests define "fairness" differently; they demand special treatment rather than universality in tax laws; and produce a U.S. tax code of several thousand pages of provisions, definitions, and interpretations.

Deciding What's Fair.   A central issue in tax politics is the question of who actually bears the heaviest burden of a tax—that is, which income groups must devote the largest proportion of their income to the payment of taxes. Taxes that require high-income groups to pay a larger percentage of their incomes in taxes than low-income groups are said to be *progressive,* and taxes that take a larger share of the income of low-income groups are called *regressive.* Taxes that require all income groups to pay the same percentage of their income in taxes are said to be *proportional.* Note that the *percentage of income* paid in taxes is the determining factor. Most taxes take more money from the rich than the poor, but a progressive or regressive tax is distinguished by the percentages of income taken from various income groups.

The federal income tax has a progressive rate structure: tax rates rise from 15 to 39.6 percent through five brackets of increasing taxable income.* The rate structure prior to 1981 was even more progressive, with numerous brackets ranging from 14 to 70 percent; following the Tax Reform Act of 1986 the rate structure was reduced to two brackets, 15 and 28 percent. President Bush agreed to the addition of a 31 percent bracket in 1990, and President Clinton pushed the 36 and 39.6 brackets through Congress in 1993. Thus, rate progressivity, which had been reduced during the Reagan presidency, has been gradually restored in recent years.

Various exemptions and deductions in tax laws can also be considered progressive or regressive, depending on whether they benefit the rich or the poor. For example, the personal exemption of $2,550 is considered progressive. Even though both rich and poor can claim their personal exemptions, four $2,550 exemptions for a family whose income is $20,000 exempts over 50 percent of their income from taxation, whereas the same four $2,550 exemptions for a family whose income is $100,000 exempts only about 10 percent of their income. In contrast, the deduction for state and local taxes is considered regressive because wealthy taxpayers who pay heavy state and local income and property taxes are more likely to claim large deductions for these items than poorer taxpayers.

The Argument for Progressivity.   Progressive taxation is generally defended on the principle of ability to pay; the assumption is that high-income groups can afford to pay a larger *percentage* of their incomes into taxes at no more of a sacrifice than that required of low-income groups to devote a smaller percentage of their income to taxation. This assumption is based on what economists call *marginal utility theory* as it applies to money: each additional dollar of income is slightly less valuable to an individual than preceding dollars. For example, a $5,000 increase in the income of an individual already earning $100,000 is much less valuable than a $5,000 increase to an individual earning only $10,000 or to an individual with no income. Hence, *added* dollars of income can be taxed at higher *rates* without violating equitable principles.

---

* Note that the same rates apply to income in each bracket for *all* taxpayers. Thus, a taxpayer with $350,000 in taxable income pays the top 39.6 percent rate only on the amount over $271,050; that same taxpayer pays only 15 percent on the first $41,200, as well as other applicable rates on subsequent income. A taxpayer with $350,000 in taxable income does not pay 39.6 percent of his or her *total* income in taxes; rather this taxpayer would pay approximately $113,000 in taxes, or 32.3 percent of total taxable income.

The Argument for Proportionality.   Opponents of progressive taxation generally assert that equity can be achieved only by taxing everyone at the same percentage of his or her income, regardless of its size. A tax that requires all income groups to pay the same percentage of their income is called a *proportional* or *flat tax.* These critics believe that progressivity penalizes initiative, enterprise, and risk and reduces incentives to expand and develop the nation's economy. Moreover, by taking incomes of high-income groups, governments are taking money that would otherwise go into business investments and stimulate economic growth. Highly progressive taxes curtail growth and make everyone poorer.

Universality.   Another general issue in tax policy is universality, which means that all types of income should be subject to the same tax rates. This implies that income earned from investments should be taxed at the same rate as income earned from wages. But traditionally federal tax laws have distinguished between "ordinary income" and *capital gains*—profits from the buying and selling of property, including stocks, bonds, and real estate. Recently the top marginal rate on capital gains was reduced to only 20 percent. The argument by investors, as well as the real estate and securities industries, is that a lower rate of taxation on capital gains encourages investment and economic growth. But it is difficult to convince many Americans that income earned by working should be taxed at a higher rate than income earned by investing. If it is true that high tax rates discourage investing, they must also discourage work, and both capital and labor are required for economic productivity and growth.

The principle of universality is also violated by the thousands of exemptions, deductions, and special treatments in the tax laws. It is true that most people wish to retain many widely used tax breaks—charitable deductions, child-care deductions, and home mortgage deductions. Proponents of these popular tax treatments argue that they serve valuable social purposes—encouraging charitable contributions, helping with child care, and encouraging home ownership. But reformers argue that tax laws should not be used to promote social policy objectives by granting a wide array of tax preferences.

Economic Growth.   High tax rates discourage economic growth. Excessively high rates cause investors to seek "tax shelters"—to use their money not to produce more business and employment but rather to produce tax breaks for themselves. High tax rates discourage work, savings, and productive investment; they also encourage costly "tax avoidance" (legal methods of reducing or eliminating taxes) as well as "tax evasion" (illegal means of reducing or eliminating taxes).

According to supply-side economists (see "Economic Theories as Policy Guides" in Chapter 9), tax cuts do not necessarily create government deficits. Rather they argue that if tax rates are reduced, the paradoxical results might be to *increase* government revenue because more people would work harder and start new businesses, knowing they could keep a larger share of their earnings. This increased

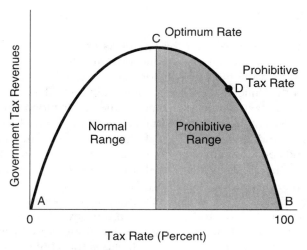

FIGURE 10–2   The Laffer Curve

economic activity would produce more government revenue even though tax rates were lower.

Economist Arthur Laffer developed the diagram shown in Figure 10–2. If the government imposed a zero tax rate, of course, it would receive no revenue (point A). Initially, government revenues rise with increases in the tax rate. However, when tax rates become too high (beyond point C), they discourage workers and businesses from producing and investing. When this discouragement occurs, the economy declines and government revenues fall. Indeed, if the government imposed a 100 percent tax rate (if the government confiscated everything anyone produced), everyone would quit working and government revenues would fall to zero (point B). Laffer does not claim to know exactly what the optimum rate of taxation should be, but he (and the Reagan administration) clearly believed that the United States had been in the "prohibitive range" throughout the 1970s.

The Economic Recovery Tax Cut Act of 1981, pushed through Congress by President Reagan, reduced personal income taxes by 25 percent over a three-year period. Although this was the largest tax cut in history, no significant changes were made in the traditional exemptions, deductions, and special treatments. When the Reagan tax cuts took effect, the nation began a long economic recovery and expansion—indeed, the largest continuous period of GNP growth in the century, lasting nine years. But the tax cuts did *not* produce the increase in revenues predicted by the Laffer curve. Instead, they slowed the rate of growth of federal revenue. Reagan had promised a balanced budget, but it proved impossible to cut taxes and maintain Social Security and other entitlement programs without increasing annual federal deficits. Indeed, during the Reagan-Bush years the federal government ran *the largest peacetime deficits in history* (see "The Burdens of Government Debt" in Chapter 9).

TAX REFORM AND THE SPECIAL INTERESTS

Nothing arouses interest groups more than the prospects of "tax reform," with its implied threats to their special exemptions, deductions, and treatments. The Tax Reform Act of 1986 was one of the most heavily lobbied pieces of legislation in the history of the Congress of the United States. President Reagan offered this reform bill as a trade-off—a reduction in tax *rates* in exchange for the elimination of many tax *breaks*. The rate structure was reduced from 14 brackets, ranging from 11 to 50 percent, to two brackets of 15 and 28 percent. To make up for lost revenue, many exemptions, deductions, and special treatments were to be reduced or eliminated.

The task fell first to the House Ways and Means Committee to try to shape President Reagan's tax reform proposal into law. The committee was chaired by Chicago Democrat Dan Rostenkowski, a man of extraordinary political skill who knew that a host of deals would have to be made with the powerful special interests to pass any tax bill. Indeed, some would argue that Rostenkowski made so many deals over tax reform that the final version of the tax reform bill had little "reform" left in it.

Industry.   Opponents of tax reform were led by the U.S. Chamber of Commerce, the National Association of Manufacturers, and the Business Roundtable. Heavy manufacturing businesses strongly opposed the elimination of the investment tax credit, accelerated depreciation, and foreign tax credit provisions in existing tax laws. The lowering of the corporation tax rate from 46 to 34 percent did not really appeal to large manufacturers because few of them paid any taxes anyway due to generous loopholes in the law.

Real Estate and Housing.   The National Association of Home Builders strongly opposed the elimination of interest deductions for second and vacation homes as well as the elimination of real estate tax shelters, which encouraged investors to put money into real estate projects that earned little or no income. The real estate industry also wanted to preserve deductions for property taxes.

Multinational Corporations.   Businesses involved in international trade opposed efforts to eliminate the foreign tax credit, which allows U.S. companies to use taxes paid to other countries to reduce their U.S. tax liability.

Oil and Gas.   The American Petroleum Institute, representing the powerful oil companies, fought bitterly against any reductions in their depletion allowance or deductions for intangible costs. Their familiar argument was that any change in their privileged status in the tax code would inhibit capital investment in energy and reduce production. But as an old Washington hand observed, "There are three reasons for keeping the oil depletion allowance—Texas, Oklahoma, and Louisiana."

Wall Street Investment Firms.   The Securities Industries Association, the American Council for Capital Formation, and the nation's large investment firms lobbied heavily to keep preferential treatment of capital gains—profits from the sales of stocks and bonds. And the investment firms joined with banks in arguing for the retention of tax-free Individual Retirement Accounts (IRAs).

Charities and Foundations.   Even before President Reagan sent his tax reform proposals to Congress, the nation's leading foundations had petitioned the president to retain deductions for charitable contributions.

Restaurants and Entertainment.   The president proposed to limit business deductions for meals to $25 per person per meal and to eliminate entertainment deductions—nightclubs, concerts, sport tickets, and so forth. The National Restaurant Association, representing high-priced restaurants, convinced Congress that business would falter without $100 meals and three-martini lunches; even the restaurant workers' union appeared to plead the same case. The National Football League, the National Basketball Association, and the National Hockey League all reported that businesses purchased most of their season tickets as tax deductions.

Labor Unions.   The AFL-CIO was unimpressed with the notion of reducing and simplifying tax rates. Instead, it focused its opposition on the proposal to tax fringe benefits, including employer-paid health insurance and group life insurance. Unions also tried to keep the deduction for union dues.

Banks.   Banking interests, led by the American Bankers Association, wished to continue unlimited deductions for all interest payments. This makes borrowing easier by shifting part of the costs of borrowing from the debtor to the government and the taxpayers who must make up the lost revenue. Interest deductions make more customers for banks.

Auto Industry.   The auto industry fought hard to keep deductions for interest paid on auto loans.

Government Lobbies.   Lobbyists from state, county, and city governments, particularly those with high taxes, convened in Washington to lobby against tax reform. The leading state and local government lobbying organizations were the National Governors' Association, the National League of Cities, the National Conference of State Legislatures, the U.S. Conference of Mayors, the Council of State Governments, and the International City Managers Association. They were joined by labor unions representing public employees, notably the American Federation of State, County, and Municipal Employees.

These lobbies understood that federal deductibility of state and local income, sales, and property taxes reduced the direct costs of their own taxing decisions. In other words, when these state and local officials voted for higher taxes in their states, they knew that their taxpayers could deduct these taxes from their federal income tax liability, in effect shifting part of the cost to the federal government.

PAC Power. An estimated one-third of all campaign contributions in congressional elections come from Political Action Committees, or PACs, which distribute their contributions on behalf of business, trade associations, and labor unions. The special interests are powerful in Congress. Most of their contributions go to *incumbent* members of Congress. Seldom do PACs try to bargain on specific pieces of legislation, that is, to "buy votes" because bribery is illegal. But every member of Congress knows who has contributed to his or her campaign costs in the past and who may do so in the future. When these same interests strongly urge him or her to vote with them on pending legislation, attention must at least be paid to their arguments.

COMPROMISING WITH THE SPECIAL INTERESTS

Representative Dan Rostenkowski devoted two months of closed-door sessions of his Ways and Means Committee to write a tax reform bill. He hammered out innumerable compromises with the special interests, restoring many popular deductions. "We have not written a perfect law," he admitted, "but politics is an imperfect process." He argued that the House bill was nonetheless a "vast improvement over current law." It limited many tax deductions and credits and shifted part of the burden of taxation away from individuals and toward corporations. All participants in tax reform agreed that the new law should be *revenue neutral;* that is, it should not raise or lower overall taxes. The Democratic-controlled House succeeded in passing the Rostenkowski tax reform bill. If tax reform failed in the Republican-controlled Senate, the Democrats could blame the failure on the Republicans.

In the Senate, the principal responsibility for tax reform fell on Senate Finance Committee Chair Robert Packwood (R-OR). Initially Packwood was lukewarm on tax reform: "I kind of like the present tax code,"[5] he said, defending special tax breaks as a way for government to shape society. He also announced that unless tax breaks for Oregon's timber industry were retained he would oppose tax reform. Lobbyists converged on Packwood's committee in droves. He initially attempted to accommodate them, writing so many special preferences into the law that little revenue remained. The result was "an orgy of special interest trading." Packwood was leading his committee through tax writing in the traditional way—by trading breaks to the special interest groups for their support. Indeed, the special interest trading became an embarrassment to members of the committee. The bill accumulated more special preferences than the existing law; tax reform was dying. The president's top legislative priority appeared to be a lost cause, and Democrats were prepared to blame the GOP-controlled Senate for failure to reform the nation's tax laws. When it became clear that Packwood himself would bear most of the responsibility for this failure, he became a convert to tax reform.

The key to overcoming the opposition of the special interests was to offer a tax rate low enough that most people would be willing to give up their deductions and preferences. Packwood decided to throw out the old bill and begin anew with a "clean" bill. The new bill had fewer deductions and lower rates than the House bill. To preserve low top rates—28 percent for individuals and 34 percent for corporations—and keep the bill "revenue neutral," senators had to reject amendments by the special interests. The strategy worked, to the surprise of everyone. The Senate Finance Committee voted twenty to zero to send the clean bill to the full Senate. In an atmosphere of nonpartisanship the full Senate passed the bill with a vote of ninety-seven to three. A political "miracle" had occurred: Democrats and Republicans, liberals and conservatives, had united against the special interests.

Nevertheless, the special interests succeeded in keeping many of their favorite exemptions, deductions, and special treatments. The real estate industry—builders, developers, mortgage lenders—succeeded in restoring deductions for vacation homes. But depreciation of housing investments was lengthened, and investors were prevented from using paper losses from real estate depreciation to "shelter" unrelated income. Indeed tax shelters of many kinds were eliminated; the act prevented taxpayers from using "passive" losses generated from investments to reduce other income for tax purposes. The oil and gas industry, however, succeeded in retaining most of their special preferences in the tax code, including "depletion allowances" and "intangible" drilling costs. But the banking and automotive industries lost their fight to retain interest deductions on auto and consumer loans. The AFL-CIO knocked out the proposal to tax employer-paid fringe benefits but lost its fight to keep union dues deductible. The restaurant and entertainment industries restored 80 percent of their favorite deductions. State and local governments were successful in retaining the exemption from taxation of interest received from state and local government bonds, and they also succeeded in keeping the deduction for most state and local government taxes. But on balance the special interests suffered their single greatest defeat in many decades.

RETURN OF THE SPECIAL INTERESTS

George Bush campaigned for the presidency in 1988 with an emphatic promise to veto any attempt to raise taxes—"Read my lips! No new taxes!" But the president's pledge did not last through his second year in office. In a budget summit with leaders of the Democratically controlled Congress, President Bush announced his willingness to support a tax increase as part of a deficit reduction agreement. Once the Democratic leaders in Congress detected the irresolution of the Republican president, they proceeded to enact their own taxing and spending program, while placing the political blame on Bush. The resulting budget plan made deep cuts in defense spending, and token cuts in domestic spending, together with major tax increases.

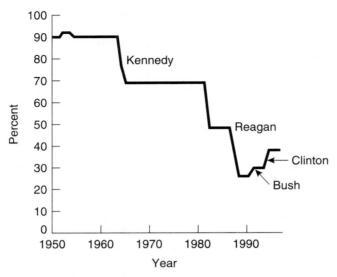

FIGURE 10–3 Maximum Income Tax Rate

"Soak the Rich."   Reversing the downward trend in top marginal tax rates, the Bush 1990 budget package raised the highest income tax rate from 28 to 31 percent (see Figure 10–3). The resulting rate structure was three-tiered—15, 28, and 31 percent. Democrats cheered the return to a more progressive rate structure They ridiculed as "trickle-down economics" the arguments by supply-side theorists that high marginal tax rates would slow economic growth. Republicans in Congress, taking their cue from President Bush, were largely silent about increasing tax rates. Instead they turned their attention to reinstituting a favorite tax break of the wealthy—the special treatment of income from capital gains.

The Capital Gains Controversy.   A central reform in the Tax Reform Act of 1986 was the elimination of preferential treatment for income from capital gains. (A capital gain is the profit made from buying and selling any asset—real estate, bonds, stocks, etc.) Before 1986, income from capital gains had been taxed at a lower rate than income from wages and salaries. But George Bush was never an enthusiastic supporter of tax reform. As vice president he pressed to retain tax breaks for the oil and gas industry, and after becoming president he pressed hard to restore preferential treatment for capital gains income.

    A reasonable argument can be made that the definition of a capital gain should exclude inflationary effects of price increases over time. That is, if the increase in the price of an asset at sale is attributable to inflation and not a true gain in value, there should be no capital "gain" tax. Capital gains should be indexed for inflation; the proportion of the capital gain that results from inflation should be deducted from the nominal capital gain. But the Tax Reform Act of 1986 did not provide for such indexing.

Restoring Preferential Treatment.   Preferential treatment for capital gains appeals to a wide variety of interests, especially Wall Street brokerage houses and investment firms and the real estate industry. Reducing taxes on capital gains increases the turnover (buying and selling) of stocks, bonds, and real estate, and hence the income of these interests. And, of course, it significantly reduces the tax burden on high-income taxpayers—those most likely to have income from the sale of these assets (see Figure 10–4).

Many Americans view preferential treatment for capital gains as a tax break for the rich. While President Bush publicly supported the proposal, many Congressional Democrats sought to favor the special interests without attracting too much public attention. So the 1990 tax increase in the top rate to 31 percent was quietly made applicable only to *earned* income. Income from capital gains continued to be taxed at a top rate of 28 percent. This ploy succeeded in restoring preferential treatment to capital gains. The same tactic was employed again in 1993 when President Clinton won congressional approval for additional increases in the top marginal tax rate on earned income to 36 and 39.6 percent. The tax on income from capital gains remained at 28 percent. Yet Republicans continued to uge further reductions in capital gains taxation.

CLINTON, DEFICITS, AND TAXES

Bill Clinton won the presidency in 1992 largely on his pledge to revive the economy—to stimulate economic growth, provide more jobs, and reduce the government's annual deficits. In Clinton's first major address to Congress, he called for a

FIGURE 10–4   Who Benefits from Capital
Gains

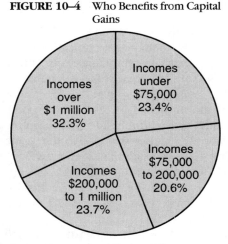

Source: Congressional Budget Office

new economic plan featuring large tax increases; cuts in defense spending; increases in federal spending for infrastructure, education, health and local development; and a plan to lower gradually annual federal deficits.

Clinton's Tax Increase.   Clinton's plan to reduce deficits centered on major tax increases on upper-income Americans, combined with an increase in the corporate income tax and new energy taxes. His campaign promise for a "middle-class tax cut" was shelved. Specifically, Clinton proposed raising taxes on

- *The affluent:* The tax rate for families with incomes above $140,000 a year to rise from 31 percent to 36 percent, and those with incomes above $250,000 to pay 39.6 percent; estate taxes to rise to 55 percent and the affluent to pay more in Medicare taxes
- *The elderly:* Retired couples with incomes above certain amounts to pay income tax on 85 percent of their Social Security benefits; premiums for Medicare also to rise
- *Corporations:* The tax rate for corporations to rise to 36 percent; firms to pay taxes on executive salaries that exceed $1 million a year; lobbying costs no longer deductible business expenses
- *Energy:* A heavy tax on all forms of energy based on heat content as measured in BTUs

Accommodating the Special Interests.   Interest group lobbying centered on the key Democratic members of the two tax-writing committees—House Ways and Means and Senate Finance—as well as the later conference committee that convened to resolve differences between House- and Senate-passed tax bills. Inasmuch as Republicans were largely united against *any* tax increase, every Democratic member's vote in the House and Senate was heavily lobbied. The principal interest groups in the struggle included the following:

- Oil, gas, and utility interests all lobbied heavily against the BTU energy tax. While the House included the tax in its bill, the Senate quickly abandoned the idea when key Democratic senators from oil-producing states threatened to sink the whole plan. The watered-down substitute was a 4.3 percent increase in the federal gasoline tax.
- Corporations fought hard against the proposed increase in the corporate income tax. They won a compromise—a raise from 34 to 35 percent instead of the 36 percent proposed by Clinton. They also won many other concessions, including repeal of luxury taxes on boats, furs, airplanes, and jewelry (enacted in 1990) and increased deductions for equipment purchases.
- Real estate interests won a partial reopening of the "passive loss" loophole (closed in the Tax Reform Act of 1986), allowing developers to shelter income from rental property.
- The powerful senior lobby, led by the American Association of Retired Per-

sons, succeeded in protecting millions of retirees from taxation by raising the threshold for taxing Social Security benefits, and they defeated all efforts to control spending for Social Security and Medicare. They also removed the income limit on the Medicare taxes on working Americans.

Clinton, Congress, and "Middle Class" Tax Cuts.   Both President Clinton and the Republican-controlled Congress agreed to a series of "middle class" tax cuts in 1997. The bipartisan legislation included a $500 tax credit for children in families making less than $110,000, an increase in the inheritance tax exemption to $1 million (from $600,000), and a tax credit of $1500 a year for each of the first two years of college. In a further concession to investors and brokerage firms, the capital gains tax was lowered from 28 to 20 percent for assets held 18 months or more. These and other tax breaks in the new law make the U.S. Tax Code even more complex than ever, guaranteeing more business for lawyers and accountants. Although both the president and Congress promise a balanced budget by 2002, these tax breaks add to the difficulty of achieving that goal.

TAX REFORM AND THE FLAT TAX

Special interest politics make comprehensive tax reform an unlikely prospect for America. Nonetheless, serious proposals have been offered in recent years to reform the nation's tax laws.

The Flat Tax.   Developed by economists over the years, the most recent legislative flat tax proposal is sponsored by House Majority Leader Dick Armey (R-TX) and his Senate co-sponsor Richard Shelby (R-AL).[6] Publisher Steve Forbes raised the profile of this idea in his 1996 bid for the Republican presidential nomination.

The elimination of all exemptions, exclusions, deductions, and special treatments would allow replacement of current progressive tax rates with a flat 19 percent tax on all forms of income. This low rate would produce just as much revenue as the current complicated system, even excluding family incomes under $25,000. It would sweep away the nation's army of tax accountants and lawyers and lobbyists, and increase national productivity by relieving taxpayers of millions of hours of record keeping and tax preparation. A flat tax could be filed on a postcard form (see Figure 10–5). Removing progressive rates would create incentives to work, save, and invest in America. It would lead to more rapid economic growth and improve efficiency by directing investments to their most productive uses rather than to tax avoidance. It would eliminate current incentives to underreport income, overstate exemptions, and avoid and evade taxation. Finally, by including a generous personal and family allowance, the flat tax would be made fair.

Opinion polls indicate that a flat tax rate is preferred over the current progressive rate system by a large majority of Americans.[7] However, many Americans also support deductions for home mortgages and charitable contributions. This

Form 1	Individual Wage Tax	1995

Your first name and initial (if joint return, also give spouse's name and initial)	Last name	Your social security number
Home address (number and street including apartment number or rural route)		Spouse's social security number
City, town, or post office, state, and ZIP code		Your occupation
		Spouse's occupation

1 Wages and salary — 1
2 Pension and retirement benefits — 2
3 Total compensation *(line 1 plus line 2)* — 3
4 Personal allowance
    (a) 0 $16,500 for married filing jointly — 4a
    (b) 0 $9,500 for single — 4b
    (c) 0 $14,000 for single head of household — 4c
5 Number of dependents, not including spouse — 5
6 Personal allowances for dependents *(line 5 multiplied by $4,500)* — 6
7 Total personal allowances *(line 4 plus line 6)* — 7
8 Taxable compensation *(line 3 less line 7, if positive; otherwise zero)* — 8
9 Tax *(19% of line 8)* — 9
10 Tax withheld by employer — 10
11 Tax due *(line 9 less line 10, if positive)* — 11
12 Refund due *(line 10 less line 9, if positive)* — 12

FIGURE 10–5 Armey-Shelby Flat Tax Postcard Return

suggests a major political weakness in the flat tax idea: even if enacted, politicians will gradually erode the uniformity, fairness, and simplicity of a flat tax by introducing popular deductions. Lobbyists for special tax treatments will continue to pressure Congress, and, over time, deductions, exemptions, and exclusions will creep back into the tax laws.

Moreover, the flat tax violates the principle of progressivity described earlier. If it is true that added (marginal) income of higher-income recipients is less valuable to them than the income of lower-income recipients, then a flat tax appears unfair. A flat tax is also opposed by those who believe that government should undertake to reduce income differences among people.

The National Sales Tax. A national retail sales tax, similar to sales taxes currently levied by many states, could replace the federal income tax and "get the IRS completely out of our lives."[8] By taxing sales rather than income, it would penalize consumption rather than production. (A value-added tax or "VAT" is comparable in effect to a sales tax, but taxes are levied on each stage of a product's development rather than on retail sale.) By eliminating taxes on income, Americans would be encouraged to engage in all of the activities that produce income—working, investing, inventing, starting businesses, and so on. It would encourage people to save money by levying taxes on their *spending* rather than their savings. It would discourage people from borrowing to purchase goods. Increased savings and reduced borrowing would bring about lower interest rates, making it easier for people to buy homes and automobiles. A sales tax would also get at the underground economy; drug dealers who do not report their income would pay a sales tax on their purchases of expensive homes, cars, and jewelry. It could be made more progressive (less regressive) by reducing or eliminating sales taxes on food, rent, medical care, or other necessities. Finally, collection costs, both in dollar terms and in lost freedom and privacy, would be greatly reduced by administering a sales tax rather than the income tax. This proposal has the support of House Ways and Means Committee Chairman Bill Archer (R-TX).

But a national sales tax is likely to be regressive, even if food, rent and other basic necessities are excluded. Low-income groups spend almost all of their income, saving very little. This means that virtually all of their income would be subject to sales taxation. In contrast, higher-income groups save larger shares of their income, thereby avoiding sales taxation on the proportion saved. A single national sales tax rate on all goods and services would violate the principle of progressivity. It would not satisfy liberals who believe that government tax policy should be shaped to serve social objectives, including the reduction of income inequality. And conservatives worry that such a tax might be adopted to supplement rather than replace an income tax. Finally, if different types of goods and services were taxed at different rates, interest groups would engage in a continuing frenzy of legislative activity seeking to lower the rate on their particular products.

Reining in the IRS.   The Internal Revenue Service (IRS) is the most intrusive of all government agencies, overseeing the finances of every tax-paying citizen and corporation in America. It maintains personal records on more than 100 million Americans and requires them to submit more than a billion forms each year. It may levy fines and penalties and collect taxes on its own initiative; in disputes with the IRS, the burden of proof falls on the taxpayer, not the agency. Its 110,000 employees spend $8 billion per year reviewing tax returns, investigating taxpayers, and collecting revenue. Americans pay an additional $30 billion for the services of tax accountants and preparers, and they waste some $200 billion in hours of record keeping and computing their taxes.

Simplifying the tax laws would not only reduce the cost of paying taxes but also reassure taxpayers that the tax structure is fair, reasonable, and understandable. It would reduce the power of the IRS to make regulations and interpretation under the tax code. Finally a "taxpayers' bill of rights" might strengthen safeguards against arbitrary actions by IRS officials.

SUMMARY

Modern pluralism praises the virtues of an interest group system in which public policy represents the equilibrium in the group struggle and the best approximation of the public interest. Yet it is clear that the interest group system puts broad segments of the American public, especially individual taxpayers, at a disadvantage.

1. Tax reform to achieve fairness, simplicity, and economic growth is an elusive goal. The interest group system, designed to protect special privileges and treatments, especially in the tax code, frustrates efforts to achieve true tax reform.

2. Special interests can take advantage of the difficulties in defining fairness. Is fairness proportionality, with everyone paying the same percentage of income in taxes? Or is fairness progressivity, with the percentage of income paid in taxes increasing with increases in income?

3. Over half of the nation's total personal income escapes income taxation through exemptions, deductions, and special treatments. Most individual taxpayers fail to itemize their deductions. Itemizers are mostly middle- and upper-income taxpayers.

4. The corporate income tax provides only 12 percent of total federal revenues. The individual income tax (43 percent) and Social Security payroll tax (36 percent) provide most of the federal government's revenue.

5. Supply-side economists are concerned about the impact of high marginal tax rates on economic behavior including disincentives to work, save, and invest, and on inefficiencies created by tax avoidance activity. According to the Laffer curve, reducing high marginal tax rates increases government revenues by encouraging productivity.

6. Supply-side ideas drove tax policy during the Reagan years. The Economic Recovery Tax Cut Act of 1981 lowered the top marginal rate from 70 to 50 percent, and the Tax Reform Act of 1986 lowered it again to 28 percent.

7. The Tax Reform Act of 1986 was one of the most heavily lobbied pieces of legislation in the history of Congress. Powerful interests opposing significant tax reform included the nation's largest manufacturers, the real estate and housing industries, multinational corporations, timber, oil, and gas companies, labor unions, banks, the restaurant and entertainment industries, and even many state and local governments. Although these special interests won some important battles, on balance they lost the war over tax reform.

8. But the special interests never abandoned the battlefield. They won an important victory in 1990 when President Bush agreed with the Democratic Congress to raise the top marginal rate on earned income, but to keep the tax on capital gains at 28 percent. President Clinton and Congress have continued this preferential treatment for capital gains.

9. President Clinton's deficit reduction plan centered on major tax increases, including raising the top marginal income tax rate to 39.6 percent, raising the corporate tax rate, and taxing some Social Security benefits of wealthy retirees. The

president won a narrow victory in Congress but only after months of hard bargaining, conciliation, and compromises with the special interests.

10. Major tax reform is regularly thwarted by special interest politics. Replacing the current federal income tax with a flat tax or a national sales tax is unlikely in the foreseeable future.

NOTES

1. Robert A. Dahl, *A Preface to Democratic Theory* (Chicago: University of Chicago Press, 1956), p. 124.
2. Text of address by U.S. Representative Dan Rostenkowski, May 28, 1985, *Congressional Quarterly Weekly Report,* June 1, 1985, p. 1077.
3. *Pollock* v. *Farmer's Loan,* 158 U.S. 601 (1895).
4. Joseph A. Pechman, *Federal Tax Policy,* 5th ed. (Washington, DC: Brookings Institution, 1987), Chap. 5.
5. *Congressional Quarterly Weekly Report,* May 10, 1986, p. 101.
6. See Dick Armey, *The Flat Tax* (New York: Fawcett, 1996).
7. See *American Enterprise,* July/August 1995, p. 69.
8. Congressman Bill Archer, "Tear the Income Tax Out by Its Roots," *Madison Review,* vol. 1, (Spring 1996), 17–21.

BIBLIOGRAPHY

ARMEY, DICK. *The Flat Tax.* New York: Ballantine Books, 1996.
BIRNBAUM, JEFFREY H., and ALAN S. MURRAY. *Showdown at Gucci Gulch.* New York: Random House, 1987.
CONLON, TIMOTHY, MARGARET WRIGHTSON, and DAVID R. BEAM. *Taxing Choices: The Politics of Tax Reform.* Washington, DC: CQ Press, 1989.
HALL, ROBERT E. and ALVIN RABUSHKA. *The Flat Tax.* Stanford, CA: Hoover Institution Press, 1985.
STOCKMAN, DAVID A. *The Triumph of Politics.* New York: Harper & Row, 1986.
WOODWARD, BOB. *The Agenda: Inside the Clinton White House.* New York: Simon & Shuster, 1994.

11

INTERNATIONAL TRADE AND IMMIGRATION
Elite-Mass Conflict

Japanese Nissan cars are unloaded at dockside. (Mathew Neal McVay/Tony Stone Images)

The elite model portrays public policy as a reflection of the interests and values of elites. The model does not necessarily require that elites and masses be locked in conflict—conflict in which elites inevitably prevail at the expense of masses. Rather, the model envisions elites determining the direction of public policy, with the masses largely apathetic and poorly informed and/or heavily influenced by elite views. The model also acknowledges that elites may choose to pursue "public re-garding" policies that benefit masses. Nonetheless, critics of the elite model often demand proof of elite-mass conflict over public policy and the subsequent shaping of policy to reflect elite preferences over mass well-being. Indeed, critics often demand proof that elites knowingly pursue policies that benefit themselves while hurting a majority of Americans. While this is not a fair test of elite theory, there is ample evidence that on occasion elites do pursue narrow self-serving interests.

Elite pursuit of narrow self-interest at the expense of mass well-being may be occurring more frequently in recent years than in the past. Certainly masses think so: public opinion is much more distrustful of national leadership today than twenty or thirty years ago. In response to the question "Would you say the government is pretty much run by a few big interests looking out for themselves or that it is run for the benefit of all of the people?" in 1965 only 28 percent chose the cynical response "a few big interests looking out for themselves." Today about 80 percent of the American public chooses this response (see Figure 11–1).

In describing immigration and international trade policy we rely on the elite

FIGURE 11–1   Public Perception of Elite Governance

Question: *Would you say that government is pretty much run by a few big interests looking out for themselves or that it is run for the benefit of all the people?*

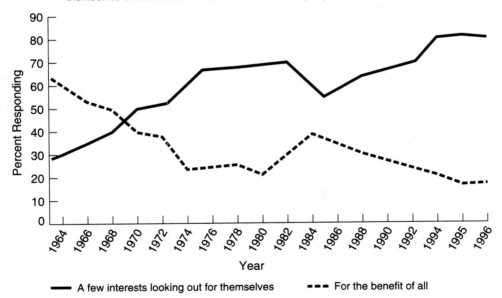

Source: Gallup opinion polls.

model. Arguably, U.S. policy, especially in international trade, serves the interests of the nation's largest multinational corporations at the expense of average American workers. We will argue that global trade policies have lowered average earnings *and* increased inequality in America. Moreover, we will argue that masses and elites have very different policy preferences regarding immigration.

THE GLOBAL ECONOMY

International trade—the buying and selling of goods and services between individuals and firms located in different countries—has expanded very rapidly in recent decades. Today, almost one-quarter of the *world's* total output is sold in a country other than the one in which it was produced. Today the United States exports about 11 percent of the value of its gross domestic product (GDP) and imports about 12 percent. Exports and imports were only about 3 percent of GDP in 1970 (see Figure 11–2). Global competition heavily impacts the American economy.

    Currently, America's leading trading partners are Canada, Japan, Mexico, China, Germany, Taiwan, Great Britain, South Korea, France, and Singapore in that order (see Figure 11–3). Note that some of these nations (Canada, Japan, Germany, for example) are advanced industrialized economies not unlike our own. But trade with developing countries (Mexico, China, Taiwan, South Korea, for example) is growing rapidly. And as we shall see, it is trade with these nations that raises the most serious problems for America's labor force.

    Years ago America's principal imports were oil and agricultural products not grown in the United States, for example, coffee. Today, however, our largest dollar-value imported products are automobiles, followed by office machinery, television

FIGURE 11–2 U.S. World Trade

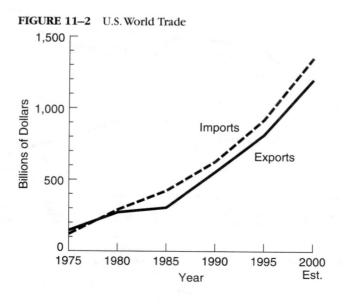

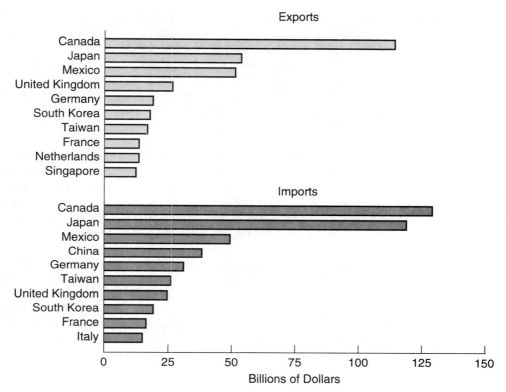

Source: Chart prepared by U.S. Bureau of the Census.

FIGURE 11–3 America's Leading Trading Partners

sets, clothing, shoes, and toys. Our largest dollar-value exports are aircraft, computers, power generators, and scientific instruments. The United States also exports wheat and corn, which can be harvested with high-tech machinery; it imports fruits, vegetables, and other agricultural products that require harvest by hand.

CHANGING ELITE PREFERENCES FOR WORLD TRADE

Historically, American business supported high tariffs, but as the U.S. economy matured and the costs of global transportation and communication declined, America's largest corporations began to look beyond the nation's borders.

Tariffs. Tariffs are simply taxes on foreign imports. Prior to World War II, U.S. tariffs on all imported goods averaged 30 to 50 percent in various decades. This suited U.S. manufacturers very well, eliminating most foreign competition from the U.S. market. U.S. firms enjoyed sheltered markets; they could raise prices to levels just below the price of imported goods with their high tariffs attached. Not only did this improve U.S. profit margins, but it also allowed U.S. firms that were less efficient than foreign producers to survive and prosper under the protection of tariffs. The pressure to cut wages and downsize workforces was less that it would be if U.S. firms had to face foreign corporations directly. American consumers, of course, paid higher prices than they otherwise would if foreign goods could enter the country without tariffs. But the U.S. steel, automobile, and electrical appliance industries grew powerful economically and politically.

Quotas. Trade quotas, where foreign producers are prohibited from selling more than a specified number of units in the United States, also protect domestic manufactures. To implement quotas, permits are granted by the U.S. State Department to favored firms in favored nations to sell specified amounts in the U.S. market. Note that quotas do not bring any revenue to the U.S. government as tariffs do; quotas allow the foreign firms exercising them to reap all of the benefits.

Protectionism. Today supporters of open global markets refer to tariffs, quotas, and other barriers to free trade as "protectionism." Protectionism, they argue, is inefficient: it not only raises prices for American consumers, but it also directs American capital and labor away from their best uses into aging, inefficient industries. This reduces a nation's overall productivity and ultimately its standard of living. Moreover, they argue that protectionist policies initiated by the United States invite retaliatory actions by other nations. U.S. exporting industries may be adversely affected by the resulting trade wars.

Enter the Multinationals. After World War II, the American economy was the most powerful in the world. American manufacturing corporations had few international competitors in most industries. Given their dominant position in world trade, American corporations sought to lower trade barriers around the world. The Council on Foreign Relations (see Chapter 14) and America's largest corporations lobbied Congress for reductions in U.S. tariffs in order to encourage other nations to reduce their own tariffs. The result was a rapid decline in average U.S. tariff rates (see Figure 11–4). In effect, the United States became an open market. Inasmuch as U.S. firms largely dominated their domestic markets in the 1950s and 1960s (steel, automobiles, aircraft, computers, drugs, electronics, appliances, agriculture, and so forth), they had little fear of foreign competition. On the contrary, they expanded their own international sales, becoming multinational corporations.

America's top exporting corporations (see Table 11–1) dictated U.S. trade policy. In 1947 GATT (General Agreement on Tariffs and Trade) was created to advance international trade (see GATT discussion below). The World Bank and International Monetary Fund (IMF) were initially formed to assist in the post–World War II recovery of European economies; today their mission has shifted to assisting developing nations in becoming world trading partners.

Prior to 1980 the United States incurred a *positive* trade balance, that is, exporting more goods and services than it imported. But since 1980 the United States

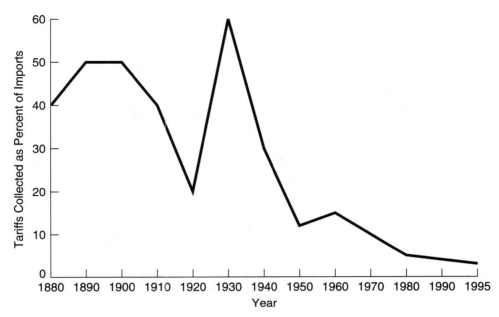

FIGURE 11–4 U.S. Tariff Policy over Time

has incurred balance of trade *deficits* every year. However, today U.S. multinational corporations receive substantial revenues from their exports. Moreover, most have manufacturing facilities as well as sales and distribution staffs worldwide. They stand to gain much more from the globalization of trade than they might lose from domestic competition from foreign firms.

ELITE GAINS FROM TRADE

The classic argument for free trade is based on the principle of "comparative advantage." If nations devote more of their resources to the production of those goods that they produce most efficiently, and trade for those goods that other nations produce more efficiently, then all trading nations benefit.

The "Comparative Advantage" Argument. Trade between two nations can improve efficiency even when one nation is much better at producing aircraft and somewhat better at producing clothing than its trading partner. Comparative advantage focuses on what each nation does *relatively* better than the other. Trade shifts resources (investment capital, jobs, technology, raw materials, etc.) in each nation toward what each does best. (Imagine a lawyer who is also a faster typist than her secretary. Even though the lawyer is better than her secretary at both law *and* typing it makes more sense for her to concentrate on law and leave the typing to her

TABLE 11-1   Top U.S. Exporting Corporations

Rank	Major Export	Value of Exports (Billions)
1 General Motors	Motor vehicles and parts, locomotives	16.1
2 Ford Motor	Motor vehicles and parts	11.9
3 Boeing	Commercial aircraft	11.8
4 Chrysler	Motor vehicles and parts	9.4
5 General Electric	Jet engines, turbines, plastics, med. sys., locomotives	8.1
6 Motorola	Communications equipment, semiconductors	7.4
7 Intl. Business Machines	Computers and related equipment	6.3
8 Philip Morris	Tobacco, beer, food products	4.9
9 Archer Daniels Midland	Protein meals, vegetable oils, flour, alcohol, grain	4.7
10 Hewlett-Packard	Measurement, computation, commun. prod. and sys.	4.7
11 Intel	Microcomputer components, modules, systems	4.6
12 Caterpillar	Engines; turbines; constr., mining, and agr. machinery	4.5
13 McDonnell Douglas	Aerospace products, missiles, electronic systems	4.2
14 E.I. Du Pont De Nemours	Chemicals, polymers, fibers, specialty products	3.6
15 United Technologies	Jet engines, helicopters, cooling equipment	3.1
16 Eastman Kodak	Imaging products	2.6
17 Lockheed	Aerospace products, missiles, electronic systems	2.1
18 Compaq Computer	Computers and related equipment	2.0
19 Raytheon	Electronic systems, engineering and constr. projects	1.9
20 Digital Equipment	Computers, software, related equipment	1.8
21 Alliedsignal	Aircraft and automotive parts, chemicals	1.8
22 Minnesota Mining & Mfg.	Ind., elec., health care, consumer, and imaging prod.	1.8
23 Westinghouse Electric	Power sys., radars, office furn., transport refrig.	1.6
24 Dow Chemical	Chemicals, plastics, consumer specialties	1.6
25 Merck	Health products	1.6
26 IBP	Fresh/frozen beef, pork, related byproducts	1.5
27 Weyerhaeuser	Pulp, newsprint, paperboard, logs, lumber	1.5
28 Textron	Aircraft, automotive systems and products	1.4
29 International Paper	Pulp, paperboard, wood products	1.4
30 Xerox	Copiers, printers, processing services and supplies	1.3
31 Rockwell Intl.	Electronics, auto parts, high-speed printing presses	1.3
32 Abbott Laboratories	Drugs, diagnostic equipment	1.2
33 Union Carbide	Chemicals, plastics	1.2
34 FMC	Armored military vehicles, chemicals	1.2
35 Deere	Farm, industrial, and lawn- and grounds-care equipment	1.1
36 Sun Microsystems	Computers and related equipment	1.1
37 UNISYS	Computers and related equipment	1.1
38 Georgia-Pacific	Pulp, building products, containerboard, paper	1.0
39 Cummins Engines	Diesel engines, related products	1.0
40 Alcoa	Aluminum products	1.0

TABLE 11-1   *Continued*

Rank	Major Export	Value of Exports (Billions)
41 Dresser Industries	Compressors, drilling fluids, drill bits	.9
42 Monsanto	Food ingredients, herbicides, chemicals, pharmaceuticals	.9
43 Bristol-Meyers Squibb	Pharmaceuticals, health care products, medical devices	.9
44 Novell	Computer software	.9
45 Exxon	Petroleum, chemicals	.8
46 Microsoft	Computer software	.8
47 Honeywell	Building, industrial, and aviation control systems	.8
48 Occidental Petroleum	Chemicals	.8
49 Ingersoll-Rand	Industrial machinery	.7
50 General Dynamics	Battle tanks and related support services	.7

Source: *Fortune,* November 13, 1995.

secretary. Their combined output of lawyering and typing will be greater than if each did some of the other's work.) Over time our nation will shift its resources to its aircraft industry and will import clothing from the other nation, and vice versa. Each nation will benefit more from trading than from trying to produce both airplanes and clothing.

Benefits from Trade.   The efficiencies achieved by trading are said to directly benefit consumers by making available cheaper imported goods. Export industries also benefit when world markets are opened to their products. American exporters benefit directly from sales abroad and they also benefit indirectly when foreign firms are allowed to sell in the American market. This is because sales of foreign goods in America provide foreigners with U.S. dollars which they can use to purchase the goods of America's exporting industries.

It is also argued that the pressure of competition from foreign-made goods in the American marketplace forces our domestic industries to become more efficient—cutting their costs and improving the quality of their own goods. Trade also quickens the flow of ideas and technology, allowing nations to learn from each other. Finally, trade expands the menu of goods and services available to trading countries. American consumers gain access to everything from exotic foods and foreign language movies to Porsches, BMWs, and Jaguars.

GATT and the World Trade Organization.   A multinational General Agreement on Tariffs and Trade (GATT) organization was created following World War II for the purpose of regulating international trade. Over the years GATT has been dominated by banking, business, and commercial interests in western nations seeking multilateral tariff reductions and the relaxation of quotas. They have been especially successful over the years in opening the giant U.S. market to foreign goods.

Indeed, average U.S. tariffs fell from more than 30 percent in 1947 to less than 3 percent today.

The most recent GATT session—the Uruguay Round—was completed in 1993 after seven years of multilateral negotiations. Among other things, it eliminated quotas on textile products; established more uniform standards for proof of dumping; set rules for the protection of intellectual property rights (patents and copyrights on books, movies, videos, and so on); reduced tariffs on wood, paper, and some other raw materials; and scheduled a gradual reduction of government subsidies for agricultural products.

The World Trade Organization (WTO) was also created in 1993 with 117 member nations. The WTO was given power to adjudicate trade disputes among countries and monitor and enforce trade agreements.

International Monetary Fund and World Bank. The IMF's purpose is to facilitate international trade, allowing nations to borrow to stabilize their balance of trade payments. However, when economically weak nations incur chronic balance of trade deficits and perhaps face deferral or default on international debts, the IMF may condition its loans on changes in a nation's economic policies. It may require a reduction in a nation's government deficits by reduced public spending and/or higher taxes, or require a devaluation of its currency making its exports cheaper and imports more expensive. It may also require the adoption of noninflationary monetary policies. Currently, the IMF as well as the World Bank are actively involved in assisting Russia and other states of the former Soviet Union convert to free market economies.

The World Bank makes long-term loans, mostly to developing nations, to assist in economic development. It works closely with the IMF in investigating the economic conditions of nations applying for loans and generally imposes IMF requirements on these nations as conditions for loans.

NAFTA. In 1993 the United States, Canada, and Mexico signed the North American Free Trade Agreement. Objections by labor unions in the United States (and independent presidential candidate Ross Perot) were drowned out in a torrent of support by the American corporate community, Democrats and Republicans in Congress, President Bill Clinton and former President George Bush. NAFTA envisions the removal of tariffs on virtually all products by all three nations over a period of 10 to 15 years. It also allows banking, insurance, and other financial services to cross these borders.

Anti-Dumping Policy. Dumping—the sale of foreign goods in the U.S. market at prices below those charged in the producing nation—presents a special trade problem. Dumping is often undertaken by foreign firms to introduce new products in the U.S. market; once Americans have accepted the product, prices go up. This pattern has been regularly followed by Japanese automobile manufactures. Dumping is also undertaken in order to destroy U.S. firms by underselling their products and forcing them out of business. Once foreign producers have driven out U.S. manufacturers, they raise their own prices. Dumping provides only temporary advantages to American consumers.

Dumping is officially illegal. The Trade Agreements Act of 1979 provides that special anti-dumping tariffs may be imposed when it is proven that a product is being sold in the United States at a price lower than that in the domestic market of a foreign producing nation. But it is a difficult and lengthy process for U.S. domestic firms to bring formal complaints to the U.S. government and obtain relief.

Trade Deficits.   For many years the United States has imported a higher dollar value of goods than it has exported. The difference is referred to as a trade deficit (the area in Figure 11–2 between the export and import lines). The trade deficit is made up by the transfer of American dollars, government bonds, and corporate securities, etc., to foreign firms. U.S. banks as well as the U.S. Treasury actually benefit from the deficit because it means that foreigners are accepting U.S. paper—currency, bonds, and securities—in exchange for their products. This makes it easier for the U.S. government to fund its own huge debt—selling bonds to foreign investors. Approximately 15 percent of the total U.S. government debt of 6 trillion dollars is owned by foreign banks and investors. U.S. interest payments on this part of the national debt flow out of the country. However, the widespread use of U.S. currency throughout the world in effect gives the U.S. Treasury an interest-free loan.

MASS LOSSES FROM TRADE

While the U.S. economy has performed very well in recent years, the benefits from that performance have been very unevenly distributed. The global economy has produced growth and profit for America's largest corporations and amply rewarded the nation's highest skilled workers. Indeed, global trade has *raised aggregate income* for the nation. But at the same time, it has contributed to a *decline in average earnings* of American workers and *worsened inequality* in America. Elite gains have been accompanied by mass losses.

Declining Worker Earnings.   Average hourly and weekly earnings of American workers have declined significantly over the past two decades (see Figure 11–5). In real dollars (controlling for the effects of inflation), average hourly earnings declined from $8.10 in 1970 to $7.40 in 1995. The earnings of unskilled and semi-skilled workers have fallen even more dramatically, by 25 to 33 percent since 1980.[1]

This decline in the earnings of American workers, especially the less skilled, has occurred simultaneously with the growth of international trade. While this coincidence does not prove that trade is causing earnings to decline, it raises a question: whether in a global economy the huge supply of unskilled labor is pushing down the wages of American workers. Increased trade, especially with less developed economies such as Mexico, China, and India, with their huge numbers of low-wage workers, creates competition for American workers. It is difficult to maintain the wage levels of American jobs, especially in labor intensive industries, in the face of

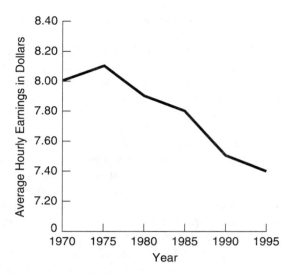

Source: Bureau of Labor Statistics, as reported in Council of Economic Advisers, *Economic Report of the President 1995,* Washington, DC: Government Printing Office, 1995.

FIGURE 11–5   Declining Real Earnings of American Workers

such competition. American corporations may initially respond by increasing their investment in capital and technology, making American workers more productive and hence capable of maintaining their high wages. But over time developing nations are acquiring more capital and technology themselves. And U.S. corporations can move their manufacturing plants to low-wage countries, especially to northern Mexico where the transportation costs of moving finished products back to the U.S. market are minimal. Harvard economist Richard B. Freeman summarizes these distressing views:

> An economic disaster has befallen low-skilled Americans, especially young men. Researchers using several data sources—including household survey data from the Current Population Survey, other household surveys, and establishment surveys—have documented that wage inequality and skill differentials in earnings and employment increased sharply in the United States from the mid-1970s through the 1980s and into the 1990s. The drop in the relative position of the less skilled shows up in a number of ways: greater earnings differentials between those with more and less education; greater earnings differentials between older and younger workers; greater differentials between high-skilled and low-skilled occupations; in a wider earnings distribution overall and within demographic and skill groups; and in less time worked by low-skill and low-paid workers.[2]

Worsening Inequality.   U.S. export industries (see Table 11–1) have thrived on international trade expansion, adding jobs to the American economy and raising the incomes of their executives and their most highly skilled workers. But the combination of effects of international trade on the American economy—*lower* wages for less-skilled workers and *higher* wages for executives and highly-skilled workers—worsens inequality in the nation. Inequality can worsen even though the aggregate income of the nation rises.

Since 1970 inequality in America has worsened. The percentage of the nation's total family income received by the poorest quintile (the lowest 20 percent of income earners) has declined from 5.4 percent to 4.2 percent between 1970 and 1995. Meanwhile the percentage of total family income of the highest income earners increased from 40.9 percent of total income to 46.2 percent. Figure 11–6 shows the percentage of losses and gains since 1979 of families in each income class. Lowest income families have lost nearly 15 percent of their real income over these years, while the highest income families have gained nearly 30 percent in real income.

Policy Options. Both Democratic and Republican presidents over the past half-century have supported expanded world trade. The U.S. market is the largest in the world and the most open to foreign-made goods. Our policy has been to maintain an open American market while encouraging other nations to do the same. Indeed the United States has led international efforts to liberalize world trade and investment and to eliminate foreign market barriers to American exports. The efforts include support for the GATT multinational trade agreement, the NAFTA, Canada, Mexico, and U.S. agreement, and a number of bilateral agreements with Japan and other Asian trading partners.

FIGURE 11–6   Worsening Inequality

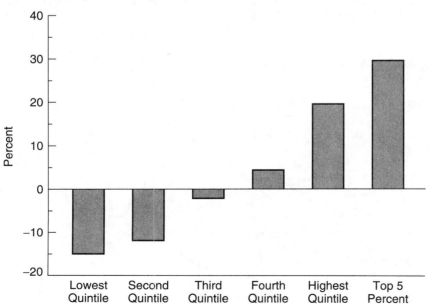

Changes in Average Real Family Income by Quintile 1979–1993

The elite response to declining real wages and worsening inequality is to stress the need for American workers to improve their productivity through better education and increased training. The "solution" found in Clinton's Economic Report of the President reads as follows:

> Ultimately, the only lasting solution to the increase in wage inequality that results from increased trade is the same as that for wage inequality arising from any other source: better education and increased training, to allow low-income workers to take advantage of the technological changes that raise productivity.[3]

ELITE-MASS DIFFERENCES OVER IMMIGRATION

The United States accepts more immigrants than all other nations of the world combined. The vast majority of immigrants in recent years come from the less-developed nations of Asia and Latin America (see Figure 11–7). Most immigrants come to the United States for economic opportunity. Most personify the traits we typically think of as American: opportunism, ambition, perseverance, initiative, and a willingness to work hard. As immigrants have always done, they frequently take dirty, low-paying, thankless jobs that other Americans shun. When they open their own businesses, they often do so in blighted, crime-ridden neighborhoods long since abandoned by other entrepreneurs.

Cultural Conflict.   The politics of immigration center on both cultural and economic issues. Elites, notably the nation's business and corporate leaders, tend to view immigration in economic terms, principally as an increase in the supply of low-wage workers in the United States. Most middle-class Americans view immigration in cultural terms, principally its impact on the ethnic composition of their communities.

FIGURE 11–7   Sources of Legal Immigration

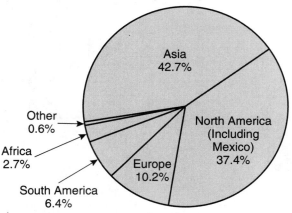

Source: *Statistical Abstract of the United States 1995,* p. 11.

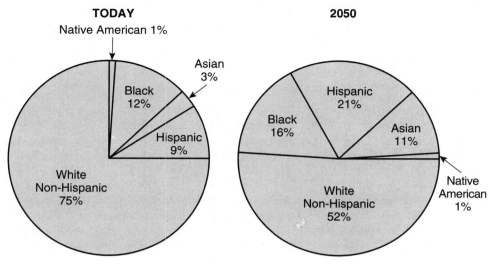

Source: *U.S. Census Bureau.*

FIGURE 11–8   Projected Ethnic Changes in the United States over Time

Until 1965 most immigrants came from Europe; today most are from Asia and Latin America. While most Americans are themselves the descendants of immigrants (Native Americans constitute about one percent of the population), most believe that today's immigrants are different from earlier waves. Population projections based on current immigration and fertility (birth) rates suggest that the ethnic character of the nation will shift dramatically over time (see Figure 11–8).

America has always been an ethnically pluralist society, but all were expected to adopt American political culture—including individual liberty, economic freedom, political equality, and equality of opportunity—and to learn American history and traditions, as well as the English language. The nation's motto is "E Pluribus Unum" (from many, one), but opponents of large-scale immigration fear that it currently represents a threat to cultural and political unity.[4] There were always Italian, Irish, Polish, Chinese, and other ethnic neighborhoods in big cities. But the children of immigrants, if not immigrants themselves, quickly became "Americanized." In contrast, today policymakers are divided over whether to protect and preserve language and cultural differences, for example through bilingual education, bilingual language ballots, and "language minority" voting districts (all currently required by amendments and interpretations of the Civil Rights Act of 1964 and the Voting Rights Act of 1965).[5]

Mass support for legal immigration appears to have declined over the years.

Question: In your view should immigration be kept at its present level, increased, or decreased?[6]

	1965	1977	1994	1995
Decreased	33%	42%	63%	62%
Kept at present level	39%	37%	27%	27%
Increased	8%	7%	6%	7%

Most Americans agree that immigrants make valuable contributions—that they "are productive citizens once they get their feet on the ground" (63 percent), "are hardworking" (58 percent), "are basically good honest people" (55 percent). However, majorities also believe that immigrants "are a burden on taxpayers" (66 percent), "take jobs from Americans" (58 percent), and "add to the crime problem" (56 percent).

Elite Support of Immigration.   Powerful industry groups that benefit from the availability of legal and illegal immigrants have led the fight in Washington to keep America's doors open. They have fought not only to expand legal immigration but also to weaken enforcement of laws against illegal immigration.

Current U.S. immigration policy—the admission of more than one million *legal* immigrants per year and weak enforcement of laws against *illegal* immigration—is largely driven by industry groups seeking to lower their labor costs. Agriculture, restaurants, clothing, hospitals, for example, all lobby heavily in Washington to weaken immigration laws and their enforcement. Large agri-businesses benefit from a heavy flow of unskilled immigrants who harvest their crops at very low wages. Clothing, textile, and shoe companies that have not already moved their manufacturing overseas are anxious to hire low paid immigrants for their assembly lines. Even high tech companies have found that they can recruit skilled computer analysts and data processors from English-speaking developing nations (India, for example) for wages well below those paid to American citizens with similar skills. These business interests frequently operate behind the scenes in Washington, allowing pro-immigration ethnic and religious groups to capture media attention. And indeed, large numbers of Americans identify with the aspirations of people striving to come to the United States, whether legally or illegally. Many Americans still have family and relatives living abroad who may wish to immigrate. Hispanic groups have been especially concerned about immigration enforcement efforts that may lead to discrimination against all Hispanic Americans. Foreign governments, especially Mexico, have also protested U.S. enforcement policies.

NATIONAL IMMIGRATION POLICY

America is a nation of immigrants, from the first "boat people," the Pilgrims, to the latest Cuban "balseros" (rafters) (see Figure 11–9). Americans are proud of their immigrant heritage and the freedom and opportunity the nation has extended to generations of "huddled masses yearning to be free"—the words emblazoned upon the Statue of Liberty in New York's harbor. Today about 8 percent of the U.S. population is foreign born.

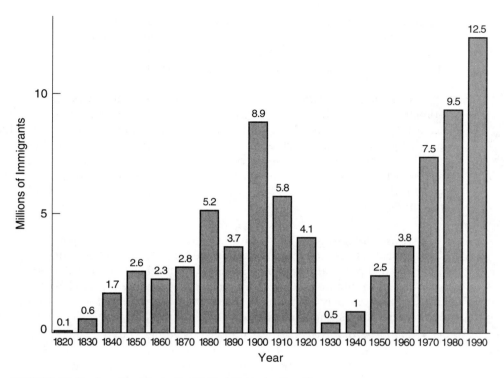

FIGURE 11–9   Immigration to the United States by Decades

Legal Immigration.   Immigration policy is a responsibility of the national government. It was not until 1882 that Congress passed the first legislation restricting entry into the United States of persons alleged to be "undesirable" as well as virtually all Asians. Following the end of World War I, Congress passed a comprehensive Immigration Act of 1921 that established maximum numbers of new immigrants each year and set a quota for each foreign country at three percent (later reduced to 2 percent) of the number of that nation's foreign born living in the United States in 1890. These restrictions reflected anti-immigration feelings that were generally directed at the large wave of southern and eastern European, Catholic and Jewish immigrants (Poland, Russia, Hungary, Italy, Greece) that had entered the United States prior to World War I. It was not until the Immigration and Nationality Act of 1965 that national origin quotas were abolished, replaced by preference categories for relatives and family members and professional and skilled persons.

Immigration "Reform."   Immigration "reform" was the announced goal of Congress in the Immigration Reform and Control Act of 1986, also known as the Simpson-Mazzoli Act. It sought to control immigration by placing principle responsibility on employers; it set fines for knowingly hiring an illegal alien, with prison terms for repeat offenders. However, it allowed employers to accept many different forms of easily forged documentation, and subjected them to penalties for discriminating against legal foreign-born residents. To win political support, the Act granted amnesty to illegal aliens who had lived in the United States since 1982. Predictably, the Act failed to reduce the flow of either legal or illegal immigrants.

Current Immigration Policy.   Today, roughly 1 million people per year are admitted *legally* to the United States as "lawful permanent residents" (persons who have relatives who are U.S. citizens or lawful permanent residents, or who have needed job skills); or as "refugees," or "asylees" (persons with "a well-founded fear of persecution" in their country of origin). In addition, more than 20 million people are awarded visas each year to enter the United States for study, pleasure, or business. Federal law recognizes the following categories of non-citizens admitted into the United States:

- *Legal immigrants* (also "lawful permanent residents" or "permanent resident aliens"). These immigrants are admitted to the United States under a ceiling of 675,000 per year, with some admitted on the basis of job skills but most coming as family members of persons legally residing in the United States. Legal immigrants may work in the United States, and apply for citizenship after five years of continuous residence.
- *Refugees and asylees.* These are persons admitted to the United States because of "a well-founded fear of persecution because of race, religion, nationality, political opinion, or membership in a social group." (Refugees are persons not yet in the United States; asylees are persons who have already arrived and apply for refugee protection.) They may work in the United States and are eligible for all federal assistance programs.
- *Parolees* (or persons enjoying "temporary protected status"). These are persons admitted to the United States for humanitarian or medical reasons or whose countries are faced with natural or man-made disasters.
- *Legalized aliens* (also called "amnesty aliens"). These formerly illegal aliens were given legal status (amnesty) under the Immigration Reform and Control Act of 1986. To qualify, they must show some evidence of having resided in the United States since 1982. They may work in the United States and are eligible for all federal assistance programs after five years.
- *Non-immigrants* (also "nonresident legal aliens"). Over 20 million people are awarded visas to enter the United States for pleasure and business. Time limits are placed on these visas usually by stamping a passport. Additionally, students, temporary workers and trainees, transient aliens, and foreign officials are eligible for temporary visas.

Illegal Immigration.   The United States is a free and prosperous society with more than 5,000 miles of borders (2,000 with Mexico) and hundreds of international air and sea ports. In theory, a sovereign nation should be able to maintain secure borders, but in practice the United States has been unwilling and unable to do so.

Estimates of illegal immigration vary wildly, from the official U.S. Immigration and Naturalization Service (INS) estimate of 400,000 per year (about 45 percent of the legal immigration), to unofficial estimates ranging up to three million per year. The INS estimates that about four million illegal immigrants currently reside in the United States; unofficial estimates range up to ten million or more. Many illegal immigrants slip across U.S. borders, or enter ports with false documentation, while many more overstay tourist or student visas (and are not counted by the INS as illegal immigrants).[7]

As a free society, the United States is not prepared to undertake massive round ups and summary deportations of millions of illegal residents. The Fifth and Fourteenth Amendments to the U.S. Constitution require that every *person* (not just *citizen*) be afforded "due process of law." The INS may turn back persons at the border or even hold them in detention camps. The Coast Guard may intercept boats at sea and return persons to their country of origin.[8] Aliens have no constitutional right to come to the United States. However, *once in the United States, whether legally or illegally, every person is entitled to due process of law and equal protection of the laws.* People are entitled to a fair hearing prior to any government attempt to deport them. Aliens are entitled to apply for asylum and present evidence at a hearing of their "well-founded fear of prosecution" if returned to their country. Localized experiments in border enforcement have indicated that illegal immigration can be reduced by half or more with significant increases in INS personnel and technology.

A national bipartisan commission on immigration reform, chaired by former Texas Democratic Congresswoman Barbara Jordan, recommended the enforcement of existing federal laws barring the hiring of illegal aliens by establishing a national computerized verification system that employers could easily access when considering job applicants. But industry groups managed to bury the recommendation in Congress. A weakened immigration reform bill was passed in Congress in 1996 that increased the number of U.S. Border Patrol guards and expedited deportation procedures for illegal aliens convicted of a crime.

Immigration and Federalism.   Although the federal government has exclusive power over immigration policy, its decisions have very significant effects on states and communities—on their governmental budgets, on the use of their public services, and even on their social character. Immigration is by no means uniform across the states. On the contrary, legal and illegal immigration are concentrated in a relatively few states. California, Hawaii, New York, Florida, and Texas have the highest proportions of legal immigrants among their populations. And these states, together with Arizona, New Mexico, Colorado, Illinois, and New Jersey, probably have the highest numbers of illegal immigrants as well. Moreover, the populations of particular cities—such as Los Angeles, Miami, El Paso, and San Antonio—may be one-third to one-half foreign born.

The U.S. Supreme Court has mandated that state and local governments may not exclude either legal or *illegal* immigrants from public education, and—perhaps by implication—from any other benefits or services available to citizens.[9] Thus, federal immigration policy heavily impacts state and local budgets, especially in states with disproportionate numbers of immigrants. (Although family "sponsors" may have pledged support of immigrants, and immigrants who become a "public charge" may be deported legally, these provisions of the law are almost never enforced.) Indeed, some states have tried unsuccessfully to sue the federal government to recover the costs of providing services to immigrants.

Welfare Benefits for Immigrants. California's Proposition 187 in 1994 set off renewed national debate over immigration. Placed on the ballot by citizen initiative, Proposition 187 denies public education, non-emergency health care, and social service benefits to illegal aliens in that state. Hispanic groups in the state feared that the passage of Proposition 187 would lead to discrimination against legal immigrants and perhaps Hispanic citizens in general. The denial of education and health care to children was branded as especially mean-spirited and cruel. Following a highly-spirited and well-publicized contest over the initiative, California voters approved it by a solid 59 to 41 percent. (The constitutionality of the measure is questionable—the Fourteenth Amendment declares that no state shall "deny to any *person* within its jurisdiction the equal protection of the laws"—and its implementation has been halted by federal courts.) National surveys report that the denial of public services to illegal immigrants has widespread support:

Question: Do you favor or oppose having a law in your state—similar to Proposition 187 in California—that requires state and local government agencies to stop providing health benefits and public education to illegal immigrants including children?"

Favor   58%
Oppose   36%

Question: Are you in favor or opposed to providing free public education, school lunches, and other benefits to children of immigrants who are in the United States illegally?

Favor   28%
Oppose   67%

Washington's reaction to the message sent by Californians was reflected in Congress's welfare reform act in 1996. The act denies most federal welfare benefits to *illegal* immigrants, and allows the states to deny federal welfare, Medicaid, and social services to *legal* immigrants if they wish to do so. Refugees and those granted asylum are exempt from these restrictions, and both legal and illegal immigrants are entitled to emergency medical care. President Clinton has pledged to repeal the restrictions on aid to legal immigrants, and federal courts may also act to block these restrictions. Nonetheless, in anticipation of the new restrictions, more immigrants applied for citizenship in 1996 (more than 1.2 million) than any previous year in history.

SUMMARY

The elite model portrays public policy as the preferences of elites. While the model does not assert that these preferences necessarily conflict with the welfare of the masses, it does imply that the elite preferences will prevail in public policy even when opposed by the masses in a democratic society.

1. The principle beneficiaries of the emergence of a global economy and the expansion of U.S. trade have been America's large multinational corporations.

2. Historically, American business supported high tariffs in order to disadvantage foreign competition in the U.S. market. But after World War II, American industry gained worldwide dominance and changed their policy preference. The United States led the worldwide effort to establish a global marketplace.

3. The principle instruments used to open world markets to U.S. goods were the General Agreement on Tariff and Trade (GATT), the International Monetary Fund, and the World Bank.

4. In 1993, elite support for the North American Free Trade Agreement (NAFTA) envisioning the removal of tariffs on virtually all goods traded between the United States, Canada, and Mexico, prevailed over the opposition of American labor unions.

5. The benefits of international trade are unevenly distributed between elites and masses in America. Average real hourly wages of American workers have declined since 1970.

6. Global trade appears to have worsened inequality in the United States in recent years. Today, greater differences exist between well-educated and less-educated workers and high-skilled and low-skilled workers than twenty years ago. America's less-educated, low-skilled workers must now compete against low-wage workers in less developed countries around the world.

7. The United States accepts more immigrants than all other nations of the world combined. More than one million legal immigrants enter the United States each year, as well as one to three million illegal immigrants.

8. Immigration today is higher than at any period in United States history. Most immigration today is from the less developed nations of Asia, and Central and South America.

9. Powerful industry groups that benefit from the availability of low-wage workers lobby in Washington to maintain high levels of legal immigration and weaken efforts to reduce illegal immigration.

10. Mass opinion generally favors efforts to control illegal immigration, including the exclusion of illegal immigrants from government benefits.

NOTES

1. *Economic Report of the President 1995,* p. 231.
2. Richard B. Freeman, "Are Your Wages Set in Beijing?" *Journal of Economic Perspectives,* vol. 9, (Summer, 1995), 15.
3. *Economic Report of the President 1995,* p. 232.

4. See Peter Brimelow, *Alien Nation* (New York: Random House, 1995).
5. For a summary of recent studies, see *America's Newcomers,* National Conference of State Legislatures, Denver, CO, 1993.
6. Data from Gallup and Yankolovich polls as reported in *The American Enterprise,* March, April 1995, p. 105; and *USA Today,* July 10, 1995.
7. American Security Council, *The Illegal Immigration Crisis,* Washington, DC: ASC, 1994.
8. *Sale* v. *Haitian Centers Council,* 125 L. Ed. 2d 128 (1993).
9. *Plyler* v. *Doe,* 457 U.S. 202 (1982).

BIBLIOGRAPHY

BARTLETT, DONALD L. and JAMES B. STEELE. *America: Who Stole the Dream.* Kansas City: Andrews and McMeel, 1996.
BATRA, RAVI. *The Myth of Free Trade.* New York: Touchstone, 1993.
BRIMELOW, PETER. *Alien Nation.* New York: Random House, 1995.
NATIONAL CONFERENCE OF STATE LEGISLATORS. *America's Newcomers.* Denver: NCSL, 1993.
THE NEW YORK TIMES. *The Downsizing of America.* New York: Times Books, 1996.
PORTER, MICHAEL. *The Competitive Advantage of Nations.* New York: Free Press, 1991.
STERN, ROBERT M. (ed.) *U.S. Trade Policies in a Changing World Economy.* Cambridge: MIT Press, 1989.

12

AMERICAN FEDERALISM
Institutional Arrangements and Public Policy

Governors actively exchange information and views on a wide range of topics at the National Governors' Association winter meeting. (National Governors' Association)

AMERICAN FEDERALISM

Virtually all nations of the world have some units of local government—states, republics, provinces, regions, cities, counties, villages. Decentralization of policymaking is required almost everywhere. But nations are not truly *federal* unless both national and subnational governments exercise separate and autonomous authority, both elect their own officials, and both tax their own citizens for the provision of public services. Moreover, federalism requires the powers of the national and subnational governments to be guaranteed by a constitution that cannot be changed without the consent of both national and subnational populations.*

The United States, Canada, Australia, India, Germany, and Switzerland are generally regarded as federal systems, but Great Britain, France, Italy, and Sweden are not. Although these latter nations have local governments, they depend on the national government for their powers. They are considered *unitary* rather than federal systems because their local governments can be altered or even abolished by the national government acting alone. In contrast, a system is said to be *confederal* if the power of the national government is dependent on local units of government. While these terms—*federal, unitary,* and *confederal*—can be defined theoretically, in the real world of policymaking it is not so easy to distinguish between governments that are truly federal and those that are not. Indeed, it is not clear whether government in the United States today retains its federal character.

There are more than 85,000 separate governments in the United States, more than 60,000 of which have the power to levy their own taxes. There are states, cities, counties, towns, boroughs, villages, special districts, school districts, and public authorities (see Table 12–1). However, only the national government and the states are recognized in the U.S. Constitution; all other governments are subdivisions of states. States may create, alter, or abolish these other governments by amending their laws or constitutions.

WHY FEDERALISM?

Why have state and local governments anyway? Why not have a centralized political system with a single government accountable to national majorities in national elections—a government capable of implementing uniform policies throughout the country?

---

* Other definitions of federalism in American political science: "Federalism refers to a political system in which there are local (territorial, regional, provincial, state, or municipal) units of government as well as a national government, that can make final decisions with respect to at least some governmental authorities and whose existence is especially protected." James Q. Wilson, *American Government,* 4th ed. (Lexington, KY: D.C. Heath, 1989), p. 47. "Federalism is the mode of political organization that unites smaller polities within an overarching political system by distributing power among general and constituent units in a manner designed to protect the existence and authority of both national and subnational systems enabling all to share in the overall system's decision making and executing processes." Daniel J. Elazar, *American Federalism: A View from the States* (New York: Thomas Y. Crowell, 1966), p. 2.

TABLE 12-1   Governments in the United States

U.S. government	1
State government	50
Counties	3,043
Municipalities	19,279
Townships	16,656
School districts	14,422
Special districts	31,555
Total	85,006

Source: *Statistical Abstract of the United States 1996*, p. 295.

Protection Against Tyranny.   The nation's Founders understood that "republican principles"—periodic elections, representative government, political equality—would not be sufficient in themselves to protect individual liberty. These principles may make governing elites more responsive to popular concerns, but they do not protect minorities or individuals, "the weaker party or an obnoxious individual," from government deprivations of liberty or property. Indeed, according to the Founders, "the great object" of constitution writing was both to preserve popular government and at the same time to protect individuals from "unjust and interested" *majorities.* "A dependence on the people is, no doubt, the primary control of government, but experience has taught mankind the necessity of auxiliary precautions."[1]

Among the most important "auxiliary precautions" devised by the Founders to control government was federalism, which was viewed as a source of constraint on big government. They sought to construct a governmental system incorporating the notion of "opposite and rival interests." Governments and government officials could be constrained by competition with other governments and other government officials.[2]

Policy Diversity.   Today, federalism continues to permit policy diversity. The entire nation is not straitjacketed with a uniform policy to which every state and community must conform. State and local governments may be better suited to deal with specific state and local problems. Washington bureaucrats do not always know best about what to do in Commerce, Texas.

Conflict Management.   Federalism helps manage policy conflict. Permitting states and communities to pursue their own policies reduces the pressures that would build up in Washington if the national government had to decide everything. Federalism permits citizens to decide many things at the state and local levels of government and avoid battling over single national policies to be applied uniformly throughout the land.

Dispersal of Power.   Federalism disperses power. The widespread distribution of power is generally regarded as an added protection against tyranny. To the extent that pluralism thrives in the United States, state and local governments have contributed to its success. They also provide a political base for the survival of the opposition party when it has lost national elections.

Increased Participation.   Federalism increases political participation. It allows more people to run for and hold political office. Nearly a million people hold some kind of political office in counties, cities, townships, school districts, and special districts. These local leaders are often regarded as closer to the people than Washington officials. Public opinion polls show that Americans believe that their local governments are more manageable and responsive than the national government.

Improved Efficiency.   Federalism improves efficiency. Even though we may think of 85,000 governments as an inefficient system, governing the entire nation from Washington would be even worse. Imagine the bureaucracy, red tape, delays, and confusion if every government activity in every community in the nation—police, schools, roads, firefighting, garbage collection, sewage disposal, street lighting, and so on—were controlled by a central government in Washington.

Insuring Policy Responsiveness.   Federalism encourages policy responsiveness. Multiple, competing governments are more sensitive to citizens' views than a monopoly government. The existence of multiple governments offering different packages of benefits and costs allows a better match between citizens' preferences and public policy. People and businesses can vote with their feet by relocating to those states and communities that most closely conform to their own policy preferences. Mobility not only facilitates a better match between citizens' preferences and public policy, it also encourages competition among states and communities to offer improved service at lower costs.

Encouraging Policy Innovation.   Federalism encourages policy experimentation and innovation. Federalism may be perceived today as a conservative idea, but it was once viewed as the instrument of progressivism. A strong argument can be made that the groundwork for the New Deal was built in state policy experimentation during the Progressive Era. Federal programs as diverse as income tax, unemployment compensation, countercyclical public works, Social Security, wage and hour legislation, bank deposit insurance, and food stamps all had antecedents at the state level. Much of the current neoliberal policy agenda—health insurance, childcare programs, notification of plant closings, government support of industrial research and development—has been embraced by various states. Indeed, the compelling phrase "laboratories of democracies" is generally attributed to the great progressive jurist, Supreme Court Justice Louis D. Brandeis, who used it in defense of state experimentation with new solutions to social and economic problems.

POLITICS AND INSTITUTIONAL ARRANGEMENTS

Political conflict over federalism—over the division of responsibilities and finance between national and state/local governments—has tended to follow traditional liberal and conservative political cleavages. Generally, liberals seek to enhance the power of the *national* government. Liberals believe that people's lives can be changed by the exercise of government power to end discrimination, abolish poverty, eliminate slums, ensure employment, uplift the downtrodden, educate the masses, and cure the sick. The government in Washington has more power and resources than state and local governments have, and liberals have turned to it to cure America's ills. State and local governments are regarded as too slow, cumbersome, weak, and unresponsive. It is difficult to achieve change when reform-minded citizens must deal with 50 state governments or 85,000 local governments. Change is more likely to be accomplished by a strong government. Moreover, liberals argue that state and local governments contribute to inequality in society by setting different levels of services in education, welfare, health, and other public functions. A strong national government can ensure uniformity of standards throughout the nation. The government in Washington is seen as the principal instrument for liberal social and economic reform.

Generally, conservatives seek to return power to *state and local* governments. They are more skeptical about the good that government can do. Adding to the power of the national government is not an effective way of resolving society's problems. On the contrary, conservatives argue that "government is the problem, not the solution." Excessive government regulation, burdensome taxation, and inflationary government spending combine to restrict individual freedom, penalize work and savings, and destroy incentives for economic growth. Government should be kept small, controllable, and close to the people.

Institutional Arenas and Policy Preferences.   Debates about federalism are seldom constitutional debates; rather, they are debates about policy. People decide which level of government—national, state, or local—is most likely to enact the policy they prefer. Then they argue that that level of government should have the responsibility for enacting the policy. Political scientist David Nice explains "the art of intergovernmental politics" as "trying to reduce, maintain, or increase the scope of conflict in order to produce the policy decisions you want." Abstract debates about federalism or other institutional arrangements, devoid of policy implications, hold little interest for most citizens or politicians. "Most people have little interest in abstract debates that argue which level of government should be responsible for a given task. What people care about is getting the policies they want."[3]

Thus, the case for centralizing policy decisions in Washington is almost always one of substituting the policy preferences of national elites for those of state and local officials. It is not seriously argued on constitutional grounds that national elites better reflect the policy preferences of the American people. Rather, federal intervention is defended on policy grounds—the assertion that the goals and priorities that prevail in Washington should prevail throughout the nation.

Concentrating Benefits to Organized Interests.   The national government is more likely to reflect the policy preferences of the nation's strongest and best-organized interest groups than are 85,000 state and local governments. This is true, first, because the costs of "rent seeking"—lobbying government for special subsidies, privileges, and protections—are less in Washington in relation to the benefits available from national legislation than the combined costs of rent seeking at 85,000 subnational centers. Organized interests, seeking concentrated benefits for themselves and dispersed costs to the rest of society, can concentrate their own resources in Washington. Even if state and local governments individually are more vulnerable to the lobbying efforts of wealthy, well-organized special interests, the prospect of influencing all 50 separate state governments or, worse, 85,000 local governments is discouraging to them. The costs of rent seeking at 50 state capitols, 3,000 county courthouses, and tens of thousands of city halls; while not multiplicative by these numbers, are certainly greater than the costs of rent seeking in a single national capitol.

Moreover, the benefits of national legislation are comprehensive. A single act of Congress, a federal executive regulation, or a federal appellate court ruling can achieve what would require the combined and coordinated action by hundreds, if not thousands, of state and local government agencies. Thus, the benefits of rent seeking in Washington are greater in relation to the costs. Lobbying in Washington is efficient.

Dispersing Costs to Unorganized Taxpayers.   Perhaps more importantly, the size of the national constituency permits interest groups to disperse the costs of specialized, concentrated benefits over a very broad constituency. Cost dispersal is the key to interest group success. If costs are widely dispersed, it is irrational for individuals, each of whom bear only a tiny fraction of these costs, to expend time, energy, and money to counter the claims of the special interests. Dispersal of costs over the entire nation better accommodates the strategies of special interest groups than the smaller constituencies of state and local government.

In contrast, state and local government narrows the constituencies over which costs must be spread, thus increasing the burdens to individual taxpayers and increasing the likelihood that they will take notice of them and resist their imposition. Economist Randall G. Holcombe explains: "One way to counteract this [interest group] effect is to provide public goods and services at the smallest level of government possible. This concentrates the cost on the smallest group of taxpayers possible and thus provides more concentrated costs to accompany the concentrated benefits."[4] He goes on to speculate whether the tobacco subsidies granted by Washington to North Carolina farmers would be voted by the residents of that state if they had to pay their full costs. Lobbying in Washington disperses costs.

The rent-seeking efficiencies of lobbying in Washington are well known to the organized interests. As a result, the policies of the national government are more likely to reflect the preferences of the nation's strongest and best-organized interests.[5]

AMERICAN FEDERALISM: VARIATIONS ON THE THEME

American federalism has undergone many changes more than 200 years since the Constitution of 1787. That is, the meaning and practice of federalism have transformed many times.

State-centered Federalism (1787–1865).   From the adoption of the Constitution of 1787 to the end of the Civil War, the states were the most important units in the American federal system. People looked to the states for the resolution of most policy questions and the provision of most public services. Even the issue of slavery was decided by state governments. The supremacy of the national government was frequently questioned, first by the antifederalists (including Thomas Jefferson) and later by John C. Calhoun and other defenders of slavery and secession.

Dual Federalism (1865–1913).   The supremacy of the national government was decided on the battlefields of the Civil War. Yet for nearly a half century after that conflict, the national government narrowly interpreted its delegated powers and the states continued to decide most domestic policy issues. The resulting pattern has been described as dual federalism, in which the state and the nation divided most government functions. The national government concentrated its attention on the delegated powers—national defense, foreign affairs, tariffs, commerce crossing state lines, money, standard weights and measures, post office and post roads, and admission of new states. State governments decided the important domestic policy issues—education, welfare, health, and criminal justice. The separation of policy responsibilities was once compared to a "layer cake," with local governments at the base, state governments in the middle, and the national government at the top.[6]

Cooperative Federalism (1913–1964).   The distinction between national and state responsibilities gradually eroded in the first half of the twentieth century. American federalism was transformed by the Industrial Revolution and the development of a national economy; the federal income tax in 1913, which shifted financial resources to the national government; and the challenges of two world wars and the Great Depression. In response to the Great Depression of the 1930s, state governors welcomed massive federal public works projects under President Franklin D. Roosevelt's New Deal. In addition, the federal government intervened directly in economic affairs, labor relations, business practices, and agriculture. Through its grants-in-aid, the national government cooperated with the states in public assistance, employment services, child welfare, public housing, urban renewal, highway building, and vocational education.

This new pattern of federal-state relations was labeled cooperative federalism. Both the nation and the states exercised responsibilities for welfare, health, highways, education, and criminal justice. This merging of policy responsibilities was compared to a marble cake: "As the colors are mixed in a marble cake, so functions are mixed in the American federal system."[7]

Yet even in this period of shared national-state responsibility, the national government emphasized cooperation in achieving common national and state goals. Congress generally acknowledged that it had no direct constitutional authority to regulate public health, safety, or welfare. It relied primarily on its powers to tax and spend for the general welfare in order to provide financial assistance to state and local governments to achieve shared goals. Congress did not legislate directly on local matters. For example, Congress did not require the teaching of vocational education in public high schools because public education was not an "enumerated power" of the national government in the U.S. Constitution. But Congress could offer money to states and school districts to assist in teaching vocational education and even threaten to withdraw the money if federal standards were not met. In this way the federal government involved itself in fields "reserved" to the states.

Centralized Federalism (1964–1980).   Over the years it became increasingly difficult to maintain the fiction that the national government was merely assisting the states in performing their domestic responsibilities. By the time President Lyndon B. Johnson launched the Great Society in 1964, the federal government had clearly set forth its own "national" goals. Virtually all problems confronting American society—from solid waste disposal and water and air pollution to consumer safety, street crime, preschool education, and even rat control—were declared to be national problems. Congress legislated directly on any matter it chose, without regard to its "enumerated powers." The Supreme Court no longer concerned itself with the "reserved" powers of the states, and the Tenth Amendment lost most of its meaning. The pattern of national-state relations became centralized. As for the cake analogies, one commentator observed, "The frosting had moved to the top, something like a pineapple upside-down cake."[8]

The states' role under centralized federalism is that of responding to federal policy initiatives and conforming to federal regulations established as conditions for federal grant money. The administrative role of the states remained important; they helped implement federal policies in welfare, Medicaid, environmental protection, employment training, public housing, and so on. But the states' role was determined not by the states themselves but by the national government.

Bureaucracies at the federal, state, and local levels became increasingly indistinguishable. Coalitions of professional bureaucrats—whether in education, public assistance, employment training, rehabilitation, natural resources, agriculture, or whatever—worked together on behalf of shared goals, whether they were officially employed by the federal government, the state government, or a local authority. One commentator referred to this type of policymaking as "functional federalism."[9] State and local officials in agencies receiving a large proportion of their funds from the federal government feel very little loyalty to their governor or state legislature.

New Federalism (1980–1985).   Efforts to reverse the flow of power to Washington and return responsibilities to state and local government have been labeled the *New Federalism.* The phrase originated in the administration of President Richard M. Nixon, who used it to describe general revenue sharing, that is, federal sharing of tax revenues with state and local governments, with few strings attached. Later the phrase "New Federalism" was used by President Ronald Reagan to describe a series of proposals designed to reduce federal involvement in domestic programs and encourage states and cities to undertake greater policy responsibilities themselves. These efforts included the consolidation of many categorical grant programs into fewer block grants, an end to general revenue sharing, and less reliance by the states on federal revenue (see "Money and Power Flow to Washington" later).

Coercive Federalism (1985–?). It was widely assumed before 1985 that Congress could not directly legislate how state and local government should perform their traditional functions. Congress was careful not to issue direct orders to the states; instead, it undertook to grant or withhold federal aid money, depending on whether states and cities abided by congressional "strings" attached to these grants. In theory, at least, the states were free to ignore conditions established by Congress for federal grants and forego the money.

However, in its 1985 *Garcia* decision, the U.S. Supreme Court removed all barriers to direct congressional legislation in matters traditionally "reserved" to the states.[10] The case arose after Congress directly ordered state and local governments to pay minimum wages to their employees. The Court reversed earlier decisions that Congress could not legislate directly state and local government matters. It also dismissed arguments that the nature of American federalism and the Reserved Powers Clause of the Tenth Amendment prevented Congress from directly legislating state affairs. It said that the only protection for state powers was to be found in the states' role in electing U.S. senators, members of Congress, and the president—a concept known as "representational federalism."

Representational Federalism. The idea behind representational federalism is that there is *no* constitutional division of powers between states and nation—federalism is defined by the role of the states in electing members of Congress and the president. The United States is said to retain a federal system because its national officials are selected from subunits of government—the president through the allocation of Electoral College votes to the states, and the Congress through the allocation of two Senate seats per state and the apportionment of representatives based on state population. Whatever protection exists for state power and independence must be found in the national political process—in the influence of state and district voters on their senators and members of Congress.

The Supreme Court rhetorically endorsed a federal system in the *Garcia* decision but left it up to the national Congress, rather than the Constitution or the courts, to decide what powers should be exercised by the states and the national government. In a strongly worded dissenting opinion, Justice Lewis Powell argued that if federalism is to be retained, the Constitution must divide powers, not the Congress. "The states' role in our system of government is a matter of constitutional law, not legislative grace. . . . [This decision] today rejects almost 200 years of the understanding of the constitutional status of federalism."

Federal Preemptions. The supremacy of federal laws over those of the states, spelled out in the National Supremacy Clause of the Constitution, permits Congress to decide whether or not there is *preemption* of state laws in a particular field by federal law. In *total preemption,* the federal government assumes all regulatory powers in a particular field—for example, copyrights, bankruptcy, railroads, and airlines. No state regulations in a totally preempted field are permitted. *Partial preemption* stipulates that a state law on the same subject is valid as long as it does not conflict with the federal law in the same area. For example, the Occupational Safety and Health

Act of 1970 specifically permits state regulation of any occupational safety or health issue on which the federal Occupational Safety and Health Administration (OSHA) has *not* developed a standard; but once OSHA enacts a standard, all state standards are nullified. Yet another form of the partial preemption, the *standard partial preemption,* permits states to regulate activities in a field already regulated by the federal government, as long as state regulatory standards are at least as stringent as those of the federal government. Usually states must submit their regulations to the responsible federal agency for approval; the federal agency may revoke a state's regulating power if it fails to enforce the approved standards. For example, the federal Environmental Protection Agency (EPA) permits state environmental regulations that meet or exceed EPA standards.

Federal Mandates.   Federal mandates are direct orders to state and local governments to perform a particular activity or service, or to comply with federal laws in the performance of their functions. Federal mandates occur in a wide variety of areas, from civil rights to minimum wage regulations. Their range is reflected in some recent examples of federal mandates to state and local governments:

- *Age Discrimination Act of 1986:* Outlaws mandatory retirement ages for public as well as private employees, including police, fire fighters, and state college and university faculty.
- *Asbestos Hazard Emergency Act of 1986:* Orders school districts to inspect for asbestos hazards and remove asbestos from school buildings when necessary.
- *Safe Drinking Water Act of 1986:* Establishes national requirements for municipal water supplies; regulates municipal waste treatment plants.
- *Clean Air Act of 1990:* Bans municipal incinerators and requires auto emission inspections in certain urban areas.
- *Americans with Disabilities Act of 1990:* Requires all state and local government buildings to promote handicapped access.
- *National Voter Registration Act of 1993:* Requires states to register voters at driver's license, welfare, and unemployment compensation offices.

State and local governments frequently complain that compliance with federal government mandates such as these imposes costs on them that are seldom reimbursed.

"Unfunded" Mandates.   Federal mandates often impose heavy costs on states and communities. When no federal monies are provided to cover these costs, the mandates are said to be *unfunded mandates.* Governors, mayors, and other state and local officials (including Bill Clinton, when he served as governor of Arkansas) have often urged Congress to halt the imposition of unfunded mandates on states and communities. Private industries have long voiced the same complaint. Regulations and mandates allow Congress to address problems while pushing the costs of doing so onto others. In 1995, Congress finally responded to these complaints by requiring that any bill imposing unfunded costs of $50 million or more on state and local governments (as determined by the Congressional Budget Office) would be

subject to an additional procedural vote; a majority must vote to waive a prohibition against unfunded mandates before such a bill can come to the House or Senate floor. But this modest restraint is not likely to be very effective.

MONEY AND POWER FLOW TO WASHINGTON

Money and power go together. As institutions acquire financial resources they become more powerful. The centralization of power in Washington has come about largely as a product of growth in the national government's financial resources—its ability to tax, spend, and borrow money.

Federal Grants-in-Aid.   The federal grant-in-aid has been the principal instrument for the expansion of national power. As late as 1952, federal intergovernment transfers amounted to about 10 percent of all state and local government revenue. Federal transfers creeped up slowly for a few years; rose significantly after 1957 with the National Defense (Interstate) Highway Program and a series of post-Sputnik educational programs; and then surged in the welfare, health, housing, and community development fields during the Great Society period (1965–1975). President Nixon not only expanded these Great Society transfers but also added his own general revenue-sharing program. Federal financial interventions continued to grow despite occasional rhetoric in Washington about state and local responsibility. By 1980, more than 25 percent of all state and local revenue came from the federal government (see Figure 12–1). So dependent had state and local governments become on federal largess that the most frequently voiced rationale for continuing federal grant programs was that states and communities had become accustomed to federal money and could not survive without it.

Reliance on Federal Aid.   President Ronald Reagan briefly challenged the nation's movement toward centralized government. Federal intergovernmental transfers fell from a high of about 25 percent of total state and local revenue to a more modest 18 percent by 1990. Most of what Reagan accomplished in this area occurred in the first years of his presidency.

The Reagan administration succeeded in eliminating general revenue sharing (GRS); consolidating many categorical grant programs in larger block grants, allowing for greater local control over revenue allocation; and reducing the rate of growth in federal intergovernmental transfer payments. Most GRS funds went for traditional services (police, fire, streets, sanitation, sewage, parks and recreation, etc.), which Reagan said local taxpayers should fund for themselves. For several years, state and local government officials successfully lobbied Congress to restore GRS funds, but federal deficit pressures finally ended GRS in 1986. The Reagan administration also consolidated many categorical grant programs into fewer block grant programs. A block grant is a payment to a state or local government for a general function, such as community development or education. State and local officials may use such

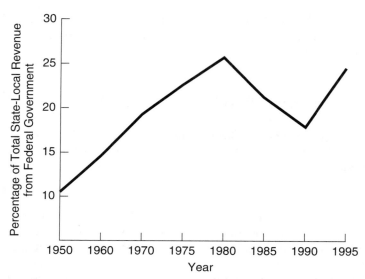

FIGURE 12–1 Trends in State-Local Reliance on Federal Grant-in-
Aid Funds

funds for their stated purposes without seeking the approval of federal agencies for specific projects.

Reasserting National Power.   It is unlikely that centralizing tendencies in the American federal system can ever be permanently checked or reversed. It is not likely that presidents or members of Congress will ever be moved to restrain national power. People expect them to "Do Something!" about virtually every problem that confronts individuals, families, communities, states, or the nation. Politicians risk appearing "insensitive" if they respond by saying that a particular problem is not a federal concern.

Bill Clinton came to Washington promising "change," but most of the changes he envisioned involved new initiatives at the federal level. As governor of Arkansas, Clinton had complained often about federal mandates and urged greater flexibility for states in federal grant programs. But under Clinton, state reliance on federal funds (the percentage of total state-local revenue derived from the federal government) has risen to about 25 percent.

Federal Grant Purposes.   Federal grants are available in nearly every major category of state and local government activity. So numerous and diverse are they that there is often a lack of information about their availability, purpose, and requirements. In fact, federal grants can be obtained for the preservation of historic buildings, the development of minority-owned businesses, aid to foreign refugees, the drainage

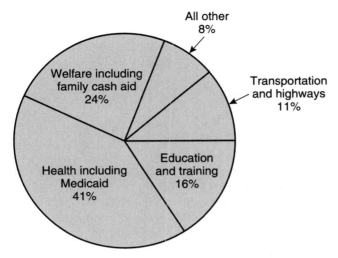

FIGURE 12–2   Purposes of Federal Grant-in-Aid Money

of abandoned mines, riot control, and school milk. However, welfare (including family cash aid and food stamps), health (including Medicaid for the poor), and highways account for more than three-fourths of federal aid money (see Figure 12–2).

A DEVOLUTION REVOLUTION?

Controversies over federalism are as old as the nation itself. Popular phrases have been employed frequently over the years to describe and promote various ideas about what level of government should do what and who should pay for it. In 1995, with new Republican majorities in both houses of Congress, the new phrase became "devolution"—the passing down of responsibilities from the national government to the states.

Welfare Reform and Federalism.   Welfare reform turned out to be the key to "devolution." Since Franklin D. Roosevelt's New Deal, with its federal guarantee of cash Aid to Families with Dependent Children (AFDC), low-income mothers and children had enjoyed a federal "entitlement" to welfare benefits. But in 1996 the welfare reform bill passed by Congress and signed by President Clinton (after two earlier vetoes) turned over responsibility for determining eligibility for cash aid to the states, ending the 60-year federal entitlement. The Temporary Assistance to Needy Families Act established block grants to the states and gave them broad responsibility for determining eligibility and benefits levels. But Congress did add some "strings" to these grants: states must not reduce their own spending for cash below 75 percent of their 1996 levels; they must place a 2-year limit on continuing cash benefits and a 5-year lifetime limit; and they must not use federal funds to pay benefits to illegal aliens nor to legal immigrants who have not yet become citizens. This is a major change in federal welfare policy (see Chapter 5) and may become a model for the future "devolution" of federal programs to the states.

INSTITUTIONS AND PUBLIC POLICY

In politics, constitutional decisions are never separated from policy outcomes. People know what the policy consequences of various institutional arrangements will be. Citizens as well as political leaders consistently subordinate constitutional questions to immediate policy concerns. History is replete with examples of the same political leaders arguing one notion of federalism at one point to achieve their immediate policy goal, and then turning around and later supporting a contradictory notion of federalism when it fits a new policy goal. No American politician, from Thomas Jefferson onward, has ever so strongly supported a view of federalism that he or she ended up conceding a policy battle.

Public Views of Institutions and Policy.   Americans generally favor governments closer to home. Most national opinion surveys show that Americans have greater confidence in their state and local governments than in the federal government (see Table 12–2). The federal income tax is usually perceived by more people as the "least fair" tax, although local property taxes are not very popular either. These responses suggest general support for decentralized government. But paradoxically, Americans want the federal government to assume even more power in many *specific* policy areas, including areas traditionally thought to be state or local government responsibilities. Thus, majorities favor a *national* policy for regulation of voting, setting penalties for murder, establishing safety standards, and setting minimum wages.

Intergovernment Competition and Public Policy.   Let us consider the impact of intergovernmental competition for different types of policy decisions. Policies have been usefully classified as allocational, developmental, or redistributional.[11] *Allocation* policies produce and distribute public goods and services to consumers-taxpayers. These policies encompass the provision of a broad range of state and local government services, including education, health, welfare, streets and highways, police and fire protection, sewers, water and utilities, garbage disposal, parks and recreation, and so on. *Developmental* policies are those that directly enhance the economic well-being of the state or community. These policies are directed toward economic growth; they include attracting industry, building transportation facilities, providing utilities, renewing urban areas, training the labor force for work, and so on. *Redistributional* policies are designed to redirect wealth and to benefit particular segments of society to satisfy equity concerns. These policies include traditional welfare services, health care for the poor, unemployment compensation, low income housing, and progressive taxation. Note that these are analytical distinctions

TABLE 12-2   Institutions and Policy: Public Views of Federalism

CONFIDENCE

How much confidence do you have in these institutions?

Your Local Government

A great deal	11
Quite a lot	20
Some	46
Very little	21

Your State Government

A great deal	6
Quite a lot	17
Some	53
Very little	23

The Federal Government

A great deal	4
Quite a lot	11
Some	47
Very little	37

POWER

Where should power be concentrated?

State government	64
Federal government	26

WASTE

From which level of government do you get the LEAST for your money?

	1990	1994
Local government	21	19
State government	26	21
Federal government	41	46

FAIRNESS

Which do you think is the worst tax—that is, the LEAST fair?

	1980	1987	1994
Federal income tax	36	30	27
State income tax	10	12	7
State sales tax	19	21	14
Local property tax	25	24	28

NATIONAL REGULATION

Which level of government should run the following programs?

Welfare		*Air/Water quality*	
Federal	38	Federal	35
State	40	State	40
Local	17	Local	22

Opportunity for minorities		*Employment and job training*	
Federal	35	Federal	15
State	30	State	59
Local	28	Local	24

Public education		*Law enforcement*	
Federal	21	Federal	15
State	47	State	36
Local	30	Local	45

INVOLVEMENT IN PROBLEMS

Which level of government should run the following programs?

Service to immigrants		*Health care for the disabled, poor, and elderly*	
Federal	60	Federal	36
State	15	State	28
Local	6	Local	18

Child care		*Job training*	
Federal	16	Federal	24
State	34	State	37
Local	29	Local	23

Note: All figures are percentages of U.S. public in national opinion surveys. "No opinions" and "Don't knows" not shown.

Source: General responses on trust, power, and regulation of specific programs from Hart and Teeter for the Council for Excellence in Government, *State Legislatures* (July/August 1995); responses on fairness, waste, and involvement in specific problems from Advisory Commission on Intergovernmental Relations, *Changing Public Attitudes on Governments and Taxes* (Washington, DC: ACIR, 1991, 1994).

among types of policies; any specific government activity may have allocational, developmental, and redistributive elements.

Allocational Policy.   Federalism directly strengthens the allocative functions of government. Decentralization permits governments to match services with variations in demand. Greater overall citizen satisfaction can be achieved with multiple governments offering different packages of public services at different prices. Competition forces governments to become more efficient in their allocative activities, providing better services at lower costs. It also forces government to be more responsive to citizens' preferences than does monopoly government. Paul E. Peterson, one of the few political scientists to incorporate the notion of competition into a coherent theory of federalism, appears to agree:

> Allocation is the function that local governments can perform more effectively than central governments, because decentralization allows for a closer match between the supply of public services and their variable demand. Citizens migrate to those communities where the allocation best matches their demand curve.[12]

Developmental Policy.   Federalism and intergovernmental competition inspires state and local governments to be concerned with the impact of their taxing and spending policies on economic growth and to become directly involved in economic development activities. The states' role in economic development has traditionally centered on the provision of *physical infrastructure,* especially transportation. Indeed for many years economic growth in the states correlated closely with state expenditures for transportation.[13] But it is likely that economic growth in the future will depend more on state investment in *intellectual infrastructure.* Economic growth is always and everywhere a function of human creativity. In practical terms, investment in education at all levels—elementary and secondary schools, trade and vocational schools, community colleges and state universities, research institutions and parks—is likely to become the key to competitive advantage in the economy of the future. Fortunately for America's future, education is largely a function of competitive state and local governments rather than of a monopoly, a centralized government. Economic competition among the states can become the driving force behind improvements in education and research. Peterson argues convincingly that the federal government would be wise to leave economic development policy to state and local government:

> Since state and local governments are well equipped to pursue developmental objectives, most public efforts of this type should be left to them. By delegating responsibility for most developmental programs to state and local governments, the federal government would frankly admit its incapacity to use those programs to help populations with special needs.[14]

Redistributional Policy.   The most serious challenge to intergovernmental competition arises in redistributional policy. Can multiple, competing governments undertake redistributive policies without creating unbearable free-rider problems for themselves? Will states and communities be restrained from providing the welfare services they would otherwise prefer because of the threat of a migration of poor people from less beneficent free-riding jurisdictions? Will each state and community wait for other states and communities to provide welfare services in the hope that their poor people will migrate to the more generous jurisdictions? Will tax burdens to support generous welfare services encourage the nonpoor—both households and businesses—to migrate to jurisdictions that impose lighter tax burdens because they provide frugal welfare services?

The argument that intergovernmental competition hurts the poor rests on a version of the free-rider problem: competing state and local governments will set welfare benefits below the true preferences of their citizens out of fear that poor people will migrate into generous jurisdictions. Governments consequently limit their welfare provisions at levels at or below those of their neighbor states. The possibility that interstate competition might drive down welfare benefits has inspired some political scientists to call for the "federalization" of welfare policy.[15]

SUMMARY

American federalism creates unique problems and opportunities in public policy. For two hundred years, since the classic debates between Alexander Hamilton and Thomas Jefferson, Americans have argued the merits of centralized versus decentralized policymaking. The debate continues today.

1. Eighty-five thousand separate governments—states, counties, cities, towns, boroughs, villages, special districts, school districts, and authorities—make public policy.

2. Proponents of federalism since Thomas Jefferson have argued that it permits policy diversity in a large nation, helps to reduce conflicts, disperses power, increases political participation, encourages policy innovation, and improves governmental efficiency.

3. Opponents of federalism argue that it allows special interests to protect positions of privilege, frustrates national policies, distributes the burdens of government unevenly, hurts poorer states and communities, and obstructs action toward national goals.

4. The nature of American federalism has changed radically over two centuries, with the national government steadily growing in power. "Coercive federalism" refers to Washington's direct mandates to state governments in matters traditionally reserved to the states. "Representational federalism" contends that there is no constitutional division of powers between nation and states and federalism is defined only by the states' role in electing the president and Congress.

5. New federalism in the Reagan administration meant an end to GRS, consolidation of many individual grant programs into block grants, and a lower rate of growth in federal aid. During the Reagan years state and local governments reduced

their dependency on federal aid, which as a share of total state and local revenue declined from a high of about 25 percent to about 18 percent. Under President Clinton federal aid returned to previous levels—about 25 percent of total state-local revenue.

6. While federal grant money is available for a wide variety of state and local government activities, welfare and food stamps, Medicaid, and highway aid account for more than three-fourths of federal aid money.

7. Policies may be broadly categorized as allocational (distributing public goods and services), developmental (enhancing economic growth), or redistributional (transferring wealth or income among groups). Most analysts believe that state and local governments are better prepared institutionally to decide and implement allocational and developmental policies.

8. The federal government may be better positioned institutionally to undertake redistributional policy. Competition between states and communities may hurt the poor. Each state and community may wait for other states and communities to provide welfare benefits in the hope that their poor people will migrate to generous jurisdictions and relieve their own taxpayers of the burdens of welfare.

NOTES

1. James Madison, Alexander Hamilton, John Jay, *The Federalist,* Number 51 (New York: Modern Library, 1958).
2. See Thomas R. Dye, *American Federalism: Competition among Governments* (Lexington, MA: Lexington Books, 1990).
3. David C. Nice, *Federalism: The Politics of Intergovernmental Relations* (New York: St. Martin's Press, 1987), p. 24.
4. Randall G. Holcombe, *An Economic Analysis of Democracy* (Carbondale: Illinois University Press, 1986), p. 174.
5. This argument is derived from public choice theory (see Chapter 2) and is developed further in Thomas R. Dye, *American Federalism: Competition among Governments* (Lexington, MA: Lexington Books, 1990).
6. Morton Grodzins, *The American System* (Chicago: Rand McNally, 1966), pp. 8–9.
7. Ibid., p. 265.
8. Charles Press, *State and Community Governments in the Federal System* (New York: John Wiley, 1979), p. 78.
9. Michael D. Reagan, *The New Federalism* (New York: Oxford University Press, 1972).
10. *Garcia* v. *San Antonio Metropolitan Transit Authority,* 469 U.S. 528 (1985).
11. Theodore J. Lowi, "American Business, Public Policy and Political Theory," *World Politics,* 16 (July 1964), 677–715.
12. Paul E. Peterson, *City Limits* (Chicago: University of Chicago Press, 1981), p. 77.
13. Thomas R. Dye, "Taxing, Spending, and Economic Growth in the American States," *Journal of Politics,* 42 (November 1980), 1085–1107.
14. Paul E. Peterson, *When Federalism Works* (Washington, DC: Brookings Institution, 1986), p. 230.
15. See Peterson, *City Limits;* Paul E. Peterson and Mark Rom, "American Federalism, Welfare Policy and Residential Choices," *American Political Science Reviews,* 83 (September 1989), 711–728.

BIBLIOGRAPHY

DYE, THOMAS R. *American Federalism: Competition among Governments*. Lexington, MA: Lexington Books, 1990.

ELAZAR, DANIEL J. *The American Mosaic*. Boulder, CO: Westview Press, 1994.

NICE, DAVID C. *Federalism: The Politics of Intergovernmental Relations*. New York: St. Martin's Press, 1987.

PETERSON, PAUL E. *City Limits*. Chicago: University of Chicago Press, 1981.

PETERSON, PAUL E. *The Price of Federalism*. Washington, DC: Brookings Institution, 1995.

RIVLIN, ALICE M. *Reviving the American Dream*. Washington, DC: Brookings Institution, 1992.

13

INPUTS AND OUTPUTS
A Systems Analysis of State Policies

The Texas House of Representatives meets during the 1995 legislative season. (Texas House of Representatives Photography Department)

COMPARING PUBLIC POLICIES OF THE AMERICAN STATES

The American states provide an excellent setting for comparative analysis and the testing of hypotheses about the determinants of public policy. Policies in education, welfare, health, transportation, natural resources, public safety, and many other areas vary a great deal from state to state. These differences are important in systems analysis because they enable us to search for relationships among different socio-economic conditions, political system characteristics, and public policies.

Nationalization of the States.   Economic differences among the states have been diminishing over time—a process that has been labeled the "nationalization" of the states. As industry, people, and money move from the Northeast and Midwest to the South, the historic disadvantage of the South gradually diminishes. As people move about the country, the distinct cultural and ethnic differences of the regions also diminish. Even regional accents become less pronounced. The impact of national television, motion pictures, and record industry adds to the "homogenization" of state and regional cultures.

Continuing Policy Variations among the States.   Nonetheless, even though the states are gradually becoming more similar over time in many respects, there is still enough variation to merit comparative analysis. Interestingly, *policy* variation among the states does *not* appear to be declining over time. There is no reliable evidence that the policy preferences of the states are becoming homogenized, or even that federal intervention is forcing uniform policies on them. For example, Table 13–1 shows that variation among the states in spending for education and in tax burdens are very large. Some states spend almost three times as much for the education of a single pupil in public schools as do other states, and some states impose per capita tax burdens that are more than twice as high as those imposed by other states.

POLICY RESPONSIVENESS AND THE MEDIAN VOTER

An important criterion in evaluating democratic political systems—including the American states—is their responsiveness to citizens' preferences. The test of responsiveness is whether state policies reflect the preferences of the "median voter" in the states.

Median voter models have provided economists and political scientists with simplified sets of assumptions about democratic political systems. In the basic model, each individual voter tries to maximize the trade-off between various public goods and services and disposable private income. Each voter balances the "utilities" obtained from higher levels of public services against the "disutilities" of higher taxes in order to choose an "optimal" benefit level. After each voter has made a choice based on his or her own preferences, tastes, needs, and so on, the choice of the median voter in any democratic political system should determine public policy.

TABLE 13-1   Policy Variation among the States

Rank	Total State-Local Taxes per Capita		Rank	Per Pupil Public Expenditures Elementary and Secondary Education	
1	Alaska	4,929	1	New Jersey	9,206
2	New York	3,655	2	New York	8,217
3	Connecticut	3,334	3	Connecticut	8,147
4	New Jersey	3,051	4	Alaska	8,120
5	Hawaii	2,984	5	Pennsylvania	6,909
6	Minnesota	2,673	6	Vermont	6,879
7	Massachusetts	2,664	7	Rhode Island	6,729
8	Maryland	2,565	8	Delaware	6,591
9	Wisconsin	2,524	9	Massachusetts	6,383
10	Washington	2,431	10	Wisconsin	6,358
11	California	2,418	11	Michigan	6,240
12	Rhode Island	2,405	12	Maryland	6,212
13	Vermont	2,379	13	Maine	6,048
14	Michigan	2,371	14	New Hampshire	5,845
15	Delaware	2,336	15	Hawaii	5,740
16	Illinois	2,332	16	Oregon	5,710
17	New Hampshire	2,305	17	Wyoming	5,582
18	Wyoming	2,295	18	West Virginia	5,565
19	Maine	2,281	19	Washington	5,563
20	Nevada	2,270	20	Ohio	5,482
21	Pennsylvania	2,260	21	Minnesota	5,413
22	Iowa	2,200	22	Kansas	5,315
23	Oregon	2,167	23	Virginia	5,303
24	Nebraska	2,128	24	Florida	5,185
25	Kansas	2,126	25	Indiana	5,158
26	Arizona	2,108	26	Iowa	5,139
27	Colorado	2,092	27	Colorado	5,101
28	Virginia	2,073	28	Montana	5,091
29	Ohio	2,059	29	Nebraska	5,018
30	Florida	2,041	30	Kentucky	5,007
31	Georgia	1,999	31	Texas	4,894
32	North Carolina	1,975	32	New Mexico	4,870
33	New Mexico	1,952	33	Illinois	4,752
34	Texas	1,933	34	North Carolina	4,739
35	North Dakota	1,923	35	South Dakota	4,693
36	Indiana	1,920	36	Nevada	4,677
37	Idaho	1,911	37	California	4,606
38	Montana	1,853	38	Georgia	4,595
39	Kentucky	1,816	39	Louisiana	4,525
40	Utah	1,803	40	Missouri	4,502

Continued

TABLE 13-1   (*Continued*)

Rank	Total State-Local Taxes per Capita		Rank	Per Pupil Public Expenditures Elementary and Secondary Education	
41	Oklahoma	1,777	41	North Dakota	4,459
42	West Virginia	1,752	42	South Carolina	4,401
43	South Carolina	1,736	43	Tennessee	4,208
44	Missouri	1,721	44	Alabama	4,194
45	Tennessee	1,706	45	Oklahoma	4,042
46	Louisiana	1,685	46	Arizona	3,982
47	South Dakota	1,668	47	Idaho	3,976
48	Arkansas	1,590	48	Arkansas	3,795
49	Alabama	1,553	49	Mississippi	3,469
50	Mississippi	1,535	50	Utah	3,431

Source: *Governing, Sourcebook 1997.*

A simple version of the median voter model treats the political system itself as a neutral conversion mechanism that transforms the needs, demands, and preferences of the median voter into public policy. The model is similar to the systems model in political science literature (see Figure 2–8 in Chapter 2). It is assumed that democratic political processes will produce public policies largely reflecting the preferences of voters-taxpayers. These preferences are usually specified in state policy studies in terms of median or average characteristics of the population—for example, median family income; median school level completed; or percentage of the population aged, young, black, urban, and so on. This requires an inferential leap that characteristics of the populations determined median voter preferences and, hence, community policy preferences. When variations in public policies among the states were shown to correlate with variations in population characteristics, this simple median voter model gains empirical support. The traditional literature on the determinants of state and local government taxing and spending policies relies implicitly on this model.[1]

Thus, the median voter model assumes that individual voter preference in a democracy determines government decisions. Elected politicians reflect the preferences of their constituents because they wish to maximize community welfare and to get reelected. Politicians seek the package of public services and taxes desired by the median voter, whose indifference curve is considered the state's indifference curve. Public spending will increase as long as the number of votes won by these increases exceeds the number of votes lost by the increasing costs of financing this spending. Politicians must estimate the numbers and preferences of voters in their separate roles as consumers and taxpayers. Their task is to balance votes won by each expenditure decision with votes lost by each revenue decision, and try to ensure that the votes won will exceed the votes lost.

ECONOMIC RESOURCES AND PUBLIC POLICY

Economists have contributed a great deal to the systematic analysis of public policy. Economic research very early suggested that government activity was closely related to the level of economic resources in a society.[2] We can picture the relationship by viewing a "plot" between per capita personal income and per pupil spending in public schools, as shown in Figure 13–1. Per capita income is measured on the horizontal, or *X*, axis, and per pupil spending is measured on the vertical, or *Y*, axis. Each state is plotted in the graph according to its values on these two measures. The resulting pattern—states arranged from the lower left to the upper right—shows that increases in income are associated with increases in educational spending. The diagonal line is a representation of the hypothesis that income determines educational spending. To the extent that states cluster around this line, they conform to the hypothesis. States that are above the line spend more for education than their income level predicts; states that are below the line spend less than their income predicts. In general, states tend to cluster around the line, indicating general support for the hypothesis.

POLITICS AND PUBLIC POLICY

The political system transforms demands generated in the environment into public policy. The traditional literature in American politics instructed students that characteristics of the political system, particularly two-party competition and voter partici-

FIGURE 13–1   Fifty States Arranged According to per Capita Personal Income and per Pupil Educational Expenditures

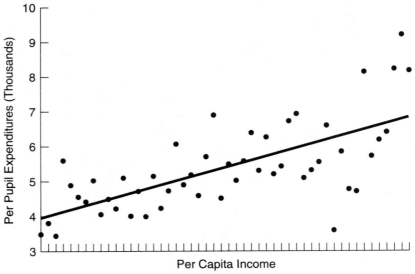

pation, had a direct bearing on public policy.[3] Because political scientists devoted most of their time to studying what happened *within* the political system, it was easy for them to believe that the political processes and institutions that they studied were important determinants of public policies. Moreover, the belief that competition and participation had important consequences for public policy reinforced the value placed on these variables in the prevailing pluralist ideology.

The assertion that political variables such as party competition and voter participation affected public policy rested more on a priori reasoning than on systematic research. It seemed reasonable to believe that an increase in party competition would increase educational spending, welfare benefits, numbers of welfare recipients, health and hospital care, and so on because competitive parties would try to outbid one another for public favor by offering such inducements, and the overall effect on such competition would be to raise levels of spending and service. It also seemed reasonable to believe that increased voter participation would influence public policy, presumably in a more liberal direction.

Political Competition Model.   The earliest systems model in the state policy field was a political competition model.

Economic resources ⟶ Competition participation ⟶ Public policies

Here, economic resources determined levels of party competition and voter participation, and these political factors in turn determined public policies in welfare, education, health, highway, taxation, and spending. For many years there was no empirical evidence to contradict this model: poor, rural, agrarian states tended to have less competitive parties (one-party systems, in contrast to two-party systems) and lower voter turnout, and these same states spent less per capita for education, welfare, health, and other social services.

However, to assess the independent effect of politics on public policy, it is important to control for the intervening effects of socioeconomic variables. For example, if it is shown that, in general, wealthy states have more party competition than poor states, it might be that differences in the level of welfare benefits of competitive and noncompetitive states are really a product of the fact that the former are wealthy and the latter are poor. If this is the case, policy differences between the states might be attributable to wealth rather than to party competition.

Economic Resource Model.   Indeed, later research demonstrated that "economic development variables are more influential than political system characteristics in shaping public policy in the states."[4] Most of the associations that occur between political variables (e.g., party competition, voter turnout, and Democratic or Republican control of state government) and policy outcomes are really a product of the fact that economic development influences both political system characteristics and policy outcomes. When political factors are controlled, economic development continues to have a significant impact on public policy. But when the effects of economic development are controlled, political factors turn out to have little influence on policy outcomes.

The resulting economic resources model may be viewed as follows:

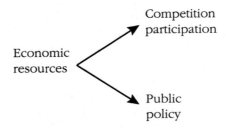

In this view, economic resources shape both the political system characteristics (competition and participation) and public policy, but characteristics of the political system have no direct causal effect on public policy.

The Politics-versus-Economics Debate.   These findings—regarded as commonplace by economists—were very disturbing to political scientists, who were committed to a pluralist ideology that asserted the importance of competition and participation in politics. Of course most of us would prefer to live in a political system in which there are high levels of competition and participation since these conditions are highly valued in any democracy. But it remains a scientific question whether these political conditions produce different kinds of policies than noncompetitive, nonparticipating political systems. We cannot assume that competition and participation will produce better public policies simply because we prefer a competitive, participating political system. There is nothing wrong with trying to find the policy relevance of differing government structures or political processes, but we should not insist that political variables must influence public policy simply because our traditional training in political science has told us that political variables should be important.

The Hybrid Model.   Nonetheless, the challenge to political scientists to prove that "politics count" in shaping public policy inspired a new systematic reexamination of its determinants.[5] One interesting model of policy determination to emerge from this research was a "hybrid model," illustrated in the following diagram.[6]

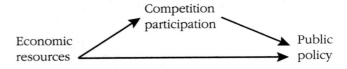

In this model, economic resources shape public policy both directly and indirectly by affecting competition and participation, which in turn affect public policy. This model appears to be more appropriate for the study of welfare policy, than the broader array of policies in education, health, highways, spending, taxation, and so on. Welfare policy is thought to magnify the conflict between "haves" and "have-nots" and therefore to magnify the effect of competition and participation. Yet most studies continue to report that economic resources are stronger determinants of welfare policies than party competition or voter turnout.[7]

PARTIES AND POLICY IN THE STATES

Political scientists have long placed great faith in party government. E. E. Schattschneider expressed this faith when he wrote, "The rise of political parties is undoubtedly one of the principal distinguishing marks of modern government . . . political parties created modern democracy and modern democracy is unthinkable save in terms of parties."[8] Sarah McCally Morehouse reaffirmed faith in the centrality of political parties in the American states: "The single most important factor in state politics is the political party. It is not possible to understand the differences in the way sovereign states carry out the process of government without understanding the type of party whose representatives are making decisions that affect the health, education, and welfare of its citizens."[9]

Why Parties May Not Matter Much.   However, "spatial" theories of parties suggest that they have little policy relevance given a normal unimodal distribution of opinion on most policy questions. Anthony Downs explained: "In the middle of the scale, where most voters are massed, each party scatters its policies on both sides of the midpoint. It attempts to make each voter in this area feel that it is centered right at his position. Naturally this causes an enormous overlapping of moderate positions." Downs acknowledged that a left or right party may "sprinkle these moderate policies with a few extreme stands in order to please its far-out voters," but overall, "both parties are trying to be as ambiguous as possible" about policy positions. "Political rationality leads parties in a two-party system to becloud their policies in a fog of ambiguity."[10]

For example, if most voters in a state were found in the middle of an opinion scale on a policy issue, the parties in that state would be encouraged to take moderate policy positions not very different from each other. Both parties would be competing for the many voters in the center. Since both parties took moderate positions on the issue, a change in party control of state government (the governor's office, the state legislature, or both) would not result in any significant shift in public policy (see top of Figure 13–2). Only if the voters were divided on a policy issue into a bimodal distribution would we expect the parties to take significantly different policy positions (see bottom of Figure 13–2). The parties would be constrained by the large number of voters on each side of the issue from moving toward the center.

In this case, a change in party control of state government might result in a significant shift in public policy.

How Much Party Competition in the States?   Another problem with the theory that party competition determines policy in the states is that traditionally many states lacked party competition. Only recently has the growth of Republican party strength

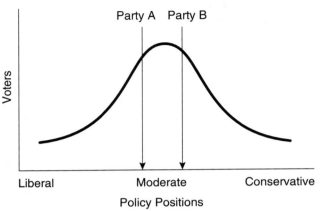

A Unimodal Distribution of Opinion

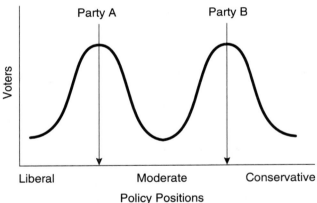

A Bimodal Distribution of Opinion

FIGURE 13–2   Parties, Opinions, and Policies. Note how the unimodal distribution of opinion produces little policy differences between parties, whereas the bimodal distribution of opinion produces large policy differences.

in the eleven southern states shifted several of them away from their traditional label as "one-party Democratic." For many years the southern states had been a partisan battleground in *presidential* elections, but remained solidly Democratic in *state and local* politics. Republican governors were occasionally elected, but very few Republicans served in southern state legislatures. However, Republican grass-roots strength in the South only began to grow in the 1990s (see Table 13–2). By 1995 six southern states (Alabama, Mississippi, South Carolina, Tennessee, Texas, and Virginia) had Republican governors. And for the first time since Reconstruction, Re-

TABLE 13-2   Party Competition in State Politics

Traditional Democratic Advantage	Traditional Democratic but Growing Republican Strength	Competitive, Leaning Democratic	Competitive, Leaning Republican	Traditional Republican Advantage
Arkansas	Alabama	Alaska	Arizona	Indiana
Hawaii	Florida	California	Colorado	New Hampshire
Kentucky	Georgia	Connecticut	Idaho	South Dakota
Louisiana	Mississippi	Delaware	Kansas	
Maryland	North Carolina	Illinois	North Dakota	
Massachusetts	Oklahoma	Iowa	Utah	
Missouri	South Carolina	Maine	Vermont	
Nevada	Tennessee	Michigan	Wyoming	
New Mexico	Texas	Minnesota		
Rhode Island	Virginia	Montana		
West Virginia		Nebraska		
		New Jersey		
		New York		
		Ohio		
		Oregon		
		Pennsylvania		
		Washington		
		Wisconsin		

publicans controlled three state legislative houses (Florida's senate, North Carolina's and South Carolina's house).

Divided Government.   Yet another problem in assessing the policy-relevance of parties is the frequency of divided party government in the states—where one party controls one or both houses of the legislature and the other party controls the governorship. In recent years, more than half of the states have experienced divided party control. A unified party government—where the same party controls both houses of the legislature as well as the governorship—is presumed to be better able to enact its program into law. While many obstacles to program enactment may remain, at least party "gridlock" is avoided.

Searching for Policy-relevant Parties.   For the parties to be truly policy relevant in a state, both parties must represent clearly differentiated socioeconomic groups; each party must have a reasonable chance of gaining control of state government; and on doing so, each party must undertake to change public policy to favor their socioeconomic constituencies. Thus, the parties are more likely to be policy relevant in states where the Democratic party represents central-city, low-income, ethnic and racial constituencies and the Republican party represents middle-class, suburban and small-town constituencies.

The United States does not have a single all-encompassing party system, but instead "a national party system that is related to, but distinct from, a set of 50 different state party systems."[11] Each state party system reflects a somewhat different alignment (coalition) of the key social groups in America. For example, Alabama represents what might be termed the "southern partisan cleavage, wherein race plays the fundamental role in differentiating the parties, with a complementing role played by rural-urban, high- and low-income, and college- and non-college-educated divisions (see Table 13–3). Vermont illustrates what might be called the

TABLE 13-3   Party System Cleavage Structures

Cleavage 1: Southern		Cleavage 2: New Deal		Cleavage 3: Post–New Deal	
Bias:		Bias:		Bias:	
Democrat	Republican	Democrat	Republican	Democrat	Republican
Black	White	Catholic	Protestant	Black	White
Low income	High income	Low income	High income	Catholic	Protestant
Rural	College	Union	College	Urban	High income
	Urban	Female		Union	College
				Low income	
				Female	
				Jewish	
South Carolina		Vermont		Illinois	
Mississippi		Maine		New York	
Alabama		New Hampshire		Michigan	
Texas		Massachusetts		Delaware	
Louisiana		Arizona		New Jersey	
Georgia		New Mexico		Maryland	
Virginia		Connecticut		California	
North Carolina		Montana		Pennsylvania	
Oklahoma		Rhode Island		Ohio	
Florida		Minnesota		Wisconsin	
Tennessee		Colorado		Missouri	
		Utah		Nevada	
		Iowa		Indiana	
		South Dakota		Kansas	
		North Dakota			
		Idaho			
		Nebraska			
		Washington			
		Oregon			

Note: Arkansas, Kentucky, West Virginia, and Wyoming do not conform to these party cleavages.

Source: Robert D. Brown, "Party Cleavages and Welfare Effort in the American States," *American Political Science Review,* 89 (March 1995), p. 28; reprinted with permission.

"New Deal" cleavage, wherein differences center on Catholic versus Protestant support of the Democratic and Republican parties, together with differential support of union members and nonmembers, and high- and low-income persons. Presumably, this is a more class-based system. Finally, Illinois illustrates a "post–New Deal" cleavage system, wherein both race and class play important roles in differentiating the parties.

The Role of Party Activists. While parties may be pushed toward the ideological center in order to win elections, the activists in the parties tend to be strong ideologues—people who take consistently "liberal" or "conservative" positions on the issues. Republican party activists in most states are more conservative than Democratic party activists. Indeed, Republican party activists tend to be more conservative than the general public, and Democratic party activists tend to be more liberal than the general public. This is true even though activists in both parties will tend to be more conservative in a conservative state and more liberal in a liberal state.

THE POLITICAL SYSTEM AS A CONVERSION MECHANISM

Perhaps we should view the political system as a conversion mechanism, rather than a direct cause of public policy. In other words, politics does not *cause* public policy; rather, it *facilitates* the conversion of demands and resources into public policy.

If we accept this view, we would not really expect variations in political systems—variations in party competition, voter participation, or Republican or Democratic party control of government—to cause public policy directly. Instead, we would expect variations in political systems to affect *relationships* between demands and resources and public policies. For example, we would not expect highly competitive political systems to produce policies different from noncompetitive systems; instead we expect the *relationships between population characteristics and public policy to be closer in competitive than in noncompetitive systems*. Our focus would shift to the impact of political system variables on relationships between environmental conditions (measures of demands and socioeconomic resources) and public policies.

In short, we expect political systems with reasonably balanced, competitive and responsible parties, and active and concerned electorates to be more responsive to popular demands than would political systems with a single dominant party and apathetic electorate.

SUMMARY

We have employed a systems model, and variations based on it, to describe linkages among economic resources, political system characteristics, and public policies in the American states. Some general propositions about public policy that are suggested by our systems model include the following:

1. Although differences among the states have been diminishing over time, considerable policy variation remains. For example, tax burdens in some states are more than twice as high as other states, and educational spending per pupil is almost three times greater in some states compared with others

2. Economic resources are an important determinant of overall levels of government taxing, spending, and service in the states. Economic differences among the states have narrowed somewhat over time, but significant policy differences remain.

3. The traditional literature in American politics asserted that characteristics of political systems—particularly party competition and voter participation—had an important impact on the content of public policy. But *systematic research* suggests that the characteristics of political systems are not *as* important as economic resources in shaping public policy. Most of the correlations between political system variables and public policy measures are a product of the fact that economic resources shape both the political system and public policy.

4. Testing alternative causal models in policy determination suggests that economic resources can affect public policy directly regardless of the character of the political system. However, in some policy areas, especially welfare, economic resources shape public policy both directly and indirectly through political variables.

5. State political systems may be classified by both the competitiveness and the policy relevance of their parties. Parties in the states are more likely to differ over policy issues when each party represents separate socioeconomic groups. Over time party competition has been growing in the states, especially in the South, and the parties have become more policy relevant.

6. However, the frequency of divided party control of state government is an obstacle to parties enacting their policy preferences.

7. Rather than think of the political system as causing public policy, perhaps we should think of it as facilitating public policy. Competition and participation may increase the responsiveness of public policies to environmental conditions.

NOTES

1. Thomas R. Dye, *Politics, Economics, and the Public* (Chicago: Rand McNally, 1966).
2. See Solomon Fabricant, *Trend of Government Activity in the United States Since 1900* (New York: National Bureau of Economic Research, 1952).
3. V. O. Key, Jr., *American State Politics: An Introduction* (New York: Knopf, 1956); also his *Southern Politics in State and Nation* (New York: Knopf, 1951).
4. Dye, *Politics, Economics, and the Public.*
5. For a summary of this literature, see Thomas R. Dye and Virginia Gray, *The Determinants of Public Policy* (New York: Lexington-Heath, 1980).
6. Charles F. Cnudde and Ronald J. McCrone, "Party Competition and Welfare Policies in the American States," *American Political Science Review,* 62 (December 1968), 1220–1231.
7. Michael Lewis-Beck, "The Relative Importance of Socioeconomic and Political Variables in Public Policy," *American Political Science Review,* 71 (June 1977), 559–566.
8. E. E. Schattschneider, *Party Government* (New York: Rinehart, 1942), p. 1.
9. Sarah McCally Morehouse, *State Politics, Parties, and Policy* (New York: Holt, Rinehart & Winston, 1981), p. 29.

10. Anthony Downs, *An Economic Theory of Democracy* (New York: Harper & Row, 1957), pp. 135–136.
11. Robert D. Brown, "Party Cleavages and Welfare Effort in the American States," *American Political Science Review,* 89 (March 1995), 23–33.

BIBLIOGRAPHY

DOWNS, ANTHONY. *An Economic Theory of Democracy.* New York: Harper & Row, 1957.

DYE, THOMAS R. *Politics, Economics, and the Public: Policy Outcomes in the American States.* Chicago: Rand McNally, 1966.

———. *Politics in States and Communities.* 9th ed. Upper Saddle River, NJ: Prentice Hall, 1997.

GRAY, VIRGINIA, and HERBERT JACOB. *Politics in the American States.* 6th ed. Washington DC: CQ Press, 1996.

KEY, V. O., JR. *American State Politics: An Introduction.* New York: Knopf, 1956.

———. *Southern Politics in State and Nation.* New York: Knopf, 1951.

MOREHOUSE, SARAH MCCALLY. *State Politics, Parties and Policy.* New York: Holt, Rinehart & Winston, 1981.

14

THE POLICYMAKING PROCESS
Getting inside the System

The Senate Judiciary Committee in session. (Paul Conklin/PhotoEdit)

THE POLICY PROCESS: HOW POLICIES ARE MADE

Policy studies often focus on *how policies are made* rather than on their content or their causes and consequences. The study of how policies are made generally considers a series of activities, or *processes,* that occur within the political system. The implication of this process model is that policymaking occurs in identifiable stages and that each stage can be examined separately. These processes are usually presented as follows:

- The *identification* of policy problems through demands for government action
- *Agenda setting,* or focusing the attention of the mass media and public officials on specific public problems to decide what will be decided
- The *formulation* of policy proposals through their initiation and development by policy-planning organizations, interest groups, government bureaucracies, and the president and Congress
- The *legitimation* of policies through political actions by parties, interest groups, the president, and Congress
- The *implementation* of policies through organized bureaucracies, public expenditures, and the activities of executive agencies
- The *evaluation* of policies by government agencies themselves, outside consultants, the press, and the public

Although it may be helpful to think about policymaking in this fashion, in the real world these activities seldom occur in a neat, step-by-step sequence. Rather these processes often occur simultaneously, each one collapsing into the others. Different political actors and institutions—politicians, interest groups, lobbyists and legislators, executives and bureaucrats, reporters and commentators, think tanks, lawyers and judges—may be engaged in different processes at the same time, even in the same policy area. Policymaking is seldom as neat as the process model. Nonetheless, it is often useful for analytical purposes to break policymaking into component units in order to understand better how policies are made.

IDENTIFYING POLICY ISSUES: PUBLIC OPINION

The influence of public opinion over government policy has been the subject of great philosophical controversies in the classic literature on democracy. Eighteenth century political philosopher Edmund Burke believed democratic representatives should serve the interest of the people, but not necessarily conform to their will when deciding questions of public policy. In contrast, some democratic theorists have evaluated the success of democratic institutions by whether or not they facilitate popular control over public policy.

The philosophical question of whether public opinion should be an important independent influence over public policy may never be resolved. But the empirical question of whether public opinion does constitute an important independent influence over public policy can be tackled by systematic research. However, even this empirical question has proven very difficult to answer.

Opinion-Policy Linkage.   The problem in assessing the independent effect of mass opinion on the actions of decision makers is that their actions help to mold mass opinion. Public policy may be in accord with mass opinion, but we can never be sure whether mass opinion shaped public policy or public policy shaped mass opinion.

In his most thoughtful book, *Public Opinion and American Democracy,* the distinguished American political scientist V. O. Key, Jr., wrote, "Government, as we have seen, attempts to mold public opinion toward support of the programs and policies it espouses. Given that endeavor, perfect congruence between public policy and public opinion could be government *of* public opinion rather than government *by* public opinion."[1] Although Key himself was convinced that public opinion did have an independent effect on public policy, he was never able to demonstrate this conclusively. Nonetheless he compiled a great deal of circumstantial evidence supporting the notion that elections, parties, and interest groups do institutionalize channels of communication from citizens to decision makers.

Policy Effects.   Public policy shapes public opinion more often than opinion shapes policy, for several reasons. First, few people have opinions on the great bulk of policy questions confronting the nation's decision makers. Second, public opinion is very unstable. It can change in a matter of weeks in response to news events precipitated by leaders. Third, leaders do not have a clear perception of mass opinion. Most communications received by decision makers are from other elites—newsmakers, interest group leaders, and other influential persons—and not from ordinary citizens.

Media Effects.   We must not assume that the opinions expressed in the news media are public opinion. Frequently, this is a source of confusion. Newspersons believe *they* are the public, often confusing their own opinions with public opinion. They even tell the mass public what its opinion is, thus actually helping to mold it to conform to their own beliefs. Decision makers, then, may act in response to news stories or the opinions of influential newsmakers in the belief that they are responding to public opinion.

Opinion Polls.   Public opinion polls frequently create opinions by asking questions that respondents never thought about until they were asked. Few respondents are willing to admit they have no opinion; they believe they should provide some sort of answer, even if their opinion is weakly held or was nonexistent before the question was asked. Thus pollsters themselves produce opinions.

Instability of Opinion.   Public opinion tends to be unstable. Mass opinion on a particular issue is often very weakly held. Asked the same question at a later date, many respondents fail to remember their earlier answers and give the pollster the opposite reply. These are not real changes in opinion, yet they register as such.

Wording of Questions.   Opinions also vary according to the wording of questions. It is relatively easy to word almost any public policy question in such a way as to elicit mass approval or disapproval. Thus, differently worded questions on the same issue can produce contradictory results.

Communicating with Policymakers.   Finally, decision makers can easily misinterpret public opinion because the communications they receive have an elite bias. Members of the mass public seldom call or write their senators or representatives, much less converse with them at dinners, cocktail parties, or other social occasions. Most of the communications received by decision makers are intraelite from newspersons, organized group leaders, influential constituents, wealthy political contributors, and personal friends—people who, for the most part, share the same views. It is not surprising, therefore, that members of Congress say that most of their mail is in agreement with their own position; their world of public opinion is self-reinforcing. Moreover, persons who initiate communication with decision makers, by writing or calling or visiting their representatives, are decidedly more educated and affluent than the average citizen.

What If We Held National Referenda on Policy Issues?   The nation's Founders were deeply suspicious of direct democracy. The U.S. Constitution makes no provision for national referenda voting. But what if Americans *could* vote on national issues? A Gallup poll in 1996 presented some 27 referenda issues to a representative sample of voters across the nation (see Table 14–1). On 13 of the 27 issues current public policy is in *dis*agreement with public opinion.

IDENTIFYING POLICY ISSUES: ELITE OPINION

When V. O. Key wrestled with the same problem confronting us—namely, the determination of the impact of popular preferences on public policy—he concluded that "the missing piece of the puzzle" was "that thin stratum of persons referred to variously as the political elite, the political activists, the leadership echelons, or the influentials."

> The longer one frets with the puzzle of how democratic regimes manage to function, the more plausible it appears that a substantial part of the explanation is to be found in the motives that activate the *leadership echelon,* the values that it holds, the rules of the political game to which it adheres, in the expectations which it entertains about its own status in society, and perhaps in some of the objective circumstances, both material and institutional, in which it functions.[2]

In view of the difficulty in finding direct links between public policy and popular preferences, it seems reasonable to ask whether the preferences of elites are more directly reflected in public policy than the preferences of masses. Do elite attitudes independently affect public policy? Or are elite attitudes so closely tied to socioeconomic conditions that elites have relatively little flexibility in policymaking and therefore little independent influence over the content of public policy?

TABLE 14-1   Public Opinion on Key Policy Issues

"Suppose that on election day this year you could vote on key issues as well as candidates. Please tell me whether you would vote for or against each one of the following propositions." (27 items read in RANDOM ORDER)

	% For	% Against	% No Opinion
1. Balanced budget amendment*	83	14	3
2. Raising the minimum wage	83	15	2
3. English as the official language*	82	16	2
4. Life sentences for drug dealers	80	17	3
5. Death penalty for murder	79	18	3
6. Congressional term limits amendment*	74	23	3
7. Prayer in public schools amendment*	73	25	2
8. Reducing all government agencies*	71	23	6
9. Two-year cutoff for welfare without work	71	24	5
10. Mandatory job retraining	69	25	6
11. Doctor-assisted suicide*	68	29	3
12. School choice*	59	37	4
13. Teaching creationism in public schools*	58	36	6
14. Ban on partial-birth abortions*	57	39	4
15. Ban on assault rifles	57	42	1
16. Five-year freeze on legal immigration*	50	46	4
17. Federal flat tax system*	49	39	12
18. Reducing social spending	44	53	3
19. Reducing defense spending	42	54	4
20. Abortion ban except to save mother's life	42	56	2
21. Reestablishing relations with Cuba	40	49	11
22. School busing for racial balance*	34	62	4
23. Legalization of gay marriages	28	67	5
24. Selling off public lands	24	70	6
25. Legalization of marijuana	24	73	3
26. Withdrawal of U.S. from United Nations	17	77	6
27. Racial preferences in jobs and school*	14	83	3

* An asterisk indicates that current public policy differs from public preference.

Source: The Gallup Poll Monthly, May 1996.

Elite preferences are more likely to be in accord with public policy than mass preferences. Public policy runs contrary to mass opinion at least one-third of the time.[3] (Note that majority opinion differs from current public policy on 13 of 27 issues presented in Table 14–1.) Of course this does not prove that policies are determined by elite preferences. It may be that government officials are acting rationally in response to events and conditions, and well-educated, informed elites understand the actions of government better than do the masses. Hence, it might be argued, on the one hand, that elites support government policies because they have greater understanding of and confidence in government, and they are more likely to read about and comprehend the explanations of government officials. On the other hand, the correspondence between elite opinion and public policy may also indicate that it is really *elite* opinion, not *mass* opinion, that determines public policy.

AGENDA SETTING AND "NONDECISIONS"

Who decides what will be decided? Defining the problems of society and suggesting alternative solutions—agenda setting—is the most important stage of the policymaking process. Conditions in society that are not defined as a problem and for which alternatives are never proposed never became policy issues. That is, they never get on the "agenda" of decision makers. The government does nothing and conditions remain the same. If certain conditions in society are defined as problems and alternative solutions are put forward, the conditions become policy issues. Governments are forced to decide what to do.

Clearly then, the power to decide what will be a policy issue is crucial to the policymaking process. Deciding what will be the problems is even more important than deciding what will be the solutions. Political scientist E. E. Schattschneider once wrote, He who determines what politics is about runs the country, because the definition of the alternatives is the choice of conflicts allocates power.[4]

Many civics textbooks imply that agenda setting just "happens." It is sometimes argued that in an open plural society such as ours, channels of access and communication to government are always open, so that any problem can be discussed and placed on the agenda of national decision making. Individuals and groups, it is said, can organize themselves to assume the tasks of defining problems and suggesting solutions. People can define their own interests, organize themselves, persuade others to support their cause, gain access to government officials, influence decision making, and watch over the implementation of government policies and programs. Indeed, it is sometimes argued that the absence of political activity such as this is an indicator of satisfaction.

But, in reality, policy issues do not just "happen." Creating an issue, dramatizing it, calling attention to it, and pressuring government to do something about it are important political tactics. These tactics are employed by influential individuals, organized interest groups, policy-planning organizations, political candidates and officeholders, and perhaps most important, the mass media. These are the tactics of "agenda setting."

Moreover, preventing certain conditions in society from becoming policy issues is also an important political tactic. *"Nondecision making"* occurs when influential individuals or groups or the political system itself operates in society. According to political scientists Peter Bachrach and Morton Baratz,

> A nondecision, as we define it, is a decision that results in the suppression or thwarting of a latent or manifest challenge to the values and interests of the decision-maker.

To be more clearly explicit, non–decision-making is a means by which demands for change in the existing allocation of benefits and privileges in the community can be suffocated before they are even voiced; or kept covert; or killed before they gain access to the relevant decision-making arena; or failing all these things, maimed or destroyed in the decision-implementing stage of the policy process.[5]

Nondecision making may occur when dominant elites act openly or covertly to suppress an issue because they fear that if public attention is focused on it something will be done and what is done will not be in their interest.

It may also occur when political candidates or officeholders or administrative officials anticipate that elites will not favor a particular idea. These officials drop the idea because they do not want to "rock the boat." Elites do not have to *do* anything. Officials are acting in anticipation of what they *might* do.

Finally, and perhaps most importantly, nondecision making occurs because the political system itself is structured in such a way as to facilitate the resolution of some kinds of issues and to obstruct the resolution of others. There is a "mobilization of bias" within the political system itself, that is, "a set of predominant values, beliefs, rituals, and institutional procedures . . . that operate systematically and consistently to the benefit of others."[6] For example, many scholars believe that the interest group system is the key to understanding how issues are identified, solutions proposed, and policies adopted. However, we know that the political system responds well to large-scale, well-organized, wealthy, active interest groups with good access to government officials. It responds less well to unorganized, poorer, inactive interest groups with few available channels of communication to government officials. The same observations might be made for the party system—that parties respond to well-organized, wealthy, skilled, active, and knowledgeable individuals and groups rather than to the disorganized, poor, unskilled, inactive, or unknowledgeable. Indeed, all governmental bodies—elected and appointed; legislative, executive, and judicial; federal, state, and local—contain this same bias.

Thus, it is difficult to maintain the fiction that anyone in a democracy can raise any policy issue anytime he or she wishes. Who, then, is responsible for agenda setting? Who decides what will be decided?

AGENDA SETTING AND MOBILIZING OPINION: THE MASS MEDIA

Television is the major source of information for the vast majority of Americans. More than two-thirds report that they receive all or most of their news from television. Television is really the first form of *mass* communication, that is, communication that reaches nearly everyone, including children. The TV viewer must see the news or else turn off the set; the newspaper reader can turn quickly to the sports and comics without confronting the political news. More importantly, television presents a visual image, not merely a printed word. The visual quality of television—the emotional impact that is conveyed by pictures—enables the TV networks to convey emotions as well as information.

Media Power. Great power derives from control over a society's media of communication. They are both players and referees in the game of politics. They not only report to the people on the struggles for power in society but also are participants in those struggles themselves. They are an elite group, competing for power alongside the more traditional leadership groups from business, labor, government, and other sectors of society. As political journalist Theodore White once observed, "The power of the press in America is a primordial one. It sets the agenda of public discussion; and this sweeping power is unrestrained by any law. It determines what people will talk about and think about—an authority that in other nations is reserved for tyrants, priests, parties, and mandarins."[7]

Media power is concentrated in the hands of a relatively small number of people: the editors, producers, anchors, reporters, and columnists of the leading television networks (ABC, CBS, NBC, and CNN) and the prestigious press (*The New York Times, The Washington Post, The Wall Street Journal, Newsweek, Time,* and *U.S. News and World Report*). Producers and editors generally work behind the scenes, and many influential print journalists are known only by their bylines. But most Americans have come to recognize the faces of the television network anchors and leading reporters: Dan Rather, Tom Brokaw, Peter Jennings, Ed Bradley, Sam Donaldson, Mike Wallace, Dianne Sawyer, and others. These media people are courted by politicians, treated as celebrities, studied by scholars, and known to millions of Americans by their television images.

The television network people who decide which issues, events, and personalities will be covered interact daily with their counterparts in the national press— the executives and editors of *The New York Times, The Washington Post, Time, Newsweek,* and so on. Even at the working level, the television and newspaper reporters interact in the Washington press corps. This interaction reinforces decisions about what the news should be. As a result, there is not much diversity in news reporting. All the networks, as well as the major newspapers and news magazines, will carry stories on the same topics at the same time.

Newsmaking. Newsmaking involves all-important decisions about what is "news" and who is "newsworthy." Television executives and producers and newspaper and magazine editors must decide what people, organizations, and events will be given attention—attention that makes these topics matters of general public concern and political action. Without media coverage the general public would not know about these personalities, organizations, or events. They would not become objects of political discussion, nor would they be likely to be considered important by government officials.

Media attention can create issues and personalities. Media inattention can doom issues and personalities to obscurity. The TV camera cannot be "a picture of the world" because the whole world cannot squeeze into the picture. News executives must sort through a tremendous surplus of information and decide what is to be "news."

In addition to deciding what is and what is not news, news executives provide cues to mass audiences about the importance of an issue, personality, or event.

Some matters are covered prominently by the media, with early placement on a newscast and several minutes of time, or with front-page newspaper coverage, including big headlines and pictures. The amount of coverage tells us what is important and what is not.

Of course, politicians, professional public relations people, interest group spokespersons, and various aspiring celebrities all know that the decisions of the media are vital to the success of their issue, their organization, and themselves. So they try to attract media attention by deliberately engaging in behavior or manufacturing situations that are likely to win coverage. The result is the "media event"—an activity arranged primarily to stimulate coverage and thereby attract public attention to an issue or individual. Generally, the more bizarre, dramatic, and sensational it is, the more likely it is to attract coverage. A media event may be a press conference to which reporters from the television stations and newspapers are invited by public figures—even when there is really no news to announce. Or it may be a staged debate, confrontation, or illustration of injustice. Political candidates may visit coal mines, ghetto neighborhoods, and sites of fires or other disasters. Sometimes protests, demonstrations, and even violence have been staged primarily as media events to dramatize and communicate grievances.

Media Bias. In exercising their judgment regarding which stories should be given television time or newspaper space, the media executives must rely on their own political values and economic interests as guidelines. In general, these executives are more liberal in their views than other segments of the nation's leadership. Topics selected weeks in advance for coverage reflect, or often create, current liberal issues: concern for problems affecting the poor and minorities; women's issues; opposition to defense spending; environmental concerns; and so forth. But liberalism is not the major source of bias in the news.

The principal source of distortion in the news is caused by the need for drama, action, and confrontation to hold audience attention. Television must entertain. To capture the attention of jaded audiences, news must be selected on the basis of emotional rhetoric, shocking incidents, dramatic conflict, overdrawn stereotypes. Race, sex, violence, and corruption in government are favorite topics because of popular interest. More complex problems such as inflation, government spending, and foreign policy must either be simplified and dramatized or ignored. To dramatize an issue the news executives must find or create a dramatic incident; tape it; transport, process, and edit the tape; and write a script for the introduction, the "voice-over," and the "recapitulation." All this means that most "news" must be created well in advance of scheduled broadcasting.

Media Effects. Media effects can be categorized as (1) identifying issues and setting the agenda for policymakers, (2) influencing attitudes and values toward policy issues, and (3) changing the behavior of voters and decision makers. These categories are ranked by the degree of influence the media are likely to have over their audiences. The power of television does not really lie in persuading viewers to take one side of an issue or another. Instead, *the power of television lies in setting the agenda for decision making*—deciding what issues will be given attention and what issues will be ignored.

The media can create new opinions more easily than they can change existing ones. They can often suggest how we feel about new events or issues—those for which we have no prior feelings or experiences. And the media can reinforce values and attitudes that we already hold. But there is very little evidence that the media can change existing values.

The viewer's psychological mechanism of *selective perception* helps to defend against bias in news and entertainment programming. Selective perception means mentally screening out information or images with which one disagrees. It causes people to tend to see and hear only what they want to see and hear. It reduces the impact of television bias on viewers' attitudes and behavior.

The networks' concentration on scandal, abuse, and corruption in government has not always produced the desired liberal, reformist notions in the masses of viewers. Contrary to the expectations of network executives, their focus on government scandals—Watergate, illicit activities by government agencies, congressional sex scandals, and power struggles between Congress and the executive branch—has produced general distrust and cynicism toward government and the system. These feelings have been labeled *television malaise:* a combination of social distrust, political cynicism, feelings of powerlessness, and disaffection from parties and politics, which seems to stem from television's emphasis on the negative aspects of American life.

Network executives do not intend to create television malaise among the masses. But scandal, sex, abuse of power, and corruption do attract large audiences and increase ratings.

FORMULATING POLICY

Policy formulation is the development of policy alternatives for dealing with problems on the public agenda. Policy formulations occur in government bureaucracies; interest group offices; legislative committee rooms; meetings of special commissions; and policy-planning organizations, otherwise known as "think tanks." The details of policy proposals are usually formulated by staff members rather than by their bosses, but staffs are guided by what they know their leaders want.

The White House.　The president and the executive branch are generally expected to be the "initiators" of policy proposals, with members of Congress in the role of "arbitors" of policy alternatives. The same division of labor is usually found at the state and local level, with governors, mayors, and even city managers expected to formulate policy proposals and state legislators and city councils to approve, amend, or reject them. The Constitution of the United States appears to endorse this arrangement in Article II Section 3: "[The president] shall from time to time give to Congress information of the State of the Union, and recommend to their consideration such measures as he shall judge necessary and expedient." Each year the principal policy statements of the president come in the State of the Union message, and more importantly, in the Budget of the United States Government, prepared by the Office of Management and Budget (see Chapter 9). Many other policy proposals are developed by executive departments in their specialized areas; these proposals are usually transmitted to the White House for the president's approval before being sent to Congress.

Interest Groups.   Interest groups may formulate their own policy proposals, perhaps in association with members of Congress or their staffs who share the same interest. Interest group staffs often bring valuable technical knowledge to policy formation, as well as political information about their group's position on the issues. Because Congress members and their staffs value both kinds of information, interest groups can often provide the precise language they desire in proposed bills and amendments. Thus, interest group staffs often augment the work of congressional staffs. Interest groups also provide testimony at congressional hearings as well as technical reports and analyses used by congressional staffs.

Legislative Staff.   Congressional staffs and the staffs in state legislatures have grown rapidly in recent years, so that this new legislative bureaucracy is itself becoming an important source of policy formulation. Committee staffs, staffs of the legislative leadership, and aids to individual legislators are all political appointees and generally reflect the political views of their legislator bosses. Over time some staffers become so knowledgeable about specific policy areas, including budget complexities, that they keep their jobs even when their original sponsor leaves the capital. Staffs are expected to research issues, schedule legislative hearings, line up experts and interest groups to testify, keep up to date on the status of bills and appropriation measures as they move through the legislative branch, maintain contact with executive agencies, write and rewrite bills, and perform other assorted chores. As legislators come to rely on trusted staffers, the staffers themselves become powerful policy formulators. Their advice may kill a bill or appropriation item or their work may amend a bill or change an appropriation, without a legislator ever becoming directly involved. Serious staffs of congressional leaders and influential committees exercise a great deal of influence in policymaking.

Think Tanks.   Policy-planning organizations are central coordinating points in the policymaking process. Certain policy-planing groups—for example, the Council on Foreign Relations, the American Enterprise Institute, Heritage Foundation, and the Brookings Institution—are influential in a wide range of key policy areas. Other policy-planning groups—the Urban Institute, Resources for the Future, the Population Council, for example—specialize in a particular policy field.

These organizations bring together the leadership of corporate and financial institutions, the foundations, the mass media, the leading intellectuals, and influential figures in the government. They review the relevant university and foundation-supported research on topics of interest, and more importantly, they try to reach a consensus about what action should be taken on national problems under study. Their goal is to develop action recommendations—explicit policies or programs designed to resolve national problems. These policy recommendations of the key policy-planning groups are distributed to the mass media, federal executive agencies, and Congress. The purpose is to lay the groundwork for making policy into law.

The following are among the more influential think tanks:

THE BROOKINGS INSTITUTION

The Brookings Institution has long been the dominant policy planning group for American domestic policy, despite the growing influence of competing think tanks over the years. Brookings staffers dislike its reputation as a liberal think tank, and they deny that Brookings tries to set national priorities. Yet the Brookings Institution has been very influential in planning the War on Poverty, welfare reform, national defense, and taxing and spending policies. *The New York Times* columnist and Harvard historian writing team, Leonard and Mark Silk, describe Brookings as the central locus of the Washington "policy network," where it does "its communicating: over lunch, whether informally in the Brookings cafeteria or at the regular Friday lunch around a great oval table at which the staff and their guests keen over the events of the week like the chorus of an ancient Greek tragedy; through consulting, paid or unpaid, for government or business at conferences, in the advanced studies program; and, over time, by means of the revolving door of government employment."[8]

THE AMERICAN ENTERPRISE INSTITUTE

For many years Republicans dreamed of a "Brookings Institution for Republicans" that would help offset the liberal bias of Brookings itself. In the late 1970s, that role was assumed by the American Enterprise Institute (AEI). The AEI appeals to both Democrats and Republicans who have doubts about big government. President William Baroody, Jr., distinguished the AEI from Brookings: "In confronting societal problems those who tend to gravitate to the AEI orbit would be inclined to look first for a market solution . . . while the other orbit people have a tendency to look for a government solution."[9]

THE HERITAGE FOUNDATION

Conservative ideologues have never been welcome in the Washington establishment. Yet influential conservative businesspersons gradually came to understand that without an institutional base in Washington they could never establish a strong and continuing influence in the policy network. So they set about the task of "building a solid institutional base" and "establishing a reputation for reliable scholarship and creative problem solving."[10] The result of their efforts was the Heritage Foundation.

THE COUNCIL ON FOREIGN RELATIONS

Political scientist Lester Milbraith observes that the influence of the Council of Foreign Relations (CFR) throughout government is so pervasive that it is difficult to distinguish the CFR from government programs: "The Council on Foreign Relations, while not financed by government, works so closely with it that it is difficult to distinguish Council actions stimulated by government from autonomous actions."[11] The

CFR itself, of course, denies that it exercises any control over U.S. foreign policy. Indeed, its bylaws declare, "The Council shall not take any position on questions of foreign policy and no person is authorized to speak or purport to speak for the Council on such matters."[12] But policy initiation and consensus-building do not require the CFR to officially adopt policy positions.[13]

POLICY LEGITIMATION: THE PROXIMATE POLICYMAKERS

What is the role of the "proximate policymakers"? The activities of these policymakers—the president, Congress, federal agencies, congressional committees, White House staffs, and interest groups—have traditionally been the central focus of political science and are usually portrayed as the whole of the policymaking process. But our notion of public policymaking views the activities of the proximate policymakers as only the final phase of a much more complex process. This final stage is the open, public stage of the policymaking process, and it attracts the attention of the mass media and most political scientists. The activities of the proximate policymakers are much easier to study than the private actions of corporations, foundations, the mass media, and the policy-planning organizations.

Many scholars concentrate their attention on this final phase of public policymaking and conclude that policymaking is a process of bargaining, competition, persuasion, and compromise among interest groups and government officials. Undoubtedly, these events continue throughout this final, law-making phase of the policymaking process. Conflict between the president and Congress, between Democrats and Republicans, between liberals and conservatives, and so forth may delay or alter somewhat the final actions of the proximate policymakers.

But the agenda for policy consideration has been set before the proximate policymakers become actively involved in the policymaking process—the major directions of policy change have been determined, and the mass media have prepared the public for new policies and programs. The formal law-making process concerns itself with details of implementation: who gets the political credit, what agencies get control of the program, and exactly how much money will be spent. These are not unimportant questions, but they are raised and decided within the context of policy goals and directions that have already been determined. The decisions of the proximate policymakers tend to center around the *means* rather than the *ends* of public policy.

PARTY INFLUENCE ON PUBLIC POLICY

Parties are important institutions in the American political system, but it would be a mistake to overestimate their impact on public policy. It makes relatively little difference in the major direction of public policy whether Democrats or Republicans dominate the political scene. American parties are largely "brokerage" organizations, more committed to winning public office than to advancing policy positions. Both the Democratic and Republican parties and their candidates tailor their policy positions to societal conditions. The result is that the parties do not have much independent impact on policy outcomes.

Both American parties subscribe to the same fundamental political ideology. Both share the prevailing democratic consensus about the sanctity of private property, a free enterprise economy, individual liberty, limited government, majority rule, and due process of the law. Moreover, since the 1930s both parties have supported the same major domestic programs—Social Security, unemployment compensation, a national highway program, a federally aided welfare system, and countercyclical fiscal and monetary policies. Finally, both parties have supported the basic outlines of American foreign and military policy since World War II. A change in party control of the presidency or Congress has not resulted in any dramatic shifts in the course of American foreign or domestic policy.

Yet there are differences between the parties that can be observed in the policymaking process. The social bases of the Democratic and Republican parties are slightly different. Both parties draw support from all social groups in America, but the Democrats draw disproportionately from labor, big-city residents, ethnic voters, blacks, Jews, and Catholics; Republicans draw disproportionately from rural, small-town, and suburban Protestants, businesspeople, and professionals. To the extent that the policy orientations of these two broad groups differ, the thrust of party ideology also differs. However, the magnitude of this difference is not very great.

Conflict between parties occurs most frequently over issues involving social welfare programs, taxation, housing and urban development, health care, antipoverty programs, and the regulation of business and labor. On some issues, such as civil rights and appropriations, voting will follow party lines during roll calls on preliminary motions, amendments, and other preliminary matters but swing to a bipartisan vote on passage of the final legislation. This means that the parties have disagreed on certain aspects of the bill but compromised on its final passage.

What are the issues that cause conflict between the Democratic and Republican parties? In general, Democrats have favored federal action to assist low-income groups through public assistance, housing, and antipoverty programs, and generally a larger role for the federal government in launching new projects to remedy domestic problems. Republicans, in contrast, have favored less government involvement in domestic affairs, lower taxes, and greater reliance on private action (see Table 14–2).

POLICY IMPLEMENTATION: THE BUREAUCRACY

"Implementation is the continuation of politics by other means."[14] Policymaking does not end with the passage of a law by Congress and its signing by the president. Rather it shifts from Capitol Hill and the White House to the bureaucracy—to the departments, agencies, and commissions of the executive branch. The bureaucracy is not constitutionally empowered to decide policy questions, but it does so, nonetheless, as it performs its task of implementation.

TABLE 14-2   Party Division on Selected Votes in Congress

| | HOUSE VOTES | | | |
| | REPUBLICANS | | DEMOCRATS | |
	Yes	No	Yes	No
Reagan income tax cuts (1981)	189	1	48	196
Federal aid for child care (1990)	47	119	218	26
Constitutional amendment to prohibit flag desecration (1990)	159	17	95	160
Clinton budget and tax increase (1993)	0	175	218	38
Additional spending cuts (1993)	156	18	57	200
Brady law, gun control (1993)	56	116	182	70
Balanced budget amendment to Constitution (1995)	228	2	72	129
Ban late term abortions, override pres. veto (1996)	215	15	70	121
Welfare reform (1996)	226	4	30	165

| | SENATE VOTES | | | |
| | REPUBLICANS | | DEMOCRATS | |
	Yes	No	Yes	No
Reagan income tax cuts (1981)	51	0	20	26
Capital gains tax cut (1989)	45	0	6	47
Constitutional amendment to prohibit flag desecration (1989)	33	11	18	37
Clinton budget and tax increase (1993)	0	44	50	6
Brady law, gun control (1993)	16	28	47	8
Balanced budget amendment to Constitution (1996)	52	1	12	34
Ban late term abortions, override pres. veto (1996)	45	6	12	35
Welfare reform (1996)	51	1	23	23

Source: *Congressional Quarterly,* "Key votes" in various issues, 1981–1997.

Implementation and Policymaking.   Implementation involves all of the activities designed to carry out the policies enacted by the legislative branch. These activities include the creation of new organizations—departments, agencies, bureaus, and so on—or the assignment of new responsibilities to existing organizations. These organizations must translate laws into operational rules and regulations. They must hire personnel, draw up contracts, spend money, and perform tasks. All of these activities involve decisions by bureaucrats—decisions that determine policy.

A society has grown in size and complexity, the bureaucracy has increased its role in the policymaking process. The standard explanation for the growth of bureaucratic power is that Congress and the president do not have the time, energy, or technical expertise to look after the details of environmental protection or occupational safety or equal employment opportunity or transportation safety or hundreds of other aspects of governance in a modern society. Bureaucratic agencies receive only broad and general policy directions in the laws of Congress. They must decide themselves on important details of policy. This means that much of the actual policymaking process takes place *within* the Environmental Protection Agency (EPA), the Occupational Safety and Health Administration (OSHA), the Equal Employment Opportunity Commission (EEOC), the National Transportation Safety Board, and hundreds of other bureaucratic agencies.

Bureaucratic power in policymaking is also explained by political decisions in Congress and the White House to shift responsibility for many policies to the bureaucracy. Congress and the president can take political credit for laws promising "safe and effective" drugs, "equal opportunity" employment, the elimination of "unfair" labor practices, and other equally lofty yet, vague and ambiguous goals. It then becomes the responsibility of bureaucratic agencies, for example, the Food and Drug Administration (FDA), the EEOC, and the National Labor Relations Board (NLRB), to give practical meaning to these symbolic measures. Indeed, if the policies developed by these agencies turn out to be unpopular, Congress and the president can blame the bureaucrats.

Regulation and Policymaking.   Policy implementation often requires the development of formal rules and regulations by bureaucracies. Federal executive agencies publish about 60,000 pages of rules in the *Federal Register* each year. The rulemaking process for federal agencies is prescribed by the Administrative Procedures Act, which requires agencies to

- Announce in the *Federal Register* that a new rule or regulation is being proposed.
- Hold hearings to allow interest groups to present evidence and assignments regarding the proposed rule.
- Conduct research on the proposed rule's economic impact, environmental impact, and so on.
- Solicit "public comments" (usually the arguments of interest groups).
- Consult with higher officials, including the Office of Management and Budget.
- Publish the new rule or regulation in the *Federal Register.*

Rule making by the bureaucracy is central to the policymaking process. Formal rules that appear in the *Federal Register* have the force of law. Bureaucratic agencies may levy fines and penalties for violations of these regulations, and these fines and penalties are enforceable in the courts. Congress itself can only amend or repeal a formal regulation by passing a new law and obtaining the president's signature. Controversial bureaucratic regulations (policies) may remain in effect when Congress is slow to act, when legislation is blocked by key congressional committee members, or when the president supports the bureaucracy and refuses to sign bills overturning regulations. The courts usually do not overturn bureaucratic regulations unless they exceed the authority granted to the agency by law or unless the agency has not followed the proper procedure in adopting them.

Adjudication and Policymaking.   Policy implementation by bureaucracies often involves adjudication of individual cases. (While rule making resembles the legislative process, adjudication resembles the judicial process.) In adjudication, bureaucrats must decide whether a person, firm, corporation, and so on has complied with laws and regulations and, if not, what penalties or corrective actions are to be applied. Federal regulatory agencies—for example, the EPA, the EEOC, the Internal Revenue Service (IRS), the Federal Trade Commission (FTC), the Securities and Exchange Commission (SEC)—are heavily engaged in adjudication. They have established procedures for investigation, notification, hearing, decision, and appeal; individuals and firms involved in these proceedings often hire lawyers specializing in the field of regulation. Administrative hearings are somewhat less formal than a court trial, and the "judges" are employees of the agency itself. Losers may appeal to the federal courts, but the history of agency successes in the courts discourage many appeals. The record of agency decisions in individual cases is a form of public policy. Just as previous court decisions reflect judicial policy, previous administrative decisions reflect bureaucratic policy.

Bureaucratic Discretion and Policymaking.   It is true that much of the work of bureaucrats is administrative routine—issuing Social Security checks, collecting and filing income tax returns, delivering the mail. But bureaucrats almost always have some discretion in performing even routine tasks. Often individual cases do not exactly fit established rules; often more than one rule might be applied to the same case, resulting in different outcomes. For example, the IRS administers the U.S. tax code, but each auditing agent has considerable discretion in deciding which rules to apply to a taxpayer's income, deductions, business expenses, and so on. Indeed, identical tax information submitted to different IRS offices almost always results in different estimates of tax liability. But even in more routine tasks, from processing Medicare applications to forwarding mail, individual bureaucrats can be friendly and helpful, or hostile and obstructive.[15]

Policy Bias of Bureaucrats.   Generally bureaucrats believe strongly in the value of their programs and the importance of their tasks. EPA officials are strongly committed to the environmental movement; officials in the Central Intelligence Agency (CIA) believe strongly in the importance of good intelligence to the nation's security; officials in the Social Security Administration are strongly committed to maintaining the benefits of the retirement system. But in addition to these professional motives, bureaucrats, like everyone else, seek higher pay, greater job security, and added power and prestige for themselves.

Professional and personal motives converge to inspire bureaucrats to expand the powers, functions, and budgets of their agencies. (Conversely bureaucrats try to protect their "turf" against reductions in functions, authority, and budgets.) "Budget maximization"—expanding the agency's budget as much as possible—is a driving force in government bureaucracies.[16] This is especially true regarding discretionary funds in an agency's budget—funds that bureaucrats have flexibility in deciding how to spend, rather than funds committed by law to specific purposes. The bureaucratic bias toward new functions and added authority and increases in personnel and budgets helps explain the growth of government over time.

POLICY EVALUATION: IMPRESSIONISTIC
VERSUS SYSTEMATIC

The policy process model implies that evaluation is the final step in policymaking. It implies that policymakers—Congress, the president, interest groups, bureaucrats, the media, think tanks, and so on—seek to learn whether or not policies are achieving their stated goals; at what costs; and with what effects, intended and unintended, on society. Sophisticated versions of the model portray a "feedback" linkage—evaluations of current policy identify new problems and set in motion the policymaking process once again.

However, most policy evaluations in Washington, state capitols, and city halls are unsystematic and impressionistic. They came in the form of interest group complaints about the inadequacies of laws or budgets in protecting or advancing their concerns; in media stories exposing waste or fraud or mismanagement in a program or decrying the inadequacies of government policies in dealing with one crisis or another; in legislative hearings in which executive officials are questioned and occasionally badgered by committee members or their staffs about policies or programs; and sometimes even in citizens' complaints to members of Congress, the White House, or the media. Yet these "evaluations" often succeed in stimulating reform—policy changes designed to remedy perceived mistakes, inadequacies, wasteful expenditures, and other flaws in existing policy.

But as we shall observe in the next chapter ("Policy Evaluation: Finding Out What Happens after a Law Is Passed") systematic policy evaluation is relatively rare in government. We define systematic evaluation to mean careful, objective, scientific assessment of the current and long-term effects of policies on both target and nontarget situations or groups, as well as an assessment of the ratio of current and long-term costs to whatever benefits are identified.

SUMMARY

The policy process model focuses on *how* policies are made, rather than on the substance or content of policies. The model identifies a variety of activities that occur within the political system, including identification of problems and agenda setting, formulating policy proposals, legitimating policies, implementing policies, and evaluating their effectiveness. Although political science has traditionally concerned itself with describing political institutions and processes, seldom has it systematically examined the impact of political processes on the *content* of public policy. Following are some general propositions about the impact of political processes on policy content.

1. It is difficult to assess the independent effect of public opinion on shaping public policy. Public policy may accord with mass opinion, but we can never be certain whether mass opinion shaped public policy or public policy shaped mass opinion. The public does not have opinions on many major policy questions, public opinion is unstable, and decision makers can easily misinterpret as well as manipulate public opinion. Public policy is more likely to conform to elite opinion than to mass opinion.

2. Deciding what will be decided—agenda setting—is a crucial stage in the policy process. Policy issues do not just "happen." Preventing certain conditions in society from becoming policy issues—nondecision making—is an important political tactic of dominant interests.

3. The mass media, particularly the three main television networks, play a major role in agenda setting. By deciding what will be news, the media set the agenda for political discussion, whether or not they can persuade voters to support one candidate or another. The continuing focus on the dramatic, violent, and negative aspects of American life may unintentionally create apathy and alienation—television malaise.

4. A great deal of policy formulation occurs outside the formal governmental process. Prestigious, private, policy-planning organizations—such as the Council on Foreign Relations—explore policy alternatives, advise governments, develop policy consensus, and even supply top governmental leaders. The policy-planning organizations bring together the leadership of the corporate and financial worlds, the mass media, the foundations, the leading intellectuals, and top government officials.

5. Policy innovation—the readiness of a government to adopt new programs and policies—is linked to urbanization, education, and wealth, as well as to competition, participation, and professionalism. Specifically, policy innovation appears to be a product of professionalism in legislatures and bureaucracies and an educated and politically active population.

6. The activities of the proximate policymakers—the president, Congress, executive agencies, and so forth—attract the attention of most commentators and political scientists. But nongovernmental leaders, in business and finance, foundations, policy-planning organizations, the mass media, and other interest groups, may have already set the policy agenda and selected major policy goals. The activities of the proximate policymakers tend to center around the means rather than the ends, of public policy.

7. The Democratic and Republican parties have agreed on the basic outlines of American foreign and domestic policy since World War II. However, there have been some important policy differences between the parties. Differences have occurred most frequently over questions of taxing and spending, welfare, housing and urban development, antipoverty efforts, health care, and the regulation of business and labor.

8. Policy implementation is an important component of the policymaking process. Bureaucrats make policy as they engage in the tasks of implementation—making regulations, adjudicating cases, and exercising their discretion. Professional

and personal motives combine to bias bureaucrats toward expanding the powers and functions of their agencies and increasing their budgets, especially their discretionary funds.

9. Most policy evaluations are unsystematic and impressionistic. They are made principally by interest groups, the media, members of Congress and their staffs, and occasionally individual citizens.

NOTES

1. V. O. Key, Jr., *Public Opinion and American Democracy* (New York: Knopf, 1967), pp. 422–423.
2. Ibid., p. 537.
3. See Robert Y. Shapiro and Lawrence R. Jacobs, "The Relationship Between Public Opinion and Public Policy: A Review," in *Political Behavior Annual,* Vol. II, ed. Samuel Long (Boulder, CO: Westview, 1989).
4. E. E. Schattschneider, *The Semisovereign People* (New York: Holt, Rinehart & Winston, 1961), p. 68.
5. Peter Bachrach and Morton S. Baratz, *Power and Poverty* (New York: Oxford University Press, 1979), p. 7.
6. Ibid., p. 43.
7. Theodore White, *The Making of the President, 1972* (New York: Bantam, 1973), p. 7.
8. Leonard Silk and Mark Silk, *The American Establishment* (New York: Basic Books, 1980), p. 160.
9. Ibid., p. 179.
10. *Heritage Foundation Annual Report 1985* (Washington, DC: Heritage Foundation, 1985).
11. Lester Milbraith, "Interest Groups in Foreign Policy," in *Domestic Sources of Foreign Policy,* ed. James Rosenau (New York: Free Press, 1967), p. 247.
12. Council on Foreign Relations, *Annual Report,* 1988, p. 160.
13. Serious students of public policy are advised to read the books and journals published by these leading policy planning organizations, especially *The Brookings Review* (published quarterly by the Brookings Institution, 1775 Massachusetts Avenue NW, Washington, DC 20036); *The American Enterprise* (published bimonthly by the American Enterprise Institute, 1150 17th Street NW, Washington, DC 20036); *Policy Review* (published quarterly by the Heritage Foundation, 214 Massachusetts Avenue NE, Washington, DC 20002); *Foreign Affairs* (published five times annually by the Council on Foreign Relations, J8 East 68th Street, New York, NY 10021).
14. Donald S. Van Meter and Carl E. Vanltorn, "The Policy Implementation Process," *Administration and Society,* 6 (February 1975), 447.
15. See James Q. Wilson, *Bureaucracy: What Governments Do and Why They Do It* (New York: Basic Books, 1989).
16. William Niskanen, *Bureaucracy and Representative Government* (Chicago: Aldine, 1971).

BIBLIOGRAPHY

Dunn, William N. *Public Policy Analysis.* Englewood Cliffs, NJ: Prentice Hall, 1994.
Erikson, Robert S., and Kent L. Tedin. *American Public Opinion.* 5th ed. Boston: Allyn and Bacon, 1995.

KEY, V. O., JR. *Public Opinion and American Democracy*. New York: Knopf, 1967.

KINGDOM, JOHN W. *Agendas, Alternatives, and Public Policies*. Boston: Little, Brown, 1984.

LINDBLOOM, CHARLES E., and EDWARD J. WOODHOUSE. *The Policy-Making Process*. 3rd ed. Englewood Cliffs, NJ: Prentice Hall, 1993.

SMITH, JAMES A. *The Idea Brokers: Think Tanks and the Rise of the New Policy Elite*. New York: Macmillan, 1991.

15

POLICY EVALUATION
Finding Out What Happens after a Law Is Passed

Senator Edward Kennedy, D-Mass., rear, center, presides over a hearing of the Senate Labor and Human Resources Committee. (John Duricka/AP/Wide World Photos)

DOES THE GOVERNMENT KNOW WHAT IT IS DOING?

Americans often assume that once we pass a law, create a bureaucracy, and spend money, the purpose of the law, the bureaucracy, and the expenditure will be achieved. We assume that when Congress adopts a policy and appropriates money for it, and when the executive branch organizes a program, hires people, spends money, and carries out activities designed to implement the policy, the effects of the policy will be felt by society and will be those intended. Unfortunately, these assumptions are not always warranted. The national experiences with many public programs indicate the need for careful appraisal of the real impact of public policy.

Does the government really know what it is doing? Generally speaking, no. Governments usually know how much money they spend; how many persons ("clients") are given various services; how much these services cost; how their programs are organized, managed, and operated; and perhaps how influential interest groups regard their programs and services. But even if programs and policies are well organized, efficiently operated, widely utilized, adequately financed, and generally supported by major interest groups, we may still want to ask, So what? Do they work? Do these programs have any beneficial effects on society? Are the effects immediate or long range? Positive or negative? What is the relationship between the costs of the program and the benefits to society? Could we be doing something else with more benefit to society with the money and workforce devoted to these programs? Unfortunately, governments have done very little to answer these more basic questions.

POLICY EVALUATION: ASSESSING THE IMPACT OF PUBLIC POLICY

Policy evaluation is learning about the consequences of public policy. Other, more complex definitions have been offered: "Policy evaluation is the assessment of the overall effectiveness of a national program in meeting its objectives, or assessment of the relative effectiveness of two or more programs in meeting common objectives."[1] "Policy evaluation research is the objective, systematic, empirical examination of the effects ongoing policies and public programs have on their targets in terms of the goals they are meant to achieve."[2]

Some definitions tie evaluation to the stated "goals" of a program or policy. But since we do not always know what these "goals" really are, and because we know that some programs and policies pursue conflicting "goals," we will not limit our notion of policy evaluation to their achievement. Instead, we will concern ourselves with all of the consequences of public policy, that is, with "policy impact."

The impact of a policy is all its *effects on real-world conditions,* including

1. Impact on the target situation or group
2. Impact on situations or groups other than the target (spillover effects)
3. Impact on future as well as immediate conditions

4. Direct costs, in terms of resources devoted to the program
5. Indirect costs, including loss of opportunities to do other things

All the benefits and costs, both immediate and future, must be measured in both symbolic and tangible effects.

Measuring Impact, Not Output. "Policy impact" is not the same as "policy output." In assessing policy impact, we cannot be content simply to measure government activity. For example, the number of dollars spent per member of a target group (per pupil educational expenditures, per capita welfare expenditures, per capita health expenditures) is not really a measure of the impact of a policy on the group. It is merely a measure of government activity—that is, a measure of *policy output*. Unfortunately many government agencies produce reams of statistics measuring outputs—such as welfare benefits paid, criminal arrests and prosecutions, Medicare payments, and school enrollments. But this "bean counting" tells us little about poverty, crime, health, or educational achievement. We cannot be satisfied with measuring how many times a bird flaps its wings; we must know how far the bird has flown. In describing public policy, or even in explaining its determinants, measures of policy output are important. But in assessing *policy impact*, we must identify changes in society that are associated with measures of government activity.

Target Groups. The target group is that part of the population for whom the program is intended—such as the poor, the sick, the ill housed. Target groups must first be identified and then the desired effect of the program on the members of these groups must be determined. Is it to change their physical or economic circumstances—for example, the percentage of blacks or women employed in professional or managerial jobs, the income of the poor, the infant death rate? Or is it to change their knowledge, attitudes, awareness, interests, or behavior? If multiple effects are intended, what are the priorities among different effects—for example, are positive attitudes toward the political system more valuable than tangible progress toward the elimination of black-white income differences? What are the possible unintended effects (side effects) on target groups—for example, does the prospect of receiving welfare cash payments, food stamps, and access to public housing encourage early teenage pregnancy and social dependency? What is the impact of a policy on the target group in proportion to that group's total need? Accurate data describing the unmet needs of the nation are not generally available, but it is important to estimate the denominator of total need so that we know how adequate our programs are. Moreover, such an estimate may also help in estimating symbolic benefits or costs; a program that promises to meet a national need but actually meets only a small proportion of it may generate great praise at first but bitterness and frustration later when this discrepancy becomes known.

Nontarget Groups. All programs and policies have differential effects on various segments of the population. Identifying important nontarget groups for a policy is a difficult process. For example, what is the impact of the welfare reform on groups other than the poor—government bureaucrats, social workers, local political figures, working-class families who are not on welfare, taxpayers, and others? Non-target effects may be expressed as benefits as well as costs, such as the benefits to the construction industry of public housing projects.

Short-term and Long-term Effects.   When will the benefits or the costs be felt? Is the program designed for short-term emergencies? Or is it a long-term, developmental effort? If it is short term, what will prevent the processes of incrementalism and bureaucratization from turning it into a long-term program, even after the immediate need is met? Many impact studies show that new or innovative programs have short-term positive effects—for example, Operation Head Start and other educational programs. However, the positive effects frequently disappear as the novelty and enthusiasm of new programs wear off. Other programs experience difficulties at first, as in the early days of Social Security and Medicare, but turn out to have "sleeper" effects, as in the widespread acceptance of Social Security today. Not all programs aim at the same degree of permanent or transient change.

Indirect and Symbolic Costs and Benefits.   Programs are frequently measured by their direct costs. We generally know how many dollars go into program areas, and we can even calculate (as in Chapter 9) the proportion of total governmental dollars devoted to various programs. Government agencies have developed various forms of cost-benefit analysis to identify the direct costs (usually, but not always, in dollars) of government programs. But it is very difficult to identify the indirect and symbolic benefits or costs of public programs. Rarely can all these factors be included in a formal decision-making model. Cost-accounting techniques developed in business were designed around units of production—automobiles, airplanes, tons of steel, and so on. But how do we identify and measure units of social well-being? Often political intuition is the best guide available to policymakers in these matters.

Calculating Net Benefits and Costs.   The task of calculating the net impact of a public policy is truly awesome. It would be all the symbolic and tangible benefits, both immediate and long range, minus all the symbolic and tangible costs, both immediate and future (see Table 15–1). Even if all these costs and benefits are known (and everyone agrees on what is a "benefit" and what is a "cost"), it is still very difficult to come up with a net balance. Many of the items on both sides of the balance would defy comparison—for example, how do you subtract a tangible cost in dollars from a symbolic reward in the sense of well-being felt by individuals or groups?

THE SYMBOLIC IMPACT OF POLICY

The impact of a policy includes both its symbolic and tangible effects. Its symbolic impact deals with the perceptions that individuals have of government action and their attitudes toward it. Even if government policies do not succeed in reducing social dependency, eliminating poverty, preventing crime, and so on, this may be a

TABLE 15-1   Assessing Policy Impact

	BENEFITS		COSTS	
	Present	Future	Present	Future
Target Groups and Situations	Symbolic Tangible	Symbolic Tangible	Symbolic Tangible	Symbolic Tangible
Nontarget Groups and Situations (Spillover)	Symbolic Tangible	Symbolic Tangible	Symbolic Tangible	Symbolic Tangible
	Sum present benefits	Sum future benefits	Sum present costs	Sum future costs
	Sum all benefits	minus	Sum all costs	
		Net policy impact		

rather minor objection if the failure of government to *try* to do these things would lead to the view that society is "not worth saving." Individuals, groups, and whole societies frequently judge public policy in terms of its good intentions rather than its tangible accomplishments. The general popularity and public appraisal of a program may be unrelated to its real impact in terms of desired results. The implication is that very popular programs may have little positive impact, and vice versa.

The policies of government may tell us more about the aspirations of a society and its leadership than about actual conditions. Policies do more than effect change in societal conditions; they also help hold people together and maintain an orderly state. For example, whether the fair housing provisions of the Civil Rights Act of 1968 can be enforced or not, the fact that it is national policy to forbid discrimination in the sale or rental of housing reassures people of all races that their government does not condone such acts. There are many more examples of public policy serving as a symbol of what society aspires to be.

Once upon a time politics was described as "who gets what, when, and how." Today it seems that politics centers on "who *feels* what, when, and how." The smoke-filled room where patronage and pork were dispensed has been replaced with the talk-filled room where rhetoric and image are dispensed. What governments say is as important as what governments do. Television has made the image of public policy as important as the policy itself. Systematic policy analysis concentrates on what governments do, why they do it, and what difference it makes. It devotes less attention to what governments say. Perhaps this is a weakness in policy analysis. Our focus has been primarily on activities of governments rather than their rhetoric.

PROGRAM EVALUATION: WHAT GOVERNMENTS USUALLY DO

Most government agencies make some effort to review the effectiveness of their own programs. These reviews usually take one of the following forms:

Hearings and Reports.   The most common type of program review involves hearings and reports. Government administrators are asked by chief executives or legislators to give testimony (formally or informally) on the accomplishments of their own programs. Frequently, written annual reports are provided by program administrators. But testimonials and reports of administrators are not very objective means of program evaluation. They frequently magnify the benefits and minimize the costs of the program.

Site Visits.   Occasionally teams of high-ranking administrators, expert consultants, legislators, or some combination of these people will decide to visit agencies or conduct inspections in the field. These teams can pick up impressionistic data about how programs are being run, whether they are following specific guidelines, whether they have competent staffs, and sometimes whether or not the clients (target groups) are pleased with the services.

Program Measures.   The data developed by government agencies themselves generally cover policy output measures: the number of recipients in various welfare programs, the number of persons in work-force training programs, the number of public hospital beds available, the tons of garbage collected, or the number of pupils enrolled. But these program measures rarely indicate what impact these numbers have on society: the conditions of life confronting the poor, the success of work-force trainees in finding and holding skilled jobs, the health of the nation's poor, the cleanliness of cities, and the ability of graduates to read and write and function in society.

Comparison with Professional Standards.   In some areas of government activity, professional associations have developed standards of excellence. These standards are usually expressed as a desirable level of output: for example, the number of pupils per teacher, the number of hospital beds per one thousand people, the number of cases for each welfare worker. Actual government outputs can then be compared with ideal outputs. Although such an exercise can be helpful, it still focuses on government outputs and not on the impact of government activities on the conditions of target or nontarget groups. Moreover, the standards themselves are usually developed by professionals who are really guessing at what ideal levels of benefits and services should be. There is rarely any hard evidence that ideal levels of government output have any significant impact on society.

Evaluation of Citizens' Complaints.   Another common approach to program evaluation is the analysis of citizens' complaints. But not all citizens voluntarily submit complaints or remarks about governmental programs. Critics of government programs are self-selected, and they are rarely representative of the general public or even of the target groups of government programs. There is no way to judge whether the complaints of a vocal few are shared by the many more who have not spoken up. Occasionally, administrators develop questionnaires for participants in their program to learn what their complaints may be and whether they are satisfied or not. But these questionnaires really test public opinion toward the program and not its real impact on the lives of participants.

PROGRAM EVALUATION: WHAT GOVERNMENTS CAN DO

None of the common evaluative methods just mentioned really attempts to weigh *costs* against *benefits*. Indeed, administrators seldom calculate the ratio of costs to services—the dollars required to train one worker, to provide one hospital bed, to collect and dispose of one ton of garbage. It is even more difficult to calculate the costs of making specific changes in society—the dollars required to raise student reading levels by one grade, to lower the infant death rate by one point, to reduce the crime rate by 1 percent. To learn about the real impact of governmental programs on society, more complex and costly methods of program evaluation are required.

Systematic program evaluation involves comparisons—comparisons designed to estimate what changes in society can be attributed to the program rather than nonprogram factors. Ideally, this means comparing what "actually happened" to "what would have happened if the program had never been implemented." It is not difficult to measure what happened; unfortunately too much program evaluation stops there. The real problem is to measure what would have happened without a program and then compare the two conditions of society. The difference must be attributable to the program itself and not to other changes that are occurring in society at the same time.

Before-versus-After Comparisons. There are several common research designs in program evaluation. The most common is the before-and-after study, which compares results in a jurisdiction at two times—one before the program was implemented and the other some time after. Usually only target groups are examined. These before-and-after comparisons are designed to show program impacts, but it is very difficult to know whether the changes observed, if any, came about as a result of the program or as a result of other changes that were occurring in society at the same time (see Design 1, Figure 15–1).

Projected-trend-line versus Postprogram Comparisons. A better estimate of what would have happened without the program can be made by projecting past (preprogram) trends into the postprogram time period. Then these projections can be compared with what actually happened in society after the program was implemented. The difference between the projections based on preprogram trends and the actual postprogram data can be attributed to the program itself. Note that data on target groups or conditions must be obtained for several time periods before the

Design 1
Before vs. After

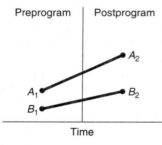

Preprogram | Postprogram

• A_2

A_1•

Time

■ $A_2 - A_1$ = Estimated Program Effect

Design 2
Projected vs. Postprogram

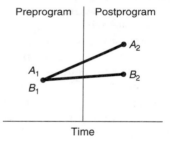

Preprogram | Postprogram

• A_2 Actual

Trend Line

A_1 Projected from Trend Line

Time

■ $A_2 - A_1$ = Estimated Program Effect

Design 3
With vs. Without Program

Preprogram | Postprogram

• A_2

A_1•   • B_2

B_1•

Time

■ A has Program; B does not.
■ $(A_2 - A_1) - (B_2 - B_1)$ = Estimated Program Effect.
■ Or difference between A and B in rate of change equals Estimated Program Effect.

Design 4
The Classic Research Design: Control vs. Experimental Groups

Preprogram | Postprogram

• A_2

A_1
B_1 • B_2

Time

■ A has Program; B does not.
■ A and B identical in preprogram period.
■ $A_2 - B_2$ = Estimated Program Effect

FIGURE 15–1   Policy Evaluation Research Designs

program was initiated, so that a trend line can be established (see Design 2, Figure 15–1). This design is better than the before-and-after design, but it requires more effort by program evaluators.

Comparisons Between Jurisdictions With and Without Programs.   Another common evaluation design is to compare individuals who have participated in programs with those who have not or to compare cities, states, or nations which have programs with those that do not. Comparisons are sometimes made in the postprogram period only; for example, comparisons of the job records of those who have participated in work-force training programs with those who have not or comparisons of homicide rates in states that have the death penalty with the homicide rates in states without the death penalty. But so many other differences exist between individuals or jurisdictions that it is difficult to attribute differences in their conditions to differences in government programs. For example, persons who voluntarily enter a work-force training program may be more motivated to find a job or have different personal characteristics than those who do not. States with the death penalty may tend to be rural states, which have lower homicide rates than urban states, which may or may not have the death penalty.

Some of the problems involved in comparing jurisdictions with and without programs can be resolved if we observe both kinds of jurisdictions before and after the introduction of the program. This enables us to estimate differences between jurisdictions before program efforts are considered. After the program is initiated, we can observe whether the differences between jurisdictions have widened or not (see Design 3, Figure 15–1). This design provides some protection against attributing differences to a particular program when underlying socioeconomic differences between jurisdictions are really responsible for different outcomes.

Comparisons Between Control and Experimental Groups Before and After Program Implementation. The classic research design involves the careful selection of control and experimental groups that are identical in every way, the application of the policy to the experimental group only, and the comparison of changes in the experimental group with changes in the control group after the application of the policy. Initially, control and experimental groups must be identical, and the preprogram performance of each group must be measured and found to be the same. The program must be applied only to the experimental group. The postprogram differences between the experimental and control groups must be carefully measured (see Design 4, Figure 15–1). This classic research design is preferred by scientists because it provides the best opportunity of estimating changes that derived from the effects of other forces in society.

FEDERAL EVALUATION: THE GENERAL ACCOUNTING OFFICE

The General Accounting Office (GAO) is an arm of Congress. It has broad authority to audit the operations and finances of federal agencies, to evaluate their programs, and to report its findings to Congress. For most of its history, the GAO confined itself to financial auditing and management and administrative studies. In recent years, however, it has increasingly undertaken evaluative research on government programs.

The GAO was established by Congress as an independent agency in 1921, in the same Budget and Accounting Act that created the first executive budget; its authority to undertake evaluation studies was expanded in the Congressional Budget and Impoundment Control Act of 1974, the same act that established the House and

Senate Budget Committees and the Congressional Budget Office (see Chapter 9). The GAO is headed by the comptroller general of the United States. Most GAO reports are requested by Congress, although the office can undertake studies on its own initiative.

According to the GAO, "Program evaluation—when it is available and of high quality—provides sound information about what programs are actually delivering, how they are being managed, and the extent to which they are cost-effective."[3] The GAO believes that evaluation efforts by federal agencies fall woefully short of what is required for rational decision making. It has been especially critical of the Defense Department for failing to test weapons systems adequately, to monitor defense contractors and their charges, or to adjust its future plans to expected reductions in defense spending (see Chapter 8). The GAO has criticized the Environmental Protection Agency for measuring its own success in terms of input measures—numbers of inspections performed and enforcement actions undertaken—rather than actual improvements in environmental conditions, such as in water quality or air quality (see Chapter 7). The GAO has also reported on the Social Security trust fund and the dangers of spending trust fund money on current governmental operations (see Chapter 5). It has reported on the high and growing cost of medical care in the United States, especially Medicaid and Medicare, and noted the lack of correlation between medical spending and measures of the nation's health (see Chapter 5). It has strongly urged Congress and the president to reduce annual deficits and has provided information on both official budget deficits and additional off-budget debts (see Chapter 9). It has undertaken to assess the overall impact of drug control policies (see Chapter 4), and it has studied the default rate on student loans and recommended collection of overdue loans by withholding tax refunds (see Chapter 6). In short, the GAO has been involved in virtually every major policy question confronting the nation.[4]

EXPERIMENTAL POLICY RESEARCH

Many policy analysts argue that policy experimentation offers the best opportunity to determine the impact of public policies. This opportunity rests on the main characteristics of experimental research: the systematic selection of experimental and control groups, the application of the policy under study to the experimental group only, and the careful comparison of differences between the experimental and the control groups after the application of the policy. But government-sponsored, experimental policy research raises a series of important questions.

A Bias toward Positive Results.   First, are government-sponsored research projects predisposed to produce results supportive of popular reform proposals? Are social scientists, whose personal political values are generally liberal and reformist, inclined to produce findings in support of liberal reform measures? Moreover, successful experiments—where the proposed policy achieves positive results—will receive more acclaim and produce greater opportunities for advancement for social scientists and administrators than will unsuccessful experiments—where the policy is shown to be ineffective. Liberal, reform-oriented social scientists expect liberal reforms to produce positive results. When reforms appear to do so, the research results are immediately accepted and published; but when results are unsupportive or negative, the social scientists may be inclined to go back and recode their data, redesign their research, or reevaluate their results because they believe a "mistake" must have been made. The temptation to "fudge the data," "reinterpret" the results, coach participants on what to say or do, and so forth will be very great. In the physical and biological sciences the temptation to "cheat" in research is reduced by the fact that research can be replicated and the danger of being caught and disgraced is very great. But social experiments can seldom be replicated perfectly, and replication seldom brings the same distinction to a social scientist as does the original research.

The Hawthorne Effect.   People behave differently when they know they are being watched. Students, for example, generally perform at a higher level when something—anything—new and different is introduced into the classroom routine. This "Hawthorne effect" may cause a new program or reform to appear more successful than the old, but it is the newness itself that produces improvement. The term is taken from early experiments at the Hawthorne plant of Western Electric Company in Chicago in 1927. It was found that worker output increased with *any* change in routine, even decreasing the lighting in the plant.[5]

Generalizing Results to the Nation.   Another problem in policy research is that results obtained with small-scale experiments may differ substantially from those that would occur if a large-scale nationwide program were adopted. For example, years ago a brief experiment involving a small number of families purported to show that a government-guaranteed income did not change the work behavior of recipients; they continued to behave as their neighbors did—searching for jobs and accepting employment when it was offered.[6] Subsequent studies of the effects of a guaranteed government income challenged even these experimental group findings but also predicted that a *nationwide* program would produce much more dramatic changes in working behavior. If everyone in the nation were guaranteed a minimum annual income, cultural standards might be changed nationwide; the resulting work disincentives might "seriously understate the expected cost of an economy-wide program."[7]

Ethical and Legal Issues.   Experimental strategies in policy impact research raise still other problems. Do government researchers have the right to withhold public services from individuals simply to provide a control group for experimentation? In the medical area, where giving or withholding treatment can result in death or injury, the problem is obvious and many attempts have been made to formulate a code of ethics. But in the area of social experimentation, what are we to say to control groups who are chosen to be similar to experimental groups but denied benefits in order to serve as a base for comparison? Setting aside the legal and ethical issues, it will be politically difficult to provide services for some people and not others.

Political Interpretations of Results.   Finally, we must acknowledge that the political milieu shapes policy research. Politics helps decide what policies and policy alternatives will be studied in the first place. Politics can also affect findings themselves, and certainly the interpretations and uses of policy research are politically motivated.

Despite these problems, the advantages of policy experimentation are substantial. It is exceedingly costly for society to commit itself to large-scale programs and policies in education, welfare, housing, health, and so on without any real idea about what works.

PROGRAM EVALUATION: WHY IT FAILS SO OFTEN

Occasionally government agencies attempt their own policy evaluations. Government analysts and administrators report on the conditions of target groups before and after their participation in a new program, and some effort is made to attribute observed changes to the new program itself. Policy experimentation is less frequent; seldom do governments systematically select experimental and control groups of the population, introduce a new program to the experimental group only, and then carefully compare changes in the conditions of the experimental group with a control group that has not benefited from the program. Let us turn first to some of the problems confronting policy evaluation.

1. The first problem confronting anyone who wants to evaluate a public program is to determine what the goals of the program are. What are the target groups and what are the desired effects? But governments often pursue incompatible goals to satisfy very diverse groups. Overall policy planning and evaluation may reveal inconsistencies in public policy and force reconsideration of fundamental societal goals. Where there is little agreement on the goals of a public program, evaluation studies may engender a great deal of political conflict. Government agencies generally prefer to avoid conflict, and hence to avoid studies that would raise such questions.

2. Many programs and policies have primarily symbolic value. They do not actually change the conditions of target groups but merely make these groups feel that the government "cares." A government agency does not welcome a study that reveals that its efforts have no tangible effects; such a revelation itself might reduce the symbolic value of the program by informing target groups of its uselessness.

3. Government agencies have a strong vested interest in "proving" that their programs have a positive impact. Administrators frequently view attempts to evalu-

ate the impact of their programs as attempts to limit or destroy their programs or to question the competence of the administrators.

4. Government agencies usually have a heavy investment—organizational, financial, physical, psychological—in current programs and policies. They are predisposed against finding that these policies do not work.

5. Any serious study of policy impact undertaken by a government agency would involve some interference with ongoing program activities. The press of day-to-day business generally takes priority over study and evaluation. More importantly, the conduct of an experiment may necessitate depriving individuals or groups (control groups) of services to which they are entitled under law; this may be difficult, if not impossible, to do.

6. Program evaluation requires funds, facilities, time, and personnel, which government agencies do not like to sacrifice from ongoing programs. Policy impact studies, like any research, cost money. They cannot be done well as extracurricular or part-time activities. Devoting resources to studies may mean a sacrifice in program resources that administrators are unwilling to make.

HOW BUREAUCRATS EXPLAIN NEGATIVE FINDINGS

Government administrators and program supporters are ingenious in devising reasons why negative findings about policy impacts should be rejected. Even in the face of clear evidence that their favorite programs are useless or even counterproductive, they will argue that

1. The effects of the program are long range and cannot be measured at the present time.

2. The effects of the program are diffuse and general in nature; no single criterion or index adequately measures what is being accomplished.

3. The effects of the program are subtle and cannot be identified by crude measures or statistics.

4. Experimental research cannot be carried out effectively because to withhold services from some persons to observe the impact of such withholding would be unfair to them.

5. The fact that no difference was found between persons receiving the services and those not receiving them means that the program is not sufficiently intensive and indicates the need to spend *more* resources on the program.

6. The failure to identify any positive effects of a program is attributable to inadequacy or bias in the research itself, not in the program.

Harvard professor James Q. Wilson formulated two general laws to cover all cases of social science research on policy impact:

Wilson's First Law: All policy interventions in social problems produce the intended effect—if the research is carried out by those implementing the policy or by their friends.

> *Wilson's Second Law:* No policy intervention in social problems produces the intended effect—if the research is carried out by independent third parties, especially those skeptical of the policy.

Wilson denies that his laws are cynical. Instead he reasons that

> Studies that conform to the First Law will accept an agency's own data about what it is doing and with what effect; adopt a time frame (long or short) that maximizes the probability of observing the desired effect; and minimize the search for other variables that might account for the effect observed. Studies that conform to the Second Law will gather data independently of the agency; adopt a short time frame that either minimizes the chance for the desired effect to appear or, if it does appear, permits one to argue that the results are "temporary" and probably due to the operation of the "Hawthorne Effect" (i.e., the reaction of the subjects to the fact that they are part of an experiment); and maximize the search for other variables that might explain the effects observed.[8]

WHY GOVERNMENT PROGRAMS ARE SELDOM TERMINATED

Government programs are rarely terminated. Even when evaluative studies produce negative findings; even when policymakers themselves are fully aware of fraud, waste, and inefficiency; even when highly negative benefit-cost ratios are reported, government programs manage to survive. Once policy is institutionalized within a government, it is extraordinarily difficult to terminate.

Why is it so difficult for governments to terminate failed programs and policies? The answer to this question varies from one program to another, but a few generalizations are possible.

Concentrated Benefits, Dispersed Costs.   Perhaps the most common reason for the continuation of inefficient government programs and polices is that their limited benefits are concentrated in a small, well-organized constituency, while their greater costs are dispersed over a large, unorganized, uninformed public. Although few in number, the beneficiaries of a program are strongly committed to it; they are concerned, well informed, and active in their support. If the costs of the program are spread widely among all taxpayers, no one has a strong incentive to become informed, organized, or active in opposition to it. Although the costs of a failed program may be enormous, if they are dispersed widely enough so that no one individual or group bears a significant burden, there will be little incentive to organize an effective opposition. (Consider the case of a government subsidy program for peanut growers. If $250 million per year were distributed to 5,000 growers, each would average $50,000 in subsidy income. If each grower would contribute 10 percent of this subsidy to a political fund to reward friendly legislators, the fund could distribute $25 million in campaign contributions. If the costs of the program could be dispersed evenly among 250 million Americans, each would pay only $1. No one would have a sufficient incentive to become informed, organized, or active in opposition to the subsidy program. So it would continue, regardless of its limited benefits and extensive costs to society.) When program costs are widely dispersed, it is irrational for individuals, each of whom bears only a tiny fraction of these costs, to expend the time, energy, and money to counter the support of the program's beneficiaries.

Legislative and Bureaucratic Interests.   Among the beneficiaries of any government program are those who administer and supervise it. Bureaucratic jobs depend on a program's continuation. Government positions with all of their benefits, pay, prerequisites, and prestige, are at stake. Strong incentives exist for bureaucrats to resist or undermine negative evaluations of their programs, to respond to public criticism by making only marginal changes in their programs or even by claiming that their programs are failing because not enough is being spent on them.

Legislative systems, both in Congress and in state capitals, are structured so that legislators with the most direct control over programs are usually the most friendly to them. The committee system, with its fragmentation of power and invitation to log-rolling ("You support my committee's report and I'll support yours") favors retention of existing programs and policies. Legislators on committees with jurisdiction over the programs are usually the largest recipients of campaign contributions from the organized beneficiaries of the programs. These legislators can use their committee positions to protect failed programs, to minimize reform, and to block termination. Even without the incentives of bureaucratic position and legislative power, no public official wants publicly to acknowledge failure.

Incrementalism at Work.   Governments seldom undertake to consider any program as a whole in any given year. Active consideration of programs is made at the margin—that is, attention is focused on proposed changes in existing programs rather than on the value of programs in their entirety. Usually this attention comes in the budgetary process (see Chapter 9), when proposed increases or decreases in funding are under discussion in the bureaucracy and legislature. Negative evaluative studies can play a role in the budgetary process—limiting increases for failed programs or perhaps even identifying programs ripe for budget cutting. But attention is almost always focused on changes or reforms, increases or decreases, rather than on the complete termination of programs. Even mandating "sunset" legislation, used in many states (requiring legislatures periodically to reconsider and reauthorize whole programs), seldom results in program termination.

Failed programs can also be "repackaged"—given new names and agency titles, while maintaining essentially the same goals, the same bureaucracy, and the same policy prescriptions. Many of the programs of Lyndon Johnson's War on Poverty in the 1960s were repackaged and placed in different federal departments following the official termination of the Office of Economic Opportunity. After much adverse publicity, the failed CETA job program (Comprehensive Employment and Training Act) was repackaged by Senators Edward Kennedy and Dan Quayle as the JTPS (Job Training and Placement Service program) with only modest reforms.

Complete program terminations in Washington are very rare. Among the precious few major terminations have been airline regulation of interstate routes and fares in 1978 and the Civil Aeronautics Board; general revenue sharing (federal sharing of general tax revenues with state and local governments) in 1986; oil price controls in 1980. Each of these terminations generated a great deal of controversy and each involved very special circumstances. Marginal policy changes are much easier to accomplish than program terminations.

POLITICS AS A SUBSTITUTE FOR ANALYSIS

Policy analysis, including systematic policy evaluation, is a rational process. It requires some agreement on what problems the government should undertake to resolve; some agreement on the nature of societal benefits and costs and the weights to be given to them; and some agreement on the formulation of a research design, the measurement of benefits and costs, and the interpretation of the results. Value conflicts intrude at almost every point in the evaluation process, but policy analysis cannot resolve value conflicts.

Politics is the management of conflict. People have different ideas about what are the principal problems confronting society and about what, if anything, the government should do about them. Value conflicts explain why policymakers rely so little on systematic policy analysis in the formulation, selection, or evaluation of policy. Instead, they must rely on political processes.

A political approach to policy analysis emphasizes

- The search for common concerns that might form the basis for identification of societal problems
- Reasonable trade-offs among conflicting values at each stage of the policy-making process
- The search for mutually beneficial outcomes for diverse groups; attempting to satisfy diverse demands
- Compromise and conciliation and a willingness to accept modest net gains (half a loaf) rather than suffer the loss of more comprehensive proposals
- Bargaining among participants, even in separate policy areas, to win allies ("I'll support your proposals if you support mine.")

At best, policy analysis plays only a secondary role in the policymaking process. But it is an important role, nonetheless. Political scientist Charles E. Lindblom explains "the intelligence of democracy":

> Strategic analysis and mutual adjustment among political participants, then, are the underlying processes by which democratic systems achieve the level of intelligent action that they do. . . .
>   There is never a point at which the thinking, research, and action is "objective," or "unbiased." It is partisan through and through, as are all human activities, in the sense that the expectations and priorities of those commissioning and doing the analysis

shape it, and in the sense that those using information shape its interpretation and application.

Information seeking and shaping must intertwine inextricably with political interaction, judgment, and action. Since time and energy and brainpower are limited, strategic analysis must focus on those aspects of an issue that participating partisans consider to be most important for persuading each other. There is no purely analytical way to do such focusing, it requires political judgments: about what the crucial unknowns are, about what kind of evidence is likely to be persuasive to would-be allies, or about what range of alternatives may be politically feasible.[9]

THE LIMITS OF PUBLIC POLICY

Never have Americans expected so much of their government. Our confidence in what governments can do seems boundless. We have come to believe that they can eliminate poverty, end racism, ensure peace, prevent crime, restore cities, clean the air and water, and so on, if only they will adopt the right policies.

Perhaps confidence in the potential effectiveness of public policy is desirable, particularly if it inspires us to continue to search for ways to resolve societal problems. But any serious study of public policy must also recognize the limitations of policy in affecting these conditions.

1. Some societal problems are incapable of solution because of the way in which they are defined. If problems are defined in *relative* rather than *absolute* terms, they may never be resolved by public policy. For example, if the poverty line is defined as the line that places one-fifth of the population below it, poverty will always be with us regardless of how well off the "poor" may become. Relative disparities in society may never be eliminated. Even if income differences among classes were tiny, tiny differences may come to have great symbolic importance, and the problem of inequality would remain.

2. Expectations may always outrace the capabilities of governments. Progress in any policy area may simply result in an upward movement in expectations about what policy should accomplish. Public education never faced a dropout problem until the 1960s, when for the first time a majority of boys and girls were graduating from high school. At the turn of the century, when high school graduation was rare, there was no mention of a dropout problem.

3. Policies that solve the problems of one group in society may create problems for other groups. In a plural society, one person's solution may be another person's problem. For example, solving the problem of inequality in society may mean redistributive tax and spending policies, which take from persons of above-average wealth to give to persons with below-average wealth. The latter may view this as a solution, but the former may view it as creating serious problems. There are *no* policies that can simultaneously attain mutually exclusive ends.

4. It is quite possible that some societal forces cannot be harnessed by governments, even if it is desirable to do so. It may turn out that the government cannot stop urban location patterns of whites and blacks, even if it tries to do so. Whites

and blacks may separate themselves regardless of government policies in support of integration. Some children may not be able to learn much in public schools no matter what is done. In other words, governments may not be *able* to bring about some societal changes.

5. Frequently people adapt themselves to public policies in ways that render the policies useless. For example, we may solve the problem of poverty by government guarantees of a high annual income, but by so doing we may reduce incentives to work and thus swell the number of dependent families beyond the fiscal capacities of government to provide guarantees. The possibility always exists that adaptive behavior may frustrate policy.

6. Societal problems may have multiple causes, and a specific policy may not be able to eradicate the problem. For example, job training may not affect the hardcore unemployed if their employability is also affected by chronic poor health.

7. The solution to some problems may require policies that are more costly than the problem. For example, it may turn out that certain levels of public disorder—including riots, civil disturbances, and occasional violence—cannot be eradicated without the adoption of very repressive policies—the forceable breakup of revolutionary parties, restrictions on the public, appearances of demagogues, the suppression of hate literature, the addition of large numbers of security forces, and so on. But these repressive policies would prove too costly in democratic values—freedom of speech and press, rights of assembly, freedom to form opposition parties. Thus, a certain level of disorder may be the price we pay for democracy. Doubtless there are other examples of societal problems that are simply too costly to solve.

8. The political system is not structured for completely rational decision making. The solution of societal problems generally implies a rational model, but government may not be capable of formulating policy in a rational fashion. Instead the political system may reflect group interests, elite preferences, institutional forces, or incremental change, more than rationalism. Presumably, a democratic system is structured to reflect mass influences, whether these are rational or not. Elected officials respond to the demands of their constituents, and this may inhibit completely rational approaches to public policy.

NOTES

1. Joseph S. Wholey, et al., *Federal Evaluation Policy* (Washington, DC: Urban Institute, 1970), p. 25.
2. David Nachmias, *Public Policy Evaluation* (New York: St. Martin's Press, 1979), p. 4.
3. *Federal Evaluation Issues* (Washington, DC: General Accounting Office, 1989).
4. *Annual Index of Reports Issued* (Washington, DC: General Accounting Office, annually).
5. See David L. Sills, ed., *International Encyclopedia of the Social Sciences,* 7 (New York: Free Press, 1968), 241.
6. David Kershaw and Jerelyn Fair, eds., *Final Report of the New Jersey Graduated Work Incentive Experiment* (Madison: University of Wisconsin, Institute for Research on Poverty, 1974).
7. John F. Cogan, *Negative Income Taxation and Labor Supply: New Evidence from the New Jersey–Pennsylvania Experiment* (Santa Monica, CA: Rand Corporation, 1978). See also SRI International, *Final Report of the Seattle–Denver Income Maintenance Experiment* (Washington,

DC: U.S. Government Printing Office, 1983), for experimental results suggesting that government job training has no effect on a person's subsequent earnings or employment and that a guaranteed income significantly lowers earnings and hours of work and contributes to marital dissolutions.

8. James Q. Wilson, "On Pettigrew and Armor," *The Public Interest,* 31 (Spring 1973), 132–134.
9. Charles E. Lindblom and Edward J. Woodhouse, *The Policy-Making Process,* 3rd ed. (Englewood Cliffs, NJ: Prentice Hall, 1993), pp. 31–32.

BIBLIOGRAPHY

BINGHAM, RICHARD D., and CLAIRE L. FELBINGER. *Evaluation in Practice.* New York: Longman, 1989.

HATRY, HARRY P., LOUIS BLAIR, DONALD FISK, and WAYNE KIMMEL. *Program Analysis for State and Local Governments.* Washington, DC: Urban Institute, 1987.

NACHMIAS, DAVID. *Public Policy Evaluation.* New York: St. Martin's Press, 1979.

PRESSMAN, JEFFREY L., and AARON WILDAVSKY. *Implementation.* Berkeley: University of California Press, 1974.

WHOLEY, JOSEPH S. *Evaluation and Effective Public Management.* Boston: Little, Brown, 1982.

WILDAVSKY, AARON. *Speaking Truth to Power.* New York: John Wiley, 1979.

INDEX